HITLER'S COMMANDERS

HITLER'S COMMANDERS

Officers of the Wehrmacht, the Luftwaffe, the Kriegsmarine, and the Waffen-SS

Second Edition

SAMUEL W. MITCHAM, JR.,
AND
GENE MUELLER

ROWMAN & LITTLEFIELD PUBLISHERS, INC.
Lanham • Boulder • New York • Toronto • Plymouth, UK

Published by Rowman & Littlefield Publishers, Inc.
A wholly owned subsidiary of The Rowman & Littlefield Publishing Group, Inc.
4501 Forbes Boulevard, Suite 200, Lanham, Maryland 20706
www.rowman.com

10 Thornbury Road, Plymouth PL6 7PP, United Kingdom

Distributed by National Book Network

British Library Cataloguing in Publication Information Available

Library of Congress Cataloging-in-Publication Data
Mitcham, Samuel W.
  Hitler's commanders : officers of the Wehrmacht, the Luftwaffe, the Kriegsmarine, and the Waffen-SS / Samuel W. Mitcham, Jr., and Gene Mueller. — 2nd ed.
    p. cm.
  Includes bibliographical references and index.
  ISBN 978-1-4422-1153-7 (pbk. : alk. paper) — ISBN 978-1-4422-1154-4 (electronic)
  1. World War, 1939-1945—Biography. 2. Generals—Germany—Biography. 3. Admirals—Germany—Biography. 4. Marshals—Germany—Biography. 5. Germany—Armed Forces—Biography. I. Mueller, Gene. II. Title.
  D757.M57 2012
  940.54'13430922—dc23
                                                                    2012020641

∞™ The paper used in this publication meets the minimum requirements of American National Standard for Information Sciences—Permanence of Paper for Printed Library Materials, ANSI/NISO Z39.48-1992.

Printed in the United States of America

CONTENTS

PREFACE AND ACKNOWLEDGMENTS

When I was growing up in America in the 1950s, evaluating Hitler's commanders was all very simple: all Germans were Nazis, and all Nazis were evil. The higher in rank a Nazi rose, the lower he sank as a human being. A German general would, then, logically be a horrible human being. A typical Nazi (i.e., German) general would be brutal, absolutely regimented, totally insensitive to human suffering, and completely ignorant of anything outside the immediate sphere of his profession. Other than a certain amount of skill in military science (and an unsurpassed talent for destruction and disorganization), he had no redeeming qualities whatsoever. He undoubtedly ate with his hands, wiped his mouth on his coat, burped loudly, interrupted people anytime he felt like it, screamed, threw things, pitched fits, and was really happy only when he was launching unprovoked invasions of innocent countries. His favorite hobbies were mass murder, bombing undefended villages, and eating small babies for breakfast.

After I became an adult, the picture I perceived became much more complex. I was somewhat shocked to discover that not all Germans were Nazis, and not all Nazis were German; furthermore, the men who came closest to doing away with Hitler (prior to 1945) were none other than German officers. Eventually my interest in military history led me to study the Wehrmacht in depth, and I discovered that there were all types of people in the German armed forces: heroes, cowards, Nazis, anti-Nazis, non-Nazis (as opposed to anti-Nazis), Christians, atheists, professionals, well-educated men, high school dropouts, backroom politicians, chameleons, innovators, dissenters, geniuses, the obtuse, men who looked to the future, and men who lived mainly in the past. They came from many social classes, with varied backgrounds, varied educations, and varied levels of skill and intelligence. Also, they had many different types of careers and various kinds of luck.

Dr. Mueller and I would like to express our appreciation to a number of people for their assistance in the completion of this work. First, we would like to thank our wives, Donna Mitcham and Kay Mueller, for their long-suffering patience and assistance in proofreading. Thanks also go to Paula Leming, professor of foreign languages, for help in translating; to Colonel Jack Angolia and Dr. Waldo Dalstead, for the loan of certain photographs; to Valerie Newborn and the staffs of Huie Library, Henderson State University, and Professor Melissa Matthews of the University of Louisiana at Monroe, for their assistance in acquiring interlibrary loans; and to the staffs of the National Archives, the Library of Congress, the Army War College, the Defense Audiovisual Agency, the Air University, and the Bundesarchiv, for their help in securing documents and photos used in this book. Also, thanks go to Colonel Edmond D. Marino and the late Theodor-Friedrich von Stauffenberg for their invaluable advice.

INTRODUCTION

The purpose of *Hitler's Commanders* is to describe the lives and careers of selected German officers from all three branches of the Wehrmacht, as well as from the *Waffen-SS* (armed SS). These officers were picked by Dr. Mueller and me on the basis of the diversity of their characters and careers, the availability of information, and our own interests. Some readers may take issue with certain of these selections, but since there were 3,663 general officers in the German Army alone during World War II, it is natural that our selections should differ from those of others; in fact, it would be quite remarkable if any author or sets of authors would choose exactly the same cast of characters we selected.

Naturally, we begin this book with the generals of the High Command, since Dr. Mueller knew the Keitel, Jodl, and Warlimont families; wrote a biography of Wilhelm Keitel; and had significant insight into the leaders of the headquarters of the armed forces. Bernhard Lossberg was selected as a subject because he is an excellent example of the kind of independent-minded, far-sighted military expert who could not be tolerated in the toxic environment around Hitler, and whose career was subsequently ruined as a result. Walter Buhle is an example of a "true believer." He was competent within his own sphere of interest but a Nazi to the core. Wilhelm Burgdorf and Hermann Reinecke are more typical of the senior officers at Fuehrer Headquarters—more Nazi than Buhle but less competent.

Friedrich Fromm is another type altogether, and the kind of man found all too frequently in the highest military echelons of the Third Reich: the opportunistic chameleon. He was more than willing to lend his considerable abilities to Hitler and his cronies when they were winning, in exchange for profession, prestige, promotions, and decorations; when they were losing, however, he wanted to be on the side of the resistance, but only if they succeeded in killing Hitler. If they failed, he wanted it to appear that he was against them all along. He was perfectly willing to commit murder to maintain this illusion.

Only two officers in Fuehrer Headquarters stand tall: Lossberg and Georg Thomas. As a member of the anti-Hitler conspiracy, Thomas was more fortunate than most: he only ended up in a concentration camp, rather than in a shallow grave with a bullet in the back of his neck.

Our second chapter deals with the commanders on the Eastern Front and discusses an entirely different cast of character types with varying degrees of competence, skill, luck, and moral clarity. They were generally very good at their profession and have only one thing in common: all were sacked by Hitler. In addition, two died in action and one faced the firing squad.

The generals of Stalingrad chapter deals with the men who directed Hitler's legions in the decisive battle of the war. Here, the blind obedience of Friedrich Paulus and Arthur Schmidt to Hitler's orders had a devastating effect on operations and even determined the final outcome of the war. How each commander dealt with this situation after the 6th Army was surrounded is an interesting character study of each individual, all of whom were under tremendous pressure. They also make an interesting case study of one of the Third Reich's major strengths: superb commanders at the corps level and below.

The commanders of the Western Front chapter was tough to write because there were so many to choose from. Nikolaus von Falkenhorst was a man who evokes some sympathy. He was a competent and basically decent non-Nazi who wanted to do the right thing but was caught in the Byzantine politics that was the Third Reich at war. Hugo Sperrle, on the other hand, engenders no sympathy. Also a non-Nazi, he was more ruthless than Falkenhorst and got caught up in the corruption of Nazi-occupied France. Friedrich Dollmann is an even more interesting character study. Certainly he was, like Sperrle, promoted above his ceiling. Originally a definite pro-Nazi, he changed his tune completely and not from self-serving motivations. When he discovered what the Nazis truly were, he suffered a genuine attack of conscience—something one finds all too rarely in the history of Nazi Germany.

The chapter on the panzer commanders could easily be expanded into an entire book, especially if the essays on Heinrich von Luettwitz, Baron Hasso von Manteuffel, and Hans Valentin Hube were included. The dominant theme of such a book would parallel that of chapter 5: professional brilliance. The generals of this chapter were all non-Nazis, although Heinz

Guderian certainly made a close pass to National Socialism, no matter what he said after the war.

The Luftwaffe was officered by a very complex set of officers with an extremely wide range of abilities, talents, and political opinions, although it contained relatively few anti-Nazis. Despite having a Jewish father, Erhard Milch was certainly pro-Nazi, and one who did not suddenly discover—after the war—that he had really been an anti-Nazi all along. Interestingly, his brother was a practicing Jew and an attorney. He defended his brother at the Nuremberg trials but without much success. Erhard certainly did not help his own case when he called the anti-Hitler conspirators "vermin" from the witness stand.

Perhaps the most competent man the reader will encounter in this book is Walter Wever. A true genius of the first order and a consummate diplomat, he is included because—in my view—he could quite literally have made all of the difference in the world. As the first chief of the General Staff of the Luftwaffe, he was constructing an air force that might well have won the war for the Third Reich. After reading the essay on Wever, the reader will, of course, have to draw his or her own conclusions. Fortunately for Western civilization, Wever was not a good pilot and was killed in an air accident in 1936.

Most of the rest of the men found in the Luftwaffe chapter are young fighter pilots. Their perspective on the war and life in general differed considerably from that of their leaders.

The naval officers covered here fall into two basic categories: admirals and U-boat aces. The admirals make interesting character studies. Here we find self-serving careerists, great efficiency, blind obedience, incompetence, and a corporate cut-throat mentality at the highest levels. (Note that I use the term *cut-throat* in a figurative, not a literal, sense.) The young aces, on the other hand, represent courage, professionalism, devotion to country, and a determination to do their duty in a fight against overwhelming odds. This is one reason why three out of every four men serving on U-boats lost his life in World War II.

The Waffen-SS (armed SS) is not an uplifting chapter. They were all Nazis. The Waffen-SS differed from the SS that ran the concentration and extermination camps, but not entirely. There was some overlap. Theodor Eicke and Helmut Becker, for example, worked in the camps prior to the war and would not hesitate to kill anyone of whom the Fuehrer decided to dispose. Even the other subjects are not an attractive lot, with the possible exception of Michael Wittmann, who was just a soldier doing his job. True, he did it much better than almost anyone else and is now internationally famous as perhaps the greatest tank ace of all kind. He killed hundreds of men, but they were all armed and capable of defending themselves. For that reason, he is the one leader in the SS chapter about whom we have not written a single negative word.

One aspect of this book that warrants specific mention is the relative lack of field marshals covered here. This is because my book *Hitler's Field Marshals and Their Battles* was published in the United States in 1990 and has been republished in paperback and hardback editions since then, so I thought it inappropriate to cover them again here. We made five exceptions: Wilhelm Keitel, Ritter Wilhelm von Leeb, Georg von Kuechler, Fedor von Bock, and Friedrich Paulus. (Field Marshal Walter von Reichenau is briefly covered also, but only superficially, and only because of his relationship to Paulus.) Keitel is included because Dr. Mueller knew his family and wrote a book on his life many years ago. Paulus is here because, in a chapter on the generals of Stalingrad, it would be impossible to leave him out. The remaining three—Leeb, Kuechler, and Bock—are discussed in the chapter on the commanders of the Eastern Front because they represented three different types of generals. Leeb was a moral, Christian, anti-Nazi, straitlaced Bavarian general of the old school, who had no use for Hitler or his party. Bock cannot be labeled pro-Nazi, non-Nazi, or anti-Nazi; he can only be described as pro-Bock. Kuechler fell somewhere in between. Even so, the current treatment of these three is considerably different from that in *Hitler's Field Marshals.* There the emphasis was on their battles; here it is on their personalities and characters.

The world has turned around many times since Dr. Mueller and I began writing the first edition of *Hitler's Commanders* in 1989. Gene has now retired, and I have left academia and am near the end of my career as a World War II historian. In the past two decades, however, more information on some of our subjects has come to light, especially in the form of personnel records. Several of our subjects have died in the interim, and other new records have become available. Also, several commanders have been added to this edition. The purposes of this edition, however, are the same as the original: to entertain the reader while simultaneously giving him or her a greater insight into the workings of the German armed forces in World War II. Dr. Mueller and I hope you enjoy the second edition of *Hitler's Commanders.*

Dr. Samuel W. Mitcham, Jr.
September 26, 2011

HITLER'S COMMANDERS

1

THE GENERALS
OF THE HIGH COMMAND

**Wilhelm Keitel. Alfred Jodl. Bernhard Lossberg.
Georg Thomas. Walter Buhle. Wilhelm Burgdorf.
Hermann Reinecke. Friedrich "Fritz" Fromm.**

WILHELM KEITEL was born on the family estate of Helmscherode in western Brunswick on September 22, 1882. Although he longed to be a farmer, as his ancestors were, the modest 650-acre estate was too small to support two families. Consequently, Keitel joined the 46th Field Artillery Regiment in Wolfenbuettler as a *Fahnenjunker* (officer-cadet) in 1901. The desire to return to Helmscherode, however, remained with him throughout his life.

Keitel was commissioned second lieutenant on August 18, 1902, entered an instructor's course in the Field Artillery School at Juterbog in 1905, and in 1908 became regimental adjutant. He was promoted to first lieutenant in 1910 and to captain in 1914. (See appendix I for a table of equivalent ranks.)

In 1909, Wilhelm Keitel married Lisa Fontaine, an attractive, intelligent young woman from Wuelfel. Her father, a wealthy estate owner and brewer, initially disliked Wilhelm due to his "Prussian" background but eventually became reconciled to the marriage. Lisa bore Wilhelm three sons and three daughters. Like their father, all three sons became officers in the German Army. Definitely the stronger partner in the marriage, Lisa wanted her husband to advance as high as possible in the ranks of the military. Incidentally, Herr Fontaine was wrong about Keitel's background: he was not Prussian at all, but Hanoverian. This same mistake was made by Adolf Hitler and the Allied prosecutors at Nuremberg later on.

In early summer 1914, Keitel took a well-earned holiday in Switzerland, where he heard the news of the assassination of Franz Ferdinand, the
archduke of the Austro-Hungarian Empire. Keitel was hurriedly recalled
to his regiment at Wolfenbuettler and was with the 46th Artillery when it
was sent to Belgium in August 1914. He saw considerable action and in
September was seriously wounded in the right forearm by a shell splinter.
After recovering he returned to the 46th, where he became a battery commander. In March 1915, he was appointed to the General Staff and transferred to the XV Reserve Corps. In late 1915 Keitel came to know a Major
Werner von Blomberg, and the two men began a friendship that continued
throughout both their careers. Keitel finished his service in the Great War
as a General Staff officer with the XIX Reserve Corps (1916–1917), the
199th Infantry Division (1917) (both on the Western Front), and the General Staff of the army in Berlin (1917–1918), and as a staff officer with the
Marine Corps, fighting in Flanders (1918).

The Treaty of Versailles, which ended World War I, was a very harsh
one. Among other things, it abolished the General Staff and limited the
German Army (now dubbed the *Reichsheer*) to 100,000 men, of whom
only 4,000 could be officers.[1] Keitel was accepted into this officer corps of
the Weimar Republic and spent three years as an instructor at the Cavalry
School at Hanover before joining the staff of the 6th Artillery Regiment at
Minden in Westphalia. He was promoted to major in 1923 and from 1925
to 1927 was assigned to the organizational branch of the *Truppenamt* (Troop
Office), as the clandestine General Staff was called. In 1927 he moved to
Muenster as commander of the II Battalion, 6th Artillery Regiment. He
was promoted to lieutenant colonel in 1929—a significant accomplishment
in the Reichsheer, which, like most small armies, was characterized by slow
promotions. That same year he returned to the General Staff as chief of the
Organizations Department.

An interesting event took place in Keitel's career in late summer
1931, when he took part in a military exchange trip to the Soviet Union.
He admired the Russia he saw, noting the vast spaces, abundance of raw
materials, the Five Year (economic) Plan, and the disciplined Red Army.
Following this trip he continued to work at his arduous task of increasing
the size of the German Army in contravention of the Treaty of Versailles.

Although Keitel did his job very well, as even his personal enemy
Field Marshal Erich von Manstein later admitted, his abilities were taxed to
the limits. The demanding (and illegal) work took its toll both physically
and mentally. The nervous Keitel smoked too much and, by 1932, was
suffering from arterial embolism and thrombosis and had severe phlebitis

in his right leg. He was recovering under the care of Dr. Guhr in the Tara Mountains of Czechoslovakia when Adolf Hitler became chancellor of Germany on January 30, 1933. Keitel's close friend Werner von Blomberg became minister of defense the same day.

In October 1933, Keitel began a year of troop duty. He served first Infantry Commander III (and one of the two deputy commanders of the 3rd Infantry Division) at Potsdam, Frederick the Great's old garrison town near Berlin. In May 1934, he heard Adolf Hitler speak at the Sportplatz in Berlin and was moved by the Fuehrer's words. That same month Keitel's father died, and Wilhelm inherited Helmscherode. He seriously considered leaving the army to manage the family estate, even though he had just been promoted to major general the month before; however, as he wrote later, "My wife was unable to keep house with my stepmother and sister, and I could not solve the problem."[2] No doubt Lisa wanted him to remain in the army, and he did so.

In July 1934, Keitel was transferred to the 12th Infantry Division in Leibnitz, more than 300 miles from Helmscherode. Because of this distance, he once again seriously considered leaving the service. General Baron Werner von Fritsch, the commander of the army, dissuaded Keitel by offering him a new assignment, which he accepted. On October 1, 1934, Keitel, now stationed at Bremen, assumed command of what was soon to become the 22nd Infantry Division.

Keitel thoroughly enjoyed his new command, organizing units and developing measures necessary to build the division up to full combat strength and effectiveness. (Many of the battalions he helped organize would later be destroyed at Stalingrad.) While he built the 22nd Division he also made frequent visits to Helmscherode and increased the value of his family estate. Then, in August 1935, War Minister von Blomberg offered Keitel the post of chief of the *Wehmachtamt* (Armed Forces Office). Although Keitel hesitated, his wife urged him to accept the appointment, which he eventually did.

Upon arriving in Berlin, General Keitel put aside his former reluctance and enthusiastically embraced his new role. Working closely with him was Lieutenant Colonel Alfred Jodl, the chief of Division "L" (national defense). The two men developed an intimate professional relationship that lasted until the end of the Third Reich. Keitel labored tirelessly to promote his idea of a unified command structure for all three services and received encouragement from von Blomberg. However, all three branches of the armed forces—the army, the navy, and most especially Goering's Luftwaffe—rejected the idea, and Blomberg quickly abandoned the concept. That result caused Keitel to gravitate to the idea of absolute and unquestioning support of the Fuehrer (the Fuehrer Principle) and subsequent personal loyalty to Hitler. After the war he presented a document at the Nuremberg Trials, wherein he stated that the Fuehrer Principle "applied throughout all areas and it is completely natural that it had a special application in military areas."[3]

Keitel was proud when, in January 1938, his eldest son, Karl-Heinz, a second lieutenant of cavalry, became engaged to Dorothea von Blomberg, one of the war minister's daughters. There was also another wedding: Field Marshal von Blomberg, whose first wife had died several years earlier, married Eva Gruhn, a 24-year-old stenographer with the Reich Egg Marketing Board, in the middle of January. The Blomberg wedding was a small, quiet, civilian affair, with Adolf Hitler and Hermann Goering appearing as witnesses. Little did anyone suspect that this simple ceremony would cause the crisis that would culminate in the final act of the Nazi revolution.

Shortly after the Blombergs exchanged vows, a minor police official happened upon the dossier of a Margarethe Gruhn, which he immediately delivered to the office of Count Wolf-Heinrich von Helldorf, the police president of Berlin.[4] When he read it, Helldorf was appalled. Margarethe's past included prostitution and an arrest for posing for pornographic pictures. Helldorf, a former military officer, took the file to Keitel, hoping the chief of the Wehrmachtamt would suggest a proper and quiet procedure for having the matter settled. Were Margarethe Gruhn and Eva Gruhn the same person? Was the sex offender the same woman the war minister had recently married? Keitel did not know and suggested the file be taken to Hermann Goering, who had met the minister's wife. Keitel was apparently unaware that Goering was waiting for just such an opportunity to have Blomberg sacked, so that he could take control of the war ministry himself. Goering went directly to Hitler and exposed the entire incident, which led to Blomberg's dismissal. Events did not work out exactly as Goering planned, however.

Following the ouster of Blomberg, Keitel was ordered to report to Hitler. The Fuehrer shocked Keitel by saying that he, Hitler, had to charge General von Fritsch, the commander-in-chief of the German Army, with the criminal offense of homosexuality under paragraph 175. Although the charges were the result of carefully produced lies by Heinrich Himmler and Goering (with the help of Reinhard Heydrich, Himmler's top man in the Security Service), and even though Fritsch was later acquitted by a military tribunal, the dismissals of Blomberg and Fritsch led to the creation of the *Oberkommando der Wehrmacht* (the High Command of the Armed Forces, or OKW) and the total subordination of the German armed forces to the will of Adolf Hitler.

On February 4, 1938, to Hermann Goering's private chagrin, the dictator personally assumed the post of war minister and simultaneously appointed Wilhelm Keitel commander-in-chief of OKW—thus providing himself with his own personal military staff.

Why was Keitel chosen as chief of the High Command of the Armed Forces? Because the Fuehrer needed someone on whom he would rely to carry out his will and to keep his "house" in order—someone who would not question his orders and who would identify with the Fuehrer Principle. Keitel fit that role. He was, as General Walter Warlimont later wrote, "honestly convinced that his appointment required him to identify himself unquestioningly with the wishes and instructions of the Supreme Commander, even though he might not personally agree with this, and to represent them faithfully to all those involved."[5]

Keitel organized the OKW into three subdivisions: the Operations Staff, under Alfred Jodl; the *Abwehr* (the intelligence/counterintelligence bureau), under Admiral Wilhelm Canaris; and the Economics Staff, directed by Major General Georg Thomas. All three sections were in direct competition with other agencies of the Third Reich. The OKW Operations Staff competed with the general staffs of the three services, but especially with the General Staff of the army; the economics office had rivals in the Todt Organization and the Four Year Plan; and the Abwehr had overlapping responsibilities with the army, air, and naval intelligence staffs; with Joachim von Ribbentrop's Foreign Office; and with Himmler's SD (*Sicherheitsdienst*, or Security Service), which finally absorbed the Abwehr in 1944.

While the preceding seems incongruous, the problems multiplied during the Nazi era. New organizational groups appeared throughout the history of the Third Reich, intensifying the competition and contributing to an eventual chaos of leadership in which only one individual could make important decisions and resolve crises—and he was named Adolf Hitler.

Crucial to the whole concept of high command was the relationship between the Fuehrer and Keitel, who trusted Hitler and served him very obediently. The OKW transmitted Fuehrer Orders and aided in coordinating the German economy to meet military demands. General Warlimont described the OKW as the "working staff" or even the "military bureau" of Hitler, the politician. Nonetheless, Keitel did exercise some early influence on at least two occasions: he succeeded in getting his own nominee, Walter von Brauchitsch, to replace General Fritsch, and in having his younger brother Bodewin named chief of the Army Personnel Office.[6]

The OKW never performed as Keitel envisioned—that is, as a real command for the armed forces. Hitler literally used Keitel during the Austrian crisis in February 1938, to bully Austrian Chancellor Kurt von Schuschnigg into surrender.[7] When the war began in 1939, the chief of OKW merely performed desk duties. Actual operational planning was carried out by Franz Halder, the General Staff of the army, and Halder's colleagues. Keitel supported Hitler's attack on Poland, as well as the successful German invasions of Denmark, Norway, the Netherlands, Belgium, and France in 1940. Although the actual plan for the Norwegian campaign (Operation Weser) was drafted by Warlimont, Jodl, and Hitler, the OKW chief created the administrative structure to carry out the operation. This 43-day campaign ended successfully and was the only military operation coordinated solely by the OKW.

Along with the other generals, Keitel applauded Hitler's victory over France in June 1940. Hitler paid tribute to Keitel by promoting him to field marshal on July 19, 1940, and by giving him an endowment of 100,000 Reichsmarks—a gift Keitel never spent because he felt he had not earned it. That same July Keitel took leave for a hunting trip to Pomerania and visited Helmscherode for a few days. Returning to duty in August, he worked on preparations for Operation Sea Lion—the invasion of England (which, however, never took place).

Rather than attack his one remaining enemy, Hitler decided to invade the Soviet Union. Keitel was alarmed and voiced his objections directly to Hitler. The Fuehrer retorted that the conflict was inevitable, and therefore Germany must strike now, while she had the advantage. Keitel then wrote a memorandum outlining his objections. Hitler rebuked the field marshal savagely. Shocked and upset, Keitel suggested that Hitler replace him and appoint an OKW chief whose strategic judgment was more amenable to the Fuehrer. Hitler rejected Keitel's request for a frontline command and sharply criticized him. He shouted that he, the Fuehrer, would decide when to replace his chief of OKW. Keitel turned and left the room without a word. From then on, Keitel submitted to the will of Adolf Hitler, almost without reservation, although he occasionally offered very weak objections to certain of the dictator's notions.

In March 1941, Hitler secretly decided to wage a new kind of warfare, in which all restraints were cast aside. This war would be vicious and aimed at the total eradication of the enemy. Accordingly, Keitel issued Hitler's draconian Commissar Order, which called for the liquidation of Soviet political officers, who always accompanied Red Army troops. Keitel also affixed his signature to a decree of July 1941, and it specified that the *Reichs-*

fuehrer-SS (Heinrich Himmler) would politically administer all rearward areas in the East. This order was tantamount to endorsing mass murder.

Although Keitel tried unsuccessfully to soften some of the decrees coming from Hitler, the field marshal continued to obey his orders. Keitel had unbounded faith in Hitler, and the Fuehrer craftily exploited this relationship. A series of decrees aimed at subduing Soviet resistance emanated from Fuehrer Headquarters, including instructions to kill 50 to 100 Communists for every German soldier who died in occupied territory.[8] These orders originated with Adolf Hitler but bore Wilhelm Keitel's signature.

The failure of the German armies to win a quick, decisive victory in Russia caused Hitler to berate his generals and call for even harsher measures. Keitel meekly succumbed to Hitler's outrages and continued to sign infamous orders, such as the *Nacht und Nebel* (night and fog) decree of December 7, 1941, which directed that "persons endangering German security" were to vanish without a trace, into the night and fog. The responsibility for carrying out this decree was assigned to the SD, and many resistance members and other anti-Nazis were secretly executed under the provisions of this order.[9] In many cases their bodies were never found.

Although on occasion the OKW chief offered quiet objections to Hitler's proposals, he remained extremely loyal and was precisely the type of individual Hitler wanted in his entourage. Unfortunately, Keitel's behavior adversely affected the behavior of his subordinates. Keitel would not defend them and submitted to the will of the Fuehrer on almost every issue.[10] Such irresoluteness led many officers to refer to him as *LaKaitel* (lackey).

On July 20, 1944, Colonel Count Claus von Stauffenberg planted his briefcase, containing a bomb, under the briefing table at the Wolf's Lair during a Fuehrer conference. At 12:42 p.m. the bomb exploded. The chief of OKW was momentarily stunned, but as soon as he recovered, Keitel rushed to Hitler, shouting, "Mein Fuehrer! Mein Fuehrer! You're still alive!" He then helped Hitler to his feet and embraced him wildly. Keitel supported the dazed Fuehrer as the two left the demolished wooden hut, which had been a briefing room only minutes before.

After the failure of this assassination attempt, Keitel became closer than ever to Hitler, and as Albert Speer observed, Hitler also leaned on Keitel.[11] The OKW marshal showed no mercy in carrying out measures against the attempted coup. He arrested his own signals chief, General Erich Fellgiebel, and ordered the arrests of Colonel General Friedrich Fromm, the commander-in-chief of the Replacement Army, and Field Marshal Erwin von Witzleben. Keitel displayed no sympathy for "disloyal" officers, such as Field Marshal Erwin Rommel, upon whom he had never wasted any love.[12]

During the final months of the war, as the Soviets continued their march to Berlin, Keitel issued decrees against enemy "terrorist activities."[13] His accepting without question the need for brutal retaliation against partisans and saboteurs clearly indicated that Keitel had reached the point where he accepted Hitler's orders verbatim. During the Battle of Berlin, Keitel completely lost his grasp of reality. He blamed General Walter Wenck and Field Marshal Ferdinand Schoemer for the fall of the capital, as well as Colonel General Gotthard Heinrici, who retreated to the west without authorization. Keitel failed to realize that Germany had lost the war—no matter what these three officers did or failed to do.

On May 8, 1945, Wilhelm Keitel performed his last official act for Germany. Appearing in full-dress uniform, with his marshal's baton in hand, he signed the surrender document in the presence of the Soviets in Berlin. He then returned to Flensburg-Muervik, the seat of the rump German government, now headed by Grand Admiral Karl Doenitz. He was arrested there a few days later by the British military police and remained in custody for the remainder of his life. He was tried at Nuremberg, where he admitted his responsibility for carrying out Hitler's orders. Although his honesty did not lessen his crimes, he nonetheless faced his accusers truthfully. He was found guilty of committing crimes against peace, of war crimes, and of crimes against humanity. On October 16, 1946, Wilhelm Keitel was hanged. As he dropped through the gaping hole, he shouted his last words: "Deutschland uber Alles!" (Germany above all!)

Field Marshal Keitel had naively believed that in serving Hitler he served the German people. He realized only after the war that his actions were wrong—something he did not grasp during the seven-year period from 1938 to 1945, when he helped Hitler carry out his demonic policies and wage his war. In the end, Keitel unconsciously aided in dooming the Prussian officer corps, which, in his own inept way, he had tried to defend.

ALFRED JODL was born in Wurzburg on May 10, 1890. His father was a retired Bavarian artillery captain who had been compelled to leave active duty because of his intended marriage to a Franconian girl from a simple milling and farming family. Alfred was one of the five children produced by this union. There were three daughters, all of whom died at an early age, and another son, Ferdinand, who rose to the rank of general of mountain troops during World War II.[14]

Educated in cadet schools, young Alfred Jodl joined the Bavarian Army as a *Faehnrich* (senior officer cadet) in the 4th Bavarian Field Artillery Regiment in 1910. He attended the Bavarian War School in Munich

(1910–1912) and was commissioned to second lieutenant on October 28, 1912. Shortly thereafter he married his first wife, Countess Irma von Bullion of an established Swabian family, despite the objections of her father, Colonel Count von Bullion. The countess, who was five years Alfred's senior, was an intelligent and vivacious socialite whom he dearly loved.

Jodl saw action as an artillery officer on both the French and Russian fronts in the Great War of 1914–1918. During the first month of the war he was wounded by a grenade splinter but soon recovered and returned to the front in December. Promoted to first lieutenant in January 1916, he served as a battery commander in the 19th Field Artillery Regiment (1916–1917), the Austro-Hungarian 72nd Honved Field Cannon Regiment (1917), and the 10th Bavarian Field Artillery Regiment (1917). He returned to the 19th as regimental adjutant in May 1917. His last World War I assignment was as adjutant, 8th Bavarian Artillery Command (Bavarian Arko 8) (December 1917–December 1918). Jodl remained in the army after the war, and after commanding batteries in four different regiments in the Augsburg area, he began clandestine General Staff training in 1921. His superiors were very happy with his performance, and a typical officer fitness report from his period described him as "very thoughtful, decisive, energetic, a good sportsman, eager, an excellent leader and suitable for higher command."[15] During the Weimar era, Jodl attended the University of Berlin (1923–1924), served on the staff of the 7th Infantry Division in Munich (1924–1927), commanded a battery in the 7th Mountain Artillery Regiment at Landsberg/Lech (1927–1928), and served as a General Staff training officer with the 7th Infantry Division (1928–1932). Promoted to captain in 1921 and major in 1931, he received an appointment to the operations branch of the Troop Office (Truppenamt), as the secret General Staff was called, on June 1, 1932.

Jodl was a highly respected officer; however, his unbridled enthusiasm for Hitler and the Nazi Party created a chasm between himself and many other officers—a gap that was never bridged. In 1935 Jodl (by then a colonel)[16] entered the Armed Forces Office (Wehrmachtamt), and when Hitler created the High Command of the Armed Forces (OKW), Jodl took charge of the National Defense Office. A few weeks later, in March, 1938, Lieutenant General Max von Viebahn suffered a nervous breakdown because he feared war would result over the Austrian crisis.[17] Jodl replaced him as chief of operations of OKW.

Colonel Jodl took on his new task with enthusiasm and leveled harsh criticisms at the army generals (such as Ludwig Beck) who, following a Hitler talk on August 10, claimed Germany was not ready for war. Jodl, writing in his diary, called the generals' attitude "pusillanimous" and wrote that they should focus on military strategy, not political decisions. He further noted that it was a tragedy that the whole nation supported the Fuehrer with one exception: army generals. He castigated the generals for not recognizing Hitler's "genius."[18] Without question, Jodl had unbridled faith in Hitler and truly believed the Fuehrer was politically infallible.

Although Jodl now assumed Hitler would utilize the OKW Operations Staff to plan his military campaigns, the Fuehrer turned instead to OKH (*Oberkommando des Heeres*, the High Command of the Army) in the early planning stages. Meanwhile, Jodl was promoted to major general in 1939 and assumed command of the 44th Artillery Command (which became the 44th Infantry Division) in Vienna in November 1938. An avid mountaineer, Jodl became hopeful when General Keitel (the chief of OKW and brother of the chief of the Army Personnel Office) discussed the possibility of Jodl's receiving command of the 2nd Mountain Division in early October 1939; however, he did not get to command this or any other mountain division because the war intervened.[19]

On August 23, 1939, Keitel telegraphed Jodl to return to OKW as chief of operations; there he would conduct the planning for the attack on Poland (Case White). Jodl would remain in this post throughout the war, receiving a promotion to general of artillery in 1940 and to colonel general on January 30, 1944 (the 11th anniversary of the Nazis' assumption of power). He bypassed the rank of lieutenant general altogether. He enjoyed his first personal conversation with Hitler on the Fuehrer's train during the Polish campaign and remained loyally at Hitler's side until the end of the war.

Due to the fact that Hitler turned to OKH to direct the campaigns against Poland (1939) and France (1940), Jodl made the decision to support Hitler whenever disagreements arose between OKH and the Fuehrer. According to his deputy, Walter Warlimont, Jodl initiated an order in May 1940, directing the 1st Mountain Division to turn south (i.e., carry out a Hitler order) without OKH approval. Such an action—in direct violation of the military principle of unity of command—is evidence of both Jodl's outspoken support for Hitler, as well as of his frustration (shared by his superior, Keitel) with the lack of command authority of the OKW.

Operation Weser (the invasion of Norway) finally gave OKW an opportunity to exercise direct operational control. The Fuehrer sealed Weser for OKW by appointing General of Infantry Nikolaus von Falkenhorst as commanding general of the operation and as commander of Group XXI.[20] Normally, such command assignments were made by OKH and then sent to Hitler for routine approval. Hitler further decreed that Falkenhorst was to serve directly under him and that Falkenhorst's staff be composed of officers from all three services. Consequently, Weser came directly under Hitler's command through the OKW.

The operation was planned principally by Jodl and his staff. The German invasion of Norway caught the British (who were themselves planning to occupy Norway) completely by surprise. Although the campaign succeeded, a particularly tense situation developed when the British destroyed 10 German destroyers that had escorted Major General Eduard Dietl's landing force to Narvik in northern Norway. The British also landed a large number of troops north of Narvik on April 14. A worried Hitler frantically ordered that Dietl's troops be instructed to fall back to the south.

Jodl realized the folly of Hitler's judgment. To abandon the battle merely because the enemy threatened the Narvik position might endanger the entire campaign. Jodl pointed out to Hitler that a march south would not only be impossible, but could well result in considerable loss of airplanes, which would then have to land on frozen lakes to resupply the mountain troops. Hitler, having calmed down, agreed to postpone a decision. However, on April 17, the navy suggested that Dietl's group might be destroyed and thus rekindled Hitler's anxieties. Even Goering entered the fray against OKW, claiming there was now no way the Luftwaffe could assist Dietl.

Hitler came completely apart and, screaming, ordered Dietl's withdrawal from Narvik (after promoting him to lieutenant general). Jodl's staff was astounded. Lieutenant Colonel Bernhard von Lossberg, of the OKW planning staff, refused to send the order to Dietl, and Jodl confronted the Fuehrer directly. Pounding the table with his fist, Jodl told Hitler that Dietl's group should fight where it stood and not give up. Jodl emphasized that the position had not been lost and should not be passively surrendered. Hitler finally succumbed to Jodl's stubbornness and allowed Dietl to remain at Narvik. By the end of the month, it was clear that Jodl had been correct and that the Germans were winning the Norwegian campaign. Hitler was pleased and asked Jodl to join him for lunch. For the next two years, Jodl sat at Hitler's table for meals. The Fuehrer had great confidence in Jodl's military judgment as a result of Operation Weser, and, for his part, Jodl's faith in Hitler remained unimpaired.

Alfred Jodl thus became invited into the so-called inner circle of Adolf Hitler. This entourage consisted primarily of civilians; furthermore, as Albert Speer told Dr. Mueller, all were silent, loyal admirers who would listen for hours on end to the Fuehrer's monologues. Jodl's participation caused the OKW general considerable grief, for it separated him from his staff; and, since he was a soldier, Jodl considered himself to be merely a "guest."[21] Nonetheless, he basked in the glory of Germany's victories in 1940.

Operation Barbarossa, the invasion of Soviet Russia, added another front for the German armed forces. Jodl was skeptical of the prospects for success (Keitel openly objected to the attack), but the OKW chief of operations believed the Fuehrer's genius would defeat the hated Bolshevist empire. Barbarossa was an OKH theater, while OKW's task was to make certain that Hitler's directives were followed. At the situation conferences Hitler turned more and more to Jodl for advice, rather than to General Franz Halder, the OKH chief of staff, even though OKH directed operations in the campaign. A Byzantine atmosphere emerged at Hitler's headquarters with Jodl and other staff officers on center stage with Hitler. As a result, Jodl "became divorced from his own staff" and even "contrived to bypass Keitel and establish a direct relationship with Hitler."[22] Jodl was drawn to Hitler by the Fuehrer's willpower, revolutionary thinking, and initial successes. Jodl believed Hitler had a "sixth sense" and would continue to achieve great victories.[23]

The strategic decisions regarding the Eastern Front brought about the first crisis between Hitler and Jodl. In August 1942, when Jodl defended Halder against Hitler's criticisms, Hitler flew into an almost uncontrollable rage and never again joined Jodl at meals or shook hands with him. A second, more serious crisis occurred in September, when Hitler became impatient with the lack of progress of Field Marshal Siegmund Wilhelm List's Army Group A in the Caucasus sector. The Fuehrer sent Jodl to List's headquarters to investigate the situation and to press for a faster advance. To Hitler's surprise and anger, Jodl returned and defended List's analysis of the situation. An argument ensued between the two men, resulting in Hitler's decision to replace Jodl with General Friedrich Paulus after the expected victory at Stalingrad.[24] This victory, of course, never came. Paulus surrendered to the Russians, and Jodl remained at OKW.

Although Hitler treated Jodl with a cold shoulder for a while, the Fuehrer came to realize that Jodl was indispensable. For his part, Jodl remained loyal to Hitler and continued to carry out his orders. Indeed, the relationship between the two strengthened during the remainder of the war. To his credit, however, Jodl flatly refused to issue Hitler's Commando Order, which called for the execution of captured enemy commando troops. Nonetheless, even though he realized that after Stalingrad the war could not be won, Jodl believed he must continue to obey and support his supreme commander.

The spring following the Stalingrad disaster Jodl suffered a personal tragedy. His loving wife went to Koenigsberg to undergo major spinal surgery. In part, the Jodls picked this city because it was farther from Allied air bases than any other German city and had not been attacked by enemy bombers. When the Allies launched their first major bombing raid against this East Prussian city, Frau Jodl was forced to seek protection in a cold and damp air raid shelter. As a result, she contracted double pneumonia, which, in her already weakened condition, proved fatal shortly thereafter.[25]

Later that year, in November, Jodl married Louise von Benda, who had admired him for some time. She stood by him throughout his agonizing postwar trial at Nuremberg and took it upon herself to successfully vindicate her husband at the *Hauptspruchkammer* proceedings in Munich in 1953.[26]

During the final 18 months of the war, Jodl continued to labor at Fuehrer Headquarters. The general suffered minor injuries during the July 20, 1944, explosion at the Rastenburg headquarters when Count von Stauffenberg narrowly missed assassinating the dictator. The blast drew both Keitel and Jodl closer to the Fuehrer. Jodl remained with Hitler in Berlin until late April 1945, when he left for Admiral Doenitz's command post. Ironically, one of the last orders Hitler issued (April 25) placed supreme command authority in the hands of OKW. It came too late and was a clear reminder of how the dispersion of authority hampered the German war effort. By then defeat was certain, and Hitler recognized that his loyal commanders were, as he told Goebbels, exhausted.[27]

The end came soon after Jodl left the Fuehrer Bunker. Colonel General Alfred Jodl bore the responsibility of signing the document by which Germany surrendered unconditionally to the Allies. He did so at Rheims on May 7, 1945, with tears rolling down his face.

Jodl (along with Doenitz and his government) was arrested on May 23, 1945, and held for trial at Nuremberg. His defense was honest and befitting a soldier who carried out his duties. As Albert Speer wrote, "Jodl's precise and sober defense was rather imposing. He seemed to be one of the few men who stood above the situation."[28] Under interrogation, Jodl insisted that a soldier cannot be held responsible for political decisions and stated that Hitler's decisions were absolute. He faithfully followed the Fuehrer, he said, and believed the war to be a just cause. The tribunal, however, rejected his arguments, found him guilty, and sentenced him to death by hanging. While at Nuremberg, Jodl dictated a letter to the wife of his defense counsel, concluding with the following words: "He [Hitler] had himself buried in the ruins of the Reich and his hopes. May whoever wishes to condemn him for it do so—I cannot."[29] At 2 a.m. on October 16, 1946, Colonel General Alfred Jodl was hanged. Later that morning his body was cremated, and his ashes were secretly scattered beside an anonymous stream somewhere in the German countryside. Despite this fact, a cross bearing Jodl's name and rank may be seen in the family plot at the Frauen-insel Cemetery near the Chiemsee. His first wife is buried to the right of his empty grave; his second wife (who died in 1998) lies on the other side.

BERNHARD LOSSBERG, who was described by David Irving as "a towering figure with a game leg and a fearless nature,"[30] was born in Berlin-Wilm-ersdorf on July 26, 1899. His father was General of Infantry Friedrich-Karl "Fritz" von Lossberg, who had a brilliant career as a General Staff officer in the Kaiser's army, ending up as chief of staff of the 4th Army in Flanders in 1918.[31] Educated in the gymnasiums at Eisenach and Stuttgart, Bernhard entered the service in 1916 (just before his 17th birthday) and saw action in the Great War as a member of the elite 2nd Grenadier Regiment in Russia and France, and was wounded three times. One of these wounds left him with a permanent limp. He was commissioned second lieutenant in 1917.

Selected for the Reichsheer, young Lossberg served in the Prussian 5th Infantry Regiment at Stettin (now Szczecin, Poland) from 1920 to 1927, where he commanded a signals platoon at Prenzlau and served as a battal-ion adjutant. He was promoted to first lieutenant in 1925, joined the staff of the 3rd Infantry Division in 1930 at Frankfurt/Oder, and later Group Command 2 (1932). Lossberg was then posted to the staff of Wehrkreis III in Berlin,[32] and while there, he received his promotion to captain on January 4, 1933. Recognized for his hard work and ability to assimilate data into meaningful military strategy, Lossberg was assigned to the operational planning department of the Defense Ministry and was promoted to major in 1936. (Lossberg was also a noted bridge player.)

With the expansion of the Wehrmacht in Hitler's Reich, Lossberg was transferred to the 44th Infantry Regiment at Bartenstein, East Prussia, where he commanded a company. He continued to impress his superiors and in 1938 was attached to the OKW to plan joint service maneuvers. In the fall of 1938, he was sent to Spain, where he worked with Special Staff W, which recruited volunteers and transported war material to the Condor Legion. On January 2, 1939, he was promoted to lieutenant colonel and later that month assumed duties with the OKW Planning Staff, where he remained for much of World War II.

Early on, Lossberg (along with Warlimont, Jodl, and others) en-visioned a unified command structure for the armed forces. Although

Wilhelm Keitel, the chief of OKW, supported this very rational concept, Hitler rejected it; indeed, the Fuehrer treated the armed forces as he did other state organizations, by dividing authority and power. In any event, Lossberg continued his work on operational plans for OKW, including Case White—the invasion of Poland. In August 1939, Lossberg and Keitel were invited to Hitler's home in Munich. The Fuehrer assured both officers that Case White would "never" be cause for a world war. Events were to prove otherwise.

The first major challenge for the OKW was the Norwegian campaign. Serving directly as Hitler's personal staff, the OKW operations staff planned the invasion, with Hitler acting as commander-in-chief of the operation. While the Germans successfully landed forces in Narvik in early April 1940, the British sank all the German Navy's destroyers there and threatened Dietl's combat group at Narvik with defeat or with internment in Sweden. Hitler was on the edge of despair. For the first time he exhibited the panic and indecisiveness that he sometimes showed later. On April 14, a nervous and agitated Fuehrer told Keitel to order Dietl to evacuate Narvik. "The hysteria is frightful," Jodl wrote in his diary. The coded message was given to Lossberg, who angrily refused to send it. Instead, he visited Jodl, who sent him to see Colonel General Walter von Brauchitsch, the commander-in-chief of the army. Lossberg wanted him to appeal to Hitler to reverse this decision, but the weak-willed Brauchitsch refused on the grounds that he had nothing to do with the Norwegian campaign. He did, however, sign another message to Dietl (apparently drafted by Lossberg), congratulating him on his promotion to lieutenant general and stating: "I am sure you will defend your position [i.e., Narvik] to the last man." Lossberg then returned to Jodl and tore up Keitel's handwritten message before his eyes.[33]

Adolf Hitler, however, still paced nervously. He sent Lossberg to General von Falkenhorst's headquarters near Oslo to observe the situation. Lossberg returned on April 22 and reported that the British had landed only five thousand troops. Once again Hitler panicked and suggested how Falkenhorst should move his forces. Lossberg rejoined that the general controlled all the key points and Hitler should leave everything in Falkenhorst's hands—in other words, Hitler should mind his own business. The Nazi dictator did not enjoy being lectured to and for weeks afterward would not allow Lossberg into his presence. The colonel's analysis, however, proved correct, and Falkenhorst's forces seized control of the entire country.

Meanwhile, Lossberg returned to his operational planning duties at OKW, and his next task was a significant one indeed. He carried out a feasibility study of a Russian campaign. Lossberg finished his 30-page report in July 1940, and gave it the code name Fritz, his son's name.[34] Lossberg stated that for Germany to defeat Russia, the Berlin and Silesian industrial areas would have to be protected from enemy bombing. Hence, the invasion must penetrate deep into the Soviet Union, allowing the Luftwaffe to devastate important rear areas.

The primary targets in the Russian campaign, Lossberg concluded, should be Leningrad and the north, where better roads and railroads existed (or at least the Abwehr reported them to exist). German success there would also remove Soviet influence from the Baltic region and would bring both Leningrad and Moscow under German artillery fire. Furthermore, the push north would be bolstered by Group XXI, operating from Norway via Finland. He proposed the thrust north as follows: "An attack by two army groups from the general line east of Warsaw to Koenigsberg, with the southern group the more powerful [the group assembling around Warsaw and southern East Prussia] and being allocated the bulk of the armored and mechanized units."[35]

The key to the success of his plan would be the encirclement of the Soviet armies from the north and their failure to withstand a rapid onslaught. Lossberg also wrote that Russia's only hope would be to take the offensive and invade the Rumanian oil fields. Such a move would be forestalled by a German-Rumanian military agreement. Besides, Lossberg argued, the Soviets would not abandon the Baltic region, which they had seized only a few months before.

Although OKH drafted the operational plan for what was to be code-named Barbarossa, it basically followed Lossberg's plan, except that a third army group (Army Group South) was added. Although the Wehrmacht invasion of Russia proceeded rapidly in the summer of 1941, the invading armies bogged down in the mud of early winter. Then they struggled forward—but only very slowly—in subfreezing temperatures. Once again concern appeared on the faces of the men at Fuehrer Headquarters, with army generals pleading for a retreat so defensive lines could be set up. Hitler, however, insisted that the Wehrmacht continue the advance. Lossberg, believing there to be a need for a firm, unified command, tried to convince Jodl to form a unitary German staff to coordinate all services. It should be commanded by an officer who clearly demonstrated exceptional leadership—General Erich von Manstein. Jodl refused, for he knew that Manstein and Hitler did not get along.

Later that winter, sensing Lossberg's criticisms, Hitler demanded that the colonel be replaced. (The Fuehrer had not forgotten the Norwegian incident, either.) On January 1, 1942, Lossberg was promoted to full colonel and became Ia (operations officer) on the staff of the Wehrmacht commander, Norway (i.e., Falkenhorst). After two and a half years in this backwater theater, Lossberg was named chief of staff to Admiral Wilhelm Marschall, the special commissioner, Danube, in June 1944, and was promoted to major general on September 1, 1944. His last assignment was as chief of staff of Wehrkreis VIII, headquartered in Breslau, a post he held until the Replacement Army was dissolved and its various components were sent to the fronts in March 1945. Without an assignment at the end of the war, Bernhard Lossberg surrendered to the British at Neustadt/ Holstein on May 5, 1945. Released in July 1946, he retired to Wiesbaden, where he wrote *Wehrmachtfuehrungsstab: Bericht eines Generalstabs-offizier* (In the Armed Forces Operations Staff: Report of a General Staff Officer). He died in Wiesbaden on March 15, 1965.

GEORG THOMAS, the son of a factory owner, was born into an upper-middle-class family in Forst, Brandenburg, on February 20, 1890. He entered the Imperial Army as a Fahnenjunker in 1908 and received his commission as a second lieutenant in the 63rd Infantry Regiment in 1910. By 1914 he was adjutant of the III Battalion of the 63rd Infantry, which fought in France and Russia. Thomas ultimately served on various regimental staffs, as well as the General Staff. He was promoted to captain on April 18, 1917, and ultimately served on the staff of the 6th Infantry Division in France. Thomas earned the respect of the men with whom he worked and proved to be daring in combat. He received several decorations, including the House Order of Hohenzollern; the Iron Cross, First Class; the Wounded Badge; the Cross of Honor for War Service, Saxe-Meiningen; and the Austro-Hungarian Military Service Award, Third Class.

After the war, Thomas joined the Reichsheer, served on the staff of the 4th Infantry Division at Dresden, and in 1928 was assigned to the staff of the Army Weapons Office. He received his promotion to major on February 1, 1929, and became chief of staff of the Ordnance Department in 1930. During his years (1928–1938) with army ordnance, the highly gifted Thomas thoroughly studied the economic aspects of preparing for war (as well as prosecuting the war) and, in applying the lessons learned from World War I to his studies, concluded that economic warfare was equally as significant as armed warfare.[36] A nation's economic resources, Thomas argued, must be constantly inventoried for their most effective wartime use, and this must also be a major factor in preparing for war. Hence, through several written memoranda to his superiors, Thomas pushed forward the concept of a centralized agency supervising a "defense economy" to enable

Germany to make the most effective use of its economic resources, especially in the production of armaments.

Although Thomas's proposal was an ambitious one, given the complexities of an industrial society, it was the stubbornness of the three services that doomed his ideas. The army, navy, and air force insisted on supervising their own armaments programs. Consequently, the armed forces looked upon Thomas as only an adviser. "Thomas' staff never managed to exert any decisive influence on essential decisions regarding armaments," Wilhelm Deist wrote later.[37] Undaunted, Thomas continued with the economic preparations for war. His accomplishments and abilities were rewarded when he was promoted to major general on January 1, 1938, and was again promoted on January 1, 1940, to lieutenant general.

Already skeptical about the Nazi government, Thomas became more disillusioned after the Fritsch affair in 1938, during which Hitler removed Colonel General Baron Werner von Fritsch as commander-in-chief of the army on trumped-up charges of participating in homosexual activity. Even though he was subsequently cleared of the false charges, Baron von Fritsch was not reemployed. After this incident, Thomas could no longer accept National Socialism and later described his decision as "my complete inner breach with this system."[38] As a result, he began discussions with two conspirators—General Ludwig Beck (who resigned as chief of the General Staff in August 1938) and Carl Goerdeler (the mayor of Leipzig)—primarily to explore ways of preventing a conflagration that Germany could not survive.

In late summer 1939, a concerned Thomas submitted a memorandum to the chief of OKW, Colonel General Wilhelm Keitel, warning that an attack on Poland would lead to a world war for which the Reich was economically unprepared. Keitel scoffed at the notion and refused to act on Thomas's memorandum. An obsessed Thomas responded with a more detailed report containing tables and graphs "illustrating the economic warfare capacity of Germany and other great powers, from which Germany's inferiority clearly emerged."[39] This time Keitel looked with astonishment at the analysis and forwarded the report to Hitler. The Fuehrer responded nonchalantly, telling Keitel that the general should not worry, as the Soviet Union (one of the great powers cited by Thomas) would cooperate with Germany. To Keitel the matter was ended; for Thomas it had just begun.

Thomas still believed that the conflict Hitler initiated when he invaded Poland on September 1, 1939, ultimately would lead to Germany's destruction. He therefore became intimately involved with the conspirators (Beck, Goerdeler, and associates) who were trying to devise a plan to remove Hitler and other top Nazis from their positions of power. During

November 1939, Thomas attempted to convince General Franz Halder, the chief of the General Staff, and General Walter von Brauchitsch, the commander-in-chief of the army, to arrest Hitler. Both men adamantly refused, with Halder citing the soldier's duty to obey his supreme commander (Hitler). Brauchitsch was even more upset and suggested to Admiral Wilhelm Canaris, the chief of the Abwehr, that Thomas be arrested. The enigmatic Canaris—himself a peripheral member of the anti-Hitler conspiracy—hushed up the whole affair. Concerned with the possibility of German armies invading neutral countries, Thomas again tried to convince Halder to take some action; Thomas showed Halder a message from Dr. Josef Mueller, a Bavarian lawyer friendly with Pope Pius XI, which stated that if both Hitler and Foreign Minister Joachim von Ribbentrop were eliminated, the Vatican would intercede to bring about peace. Halder again rejected Thomas's pleas.

Failure to convince others to act against Hitler subdued Thomas's conspiratorial activities for a while. Following the successful German invasion of Denmark and Norway in the spring of 1940, a discouraged Thomas decided to let fate run its course. By then he had been promoted to general of infantry (on August 1, 1940) and had become head of the Economic Department and Armament Office of the army (in addition to his duties at OKW). Although he conscientiously carried out his duties, his efforts were still plagued by the interservice rivalry mentioned earlier.

Operation Barbarossa, the invasion of the Soviet Union in June 1941, once again stirred the despondent Thomas. During late August and early September, he journeyed to the Russian Front, visiting several army groups to gauge possible support for a coup against Hitler. Although he received no direct assent to such a plan, General Thomas was "moderately satisfied," according to fellow conspirator Ulrich von Hassell, the former ambassador to Italy.[40]

It was during this trip to the Eastern Front that Thomas witnessed the murder of Jews by the *Einsatzgruppen*—the mobile killing units of the SS and SD. An infuriated Thomas shared his experience with Baron Friedrich von Falkenhausen, another active conspirator, and the two of them visited Field Marshal von Brauchitsch. They wanted to ascertain how Brauchitsch now felt about the Hitler regime. Brauchitsch responded by pointing out to his visitors that it was his duty to obey his Fuehrer. Thomas then blurted out that Brauchitsch was partly responsible for the murder of the Jews. The field marshal walked away without replying.

A rebuffed Thomas returned to his duties and on May 6, 1942, was appointed to the Armaments Council. Although he still disdained the Nazi

regime, he carried out his duties and participated in the planning, for example, of the economic exploitation of occupied Russia. Later that month,
in fact, he was appointed chief of the new Armaments Office of the Reich
Ministry for Armaments and Munitions. Although he had an impressive
title, economic authority was still divided, with Albert Speer (Hitler's designated munitions expert) assuming more and more control. Consequently,
Thomas resigned his post in the armaments and munitions ministry on
November 20, 1942. He continued his duties at OKW, however.

Thomas took no further part in the anti-Hitler conspiracy after the
Casablanca Conference of January 1943. At the conclusion of these meetings, U.S. President Franklin D. Roosevelt announced that the Allies
would accept nothing less than the unconditional surrender of Germany,
Italy, and Japan. Since Thomas saw that the war was clearly lost and that
no alternative German government could expect any softening of the Allied terms, the general felt that the assassination of Hitler would serve no
purpose except to make Hitler a martyr in the eyes of the German people.[41]

After the July 20, 1944, assassination attempt, papers were discovered
that implicated Thomas as a possible conspirator. Although the Nazi tribunal failed to uncover any direct evidence linking Thomas with the attempt
on Hitler's life, he was nevertheless arrested and sent to the prison camp at
Flossenburg. He also spent time at Dachau Concentration Camp and was
finally imprisoned in a concentration camp in South Tyrol, Italy. As the
war came to an end, Thomas was rescued by American troops and quickly
freed. He moved to Frankfurt-am-Main, but his health had been broken
during his imprisonment, and he died there on December 29, 1946.

WALTER BUHLE was born in Heilbronn, Wuerttemberg, on October 26,
1894. He joined the Imperial Army as a Fahnenjunker on July 10, 1913,
received his commission in August 1914 (just as World War I broke out),
and served mainly with the Wuerttemberger 124th Infantry Regiment
(27th Infantry Division) in Lorraine and the 122nd Fusilier Regiment
(26th Infantry Division) on the Eastern Front. Severely wounded in June
1915, he recovered, underwent mortar training, and served with a mortar battalion for the rest of the war. After serving as a signals officer with
the Reichsheer's 13th Infantry Regiment at Ludwigsburg, Wuerttemberg
(1921), he transferred to the Wuerttemberger 18th Cavalry Regiment,
where he began his General Staff training. After attending the College for
Politics in Berlin (1925–1926), Buhle worked in the Defense Ministry and
Group Command 1 in Berlin (1926–1930). Promoted to captain in 1926,
he commanded a company in the 13th Infantry Regiment from 1930 to

late 1932, when he returned to the Defense Ministry and was assigned to the Organizations Department (T-2). Promoted to major in 1933 and lieutenant colonel in 1936, he commanded II/87th Infantry Regiment, a former provincial police unit in Aschaffenburg, northwest Bavaria, from October 1936 to October 1937. He was Ia of Wehrkreis V at Stuttgart from October 1937 to November 1938, when he was posted to the army General Staff. He was promoted to full colonel in early 1939 and, in recognition of his knowledge and technical expertise in the field of armaments, he was named head of the Organizations Section of OKH five days before World War II began. A convinced Nazi, Buhle was rewarded for his loyalty and hard work by promotion to major general in 1940 and to lieutenant general in 1942.

Buhle was given greater responsibility when he was assigned to the post of chief of the army staff at OKW in January 1942. He was disliked by other generals, for he meddled in everything and was a trusted informant for Hitler. General Warlimont noticed his personality flaws and wrote that Buhle bypassed Keitel (the chief of OKW and his direct superior) and established a direct, personal relationship with Hitler.[42]

Buhle's isolation at Fuehrer Headquarters, along with his propensity for offering a view on all matters (his "meddling") was apparent at a Fuehrer conference on July 25, 1943. The conference centered on the Italian situation, which had deteriorated, as Mussolini had been removed from power the previous day, and the German situation in the Mediterranean was potentially desperate. Hitler was discussing the situation with Jodl and Keitel when Buhle interjected that Italy must be given top priority for all transport vehicles. He even insisted that everything on the assembly line or on the way to the East should be sent to the German troops in the Rome area. He made this recommendation at a time when army groups Center and South were fighting the largest armored battle in history at Kursk and needed all the vehicles they could possibly get to supply and reinforce their regiments.

Buhle, in charge of army transport, fumed at the generals who always demanded more and, Buhle believed, interfered with his allocation plans. In December 1943, for example, Buhle complained during a Fuehrer briefing that he could assure that there would be adequate tank battalions in the West, provided no one took them away. "No sooner have I got something together," he went on, "than it's gone."[43] Hitler angrily asked if Buhle was referring to him, which of course he was not. His remark was aimed at Colonel General Kurt Zeitzler, who had replaced Halder as the chief of OKH in September 1942.

This type of criticism of OKH by Buhle and others contributed to Hitler's declining confidence in General Zeitzler. On the other hand, Hitler demonstrated his faith in Buhle by promoting him to general of infantry on April 1, 1944. The Fuehrer wanted to make him chief of the General Staff in place of Zeitzler later that year; however, Buhle was severely wounded by the July 20 explosion at Hitler's headquarters and was in the hospital for some time. He did not fully recover for weeks after that. Ironically enough, the would-be assassin was Colonel Count Claus von Stauffenberg, a talented General Staff officer who had been one of Buhle's principal assistants in the Organizations Branch from 1940 to 1942. After some initial friction the two had worked well together, although the aristocratic Stauffenberg commented at the time that Buhle was "not altogether" a gentleman.[44]

In January 1945, Hitler chose Buhle to replace Emil von Leeb as head of the Army Weapons Office (i.e., chief of armaments for the army).[45] Buhle did his best to supply the German field forces, but the combination of Allied bombing and lack of labor made his task nearly impossible. Nonetheless, he gave it his best effort. It is interesting to note that it was Buhle who by chance found Admiral Wilhelm Canaris's diaries, which clearly indicated that the former chief of the Abwehr had been in contact with the anti-Hitler conspirators of July 20. Ever the pro-Hitler informer, Buhle handed the evidence over to the Gestapo. As a result the admiral was stripped naked, taken out, and hanged by the SS on April 9, 1945.

General Buhle survived the war and the subsequent trials. Released from Allied captivity in 1947, he retired to Stuttgart, where he died on December 28, 1959.

WILHELM BURGDORF was born on February 15, 1895, in Fuerstenwalde/ Spree. On August 3, 1914, as World War I was breaking out, the 19-year-old Burgdorf joined the Imperial Army as a Fahnenjunker in the 12th Grenadier Regiment of the Brandenburger 5th Infantry Division. Commissioned second lieutenant in 1915, he rejoined the main body of his regiment on the Eastern Front in the spring of 1915 and was named adjutant of its fusilier battalion. Burgdorf fought in Belgium and France, including the battles of Verdun and the Somme. He became regimental adjutant in 1916 and held the post until after the end of the war, fighting in Alsace, Champagne, the Russian Front, and Italy. Returning to the Western Front in early 1918, he fought in the Battle of Picardy, the Aisne, the Marne, and the Ardennes.

After the armistice, Second Lieutenant Burgdorf joined the Reichsheer as adjutant of the 54th and then 10th Grenadier Regiment, a platoon leader in the Prussian 10th Grenadiers (1920–1921) and its successor unit, the 8th Infantry Regiment at Frankfurt/Oder (1921–1923). He became adjutant of the I/8th Infantry at the start of 1923, and began his General Staff training in the fall of that year. Despite a solid record, he was not promoted to first lieutenant until 1925.

After a thorough training program, Burgdorf returned to the 8th Infantry at Frankfurt/Oder (1925–1933), where he worked as a signals officer, regimental adjutant, and company commander. He was on the staff of the 4th Infantry Division at Dresden (1934–1936) and, by the end of 1936, was serving as adjutant of Wehrkreis IX (IX Corps) at Kassel. He was promoted to captain in 1930, major in 1935, and lieutenant colonel in August 1938.

During the early days of the war Burgdorf served as adjutant of the IX Corps on the virtually inactive Western Front. Prior to the invasion of France, however, he was named commander of the 529th Infantry Regiment, which he led in Belgium and France (1940) and in the savage battles on the central sector of the Russian Front (1941–April 4, 1942). After the Soviet winter offensive of 1941–1942 had been checked, Burgdorf (who had been promoted to full colonel in September 1940) was made a department chief in the Army Personnel Office (*Heerespersonelamt*, or HPA), a part of OKW, in May 1942. On October 1, 1942, he was promoted to major general and named deputy chief of the Army Personnel Office; he was elevated to lieutenant general in October 1943. No doubt his overt allegiance to the Nazi Party played a major role in his rapid advancement.

The failed assassination attempt by Colonel von Stauffenberg on July 20, 1944, led to further advancement for Burgdorf, as well as his participating in the extraction of revenge on the anti-Hitler conspirators. General of Infantry Rudolf Schmundt, the Fuehrer's Army adjutant and chief of the HPA, was mortally wounded by the explosion, which only slightly injured Hitler. Taken to the Rastenburg hospital, Schmundt succumbed to his injuries on October 1, 1944, and Hitler named Burgdorf his successor.

Adolf Hitler demanded quick and brutal revenge be meted out to the conspirators. One victim was Germany's most popular commander, Field Marshal Erwin Rommel, the legendary Desert Fox, who was implicated in the plot. Field Marshal Keitel called upon Burgdorf to carry out a secret mission—to confront Rommel with the testimony that accused him of complicity in the "treason." If the statements were true, the popular Rommel was to be given a choice: suicide or a trial before the People's Court.

Obediently, Burgdorf and his deputy, Lieutenant General Ernst Maisel, went to Rommel's home at Herrlingen on October 14, armed with the letter and a box of poison ampules. Burgdorf had the residence surrounded by SS men; then he and Maisel went inside and confronted the gallant field marshal with Keitel's letter. To Maisel's surprise, Rommel admitted that he had plotted to help have Adolf Hitler deposed. Burgdorf then presented the field marshal with his choices. If he chose suicide, Hitler promised him a state funeral with full military honors and guaranteed safety for his family, including a pension for his wife and son. If the Desert Fox chose the People's Court, he could expect his family to share his fate. Erwin Rommel chose the poison and was dead within an hour.

While one can only speculate about Burgdorf's thoughts when he carried out his mission at Rommel's house, his later remarks clearly demonstrate his unwavering loyalty to Hitler and the Nazi cause. As the new chief of the Army Personnel Office and now an accessory to the murder of one of the Fuehrer's opponents, Burgdorf became part of Hitler's inner circle and remained at his side until almost the moment of his death. Hitler appreciated Burgdorf's absolute loyalty and rewarded him with a promotion to general of infantry, effective November 1, 1944. Also, it was on Burgdorf's recommendation that Hitler appointed General of Infantry Hans Krebs to replace Colonel General Heinz Guderian as chief of the General Staff in March 1945.

Wilhelm Burgdorf was a stocky, brutal man. He was a heavy drinker and was hated by much of the officer corps because of his slavish devotion to Nazism. During the last two months of the war, Burgdorf did his best to maintain order and did not believe the situation in Berlin was utterly hopeless—as in fact it was. As Goebbels recorded in his diary on March 13, 1945, "The Army Personnel section is the first Wehrmacht organization where everything is totally in order and of which no criticism can be made. Obviously therefore General Burgdorf has done a good job here too."[46] Indeed, although Hitler raged about army officers, SS officers, and even long-time party faithfuls, there is no record of him ever berating Burgdorf. Meanwhile, the general allied himself with Goebbels and Martin Bormann, the inner sanctum of Hitler's unreal world in the last days of the Reich. Burgdorf and Bormann got along particularly well. At a party at Rastenburg, for example, the two hard-drinking Nazis actually danced together and denounced the treacherous field marshals.[47]

Burgdorf briefly recognized his flaunting of duty and integrity as a German officer; on April 8, 1945, he told Krebs, "Ever since I took on this job, nearly a year ago, I've put all my energy and idealism into it. I've tried every way I know to bring the army and party closer together. . . . In the end they accused me in the forces of being a traitor to the German officer class, and now I can see that those recriminations were justified, that my work was in vain, my idealism wrong—not only wrong but naive and stupid."[48]

The chief of HPA soon recovered from his moroseness, however, and remained loyal to the Fuehrer and the Nazi cause until the end. As the Soviets closed in, Burgdorf made it clear that he would remain in the bunker. He was among those who were present at Hitler's final farewell, shortly before the Fuehrer committed suicide. General Burgdorf, General Krebs, and an SS bodyguard were the only ones who remained in the bunker following Hitler's death. It is generally believed that Burgdorf and Krebs shot themselves in the cellar of the New Chancellery on May 1, 1945, shortly before the Russians arrived. Their bodies were lost in the confusion accompanying the fall of Berlin, and their final resting places are unknown.

HERMANN REINECKE was born at Wittenburg/Elbe on February 14, 1888. Educated in cadet schools, he joined the army as a Faehnrich in 1905 and was commissioned second lieutenant in the 79th Infantry Regiment in 1906. During World War I he served the Kaiser enthusiastically and courageously, fighting on both the Eastern and Western fronts and receiving the Hohenzollern House Order; the Iron Cross, First Class; the Hamburg Hanseatic Cross; and the Austro-Hungarian Military Service Cross. He became a first lieutenant during the first months of the war and in 1916 was promoted to captain.

Remaining in the army after World War I, Reinecke served on the staff of the 2nd Infantry Regiment at Allenstein, East Prussia (now Olsztyn, Poland) and from 1928 to 1932 was on the staff of the Defense Ministry, where his duties varied but included working with the staffs of technical schools and supply services. He was promoted to major in February 1929 and in October 1932, assumed command of the II Battalion, 6th Infantry Regiment at Luebeck. He was promoted to lieutenant colonel in June 1933.

In August 1938, Reinecke was appointed head of the General Military Affairs Office of the Armed Forces High Command (OKW). He excelled in his new role, which included supervision of indoctrination training, and he enjoyed hobnobbing with Nazi bigwigs. His attitudes and connections naturally did his career no harm. He was promoted to major general on January 1, 1939, and to lieutenant general on August 1, 1940.

Reinecke made every attempt to please both his superiors in OKW and party officials at the Reich Chancellery. Many army officers referred to him as "little Keitel," comparing him unfavorably to Wilhelm Keitel, the chief of OKW, who practically threw himself at Hitler's feet. This nickname was also a slap at his height: Reinecke was only five foot seven and weighed 150 pounds.

At a meeting in July 1941, with Major General Erwin Lahousen of the Abwehr, Colonel Breuer of the POW Department, and Gestapo Chief Heinrich Mueller, Reinecke declared that the only goal of every Russian was to destroy Germany; the Soviets should, therefore, be considered mortal enemies and treated accordingly. He then accused the German officer corps of failure to recognize this, claiming it was still "in the ice age."[49]

Appropriately enough, under Nazi logic, Reinecke was placed in charge of Soviet prisoners of war, and his handling of this task reflected his pathological hatred of Communism. Repeating his earlier sentiments, on September 8, 1941, he issued the following order:

> Bolshevism is the mortal enemy of National Socialist Germany. For the first time the German soldier faces an enemy not trained merely as a soldier but with Bolshevisk political schooling, which is so pernicious to the people. For this reason the Russian soldier loses all claim to treatment as an honorable soldier according to the Geneva Convention.[50]

Furthermore, Reinecke ordered, Russian prisoners of war were to be beaten if they demonstrated any sign of resistance and were to be immediately shot if they tried to escape. These measures, along with similar actions taken by the army and the SS, resulted in a 65 percent death rate for Soviet prisoners of war. The Geneva Convention accords regarding treatment of POWs were completely ignored. Recognizing Reinecke's loyalty to Nazism, the government appointed him an honorary member of the People's Court in 1942 and on June 1 of the same year promoted him to general of infantry.

Reinecke gloated in the limelight of Nazi recognition and continued to emphasize how important it was for OKW officers to be properly indoctrinated politically. Indeed, in 1943, he informed Hitler that he and Bormann's staff were recruiting hard-core, veteran party warriors to work with young "battle-hardened" army officers. Such enthusiasm did not go unnoticed, and in July 1943, Reinecke became chief of the Combined Armed Forces Office (Personnel). In this new position he introduced what for Germany was a new idea for indoctrination: the National Socialist Leadership Officers, who, modeled on their Soviet counterparts, would serve as German "Commissars."

Reinecke's concept became formalized in February 1944, when Hitler approved the appointment of National Socialist Leadership Officers (NSFOs) to the OKW and OKH. The OKW established its NSFO staff under General Reinecke, while General of Mountain Troops Ferdinand Schoerner was named chief of the NSFOs for the army. Almost immediately friction occurred between Reinecke and Schoerner over the role NSFOs should have with the regular armed forces.

Major General Ernst Maisel of the Army Personnel Office voiced the army's disdain when he criticized Reinecke's speech, "The Duties of the NS-Leadership Staff of OKW and the Purpose and Objectives of the NS-Leadership," given at Sonthofen on May 15, 1944. In it, Reinecke had told future NSFOs that it was their duty to instill a patriotic, Nazi belief among soldiers to defend Hitler's Reich. General Maisel caustically remarked that Reinecke did not speak with the "heart of a combat soldier"—nor could he.[51] How could Reinecke, a desk general, have any idea how to motivate fighting men, Maisel asked, or understand how little importance political indoctrination really had? Nonetheless Reinecke set up a training program for NSFO recruits (most were reserve officers who were simultaneously Nazi Party members). The program concentrated on instilling a so-called Nazi fighting spirit into the men in uniform. To assist in these efforts, Reinecke sought the support and the approval of Nazi stalwarts Bormann and Himmler.

Reinecke also advocated making NSF training part of normal operations—that is, political indoctrination would take place on a continual basis as part of the daily routine. He wanted NSFOs to share privileges granted to other army officers—an idea that infuriated regular Army officers, who felt NSFO men did not deserve such privileges because they were not combat soldiers.

The July 20, 1944, attempt on Hitler's life directly affected Reinecke's role in the Third Reich. During the chaotic hours following the explosion, Reinecke (acting on the orders of Keitel) assumed command of Berlin, after ordering Lieutenant General Paul von Hase, the incumbent commandant, to hand his forces over to him. Even though Hase was one of the conspirators, he obviously realized that the coup attempt had failed, and he did as Reinecke instructed, apparently hoping that this last-minute change of face would save him from the gallows (which it did not).[52] Meanwhile, Reinecke quickly restored order in the capital and made it clear to the Berlin garrison that Hitler was alive and very much in command.

Reinecke later served as president of the Court of Honor, which tried officers who were involved in the plot against Hitler, quickly expelled them from the army, and handed them over to the People's Court.

During this same period, Bormann told him that the NSFO program had to be strengthened. To accomplish this, Reinecke issued an order on August 8, instructing NSFOs to "concentrate their entire energy toward the utmost activation and fanaticization of the soldiers."[53] He directed them to get the most out of the troops and to ignore standard operating procedures. Now, more than ever, fanatical loyalty to the Fuehrer and Germany must be stressed.

Reinecke amplified his views in an article that appeared in the October 1944 issue of the *Political Soldier*, a magazine published by OKW in cooperation with the Nazi Party. He wrote that the goal was to have the soldier act as if the Fuehrer were with him; soldiers, he wrote, must realize that they carry Hitler's vision with them. The NSFOs must talk to all officers and men and have the troops reaffirm their oath of allegiance to the Fuehrer. However, not even the Hitler mystique could stop the Soviet steamroller in the East or the Allied thrust into France. Consequently, the NSF program failed to accomplish its objectives, as war-weary soldiers paid little attention to political indoctrination, and combat officers stonewalled NSFOs at every opportunity. Party stalwarts blamed Reinecke for the NSF failure, but Field Marshal Keitel supported him and fended off the criticisms of the party. Martin Bormann, as head of Hitler's chancellery and secretary of the party, received the criticisms but, because of Keitel's interference, hesitated to take any action. As the reprobation continued, however, Reinecke felt more and more responsible for the failure of the program and suggested to Bormann that he, the party secretary, assume command of the NSFO system. Loyal Nazi supporter that he was, Reinecke could no longer bear the pain of having failed to politically acclimate the fighting men of Germany. The general further volunteered to dismantle his staff and to support any reorganization Bormann proposed. Reinecke's condescending to party opinion infuriated Keitel, who had stood by his general. A rift subsequently occurred between the two that never healed. Even so, Bormann refused to take any decisive action, and Reinecke retained command of the NSFOs. He finally gave up hope of effective political indoctrination and, on April 9, 1945, virtually admitted defeat when he ordered the NSFOs to actively fight the enemy and refrain from any political proselytizing.

At the end of the war Reinecke surrendered to the Allies and was placed in a detention camp by the U.S. Army. Shortly thereafter, as his activities became known (especially his brutal treatment of prisoners of war), he was tried by a U.S. military tribunal and sentenced to life in prison on October 28, 1948.[54] Incarcerated at Landsberg, Reinecke later had his sentence reduced to 27 years, and he was released in October 1954. He retired to Hamburg and died on October 10, 1973, at the age of 85.

★ ★ ★

FRIEDRICH "FRITZ" FROMM was born in Berlin-Charlottenburg on October 8, 1888. He entered the Imperial Army as a Fahnenjunker in the 55th Field Artillery Regiment in late December 1906, and was commissioned second lieutenant in 1908. He was adjutant of the I Battalion when World War I broke out and was promoted to first lieutenant in November 1914. As part of the Alsacian 38th Infantry Division, Fritz Fromm fought in Belgium, East Prussia, and Poland; was wounded at least once; and was admitted to the General Staff in 1915. He became adjutant of the 38th Artillery Brigade of the 38th Division in 1915, and fought at Aisle, at Verdun, at the Somme, and in Flanders. He received an accelerated promotion to captain in the spring of 1916. He spent the last two years of the war on the staff of the 30th Infantry Division (also an Alsacian unit) and fought in Champagne, including the Battle of Cambrai.

After the armistice, Fromm was retained in the Reichsheer and by 1920 was commanding a battery in the Prussian 3rd Artillery Regiment at Frankfurt/Oder. He was transferred to the staff of the 3rd Infantry Division (also at Frankfurt/Oder) in 1922 and to the Defense Ministry in 1927. From June 1932 to January 1933, he commanded the IV Battalion of the 3rd Artillery Regiment at Potsdam.

On February 1, 1933—two days after Hitler took power—Fromm was named chief of the Defense Office in the Defense Ministry. He remained in Berlin the rest of his career, rising to chief of the General Army Office in the Defense Ministry and later the War Ministry and OKH. When Germany mobilized, he was named commander-in-chief of the Replacement Army, effective August 31, 1939. Headquartered in the Bendlerstrasse, a huge building complex that served as Nazi Germany's Pentagon and was formally the site of the Defense Ministry, Fromm was also named chief of army armaments and equipment in November 1939. He did not relinquish control of the General Army Office to his deputy, General of Infantry Friedrich Olbricht, until June 1940. Meanwhile, Fromm was promoted to major (1927), lieutenant colonel (1931), colonel (February 1, 1933), major general (November 1, 1935), lieutenant general (January 1, 1938), and general of artillery (April 20, 1939).

Fromm did not look like a typical Prussian general. He was a heavy cigar smoker, very overweight, and out of shape. He was, however, an enthusiastic hunter and enjoyed the pleasures of life. He was also a corporate climber who first and foremost looked after the career and well being of Fritz Fromm. This, however, did not mean that he was not competent. German mobilization functioned smoothly, as did the German draft.

Fromm was also responsible for supervising the German Wehrkreise, train-ing German soldiers and officers, rebuilding battered divisions and forming new ones. He did not lose control of the panzer replacement and training units and facilities to Heinz Guderian until early 1943, after the fall of Stalingrad. Despite his best and repeated efforts, Guderian was never able to take the assault gun arm from the Replacement Army, where Fromm kept it under the artillery branch. This was probably a good thing for the German Army. Assault guns flowed smoothly from the Replacement (or Home) Army to the field forces, along with exceptionally well-trained of-ficers and crews. In the period from June 1941 to January 1944, the assault guns (most of which were mounted on obsolete Panzer Mark III chassis), knocked out more than 20,000 Soviet tanks. It is difficult indeed to imagine them performing any better than they did.

Fromm succeeded in ingratiating himself with Hitler, who recognized how well the Replacement Army functioned and the part it played in his victories. On July 19, 1940, after the fall of France, Hitler rewarded Fromm by promoting him to colonel general and decorating him with the Knight's Cross, which was normally reserved for combat soldiers. As the war progressed, however, Fromm's standing at Fuehrer Headquarters began to slip. Heinrich Himmler wanted control of the Home Army for himself; Wilhelm Keitel, the commander-in-chief of OKW, hated Fromm bitterly, and the feeling was mutual.

For his part, Fromm realized that Germany was losing the war. He wanted to remain on top, even if Germany fell.

Meanwhile, a crippled lieutenant colonel returned from the hospital. General Olbricht named the man his chief of staff. Recognizing that this man was brilliant, Fromm took him from Olbricht, named him chief of staff of the Replacement Army, and promoted him to colonel. His name was Claus von Stauffenberg.

Fromm soon learned that Stauffenberg was the de facto leader of the plot to overthrow Adolf Hitler. He allowed him to proceed and is even said to have told Stauffenberg, "Don't forget Keitel!" when he launched his coup. The general, however, refused to join the conspiracy himself. His attitude was that he would join it (and take the credit) if it were successful, but he would deny all knowledge and suppress it if it were unsuccessful.

Using a delayed-action fuse, Stauffenberg detonated a bomb in Hitler's briefing hut at the Fuehrer Headquarters near Rastenburg, East Prussia, on July 20, 1944. After he returned to Berlin, the conspirators launched a mili-tary coup against the Nazi regime, without informing Fromm. The general, however, soon learned that Hitler was still alive and, when the one-eyed colonel announced that he had detonated the bomb himself, urged him to commit suicide. Instead, Stauffenberg arrested his commander-in-chief.

Late that evening, the coup collapsed, and pro-Nazi forces freed General Fromm and arrested several conspirators. With Fromm's permission, Colonel General Ludwig Beck, the former chief of the General Staff, was allowed to shoot himself. When his wound did not kill him, Fromm ordered a sergeant to finish him off. Then, acting with lightning speed, Fromm announced that a court-martial (consisting of himself) had convicted four other officers and sentenced them to death. Major Otto Ernst Remer, the commander of the Watch Battalion that had captured the Bendlerstrasse and freed Fromm, objected, because the executions were against the orders of the Fuehrer (who wanted them taken alive), but he was quickly and firmly overruled by Fromm. At 10 minutes after midnight on July 21, a firing squad executed Stauffenberg, Olbricht, Lieutenant Werner von Haeften (Stauffenberg's aide), and Colonel Albrecht Mertz von Quirnheim, another prominent conspirator. Fromm was preparing to execute others at 12:30 a.m., when SS Colonel Otto Skorzeny arrived and put an end to the killings. Fromm then went to see Propaganda Minister Dr. Paul Joseph Goebbels, to take credit for suppressing the coup.

Goebbels listened to Fromm's remarkable claim in disbelief and said "You have been in a damn hurry to get your witnesses below ground." He then had Fromm locked in the basement. Typically, Fromm asked for a bottle of wine. After drinking that, he asked for another. Somewhat put out, Goebbels agreed, but remarked that he was not going to provide an unlimited supply.

Although Fromm was expelled from the army by the so-called Court of Honor, the People's Court and Gestapo did not have enough evidence to convict Fromm of treason because too many of the witnesses were dead. Hitler had him tried for cowardice instead. He was sentenced to death on March 7, 1945, and was executed by a firing squad at the Brandenburg-Goerden Prison on March 12. His last words were, "I die because it was ordered. I had always wanted only the best for Germany."[55]

2

THE WARLORDS
OF THE EASTERN FRONT

**Fedor von Bock. Ritter Wilhelm von Leeb.
Georg von Kuechler. Georg Lindemann. Friedrich Mieth.
Count Hans Emil Otto von Sponeck. Gotthard Heinrici.**

FEDOR VON BOCK was born in Kuestrin, Brandenburg province, on December 3, 1880, the son of Moritz von Bock, a distinguished Prussian general. He spent his childhood in the old fortress city of Kuestrin on the Oder River, quartered in buildings dating back to Frederick the Great. He spent hours playing on the banks of the fortress moat, imbibing the lessons of history—especially Prussian military history. All of this left an indelible mark on his development and character. All he ever wanted to do in his entire life was reach the top ranks of the army, and indeed he had a lifelong contempt for anything that was not Prussian or military. He once confessed that the only kind of art to which he could respond was the performance of a brass band. Indifferent to good food or drink, he could fast for days and still execute his duty in a demanding—indeed, fanatical—manner. He grew up to be overly serious, extremely ambitious, arrogant, opinionated, and humorless. One officer recalled that his "piercing gray eyes, in a severely lined face, look through you, their appraising regard not softened by any amiable pretense . . . his cold detachment would just as well become a hangman. . . . If he has a mental awareness of spheres of life other than that of the Army, and human beings other than those in uniform, he gives them no consideration."[1]

Capable but not brilliant, von Bock threw himself into his career with a fanatical zeal. Educated in cadet schools at Potsdam and Gross Lichterfelde, he was commissioned into the elite 5th Potsdam Foot Guards Regiment in 1898. He became a battalion adjutant in 1904 and regimental adjutant in 1906. After attending the War Academy, he joined the General Staff as a provisional member in 1910 and became a permanent member in 1912, the year he was promoted to captain. He then became Ib (General Staff officer, supply) for the elite Guards Corps, a post that he held when the war began. In September 1914, he became Ia (chief of operations) of the Guards Corps, before joining the staff of the 11th Army on the Eastern Front in May 1915.[2] In January 1916, Bock temporarily assumed command of a battalion in the Prussian 4th Foot Guards Regiment. He led this unit with such fanatical courage that he won the *Pour le Merite* in the process. The official citation did not state the circumstances leading to the award, but it did not use the usual adjective "conspicuous" when referring to his bravery; instead, it described his courage as "incredible": almost unique praise for the Imperial German Army.[3]

After his tour as a battalion commander, Bock became first General Staff officer (Ia) of the 200th Infantry Division, a reserve unit of southern Germans not up to the standards of the Guards. Here Bock was almost universally hated by the other officers of the staff.[4] This was a trend that would endure: none of Bock's staff officers ever liked him or had much respect for him, largely because he took credit for their ideas himself.[5] Nevertheless, Bock was promoted to major at the end of 1916, and the division did well on the Russian Front. A 1918 American intelligence report called it "one of the best divisions in the German Army."[6]

In April 1917, Bock returned to France as Ib on the staff of Army Group Crown Prince, which was commanded by Crown Prince Rupprecht of Bavaria, with whom he was friendly. On July 27, 1917, he became the chief of operations, working under Rupprecht's chief of staff, Count Frederick von der Schulenberg.

Following the armistice, von Bock served on the Army Peace Commission and then became an associate of Hans von Seeckt, commander-in-chief of the Reichsheer. As chief of staff of Wehrkreis III in Berlin, Major von Bock was involved in the clandestine activities of the Black Reichswehr, a secret organization of illegal military formations operating under the disguise of volunteer civilian laborers. In September 1923, this group got out of hand and rebelled against the Weimar Republic, forcing General von Seeckt to suppress it by force of arms. At the ensuing trial, the recently promoted Lieutenant Colonel von Bock was called to the witness stand, where he denied any knowledge of the Black Reichswehr. He was lying, of course, but he got away with it, as did Kurt von Schleicher and Baron Kurt von Hammerstein. The left-wing press also accused Bock of being involved in several political murders conducted by the *Femegerichte* (Secret

Court), another illicit right-wing organization. Again, however, they were unable to prove their allegations.

Bock's subsequent Reichsheer career was less controversial. He became commander of the II Battalion, 4th Infantry Regiment at Kolberg, Pomerania (now Kolobrzeg, Poland) (1924–1926); commander of the 4th Infantry (1926–1929); commander of the 1st Cavalry Division at Frankfurt/ Oder (1929–1931); and commander of Wehrkreis II at Stettin (1931–1935). He was successively promoted to full colonel (1926), major general (1928), lieutenant general (1931), and general of infantry (1931), the rank he held when Hitler came to power.

General von Bock was a non-Nazi but certainly not an anti-Nazi. He wholeheartedly supported Hitler's military policies and was not concerned with his domestic or foreign policies; as a result Bock was considered acceptable by the Fuehrer and his Nazi Party cronies. When many of Bock's colleagues and peers were relieved or forced into retirement on the thinnest of pretexts, Bock would not lift a finger to help them or utter a single word of protest. Hitler thus saw him as a willing tool. Bock, of course, was well aware that the removal of senior generals only helped him move up the professional ladder. He was given command of Army Group 3 at Dresden in 1935 and was promoted to colonel general on March 1, 1938.

Bock's army group (temporarily redesignated 8th Army) was in charge of the occupation of Austria in 1938 and had the task of incorporating the units of the former Austrian Army into the German Army. Here Bock's true personality came out again. He openly displayed his contempt for everything Austrian, including his own war decorations from the Austro-Hungarian Empire, which he referred to as "scrap iron." During this period, Hermann Goering invited him to parades, ceremonies, and other social events celebrating the *Anschluss*. Bock, however, considered Hitler's deputy a civilian and therefore beneath him. He rejected all invitations, without even the pretense of politeness. Because of Bock's lack of social adroitness, Hitler soon had to transfer his difficult general back to Dresden. His own patrimony notwithstanding, Hitler himself held many Austrian traits in low regard, however, so Bock's attitude was not to count against him.

Later in 1938, Bock commanded some of the forces that occupied the Sudetenland. He was accompanied by his nine-year-old son, who was wearing a sailor's suit and a beret. He wished, Bock told foreign journalists, to impress the boy with "the beauty of and exhilaration of soldiering."[7] Shortly thereafter, another general ran afoul of the Nazis, and Bock was summoned to Berlin to replace Gerd von Rundstedt as commander-in-chief of Army Group 1.

For the 1939 invasion of Poland, Bock's headquarters was redesignated Army Group North, and it had a strength of about 630,000 men. Rundstedt was called out of retirement to command the other army group used in Poland (Army Group South) and had the major responsibility for the campaign. Bock nevertheless relished his role, for he liked Poles even less than south Germans or Austrians. He overran the Polish Corridor and drove all the way to Brest-Litovsk in eastern Poland, where he linked up with the Soviets. By early October Bock had successfully completed all his assignments and was on his way to the Western Front.

According to the original German plan, Bock's headquarters (now designated Army Group B) was supposed to direct the major effort against the Western Allies. Unfortunately (from Bock's point of view) the German plan was an unimaginative rehash of the Schlieffen Plan, which had failed in 1914. Bock wrote a memorandum criticizing it, and Hitler agreed. Then, early in 1940, Erich von Manstein proposed a superior plan, which envisioned Rundstedt's Army Group A delivering the main blow. Subsequently adopted, the Manstein Plan left Bock with a vital but secondary mission: drive into the Low Countries with enough vigor to convince the Allies that his was the main attack. That he succeeded in this mission no one can doubt. His two armies (the 18th and 6th) overran Holland and most of Belgium and finished off the remnants of the French forces at Dunkirk, taking tens of thousands of prisoners in the process.

During the second phase of operations in the West, Bock, with three armies and two panzer groups under his control, overran western France. After the French capitulated, Bock was promoted to field marshal on July 19, 1940. After this he briefly commanded occupation forces in France but made himself so obnoxious that Hitler transferred him back to Poland, where he directed defenses on the Eastern Frontier. The dour field marshal was ill with stomach ulcers much of the winter.

By now even Fedor von Bock was sick of the excesses of the Nazi regime and went so far as to knowingly tolerate having members of the anti-Hitler conspiracy on his staff. These men hoped to gain his support in a coup d'état against the Nazi government but were doomed to disappointment. Bock's attitude was characteristic: "I will join you if you succeed but will have nothing to do with you if you fail." Bock did not modify this position for the rest of the war.

Field Marshal von Bock was opposed to the invasion of the Soviet Union in 1941; nevertheless, his headquarters (now called Army Group Center) had the most important objective of the campaign—Moscow. Initially he was assigned 51 of the 149 German divisions committed to

Operation Barbarossa, including nine panzer and seven motorized divisions. Despite his pessimism over Germany's chances, Bock initially did very well in the invasion—perhaps even showing a flash of military genius in the process. Less than a week after the campaign began, Bock's panzer spearheads closed in on Minsk, 170 miles behind the Soviet frontier. Hitler grew nervous at his own success and suggested that Bock switch to a much shorter envelopment. Bock protested so strongly against this timidity that Hitler let him have his way. Minsk was surrounded on June 29, and the battle ended on July 3. Bock had captured 324,000 men and captured or destroyed 3,332 tanks and 1,809 guns.[8]

Spearheaded by his two panzer groups under Hermann Hoth and Heinz Guderian, Bock's forces continued to win victory after victory in several major battles of encirclement. In the Smolensk pocket, which was cleared on August 5, he took 310,000 prisoners and captured or destroyed 3,205 tanks and 3,120 guns. At the battle of Roslavl, which ended on August 8, he took 38,000 prisoners and captured or destroyed 250 tanks and 359 guns. The Gomel pocket had yielded 84,000 prisoners, 144 tanks, and 848 guns by August 24.[9] By the last week of August, Bock had advanced more than 500 miles and was only 185 miles from Moscow. He had inflicted more than 750,000 casualties on the Soviets and captured or destroyed some 7,000 tanks and more than 6,000 guns, while Army Group Center had lost fewer than 100,000 men. The road to the Soviet capital was open when, much to von Bock's disgust and over his protests, Hitler shifted the focus of the war to the north and south, against Leningrad and Kiev. Bock was forced to give up four of his five panzer corps and three infantry corps—giving the Soviets the time they desperately needed to organize the defense of their capital, their most important city.

It was one of the greatest mistakes of the war.

Field Marshal von Bock had little choice but to go over to the defensive in early September, while Stalin poured reinforcements into this critical sector. After a series of fierce attacks, he forced Bock to evacuate the Yelnya salient, but otherwise Army Group Center held its line against continually worsening odds. By the end of September, Bock was facing 1.5 million to 2 million men.

After the fall of Kiev in early September, Hitler considered going into winter quarters, but Bock, Brauchitsch, and Luftwaffe Field Marshal Albert Kesselring, among others, argued against it. Bock still felt that he could capture Moscow, despite the exhaustion of his men, the worn condition of his tanks, and the questionable campaign weather.

Bock got off to a good start in the double battle of Vyazma-Bryansk, which Carell calls "the most perfect battle of encirclement in military history."[10] Beginning on September 30, Bock smashed and encircled 81 Soviet divisions in two huge pockets. Although several Russian units succeeded in breaking out before the battle ended on October 17, Bock nevertheless captured 663,000 men and captured or destroyed 1,242 tanks and 5,412 guns.[11] The offensive was halted only by heavy rains, which immobilized the German advance.

Bock was now only about 70 miles from Moscow, but the first snows had already fallen, and the Russian roads had turned into rivers of mud. Motorized supply columns could make only about five miles per day, and there were more than 2,000 vehicles stuck on the unpaved Moscow Highway alone. Furthermore, OKH was unable to provide the troops with winter clothing. Rundstedt and Leeb, the other two army group commanders in the East, now wanted to go over to the defensive, but Bock stubbornly insisted that the drive be resumed as soon as the ground froze and he could bring up food and ammunition.

The advance resumed on November 15. Struggling forward without winter clothing in temperatures below zero, with 70 percent of their vehicles inoperative, the German soldiers made a magnificent effort and pushed to within six miles of the Kremlin. Moscow could not be taken, however, and Bock's stubbornness had placed his entire army group in jeopardy. Exhausted and at the end of a long and tenuous line of communications, the forward German divisions simply could not be supplied. Many units lived on a diet of horse meat for days at a time.

Stalin launched his counteroffensive on December 6. Despite Hitler's orders that all units stand and if need be die where they were, Army Group Center was slowly pushed back in heavy fighting. Some divisions were forced to abandon all their artillery, while some panzer divisions lost almost all their tanks because there was not enough fuel to withdraw them. Soon 9th Army was in danger of being encircled, and it looked as if Army Group Center might be destroyed. Casualties were appalling.

Fedor von Bock had suffered his first defeat. As disaster closed in on his divisions, Bock's reaction was to contact Colonel Rudolf Schmundt, Hitler's personal adjutant, and complain about his deteriorating health, especially his stomach ulcers. He asked Schmundt to relay the details of his illnesses to Hitler, which Schmundt no doubt did. Two days later, on December 18, 1941, Field Marshal Keitel telephoned and said that Hitler suggested he take an extended leave to restore his health. Bock jumped at the chance. He was replaced that same day by Field Marshal Guenther von Kluge.

One month later, on January 17, 1942, Field Marshal Walter von Reichenau died, probably from a heart attack. The next day Hitler summoned Bock (now miraculously recovered) to Fuehrer Headquarters and offered him command of Army Group South, which Bock quickly accepted. By March, the Red Army offensives on this sector had been halted, largely because of Soviet troop exhaustion, supply failures, and deep snow. Now both sides began a race to build up supplies for a renewed offensive in the spring.

Bock's command in 1942 was characterized by much greater caution than before. The field marshal obviously had been affected by his defeat at Moscow. When the Soviets launched their spring offensive on May 12, Hitler rejected several nervous requests from Bock and did not authorize the commitment of his reserves until May 17, when the Reds were within 12 miles of Kharkov. As a result, Army Group South won a major victory, capturing 240,000 men and capturing or destroying more than 1,200 tanks and 2,000 guns. The German forces suffered only 20,000 casualties. Hitler, however, was understandably unhappy about the lack of nerve Bock had displayed before Kharkov.[12]

Hitler now began the second phase of his summer offensive (Operation Blue) by ordering Bock to clear the Don in preparation for drives against Stalingrad and the Caucasus. Bock was openly critical of this plan because it relied too heavily on undependable foreign armies to guard the flanks of the German advance. He nevertheless attacked with more than a million men on June 28. In contrast to 1941, however, his advance was very slow, and he appeared to be preoccupied with the security of his left flank. Against Hitler's orders, he allowed himself to be pinned down in a prolonged battle at Voronezh—a fruitless battle, which he continued even after Hitler ordered him to break it off. As a result, several large Soviet formations escaped across the Don, and the expected large haul of prisoners did not materialize. For this reason Hitler relieved Bock on grounds of illness on July 15 and never employed him again. Privately Hitler told Rudolf Schmundt that he still admired Bock but could work only with commanders who obeyed orders to the letter.

In early May 1945, with Hitler dead and the Russians already in Berlin, Fedor von Bock received a telegram from Manstein, informing him that the Grand Admiral Karl Doenitz was forming a new government in the vicinity of Hamburg. The ambitious Bock left for that city at once—even this late in the war angling for a new command. Accounts of his death vary. On or about May 4 his car was on the Kiel Road when it was attacked by a British fighter-bomber.[13] According to some accounts, British soldiers found his bullet-riddled body several days later, along with those of his wife and daughter. Other reports have that Bock was still alive when the British arrived. He was rushed to the Oldenburg Naval Hospital, where he died without regaining consciousness. He was 64 years old.

RITTER WILHELM JOSEPH FRANZ VON LEEB is the least known of the three Germans who commanded army groups from 1939 to 1941 and the only one of the three who could properly be classified as an anti-Nazi. Ironically, he was the last to be dismissed, and the only one to be relieved at his own request. Unlike Rundstedt and Bock, however, he was never reemployed.

He was born in Landsberg-am-Lech, Bavaria, on September 5, 1876, into an old Bavarian military family. His father was Major Adolf von Leeb, and his future wife, Maria Schrott, was the daughter of a general of cavalry. Young Wilhelm entered the Bavarian 4th Field Artillery Regiment at Augsburg as an officer-cadet (Fahnenjunker) in 1895. Duly commissioned on March 3, 1897, he first saw action as a platoon leader in the East Asian Field Artillery Regiment at Peking, China, in 1900, during the Boxer Rebellion. After returning to Europe he attended the Bavarian War Academy at Munich, graduated in 1909, and served on the Bavarian General Staff in Munich, the Greater General Staff in Berlin, and as a battery commander in the 10th Artillery Regiment at Erlangen prior to the outbreak of World War I. He was a captain and Ib of the I Bavarian Army Corps in Munich in 1914, when World War I began.

Captain von Leeb served on the Western Front, primarily as Ia of the Bavarian 11th Infantry Division, during the first two years of the war. His division was transferred to the East in 1916, and during operations in Galicia and Serbia, Leeb won the Bavarian Military Order of Max Joseph for exceptional bravery. This decoration carried with it an honorary non-hereditary knighthood—hence he held the title *Ritter* (knight) but could not pass it on to his descendants.

Leeb was promoted to major in the summer of 1916 and fought against the Russians in the Battle of Kovel, and later took part in the conquest of Rumania. In May 1917, he was transferred back to the Western Front, as the second General Staff officer (Ib) on the staff of Crown Prince Rupprecht of Bavaria, and remained there (like Fedor von Bock) until the end of the war. According to one source, he served briefly with the Freikorps in 1919.[14] In any event he was a department chief in the Reich's Defense Ministry in Berlin in October 1919. Selected for retention in the 100,000-man army, he rose rapidly in the Reichsheer. Promoted to lieutenant colonel in 1920, he became chief of staff of Wehrkreis II at Stettin in 1921 and in 1922 returned to Munich as chief of staff of Wehrkreis VII. He was a year at Landsberg as commander of the II Battalion of the 7th Mountain Artillery Regiment (1924), before being promoted to colonel in February 1925. In 1926 he was commander of the 7th Artillery Regiment, then stationed at Nuremberg. Two years later Wilhelm von Leeb was named *Artilleriefuehrer V* (Artillery Leader V) and one of the two deputy commanders of the 5th Infantry Division at Stuttgart. He was promoted to major general and named Artilleriefuehrer VII and deputy commander of the 7th Infantry Division in Munich in 1929. On December 1, 1929, while serving as commander of the 7th Infantry Division at Munich, Leeb was promoted to lieutenant general and in 1930 became commander of Wehrkreis VII.

By the time the Nazis came to power in 1933, Leeb was known as an austere and forbidding, no-nonsense Christian officer with a high moral code. He was openly suspicious of the Nazi Party and its leader at a time when almost all of the other generals were enthusiastically supporting Hitler's rearmament program. A practicing Catholic, he made a point of going to mass in uniform (with his family), much to the displeasure of the party, whose ideals he rejected. Uncompromising in matters of principle, Ritter von Leeb refused to attend a dinner for Alfred Rosenberg, a top Nazi, because he was an anti-Christian.

For his part, Adolf Hitler privately denounced Leeb as "an incorrigible anti-Nazi" and had him placed under Gestapo surveillance—one of the first generals to earn this dubious distinction.[15] Leeb, however, was a thinker and an intellectual, not a plotter or a conspirator. He was not a member of the German resistance and did not even know of the Stauffenberg assassination plot of July 20, 1944, until after it had failed.

An anti-Nazi attitude was not yet an impediment to advancement in the German Army, so von Leeb was named commander-in-chief of Army Group 2 at Kassel in late 1933, and on January 1, 1934, was promoted to general of artillery. In the mid-1930s his book, *Defense*, was published, and in 1938 it was republished by the German War Ministry in the prestigious *Militarwissenschaftliche Rundschau* (the Scientific Military Review), adding to Leeb's international reputation as an authority on defensive warfare. His work on the subject was translated into English and Russian and was even incorporated into the Soviet Field Service Regulations.

Despite his preeminence, Leeb was one of the first commanders removed after General Walter von Brauchitsch assumed command of the army on February 4, 1938, and immediately began sacking commanders whom Hitler considered hostile to National Socialism. Leeb was involuntarily retired effective March 1, 1938, with the honorary (*charakterisierte*) rank of colonel general. Simultaneously, he received a singular honor when he was named honorary commander of the 7th Artillery Regiment. He was recalled to duty in August, as commander of the newly activated 12th Army, when it seemed certain that the Sudetenland crisis would lead to war. After the Anglo-French diplomatic capitulation at Munich, Leeb's forces occupied southern Bohemia in October 1938, and shortly thereafter the general returned to his retirement home in Bavaria. He was recalled to active duty again the following year, however, and this time Hitler's policies really did lead to war.

During the Polish campaign, Leeb's Army Group C (which had evolved from his old headquarters, Army Group 2) was charged with defending the Western Front, while the main German armies conquered Poland. His three armies (the 1st, 5th, and 7th, plus Army Detachment A) controlled 51 divisions—mostly older-age or reserve formations. None of them was armored or motorized, so Leeb might have been in serious trouble had the French launched a major offensive. Leeb was not particularly worried about his situation, however, because he, like Hitler, considered an early Allied reaction unlikely. They were right—the French attempted only one limited offensive in the Saar area, beginning on September 9. It was halted on September 13 after a gain of only 16 miles, and Leeb regained all the lost ground by October 24, at a cost of less than 2,000 dead.

Wilhelm von Leeb was opposed to the Western campaign of 1940 from the beginning—on moral grounds. The death of his son, Lieutenant Alfred von Leeb of the 99th Mountain Infantry Regiment, no doubt contributed to his outspoken opposition to the operation. Young Leeb was killed in the Battle of Lvov—a city subsequently turned over to Stalin under the terms of the Soviet-German Non-aggression Pact—a fact hardly calculated to endear Hitler's policies to the elder von Leeb. In the fall of 1939, Leeb wrote the "Memorandum on the Prospects and Effects of an Attack on France and England in Violation of the Neutrality of Holland, Belgium and Luxembourg," in which he predicted that the entire world would turn on Germany if she violated Belgian neutrality for the second time in 25 years.[16] He urged the commander-in-chief of the army to confront Hitler on this issue, but the weak-willed General von Brauchitsch would have none of it. Therefore, on November 9, 1939, Leeb met with his fellow army group commanders, Gerd von Rundstedt and Fedor von Bock, at Koblenz. Leeb wanted all three of them to resign if Hitler continued with his plans for an invasion of the West. Faced by the united front of his army group commanders, Leeb felt, Hitler might be compelled to change his plans. Rundstedt and Bock, however, were not troubled by Leeb's sort of scruples, and the commander of Army Group C returned to his headquarters in disgust. He even considered resigning his command unilaterally but concluded that it would be an empty gesture, since it would do no good.

In the Western campaign, which began on May 10, 1940, Army Group C had only 17 divisions (all infantry) under the 1st and 7th armies. Its mission was purely secondary: feint against the Maginot Line to prevent the French from reinforcing the critical sector to the north. In this mission Leeb was entirely successful. After the French campaign he was rewarded with a field marshal's baton on July 19, 1940.

After a brief period of occupation duty in southern France, the headquarters of Army Group C was transferred to Dresden in October, to begin preparations for the invasion of the Soviet Union. Characteristically, Leeb protested against Hitler's latest military adventure, but to no avail.

For the invasion of Russia, which began on June 22, 1941, Army Group C was redesignated Army Group North and controlled the 18th Army (Colonel General Georg von Kuechler), the 16th Army (Colonel General Ernst Busch), and the 4th Panzer Group (General of Panzer Troops Erich Hoepner). Leeb's objectives were to advance rapidly, cut off and destroy the main Soviet forces in the Baltic States, and drive on to Leningrad.

Leeb's problems in this campaign were mammoth: difficult terrain, poor roads, and insufficient forces for his mission. He had only 26 divisions, of which only three were panzer and three were motorized, and he faced 30 Soviet divisions, including four armored and two motorized divisions—and his opponents had 20 more divisions in reserve. In addition to all this, Leeb himself was neither trained nor suited to handle large mobile formations, which he commanded here for the first time in his long career. Nevertheless Leeb's regiments struggled forward down dirt roads, through thick forests, across a landscape broken by many swamps, lakes, marshes, and streams. They breached the Dvina River line, took Ostrov, repelled repeated Soviet counterattacks, smashed entire opposing armies, and pushed on to Staraya Russa, which fell in bitter house-to-house fighting.

There can be little doubt that Leeb mishandled his armor during this campaign, forcing it to advance on a broad front, instead of thrusting forward in a concentrated drive, as Hoepner proposed. At one point Leeb even used a whole panzer division (the 8th) to clear his lines of communication. This process took an entire month and constituted a terrible waste of valuable armor. Leeb's approach to the campaign was conservative and cautious—perhaps overly cautious. Nevertheless, on September 8, 1941, Leeb began his climactic push on Leningrad, which was already within range of his 240mm guns. Stalin hurled three fresh armies into the battle and committed three more against Leeb's right flank at Staraya Russa and Kholm. Leeb's men repulsed every attack and, on September 11, the 6th Panzer Division penetrated through the Duderhof Hills and the Leningrad fortifications to positions overlooking the city. Meanwhile, the 58th Infantry Division broke into the suburbs and captured a tram car only six miles from the heart of Leningrad, while the 126th Infantry Division took Schleusselburg off to the east on Lake Ladoga, sealing off the city. Leeb was poised for the final attack, and the second city of the Soviet Union seemed doomed when, on September 12, 1941, a message arrived from Adolf Hitler, ordering him not to take the city. Leningrad was to be starved to death instead, and Leeb was to immediately transfer the 4th Panzer Group (with five panzer and two motorized divisions) as well as the entire VIII Air Corps to Army Group Center.

Leeb at once protested against this strategically ridiculous order, but it did no good: Hitler was insistent. This decision turned out to be one of the great blunders of the war. It tied down two German armies in a useless siege, which was finally broken in January 1944. Leningrad never fell.

Meanwhile, despite the lateness of the season, Hitler ordered a frustrated Field Marshal von Leeb to take the Tikhvin bauxite-producing region and occupy the eastern shore of Lake Ladoga—which would require an advance of 250 miles—in the middle of the Russian winter. Juergen von Arnim's XXXIX Panzer Corps smashed the Soviet 4th Army and actually succeeded in capturing Tikhvin on November 8, but was met with fierce counterattacks from Stalin's Siberian reserves, which forced it to retreat on November 15. By the time it limped back to its starting line, the XXXIX Panzer had been more than decimated. The 18th Motorized Division alone had suffered 9,000 casualties in the Tikhvin operation and was reduced to a strength of 741 men—about the size of a normal peacetime battalion.

By mid-December the Soviet winter offensive was in full swing, and Ritter von Leeb was wondering aloud if Hitler and Stalin were secretly allied against the German Army. Leeb also annoyed Hitler and the Nazis by protesting against the massacres of Soviet Jews by the SS, SD, and Lithuanian irregulars, and by his requests to retreat in spite of Hitler's hold-at-all-costs orders. Still, there is no evidence that Hitler planned to sack Leeb, as he had done with Rundstedt, Guderian, and others who were much less anti-Nazi than Leeb. Instead, it was the marshal's own growing sense of frustration that led to his downfall. On January 12, 1942, he requested permission to pull Count Walter von Brockdorff-Ahlefeldt's II Corps out of Demyansk, to keep it from being encircled. Hitler rejected this request on the grounds that such salients tied down more Soviet than German troops. As a result, 100,000 badly needed German soldiers were surrounded a few days later; Leeb, however, refused to accept this kind of strategic reasoning and, on January 16, asked to be relieved of his command. He was placed in Fuehrer Reserve the next day and not employed again.

Leeb was arrested by the Western Allies at the end of the war and, in October 1948, at the age of 72, was sentenced to three years' imprisonment as a minor war criminal—a sentence that seems severe, given his record. After his release the old marshal, a relic of a bygone era, returned to Bavaria, where he died in the town of Hohenschwangau on April 29, 1956. He was 79 years old.

Wilhelm's younger brother, Emil von Leeb (1881–1969), commanded the 15th Infantry Division (1936–1939) and Wehrkreis XI (1939) prior to World War II. Promoted to general of artillery on April 1, 1939, he led the XI Corps in the Polish campaign and was chief of the extremely important Army Weapons Office (*Heereswaffenamt*, or HWA) from March 1940 until January 1945, when he was replaced by Walter Buhle. He was discharged from the army on May 1, 1945.

GEORG VON KUECHLER succeeded Wilhelm von Leeb as commander-in-chief, Army Group North, on January 17, 1942, and was charged with the task of maintaining the Siege of Leningrad. As was the case with Leeb, this turned out to be his last command.

Kuechler was born in Schloss (Castle) Philippsruh, near Germersheim, on May 30, 1881, the son of an old Prussian Junker family. Educated in cadet schools, he joined the Imperial Army as an officer-cadet in the 25th Field Artillery Regiment at Darmstadt in 1900 and received his commission the following year. He continued to serve in the artillery until 1907, when he was transferred to the Military Riding School in Hanover. Promoted to first lieutenant in 1910, he spent the next three years at the War Academy, undergoing General Staff training. In 1913 he was assigned to the topographical section of the Greater General Staff in Berlin. When World War I broke out the following year, he was promoted to captain and given command of an artillery battery.

Captain von Kuechler distinguished himself in World War I, which he spent primarily on the Western Front. He served as a battery commander in the 9th Reserve Field Artillery Regiment on the Western Front (1914–January 1915), on the General Staff of the IV and VIII corps and as first General Staff officer (Ia) of the 206th Infantry and 9th Reserve divisions, all on the Western Front. After the war he was a General Staff officer to General Count Ruediger von der Goltz, who fought the Reds in the Baltic States in 1919 and 1920. Briefly a member of the Freikorps, Kuechler joined the Reichsheer in 1920 as a staff officer with the I Corps (later Wehrkreis I) in East Prussia.

Thoroughly Prussian in his attitude, despite a curious untidiness in his personal appearance, Kuechler advanced steadily during his postwar career. Initially, he served as an instructor in the Infantry School at Munich (1920–1921), followed by tours in the Army Construction Department (T-4) (1921–1923); as battery commander in the Hessian-Wuerttemberg 5th Army Regiment at Ulm (1923–1926); in the Infantry School at Ohrdruf, Thuringia, and then Dresden, Saxony (1926–1928); and in the Artillery School at Jueterbog, about 40 miles southwest of Berlin (1930–1932). He became Artillery Commander I at Koenigsberg, East Prussia, on October 1, 1932.[17] He was promoted to major (1923), lieutenant colonel (1929), colonel (1931), and major general (April 1, 1934). In 1935, he was named inspector of army schools and promoted to lieutenant general. In 1937, he succeeded Brauchitsch as commander of Wehrkreis I and, on April 1, 1937, was promoted to general of artillery.

Kuechler had a very important and potentially dangerous command in those days, as East Prussia was surrounded on all three land sides by a hostile Poland. Kuechler coordinated with Nazi Party formations in matters of frontier defense, expanded the military forces in his area, and supported Hitler in the Blomberg-Fritsch crisis. Accompanied by Heinrich Himmler and Gauleiter Erich Koch, his forces occupied Memel, Lithuania, on March 23, 1939, in the last of Hitler's bloodless conquests.

When the war broke out on September 1, 1939, Kuechler's headquarters (redesignated 3rd Army) controlled seven infantry divisions, an ad hoc panzer division, and four brigade-size units. His forces took Danzig, helped clear the Polish Corridor, and pushed south toward Warsaw, against the Polish Modlin Army. Later, 3rd Army was diverted to the east, where it overran the Polish defenders on the Narew and Bug, and linked up with the Soviets.

After the fall of Poland, Kuechler's headquarters was redesignated 18th Army (to fool Allied intelligence) and was sent west, where it was given the mission of conquering the Netherlands the following spring. For this task, Kuechler was given five infantry divisions, the SS-Verfuegungs Motorized Division, and the weak 9th Panzer Division, which was equipped mainly with light Czechoslovakian tanks. He also had the support of strong Luftwaffe forces and of the XI Air Corps—Germany's parachute, glider, and air-transported combat forces, which seized key towns and bridges in the Dutch interior and held them until the ground forces arrived. As a result, Kuechler conquered the Netherlands in only five days, before the Dutch Army had time to mobilize. He then turned south, where his forces occupied Antwerp, and launched the final assault on Dunkirk on June 4, capturing 40,000 French soldiers whom the British Navy had been unable to evacuate.

During the second phase of the Battle of France, Georg von Kuechler was given the historic task of capturing Paris. Initially in reserve with six infantry divisions, 18th Army was not committed until the French were in full retreat. Paris was declared an open city on June 13, and the 218th Infantry Division took possession of the city on the morning of June 14, marching down the Champs-Elysees in parade formation. Kuechler, however, was always prouder of his capture of Dunkirk than of the French capital, which was already doomed before 18th Army was committed and fell virtually without opposition.

General von Kuechler had performed brilliantly in the campaign of 1940, often leading his men from the sidecar of a motorcycle, frequently exposing himself to enemy fire in order to help wounded enlisted men—a habit well calculated to inspire admiration in the ranks. His men loved him for these demonstrations of the compassion he felt for them. For his services in Poland, the Netherlands, Belgium, and France, Kuechler was promoted to colonel general on July 19, 1940. Then he was sent back to Poland, to guard the Reich's new eastern borders against the Soviets. During Operation Barbarossa, his 18th Army formed the left wing of the German invasion, conquered the Baltic States (Lithuania, Latvia, and Estonia), and, on Hitler's orders, laid siege to Leningrad. When Ritter von Leeb asked to be relieved, he was replaced by Georg von Kuechler on January 17, 1942.

When Kuechler took command of Army Group North, the situation was already desperate. He controlled the 18th Army (General Georg Lindemann) and the 16th Army (Colonel General Ernst Busch), which together faced 12 Soviet armies. Kuechler had virtually no reserves, and his exhausted men had very little winter equipment or clothing in temperatures that dropped to 49 degrees below zero Fahrenheit. Kuechler simply did not have the forces to man a continuous line, so he made the winter campaign in the northern sector a battle for the major crossroads, reasoning that the Soviets would not be able to resupply their spearheads once the spring thaw set in if he continued to hold these key positions. This strategy took considerable nerve, but Kuechler pulled it off.

The fighting centered on Novgorod, Staraya Russa, Kholm, and Demyansk. Because Hitler had forbidden withdrawals, Kholm was encircled on January 21 and Demyansk was surrounded on February 8. Both garrisons were resupplied by the Luftwaffe despite terrible losses. At Staraya Russa, the Soviets were thrown back only after hand-to-hand fighting in the streets.

Kuechler resorted to many improvised and patchwork measures to hold his strongpoints and to limit or seal off breakthroughs. He created ad hoc battalions of Latvian volunteers, used service troops and Luftwaffe ground units as infantry, and weakened several sectors (and took the risk of more Soviet breakthroughs) to reinforce key strongpoints. By early March, however, it became evident that he had mastered the crisis, and his front was more or less stabilized. Now he began a series of counterattacks aimed at destroying Soviet penetrations and rescuing the surrounded garrisons.

On March 15, Kuechler began an offensive on either side of the Soviet's Volkhov salient. Four days later two Soviet armies were cut off. The battle to collapse the pocket was fierce, and fighting continued until July, but in the end 17 Red Army divisions were destroyed. Most of the defenders were killed; only 32,000 men surrendered.

Meanwhile, Kuechler made two unsuccessful attempts to rescue the garrison at Kholm. On May 5, however, the third attempt was successful, and the defenders were saved after a siege of 103 days.

To relieve the 100,000 men trapped around Demyansk, Kuechler created a special assault force of five divisions he carefully mustered near Staraya Russa. Under Lieutenant General Walter von Seydlitz-Kurzbach, these divisions began to advance on March 21 and penetrated five separate Soviet defensive lines and 24 miles of mud. Seydlitz reached the western edge of the pocket on April 20. It was May 2, however, before the German gains could be consolidated and a tenuous overland supply line established with the II Corps at Demyansk.

For Kuechler's part in checking the Soviet winter offensive of 1941–1942 and for his subsequent victories, Adolf Hitler promoted him to field marshal on June 30, 1942.

The Siege of Leningrad was a problem that plagued Kuechler throughout his tenure of command at Army Group North and eventually ended his career. A planned German offensive in the fall of 1942 had to be cancelled because of the Stalingrad crisis, and after that about all Kuechler could do was to try to maintain his siege lines. He repelled several massive attacks in October, but on January 12, 1943, a dozen Red Army divisions struck at Schluesselburg and by the 19th had established a six-mile-wide corridor to the city, linking Leningrad to the outside world for the first time in 17 months.

Throughout 1943 Army Group North was neglected by Hitler and the High Command of the Army. From December 22, 1942, Kuechler lost eight divisions to other theaters, including both of his panzer divisions and two of his three motorized divisions. By October 10, 1943, he had 43 divisions: 30 infantry (almost all understrength), three jaeger (light divisions with only two infantry regiments), and three security divisions (with only two infantry regiments and no organic artillery). He had only one motorized infantry division. His other five divisions (four Luftwaffe Field divisions and a training division) were of little combat value. Nevertheless, in November 1943, Hitler forced him to commit five infantry divisions to the Battle of Nevel, on the extreme southern end of his line. Kuechler protested against this depletion of his reserve because he feared an imminent Soviet attack in the Leningrad sector but was curtly overruled.

Kuechler was right. In late December 1943, he was forced to give up three more divisions.[18] He now had only 40 understrength divisions to defend some 500 miles of front at a time when a full-strength division could expect to successfully defend only about six miles against a determined attack. In late December, Kuechler urgently requested permission to abandon the Siege of Leningrad and retreat to the Panther Line in the west, a move that would shorten his defensive line by 120 miles. Hitler not only denied him permission but, as if to add injury to insult, also transferred three more infantry divisions (the veteran 1st, 96th, and 254th) to other sectors. All three were taken from 18th Army, which was facing Leningrad. Again Kuechler protested; again he was ignored.

The Soviet offensive struck 18th Army in full fury on January 14, 1944. On January 17 Georg Lindemann, the commander of 18th Army, requested permission to retreat, but Hitler refused to allow it. The situation continued to deteriorate until the following evening, when Kuechler signaled OKH that he intended to retreat that night, whether Hitler approved or not. Hitler did approve that night, but only after General Kurt Zeitzler informed him that the retreat was already in progress. The Fuehrer, however, would agree only to local withdrawals. No general withdrawal to the Panther Line was permitted. Finally, however, on the orders of Army Group North, 18th Army did begin a general retreat on January 30. It had suffered 31,000 casualties (including 14,000 killed) and was down to a strength of 17,000 men.

Hitler approved the order of January 30 but the next day summoned Kuechler to Fuehrer Headquarters and relieved him of his command. He was made the scapegoat for the entire disaster and was never reemployed.

★ ★ ★

Field Marshal von Kuechler was not a great general and has been accused of moving too slowly in conquering the Baltic States in 1941. These charges seem unjust, considering that all of his divisions were non-motorized infantry. Although Kuechler is almost unknown in the West, he in many ways typifies the anonymous German general in the East. He was a tough, respected, highly competent commander who was neglected and ignored by Berlin until a disaster occurred. Then he was relieved, made the scapegoat, and sent into permanent retirement. Hitler would have done much better to have followed his advice in 1943 and 1944, even if it meant giving up Leningrad a few weeks earlier.

After his forced retirement, von Kuechler faded into obscurity. He was approached by Dr. Carl Goerdeler and Johannes Popitz, the civilian leaders of the anti-Hitler conspiracy. Like many others he expressed sympathy for their goals but refused to join them himself.

Throughout World War II, Georg von Kuechler dealt with enemy civilians in a civilized manner. He refused to cooperate with SS and SD murder squads and had several violent clashes with Erich Koch over that Nazi Gualeiter's brutal policies. He even halted the forced evacuation of civilians from eastern Estonia in the fall of 1943 because it was causing too much suffering among the enemy's population. Partisans, however, he treated like terrorists and bandits; some of them were. For this he was arrested at the end of the war and, at Nuremberg, was convicted as a minor war criminal. On October 27, 1948, he was sentenced to 25 years in prison. He was released in February 1955 and faded back into obscurity. In 1959 he was living in retirement with his wife in the village of Zurueckgezogenheit, in the Garmisch-Partenkirchen area. Unfortunately he wrote no memoirs. He died on May 25, 1968.

Georg von Kuechler was replaced as commander-in-chief of Army Group North by Colonel General Walter Model, who was promoted to field marshal on March 1, 1944, and was named commander-in-chief of Army Group North Ukraine the same day. He, in turn, was succeeded by Colonel General Lindemann, the commander of the 18th Army.

GEORG LINDEMANN was born at Osterburg in Altmark on March 8, 1884, and entered the Prussian Army as a Fahnenjunker in 1903. He was commissioned into the Magdeburger 6th Dragoon Regiment in the Rhineland in 1904 and was a first lieutenant in the 13th Hussar Regiment in 1913. He served with 5th Army during the drive on Paris in 1914 and then finished his General Staff training. Promoted to captain on November 28, 1914, he had returned to the Western Front as a General Staff officer by the spring of

1915 and was on the staff of the 1st Army in France by the summer of 1916. In the latter stages of the war, he was on the General Staff of the West-phalian 220th Infantry Division, which suffered heavy casualties at Lens in early 1918. Lindemann was chief of operations of the 200th Infantry Division on the Western Front when the war ended. He emerged from the conflict with both grades of the Iron Cross and the Hohenzollern House Order with Swords. When he returned to Germany, he was assigned to border protection duties with the staff of Volunteer Division von Lettow-Vorbeck. Late in 1919, he became an instructor at the Infantry School at Munich. Selected for retention by the Reichsheer, he spent the Weimar era in the cavalry, first with the 7th (Prussian) Cavalry Regiment at Breslau (1922–1925), where he commanded a squadron (1923–1925); on the staff of the 2nd Cavalry Division, also at Breslau (1925–1928); as commander of an instructional group at the Cavalry School at Hanover (1928–1931); and as commander of the 13th (Prussian) Cavalry Regiment at Hanover (1931–1934). He became a major in 1926 and a lieutenant colonel in 1931. Promoted to full colonel in 1933, he served as commandant of the War School at Hanover (1934–1936) and assumed command of the newly authorized 36th Infantry Division at Kaiserslautern. He was promoted to major general on April 20, 1936, and to lieutenant general on April 1, 1938.

Lindemann led the 36th Infantry during the so-called Phoney War of 1939–1940 and directed it in the attacks against the Maginot Line during the Western campaign of 1940, where he had little opportunity to distinguish himself.[19] Nevertheless the ambitious and pro-Nazi Lindemann was awarded the Knight's Cross on August 5, 1940, and on October 1 was given command of the L Corps, which was then forming in Baden-Oos, Germany. One month later he was promoted to general of cavalry.

General Lindemann's L Corps was rushed to the Balkans with the 46th, 76th, and 198th Infantry divisions in the spring of 1941, but arrived too late to participate in the fighting in Greece and Yugoslavia. After detraining in Rumania, the corps headquarters was sent to Bulgaria and then back to Berlin, where it was stationed when Germany invaded the Soviet Union. In August it was sent to Smolensk and then to the Leningrad sector, where Lindemann (with the 269th Infantry and the SS Motorized Division "Police") covered the right flank of Leeb's major thrust into the Duderhof Hills. After Hitler's halt order robbed Leeb of his opportunity to capture the city, Lindemann's troops dug in and spent the rest of 1941 in the siege lines west of Leningrad. They would still be there when 1944 began.

Why Georg Lindemann was given command of the 18th Army when Colonel General von Kuechler replaced Leeb as commander-in-chief of

Army Group North on January 17, 1942, can only be explained by political intrigue, Lindemann's pro-Nazi attitude, and his willingness to do the Fuehrer's will, since Lindemann had done nothing to warrant such a rapid advancement and there were dozens of generals with better claims to army-level command than he. In fact, of the three other corps commanders in the 18th Army, two (General of Artillery Albert Wodrig and General of Infantry Kuno-Hans von Both) were senior to Lindemann. The other, General of Infantry Mauritz von Wiktorin, had the same date of rank. The pro-Nazi Lindemann nevertheless took charge and played a creditable role in the Battle of the Volkhov Pocket, where two Soviet armies were cut off and destroyed. After this battle he was promoted to colonel general (on July 3, 1942). Later in 1942 and in 1943, he turned back several Soviet attempts to raise the Siege of Leningrad, although he could not prevent the Red Army from establishing an overland supply corridor to the city in January 1943.

Grateful to Lindemann nevertheless, the Fuehrer presented him with Oak Leaves to his Knight's Cross on August 21, 1943. Hitler's gratitude took on more tangible form than decorations, commendations, and verbal praise, however; in the fall of 1943, the 18th Army commander received a check for 200,000 Reichsmarks, sent by his Fuehrer for "true and faithful service."[20] What effect this "gift" had on Lindemann's subsequent attitude can only be speculated upon, but it probably was considerable.

In late 1943, Georg von Kuechler pleaded with Adolf Hitler to allow him to lift the Siege of Leningrad and retreat to the Panther Line, well to the rear, before the Soviets could launch their next massive offensive against the 18th Army. When Hitler asked Lindemann's opinion, the cavalryman confidently stated that his army could hold its positions against the Russian onslaught.

Hitler, who had now heard exactly what he wanted to hear, naturally took Lindemann's word for it and refused to sanction a retreat.

On January 4, 1944, seeing disaster on the horizon, Field Marshal von Kuechler showed up at Lindemann's headquarters and practically begged him to reconsider his opinion. Once again, however, the army commander expressed his confidence in his ability to hold his lines despite a lack of reserves.

Lindemann's optimism led to disaster, for he had badly underestimated the strength of the Soviet attacks and overestimated the ability of his 21 divisions (five of which were Luftwaffe Field units) to check them. He should have known better. He had no reserves, no armor, very few assault guns, and his air support was virtually nil. In addition, his depleted divisions held frontages as wide as 25,000 yards—about twice as much as they could reasonably have been expected to hold. Kuechler believed that Lindemann's lack of realism stemmed from his desire to draw attention to himself—to show what he could do under the very eyes of the Fuehrer. This much he accomplished—and proved that under such circumstances he could not do very much.

The Soviet offensive struck on January 14 with a clear superiority of six to one, and by January 17 the poorly trained Luftwaffe ground units were crumbling. Only the determined resistance of Felix Steiner's III SS Corps (which included the SS Police and Nordland divisions, as well as the nearly useless 9th and 10th Luftwaffe Field divisions) prevented the complete collapse of the army's left wing, but even so it was thrown back with heavy losses. Lindemann's left flank was on the verge of being over-whelmed, and 18th Army was threatened with a double envelopment.

Although Kuechler ordered a retreat (against Hitler's wishes) on January 18, 18th Army was crushed by the end of the month and had lost more than two-thirds of its combat strength. Adolf Hitler and Colonel General Lindemann must bear primary responsibility for this disaster, even though the Fuehrer blamed Kuechler and replaced him with Walter Model. Incredibly, when Model was named commander of Army Group North Ukraine on March 1, 1944, Georg Lindemann succeeded him as commander-in-chief of Army Group North.

By March 31, the situation in the northern sector had stabilized, largely because Hitler had allowed Model to retreat to the Panther Line and because bad weather (snow, thaw, and rain) had caused the Russian advance to flounder. Army Group North enjoyed a period of relative calm until June 22, when, south of Lindemann's forces, the Soviets struck Army Group Center in an offensive of almost unbelievable strength. Entire corps and divisions were overwhelmed and erased from existence. Army Group North also came under attack—not as immense but very heavy nonetheless. Also, the near annihilation of Army Group Center left Lindemann's right flank exposed. At the end of June, he requested permission to pull back his uncovered southern wing. Colonel General Kurt Zeitzler, the chief of the General Staff, not only supported this request but also suggested that Army Group North be allowed to shorten its line (and thus release more combat formations) by evacuating Estonia and falling back to the Riga-Daugavpils (Duenaburg) line. Hitler responded by denying Lindemann's request to retreat and ordering him to attack to the southeast, to take some of the pressure off Army Group Center. When Lindemann was unable to accomplish this impossible mission, Hitler relieved him of his command on July 3, 1944, and replaced him with Colonel General Johannes Friessner.

General Lindemann was unemployed for six months but gradually regained favor with the Fuehrer and on January 27, 1945, was named Wehrmacht commander, Denmark. His command was territorial in nature and consisted of a few older-age units, some garrison troops, and a few coastal defense batteries. None of these had particularly high morale. Even after Hitler's death, however, Lindemann ordered his men to refuse any orders to lay down their arms and to resist with force any attempt to make them do so—even though this order ran counter to the policies of Hitler's designated successor, Grand Admiral Karl Doenitz, who had told Lindemann that he wanted the war ended with a minimum of casualties. Fortunately, Lindemann's pleas fell on deaf ears. Finally seeing that the situation was hopeless and that his men would not obey his fanatical orders, Lindemann surrendered to the British at Copenhagen on May 8, 1945. He was released from captivity in May 1948 and retired to Freudenstadt, in the Black Forest, where he died on September 25, 1963.

FRIEDRICH MIETH, an officer of great physical and moral courage, was born in Eberswalde, Brandenburg, about 30 miles northeast of Berlin, on June 4, 1888. He entered the army in 1906 as a Fahnenjunker in the 2nd Jaeger Battalion and was commissioned in the infantry in 1907. He served with distinction in World War I, where he fought on the Western Front, in Rumania, and with the Turkish Army. He performed well, became a company commander, and was wounded at least once. He remained in the army throughout the Weimar era, joined the General Staff, worked in the Defense Ministry, and was promoted to major in 1928. After Hitler came to power, the highly capable Mieth rose rapidly as the Wehrmacht expanded, being promoted to lieutenant colonel (1933), colonel (1935), and major general on April 1, 1938. In the meantime he commanded the 27th Infantry Regiment at Rostock, Pomerania (1936–1938) and served as chief of staff of Wehrkreis XII (1938–1939), which headquartered in Wiesbaden, Hesse. He was chief of staff of the 1st Army on the Western Front when World War II broke out.

Mieth was one of the first officers to clash with Hitler and the Nazis over the Einsatzgruppen (murder squads) and the SS and SD atrocities in Poland. In January 1940, Reinhard Heydrich, the brutal chief of the SD, set up a liquidation camp at Soldau, Poland, near the East Prussian border. When Mieth learned of this, he assembled the officers of the 1st Army and told them, "The SS has carried out mass executions without proper trials. The SS has besmirched the Wehrmacht's honor."[21]

Prior to Mieth's speech Hitler may have been unaware of Heydrich's specific actions, but he certainly endorsed them in principle. In this clash between the army and the SS he quickly demonstrated which side he was on. Mieth was dismissed from his post on January 22 and sent into retirement. General Franz Halder, chief of the General Staff of the army and sometimes an anti-Hitler conspirator, rescued Mieth from professional oblivion three weeks later by naming him chief of the Operations Department (O Qu I) of OKH. This took a considerable amount of courage on Halder's part. Remarkably, Mieth was promoted to lieutenant general on March 1, 1940—only five weeks after Hitler had sacked him.

In his new job, Mieth was involved in planning and executing the Western campaign of 1940—especially the operations on the Upper Rhine. During the last phase of the Battle of Dunkirk he served as OKH liaison officer with the 18th Army in a successful effort to transfer its divisions to the south as rapidly as possible. Partially as a result of these efforts, elements of the 18th Army took Paris on June 14. Later Mieth helped coordinate the buildup of forces between Army Group A (von Rundstedt) and OKH for the final phase of the conquest of France and toured the 9th Army's front as the representative of General Halder. He was named chief of staff of the Armistice Commission on June 25, 1940.

After France capitulated and Operation Sea Lion, the invasion of the United Kingdom, was cancelled, Friedrich Mieth apparently tired of his duties in Berlin and asked for a command. He took over the 112th Infantry Division near Mannheim on December 10, 1940, the day it was officially activated. Sent to Russia in July, the 112th fought at Bobruisk, Kiev, and Bryansk and suffered heavy losses during the retreat from Moscow in the winter of 1941–1942. It was occupying a relatively static sector of Army Group Center's line when Stalingrad was encircled on November 23, 1942.

When the Rumanian armies collapsed, Hitler upgraded headquarters' 11th Army to Headquarters, Army Group Don, and called upon the brilliant Field Marshal Erich von Manstein to stabilize the front and save 6th Army. Manstein hastily summoned Mieth and named him commander of security and rear-area troops for the new army group. Because of the rapid speed of the Soviet breakthroughs, however, Mieth's real function was to organize ad hoc units and lead them into combat to help stem the Russian tide. On New Year's Day 1943, for example, he was in the Zymlia sector, commanding four ad hoc combat groups, each of approximately regimental strength, plus the 336th Infantry Division and what was left of the 7th Luftwaffe Field Division. With these forces he was conducting a delaying action near the Don River.[22] His hastily organized headquarters was already known as Korps Mieth.

From January to July 1943, Mieth fought in the battles along the Don, in the Donetz, and in the retreat to the Mius. During this period he had to maintain constant flexibility because his units were always changing, as the southern sector of the Eastern Front underwent crisis after crisis. On March 4, for example, Mieth controlled the 336th and 384th Infantry divisions and the 23rd Panzer Division. Five weeks later all these units had been transferred, and Mieth was directing the 3rd Mountain and the 304th and 335th Infantry divisions. Mieth, however, proved himself to be an excellent field commander, and on April 20, 1943 (Hitler's birthday), he was promoted to general of infantry. His headquarters was recognized as a permanent formation on July 20, when it was upgraded to IV Corps—named after a unit destroyed at Stalingrad. In the meantime, it received its corps units, including the 404th Artillery Command (Arko 404), the 44th Signal Battalion, and the 404th Supply Troop.[23]

Friedrich Mieth continued to distinguish himself on the Russian Front throughout 1943 and into 1944, earning his Knight's Cross and Oak Leaves in the process. He did not make headlines in America or Britain, or even in Germany, for that matter. He was, rather, one of many solid, dependable, highly competent German generals, fighting very skillfully against heavy odds, for a cause in which he did not believe and for a leader and regime he did not love, but for a country he did love. Meanwhile, IV Corps was pushed inexorably back, across the Dnieper, out of the Nikopol Bridgehead, across the Nogay Steppe and over the Bug and Dnestr, all the way to Moldavia in the eastern Carpathians, where the Soviet spring offensive of 1944 was finally brought to a halt. Here, as part of Colonel General Johannes Friessner's Army Group South Ukraine, it awaited the next, inevitable Soviet attack.

In the meantime, secret negotiations were taking place between representatives of the Soviet Union and the political enemies of Hitler's ally, Rumanian dictator Ion Antonescu. On August 20, the anticipated Soviet offensive began with a massive artillery bombardment, followed by strong ground attacks. In all, the Soviets had 90 infantry divisions and six tank and mechanized corps, or more than 925,000 men. Friessner met them with 360,000 German soldiers (23 divisions, of which 21 were infantry) and 23 Rumanian divisions—all of which had lost the will to fight. Of the army group's 392-mile front, 160 miles were held by unreliable Rumanian troops. Although the Germans held their positions, the Rumanian front broke in a number of places, and there were incidents of Rumanians disarming and arresting German liaison staffs and cutting German communications and even firing on German troops. Friessner was already retreating when the Soviets sprang the trap.

On the afternoon of August 23, Antonescu was deposed and arrested and Rumania defected from the Axis, and that night the king broadcast a message to the Rumanian people stating that Rumania would join the United Nations against their common enemy—Germany. Meanwhile, the Rumanian Army stopped fighting the Soviets, whose motorized columns surged unopposed into the German rear. They were already 40 miles behind IV Corps before Mieth learned what was going on in Bucharest. Two days later Rumania formally declared war on Germany.

Meanwhile, on the morning of August 24, Friessner made the difficult decision to save what little of his army group he could save (for the defense of Hungary) and abandon the rest. Those forces already cut off in Rumania would have to break out and escape on their own—if they could. These included virtually the entire 6th Army (resurrected since Stalingrad) and the IV Corps of the 8th Army.

On August 21, Mieth's corps consisted of the German 370th, 79th, and 376th Infantry divisions and the 11th Rumanian Division. Outflanked by a major Red Army attack to the west, Mieth at once retreated to the south, parallel to the Pruth River, although he lost a number of heavy guns in the process. (It had rained, and his horses could not move them out of the heavy mud.) Mieth had already lost contact with the corps on both his flanks.

August 22 was a day of continuous fighting with Soviet vanguards, as IV Corps slowly fell back to the previously prepared Trajan position. The sky was cloudless and the heat oppressive. The rainwater had already evaporated, and dust choked the veteran foot soldiers, who nevertheless beat back every Soviet attack. By this point of the war, the Luftwaffe was long since a spent force even in the East. Soviet airplanes bombed and strafed all the roads more or less continuously. No one had seen a German fighter plane for a long time.

Despite these difficulties, Mieth managed to keep his corps together—except for the 11th Rumanian, which had been engaged but was still not conforming to his instructions. Mieth ordered Lieutenant General Friedrich-August Weinknecht, the commander of the 79th Infantry, to visit the Rumanian commander, to coordinate operations and bring the 11th back into the battle. While the two divisional commanders were talking, panic-stricken hordes of Rumanians—led by their officers—suddenly appeared and rushed by them, babbling something about being under tank attack even though not one vehicle could be heard. The Rumanian commander tried to halt the rout and even resorted to using his whip, but he could not perform a miracle. The next day he was forced to report that his division had dissolved.

Fourth Corps continued its withdrawal on August 23, under the remorseless sun and cloudless sky. Soviet mechanized and armored attacks against the rearguards were bolder now and beaten off with difficulty. No food had arrived for some time, and the troops ate their Iron Rations or lived on what little corn they could find in the poor Rumanian fields.[24] The wounded, without medication or proper attention, were carried along in primitive farm carts and died like flies in the scorching heat. By August 24 the men were nearing exhaustion when Mieth learned from a radio interception that Soviet armor had overrun Husi, cutting IV Corps off to the south and destroying or dispersing the supply units in the process. Any possibility of help or resupply was now gone. Meanwhile, stragglers from two other crushed German infantry divisions joined Mieth's columns in an effort to escape the impending disaster. On August 25 and 26, with strong Soviet forces to his front and rear, Friedrich Mieth launched a series of desperate attacks against Husi; however, due to the swampland that almost surrounded the town, the stiffness of the Soviet resistance, and the rapidly diminishing combat strength of his exhausted corps, he was unable to take the place and reopen the escape route to the south. He therefore ordered all carts burned and all unwanted horses shot.

General Mieth's new plan was desperate, although definitely in line with the situation. He planned to change direction and march to the west. Fourth Corps would attack across the Berlad River, destroy all its remaining equipment, and break into small groups. These parties were then to head for German lines in the Carpathian Mountains, about 70 miles away— or at least Mieth hoped they were heading for German lines. He had had no contact with any higher or adjacent headquarters for days (although he must have assumed—correctly—that the latter had already been destroyed). In reality, Mieth had no way of knowing where either German or enemy forces were located.

The German assault group was supposed to form up for the attack on the night of August 27–28. It was to be spearheaded by the 79th Infantry Division and led by the four assault guns still left to the division, followed by its two combat engineer companies. The infantry by now was low in ammunition and too exhausted to be of much use. The foot soldiers who could still walk followed like zombies, in stupefied silence.

General Weinknecht tried to carry out the assault as scheduled, but it proved to be impossible. The combat organization of the 79th Infantry Division was breaking down, communications were gone, and the exhausted troops, many of whom had not eaten for days, simply could not be aroused in sufficient numbers. Delay followed delay until well after daybreak. Meanwhile, a hollow-eyed General Mieth showed up at the division command post, shaken and disheveled. He told how his headquarters had been overrun by Soviet troops a few hours before. With the Reds pressing heavily into his rear, Mieth was not happy that Weinknecht had not yet crossed the river, and the two exchanged harsh words, largely brought on by the physical and mental strain of the preceding nine days.[25] In any event, the 79th Infantry, followed by other units and stragglers, crossed the river under artillery and mortar fire and overran the Soviet blocking positions on the morning of August 29. Friedrich Mieth himself was right up front with the engineers in close combat, and this is where he died. Due to conflicting reports, we do not know for sure whether he fell to a Soviet bullet or to a heart attack, but he certainly would have preferred the former.

Once across the Berlad, IV Corps broke up as planned. Later that day, Red Army radio traffic revealed that Mieth's men had broken across the river in strength and that about 20,000 of them had pushed southwest of Husi. Almost all of these were run down and killed or captured by the Soviets or the Rumanians. Only one member of the 79th Infantry Division reached German lines in Hungary 12 days later.[26] He was now 300 miles from Iasi, where the ordeal began. The detailed reports of the other divisions of the IV Corps are lacking, but they could not have done much better. In sum, Army Group South Ukraine lost all but five of its divisions in the Rumanian disaster. Three of these were west of the Soviet offensive when it began and were not engaged, and two (the 13th Panzer and 10th Panzer Grenadier) were mobile enough and acted quickly enough to escape. Some rear-area units, of course, were far enough behind the front to escape as well, and a few isolated bands of infantry made their way back to German lines weeks after the fighting began. Exact losses will never be known but could not have been much below 200,000 men. Most of these were never heard from again.

COUNT HANS EMIL OTTO VON SPONECK was born in Duesseldorf in the Rhineland on February 12, 1888, the fourth child and only son of Count Emil von Sponeck, a *Rittmeister* (captain of cavalry) and squadron commander in a Westphalian *ulan* (lancer) regiment. His father died eight months later and his mother raised her children in Freiburg/Breisgau, an area in southwestern Germany between the Rhine River and the Black Forest. Sponeck entered the Karlsruhe Cadet School in 1898 and graduated at the head of his class in 1905. He then enrolled in the senior German cadet school at Gross-Lichterfelde—Imperial Germany's West Point. He joined the army as a second lieutenant in the 5th Guards Grenadier Regiment on March 19, 1903.

Sponeck was an outstanding junior officer and athlete who excelled in soccer and gymnastics. He also got on well with the ladies. He married Anneliese Honrichs, a Berliner, on October 29, 1910. She gave him his first child, Hans-Curt, on July 23 of the following year. A second son, Hans Wilhelm Otto, was born in 1913.

Hans von Sponeck became adjutant of the 5th Guards' II Battalion in 1913. He went to war with the 2nd Guards Division in 1914 and fought in France and Russia. Severely wounded in February 1915, he returned to duty as adjutant of the less elite 262nd Reserve Infantry Regiment. In the fall of that year, he was given the great honor of being admitted to the General Staff (on probationary status) without undergoing the usual abbreviated wartime training course. He spent the rest of the war in army group level staff positions. He was promoted to captain in 1917.

Selected for retention in the Reichsheer, Sponeck was a company commander in the 4th Infantry Regiment at Kolberg (1921–1923) and as a company commander in the prestigious 9th Infantry Regiment at Potsdam (1923–1924). Then followed staff assignments with Artillery Command III in Berlin (1924), the Army Organizations Department in the Defense Ministry in Berlin (1927–1930), and as Ia of the 3rd Infantry Division in Frankfurt/Oder (1930–1934). He was progressively promoted to major (1928), lieutenant colonel (1932), and colonel (1934).

In 1934, even before Hitler's military expansion was fully underway, Sponeck was given another choice assignment: commander of the 48th Infantry Regiment at Neustrelitz, Mecklenburg, in the Lake District of northeastern Germany. While here, he set aside his wife and filed for divorce.

Meanwhile, the Luftwaffe was expanding from virtually nothing and needed qualified senior commanders and experienced General Staff officers. On December 12, 1937, Sponeck was attached to the air force as commander of *Luftgau III* (Air District III) in Berlin, a post similar to the army's Wehrkreis and normally commanded by a full (three-star) general. Sponeck was promoted to major general on February 1, 1938.

General von Sponeck soon ran afoul of Hermann Goering because of his support of Colonel General Baron Werner von Fritsch, the former commander-in-chief of the army, who was dismissed on trumped-up charges of homosexuality. Sponeck even went so far as to serve as a character witness for Fritsch at his court-martial, for which he was severely reprimanded by the *Reichsmarschall*, who was also president of the court-martial. On March 11, Sponeck was transferred out of Berlin to Munich, where he assumed command of Luftgau VII.

Shortly after moving to Bavaria, Sponeck married Gertrud Konitzer, another Berliner, on April 7, 1938. She would give him one child, Hans-Christof, who was born in August 1939, just as her husband marched off to war. Meanwhile, Sponeck was transferred to Bremen, where he assumed command of the 22nd Infantry Division on November 11, 1938. He was given the task of converting it into an air landing unit. Perhaps he was given this mission because of his familiarity with the Luftwaffe; in any case, he was promoted to lieutenant general on February 1, 1940.

The 22nd Air Landing was held in reserve behind the Western Front during the Polish campaign of 1939. In the Western campaign of 1940, however, it and the 7th Air Division (Germany's first parachute division) were heavily engaged from the first day. They had the task of capturing key positions in the Netherlands and holding them until help arrived. Sponeck was supposed to capture The Hague, the capitol, and the Royal Family. The Dutch reaction, however, was too prompt, and Sponeck failed in all three missions; in addition, he was severely wounded and almost captured. He was nevertheless awarded the Knight's Cross by Adolf Hitler.

After the fall of France and the Low Countries, the 22nd remained in the Netherlands, preparing for the invasion of Great Britain, which never came. At the beginning of 1941, it was sent back to Germany, and that spring it was transferred to Rumania and placed in the 11th Army's reserve. It fought in the battles of southern Russia and southern Ukraine and pushed all the way to the entrance of the Crimea. In September, it pushed across the Perekop Isthmus, despite heavy resistance; helped overrun the western Crimea; and took part in the first, unsuccessful attempts to capture Sevastopol, the main Soviet naval fortress on the Black Sea. On October 10, Sponeck was given command of the XXXXII Corps, covering the 11th Army's eastern flank on the Kerch peninsula. With only two German "marching infantry" divisions (the 46th and 170th), a few infantry battalions from the 72nd and 73rd Infantry divisions, some corps units (most notably the 107th Artillery Command), and a few marginal Rumanian mountain formations, it was in an exposed and dangerous position.

On November 21, Army Group South's 1st Panzer Army captured the vital city of Rostov, north of the Crimea. They were almost immediately faced with massive Soviet counterattacks. Hitler ordered that the city be held at all costs. Rather than lose most of the 1st Panzer Army, Field Marshal Gerd von Rundstedt, the commander-in-chief of Army Group South, retreated anyway. Hitler sacked him on November 30.

On December 6, Stalin unleashed his huge winter offensive all along the line, from Leningrad to the Mius. Hitler responded by commanding that the German Army hold where it was, all along the front, even if it meant encirclement. Soon 103,000 men were needlessly surrounded at Demyansk, and another 5,500 were trapped at Kholm. But several senior German commanders—faced with the annihilation of their divisions and the needless sacrifice of their men—acted responsibly and retreated anyway. Among these was Colonel General Heinz Guderian, the commander of the 2nd Panzer Army and the "father of the Blitzkrieg." He was fired on December 26. But still, brave generals retreated. Others simply resigned or went on sick leave and left the decision to their successors. It became clear to the Fuehrer that some of the army generals were going to act in accordance with the tactical situation and were not prepared to obey his senseless orders without question. To bend them to his will and force him to accept his amateurish micromanagement of the Eastern Front, harsher measures would be required.

On December 26, the Reds launched an amphibious invasion of the Kerch peninsula. Their plan included the establishment of two major beachheads and several secondary landings. By December 28, Sponeck had wiped out one of the two major beachheads near the city of Kerch, but, since his infantry was non-motorized and he had no panzers, he was unable to defeat them all, and several of the landings were behind his fronts and were being reinforced by the Soviet Navy. Seeing that he would eventually be cut off and destroyed, Sponeck signaled Erich von Manstein, the commander of the 11th Army, and requested permission to retreat. In accordance with Hitler's orders, permission was denied. Sponeck's second and third appeals—each stronger and more desperate than the last—were also rejected.

By December 29, Sponeck's forward units—the 46th Infantry Division and a few smaller formations—were down to 10,000 men. Despite heavy casualties, the Soviets had more than 40,000 men ashore north and south of Kerch, on the eastern extremity of the Crimea. Then came the news of fresh Russian landings on the southern coast, in the vicinity of Theodosia. With all of Sponeck's reserves committed, it was clear that there was no way XXXXII Corps could defeat this new threat, and that it was only a matter of time before the 46th Infantry was cut off and destroyed.

It took General von Sponeck only 30 minutes to decide. In disobedience to the Fuehrer's orders, he commanded his men to fall back to the Parpach neck, where the Kerch peninsula narrowed and a defensible position might be established.

The retreat from Kerch lives on in the minds of the old men who survived it because of its horror. The temperature was minus 22 degrees Fahrenheit, but it felt much colder because of the strong winds that were blowing ice and snow. Unprepared for winter, the column was soon strung out for 80 miles, and most of the trucks and motorized vehicles broke down or slipped off the icy roads and had to be abandoned. Horses, which were mostly without food, collapsed and had to be shot. This meant that the division's artillery and Arko 107's guns had to be abandoned, because they were horse-drawn. The retreat through this frozen hell lasted 46 hours. Most of the men who fell asleep in the snow never woke up, and there were thousands of cases of frostbite, often resulting in amputations. Most of the division's heavy weapons and equipment were lost. The 46th Infantry Division was crippled in a movement that did not involve enemy contact.

Sponeck was right in his assessment of the defensive value of the Parpach neck, where he established his defensive line. The next day, the pursuing Soviet tanks attacked and, with the help of some timely reinforcements from Manstein, were beaten off with serious losses. Later that day, January 1, 1942, Sponeck received orders to turn over command of the XXXXII Corps to Lieutenant General Franz Mattenklott, the commander of the 72nd Infantry Division. He was to report to Berlin for court-martial proceedings. The trial began on January 23.

Sponeck was charged with disobeying the orders of a superior officer. The outcome of the trial was preordained, as the president of the court-martial was Hermann Goering, the number two Nazi and a man who had clashed with General Sponeck before. Sponeck contended that, as a Prussian officer, he had been taught to act on his own initiative—even against orders—if the tactical situation demanded it in order to save his men. This defense was brushed aside, and General von Manstein did not lift a finger to help him. He was found guilty and sentenced to death.

Having found his example and made his point to the other generals, Hitler commuted Sponeck's sentence to six years in prison. He was sent to the Germersheim Fortress, where he enjoyed a privileged life for a prisoner. He was allowed an occasional visit to town, where he could buy books and cigarettes. His wife was allowed to visit him one week per month, and his youngest son (who turned three in 1942) could visit as well. Then came the Stauffenberg assassination attempt of July 20, 1944. In the aftermath,

Heinrich Himmler acquired vast new powers. One of his first acts was to order the execution of Hans von Sponeck.

On July 23, Lieutenant General Count von Sponeck faced the firing squad. He was allowed to take Holy Communion and his request to be neither bound nor blindfolded was honored. He was shot at 7:13 a.m.

Both of Sponeck's wives were present at his execution and jointly asked for his body, which was given to them. They buried him in a local cemetery. No speeches or eulogies were allowed at his funeral, but the Lord's Prayer was said. After the war, his remains were moved to the Soldiers' Cemetery at Dahn, in the Palatinate, where they still lie.

Anneliese, Sponeck's first wife, died in Berlin in 1961. His second wife was still alive at last report. Hans-Curt, his oldest son, became a fighter pilot in Norway and over Germany, and ended the war as a captain and chief of operations of the 3rd Fighter Division of Air Fleet Reich. He died in 1999.

Count Hans Wilhelm von Sponeck, the general's second son, also became a captain, but in the cavalry. He was killed on the Don sector of the Russian Front in 1943.

Hans-Christof von Sponeck, the general's youngest son, was only five years old when his father was shot. He became a conscientious objector and had a career as a diplomat, retiring recently as assistant secretary general of the United Nations. In the 2000s, he headed the Oil-for-Food Program in Iraq. He held a requiem at his father's grave on the 55th anniversary of his death.

General von Sponeck had several grandchildren, at least one of whom now lives in the United States.

GOTTHARD HEINRICI was born in Gumbinnen, East Prussia (now Gusev, Russia) on December 21, 1886. His father, Paul, was the local Lutheran minister, and he instilled a sense of religious values in Gotthard that lasted all of his life. Even after the Nazis told him it was in the best interests of his career to stop attending church every Sunday, he continued to do so, and in full uniform—much to their annoyance. The Prussia military tradition was also in his blood, since members of his family had served in the Kaiser's army since the 12th century. Gotthard entered the Imperial Army as a Fahnenjunker in the 95th (6th Thuringian) Infantry Regiment on March 8, 1905. He attended the War School at Hanover and was commissioned second lieutenant on August 18, 1906. He served as adjutant of the II Battalion, was promoted to first lieutenant in early 1914, and was regimental adjutant when World War I began. Initially he saw action with the 3rd Army in the Belgian Ardennes and in the capture of Namur. His division (the 38th Infantry) was then ordered to turn around and head back to Germany, because the Czar's armies had invaded East Prussia. Heinrici fought in the Battle of Tannenberg and then in Poland, as the Russians retreated toward Moscow. By 1915, he was a company commander in the II Battalion. He did his job so well that he was named acting battalion commander, despite his very junior rank. His generals remedied this situation with a special accelerated promotion to captain. It is safe to conclude that Heinrici's performance did not go unnoticed at higher headquarters. In the spring of 1916, he was named adjutant of the 83rd Infantry Brigade, which was also part of the Thuringian 38th Division, and was recommended for General Staff training.

Meanwhile, in September 1915, the 38th was transferred from the Eastern to the Western Front. After fighting in the trenches, it was committed to the Battle of Verdun, where it held Hill 304 for five months, despite serious casualties. One of them was Lieutenant Heinrici, who was severely wounded in a poisonous gas attack. When he recovered that fall, he was assigned to the staff of the XXIV Reserve Corps, to begin his General Staff training. His on-the-job training continued when he was assigned to the staff of the 115th Infantry Division, with which he took part in the conquest of Rumania. He was temporarily assigned to the General Staff of the army in March 1917 and attended the abbreviated General Staff course at Sedan in September and October. Following graduation, he was named Ib (second General Staff officer and chief supply officer) of the VII Corps. After serving with the VIII Corps, Heinrici was named chief of operations (Ia) of the 203rd Infantry Division in February 1918.

Heinrici's division (which was previously considered only mediocre), was full of new recruits, and it played an important role in the Ludendorff Offensives. By the end of the war, it was decimated and exhausted.[27]

After the armistice, Heinrici returned to East Prussia, where he joined the staff of the I (Eastern Prussian) Military District. He was named Ia of Volunteer Division von Tschischwitz, which defended the border areas from Polish incursions. In the fall of 1920, after the Treaty of Versailles, he became a tactics instructor for the 1st Infantry Division in Koenigsberg. Four years later, he became a company commander in the 14th Company of the 13th Infantry Regiment at Schwaebisch-Gmuend in eastern Wuerrtemberg (1924–1927). He then returned to General Staff assignments as a group leader in the Army Organization Department in Berlin (1927–1930). From 1930 to 1932, he commanded the III Battalion of the Prussian 3rd Infantry Regiment at Osterode (now Ostroda, Poland).

Heinrici became Ia of Group Command 1 (one of Weimar Germany's two army-level headquarters) in Berlin in 1932, and the following year he became a department chief in the Defense Ministry. In this post, he was promoted to major general on January 1, 1936. He had previously been promoted to major (1926), lieutenant colonel (1930), and colonel (1933).

Heinrici continued his advancement on October 12, 1937, when he became commander of the 16th Infantry Division at Muenster, Westphalia. Promoted to lieutenant general on March 1, 1938, he took his unit to the northern sector of the Western Front when World War II began. The Western campaign had not yet begun, however, when Heinrici was promoted again, this time to commander of the XII Corps.[28] A general of infantry as of June 1, he was part of the 1st Army during the fighting against the Maginot Line. Before the conquest of France was completed, however, Heinrici was given command of the recently formed XXXXIII Corps, which he led while Hitler's Wehrmacht finished off the French Army. He prepared his corps for the invasion of Great Britain and, after Operation Sea Lion was cancelled, took it to Poland in the spring of 1941.

From the beginning of Operation Barbarossa, the XXXXIII Corps was in the middle of the fighting on the Eastern Front. It took part in the major victories at Brest-Litovsk, Minsk, Bobruisk, Kiev, and Bryansk. During the Battle of Moscow, it pushed as far as Tula and was actually east of Moscow when the Soviets launched their winter offensive. Despite being badly outnumbered and surrounded on three sides, Heinrici successfully extricated his corps, like the superior general he was.

Meanwhile, Guenther von Kluge succeeded Fedor von Bock as commander of Army Group Center. General of Mountain Troops Ludwig Kuebler replaced Kluge as commander of the 4th Army on December 19, but he was not up to the task. When he was replaced by Gotthard Heinrici on January 20, 1942, 4th Army was scattered, exhausted, frozen, under attack by several Soviet armies, and on the verge of disaster.[29]

When the great commanders of World War II are discussed, Gotthard Heinrici is never mentioned. Perhaps he should be. He was certainly not charismatic like Rommel or Guderian or Patton; in fact, he was about as charismatic as a 20-pound sack of fertilizer. But he was incredibly competent and, by early 1942, everybody in the German Army knew it. Short and small (he weighed only 160 pounds and was five foot seven, with blue eyes and gray hair), he was nicknamed *Giftzwerg*, which literary translates into "our poisonous dwarf." A better translation into the American vernacular would be "our tough little bastard." The sagging morale of the 4th Army picked up immediately when they learned who was their new commander.

It picked up even more in the days ahead. Heinrici was good in the attack, but he proved to be a genius in the defense. He had an almost clairvoyant ability to discern when and where the Soviets were about to launch a major attack or full-scale offensive. Only a few hours before they attacked, he would pull his front line back one or two miles, to a carefully prepared second line of defense, which was usually superior to his forward position. Right on schedule, the Russians would pound his original line with thousands of guns, mortars, bombs, and rocket launchers. They never hit a thing. When they advanced at dawn, there were bomb and artillery craters all over the place, but no dead Germans. Except for the tanks, their fighting vehicles and trucks would bog down in the craters while the German artillery—also in new positions—had a field day, slaughtering the stuck infantry. The Soviet tanks, meanwhile, pushed forward without infantry support. They were slaughtered by German armored vehicles and anti-tank weapons, which, in their new positions, were fully supported by Heinrici's artillery, flak guns, infantry, and combat engineers, who frequently placed sticky shape charges right on the Soviet tanks. There were, after all, no Red infantrymen around to stop them. Heinrici did this again and again and again, winning victory after victory after victory. And 4th Army's front was never broken.

Gotthard Heinrici was promoted to colonel general on January 30, 1943, a year after he assumed command of his army. This was far later than it should have been. But the Nazis were very suspicious of Heinrici. He was too religious and, as a thorough professional, clearly looked down on and despised the Nazis and their political soldiers, and refused to cooperate with the SS and their murder squads. On the other hand, helping to overthrow the German head of state—even if it was Hitler—was something he would never consider. It went against his Prussian concept of loyalty.

In May 1944, Heinrici fell seriously ill with hepatitis. He was evacuated back to Karlsbad for treatment, but it took him months to recover. He was succeeded as commander of 4th Army by General of Infantry Kurt von Tippelskirch, who was a fine commander but who lacked Heinrici's tactical genius.[30] Meanwhile, Stalin concentrated 2.5 million men, more than 6,000 tanks, more than 45,000 guns and 7,000 aircraft against Army Group Center (3rd Panzer, 9th and 4th armies), which had 700,000 men and a few hundred tanks and assault guns, and practically no air support. On June 22, 1944, Stalin unleashed Operation Bagration. By the time it was over, 4th Army had lost 130,000 of its 165,000 men.

Heinrici recovered from his illness and returned to the Eastern Front on August 16, 1944, but this time as commander of the 1st Panzer Army.

A few days later, the 1st Hungarian Army was attached to his command, which was now known as *Armeegruppe Heinrici*. The 1st Panzer was not really a tank army any longer, but rather consisted mostly of second-rate infantry units. Heinrici's main task, however, was to defend the mountainous terrain and passes of Slovakia, which for a man of his talents was not much of a challenge. He was still holding them on March 20, 1945, when he replaced Heinrich Himmler as commander-in-chief of Army Group Vistula. He was assigned the task of defending Berlin.

Heinrici's new assignment was not difficult: it was impossible. With two armies (the 3rd Panzer and 9th), Heinrici faced three Soviet fronts (army groups) and dozens of Russian and Polish armies—more than 2.5 million men; 6,250 tanks; 7,500 aircraft; 41,000 guns; and more than 3,000 self-propelled rocket launchers. Heinrici had 700,000 men; perhaps 1,000 worn out tanks and assault guns; 9,000 artillery pieces; and virtually no air support. Since he knew he could not win this battle, General Heinrici did not even try. His plan for this campaign was to (1) hold the Soviets off as long as possible; (2) avoid a battle in the city of Berlin, insofar as that was possible; and (3) make sure as many of his men could surrender to the Western Allies as was possible. He accomplished all three tasks to as high a degree as was humanly possible.

The Battle of Berlin (as the last Soviet European offensive of World War II was called) began on April 16. The Red High Command thought that they would be in Berlin in three days. It took them two weeks to reach the Reich Chancellery. This was in large part because their initial, overwhelming bombardment—fired by tens of thousands of artillery pieces, mortars, heavy guns, and rocket launchers—had struck thin air and missed the Germans entirely. Army Group Vistula had pulled back to its second line of defense a few hours before. General Heinrici had done it again.

After wading through terrain that looked like a moonscape—and suffering tens of thousands of casualties in the process—the Red Army finally managed to push through the German line. Heinrici's main body, the 3rd Panzer Army and the 9th Army, retreated north and south of Berlin, respectively, although much of the less mobile 9th Army was encircled at Halbe, southeast of Berlin. The battle for the city itself was left to LVI Panzer Corps, and had it been left up to Heinrici, the city would have been given up without a fight. Since this was not possible, Heinrici attempted to stop the Russians before they reached the urban area. What has gone down in history as the Battle of Berlin was really nothing more than a contested mopping-up operation. General of Artillery Helmuth Weidling, the commander of the LVI Panzer, had 45,000 soldiers, police, and Hitler Youth, augmented by 40,000 *Volkssturm*, the old men and boys of the German home guard.

Berlin was surrounded on April 25. By April 26, the Reds were nearing the Fuehrer Bunker and Hitler and his cronies were screaming for Heinrici to save them. Since he could not do this, he had determined not to even try—he refused to waste the life of a single soldier. Hitler's orders to the contrary were ignored. Field Marshal Keitel figured this out on April 29, when he caught up with Heinrici and relieved him of his command. (He was temporarily succeeded by Kurt von Tippelskirch, because General Hasso von Manteuffel refused to accept the post.) Heinrici was ordered to report to Berlin and he actually considered going, but was dissuaded from doing so by his aide, Captain Helmuth Lang. Lang told him that he would be murdered in Berlin, like Field Marshal Rommel. A startled Heinrici asserted that the Desert Fox had died of a brain hemorrhage—the story that the Nazi Propaganda Ministry had told the German people. No, Lang replied—that is what the Nazis wanted people to believe. He had been Rommel's aide and had been in Rommel's home when Generals Wilhelm Burgdorf and Ernst Maisel arrived, carrying cyanide capsules. The Desert Fox had been forced to commit suicide.

Instead of going south to Berlin, Heinrici traveled north, initially to Ploen. The British took him prisoner at Huerna bei Flensburg on May 28.

Heinrici spent the next three years in various prisons, mainly at Island Farm Special Camp 11. He spent most of his time there with his cousin, Field Marshal Gerd von Rundstedt, with whom he was very close.[31] He was released on May 19, 1948. He died at Waiblingen, Wuerttemberg on December 13, 1971.

3

THE GENERALS OF STALINGRAD

Friedrich Wilhelm Paulus. Walter von Reichenau. Gustav von
Wietersheim. Victor von Schwedler. Walter Heitz. Karl Strecker.
Walter von Seydlitz-Kurzbach. Arthur Schmidt. Wolfgang
Pickert. Erwin Jaenecke. Hans Valentin Hube.

FRIEDRICH WILHELM PAULUS will forever be associated with the Battle
of Stalingrad, one of the greatest disasters for one nation in military
history. There was nothing in his background or early life to indicate that
he might suffer such a fate. He was born on the evening of September 23,
1890, in the parish of Breitenau-Gershagen, in the Hesse-Nassau region.
Although Paulus later tried to give the impression that he was of the nobility (and many distinguished authors still incorrectly refer to him as "von
Paulus"), his father was, in fact, a minor bookkeeper in the civil service,
and his army personnel file never refers to him by the aristocratic "von."[1]
Well educated in the Wilhelms-Gymnasium at Kassel, he applied for an
officer-cadet slot in the navy but was rejected. After briefly studying law at
the University of Munich, he joined the 111th (3rd Baden) Infantry Regiment, Markgraf Ludwig Wilhelm, at Rastatt as a Fahnenjunker on February
18, 1910, and was commissioned second lieutenant on October 18, 1911.

Lieutenant Paulus married into the nobility in 1912, when he exchanged vows with Elena Constance "Coca" Rosetti-Solescu, a beautiful,
strong-willed Rumanian aristocrat who was very ambitious for her husband, constantly helping and/or pushing him up the professional ladder.
She also gave him three children: a daughter born in 1914 (who later married a baron) and twin sons, Friedrich and Alexander, born in 1918. Both
became captains in the army of the Third Reich.

Paulus was adjutant of the III Battalion, 3rd Baden Infantry Regiment, when World War I broke out. He served in various staff positions on both the Eastern and Western fronts and also in the Rumanian campaign. His only command experience, however, was extremely brief: for seven weeks he directed a machine-gun detachment on a relatively inactive sector of the Russian Front in 1916.[2] He nevertheless emerged from the war as a captain on the staff of the 48th Reserve Division. After the war, he helped form (and apparently fought with) the Freikorps Grenzschutz Ost, a band of paramilitary volunteers who helped check the Poles in 1919.

Selected for the 4,000-man officer corps, Paulus served as commander of a Reichswehr security company (1919–1920) and as the regimental adjutant of the 14th Infantry at Konstanz on Lake Constance (or Bodensee) (1920–1922), before being selected to attend the "R" Course in Berlin in 1922. Here he received clandestine General Staff training. Further staff assignments followed. He served on the staff of Infantry Command V at Stuttgart (1925–1926) and Artillery Command V (1926–1927). On October 1, 1927, he assumed command of the 2nd Company of the 13th (Wuerttemberger) Infantry Regiment at Ulm, where Erwin Rommel, the future "Desert Fox," commanded the machine gun company. The two were very different people and different kinds of officers, and they did not care for each other.

Paulus returned to staff duties with the 5th Infantry Division in Stuttgart in the fall of 1930, and was promoted to major on February 1, 1931. That autumn, he returned to the Defense Ministry as a staff officer with the Army Training Office. He did not receive another command until 1934, when he was named leader of the 3rd (Prussian) Motor Transport Battalion in Berlin, an experimental formation that later grew into one of Germany's first panzer/reconnaissance units.

Friedrich Paulus was only a relatively junior major when Adolf Hitler came to power in 1933 and was marked by his officer efficiency reports as a dedicated and thorough officer, although one who lacked decisiveness.[3] Such reports, however, were not taken too seriously. He had developed impeccable social graces and perfect manners and was both handsome and a gentleman. Not only had he taken great pains not to make enemies, he had made some excellent contacts in the process, including General Oswald Lutz, the commander of motorized and panzer forces, and Walter von Reichenau, the chief of the Armed Forces Office in the Ministry of Defense and the most prominent Nazi officer of the time.

Like so many others, Paulus also fell under the Fuehrer's spell, although his rapid advancement in the 1930s and early 1940s can be attributed more to his excellent staff work, his meticulous attention to detail, and the accelerated expansion of the 100,000-man army than to any other factors. In any event, Paulus received rapid promotion under the Nazis. He became a lieutenant colonel in 1933, colonel in 1935, major general on January 1, 1939, and lieutenant general on August 1, 1940. In the meantime he served as chief of staff to General Lutz, chief of staff of the XVI Motorized Corps in Berlin, and chief of staff of Reichenau's Army Group 4 in Leipzig in 1939. This headquarters was redesignated 10th Army for the invasion of Poland and, in late 1939, changed its name again (to 6th Army) to deceive Allied intelligence. Through all these changes, Reichenau remained its commander, and Paulus stayed on as its chief of staff.

In **WALTER VON REICHENAU**, Paulus found the ideal mentor. As brilliant as Paulus was methodical, the unconventional Reichenau hated desk work as much as Paulus thrived on it. They made a perfect team, this decisive, dynamic man of action and his thorough, desk-bound, unquestioning chief of staff. Reichenau led his army to major victories in Poland (1939), Belgium and France (1940), and Russia (1941). Then, on November 30, 1941, Adolf Hitler relieved a frustrated Field Marshal Gerd von Rundstedt as commander-in-chief of Army Group South and selected his senior army commander in the sector, Field Marshal von Reichenau, to succeed him. By now, Paulus was deputy chief of the General Staff of the army and was working for another friend, General Franz Halder. Reichenau, however, remembered the previous services of his former chief and on December 3, 1941, over a vegetarian dinner, suggested to Adolf Hitler that Paulus be given a chance to command 6th Army. Reichenau knew that Paulus was inexperienced in the area of troop command but calculated that he (Reichenau) could guide the Hessian staff general through the initial, difficult period, while he learned the ropes. Hitler, who also liked Paulus, concurred, and on January 1, 1943, Friedrich Paulus was promoted to general of panzer troops. Despite his junior rank and absolute lack of time in grade, he assumed command of 6th Army four days later.

Although delighted by his promotion and his new assignment, Paulus was, in fact, unqualified for such a high command, both temperamentally and on the basis of experience. His highest previous command was that of an experimental motorized battalion. He had bypassed the vital experiences of commanding a regiment, brigade, division, or corps. Perhaps this lack of experience was not too critical a factor, for other men have been promoted even more rapidly and succeeded brilliantly as army commanders (Napoleon and Robert E. Lee, for example). Paulus, however, lacked the temperament to command an army. A confirmed desk soldier, he hated dirt, habitually wore gloves so that his hands would never be soiled, and bathed and changed clothes twice a day so he would always be very clean. His more combat-oriented peers sarcastically referred to him as "The Noble Lord" and "Our Most Elegant Gentleman."[4] More dangerous still, he was one of those generals convinced of the genius and infallibility of the Fuehrer and an officer who believed in the principle of blind, unquestioning obedience to orders from superiors—no matter what the tactical circumstances.

On the other hand, unlike Reichenau, Paulus believed in the humanitarian treatment of prisoners and enemy civilians whenever possible. Reichenau, for example, had instructed 6th Army to cooperate with the Einsatzgruppen (special extermination groups—see chapter 8) to the fullest possible extent—until they were shooting so many Jews that they were making inroads on his ammunition reserves. Then he suggested to the SS and SD that they use no more than two bullets per Jew. Nearly a million Jews and other civilians had been executed in 6th Army's zone by the beginning of 1942. Paulus, however, rescinded Reichenau's "Severity Orders" almost as soon as he assumed command, terminating 6th Army's cooperation with the Einsatzgruppen and effectively ending the genocide in his area of operations. Sixth Army also had standing orders to execute Soviet political commissars even if they were captured in uniform. These, too, were revoked by the new commander. To his everlasting credit, Paulus brought the 6th Army out of the mass murder business.

Shortly after his appointment was announced, Paulus lost his mentor. On January 12, 1942, Walter von Reichenau went on his usual cross-country run of several miles despite the fact that the temperature was well below minus 20 degrees Fahrenheit. Later that morning, he collapsed in the officers' mess with a severe heart attack. Still unconscious and near death on January 17, he was strapped into an armchair for a flight to Leipzig, where a team of distinguished surgeons stood by. The airplane, however, crashed en route, and Reichenau suffered severe head injuries. Whether he succumbed to heart failure or to the head injuries is neither clear nor significant. What is important is that he was dead shortly after he reached Leipzig on the evening of January 17. Friedrich Paulus had lost his teacher before the lessons could be completed.

Despite the fact that he had been promoted above his ceiling, Paulus was fortunate in that he inherited a reasonably good set of corps commanders from Reichenau.[5]

* * *

GUSTAV VON WIETERSHEIM, leader of the XIV Panzer Corps, was the senior corps commander. Born in Breslau on February 11, 1884, Wietersheim came from a military background. Educated in various cadet schools, he entered the army as a Faehnrich on December 30, 1902. Commissioned second lieutenant in the 4th Grenadier Guards Regiment "Queen Augusta" within a year, Wietersheim was a first lieutenant when World War I began in August 1914, but was promoted to captain in October. Part of the elite 1st Guards Division, he fought in the invasion of Belgium, on the Marne, and in Flanders and Champagne, before being sent to the Eastern Front in the spring of 1915. Here the 1st suffered heavy casualties in the conquest of Galicia (the 1st Guards Grenadier Regiment, for example, lost 3,000 men), but inflicted even more of the Russians. Sent back to France, it fought in the Artois sector, and spent much of the first half of 1916 rebuilding in the rear areas or in quiet sectors of the front. This changed in August, when it fought in the Battle of the Somme, where it lost 5,000 men. Captain von Wietersheim, however, was not one of them. He continued to perform efficiently and was marked for bigger things. He was admitted to the General Staff in 1917. He was then assigned to the staff of the 3rd (Pomeranian) Infantry Division on the Eastern Front and apparently ended the war on the staff of the XXV Reserve Corps. Selected for the 100,000-man army, he became a company commander in the 5th (Prussian) Infantry Regiment in Pomerania in 1924. Wietersheim was promoted to major in 1925 and posted to the Defense Ministry in Berlin as a member of the (T-4) Training Directorate.

On February 1, 1929, Major von Wietersheim assumed command of the II (Jaeger) Battalion of the 17th Infantry Regiment in Goslar. Promoted to lieutenant colonel exactly one year later, he became chief of staff of the 1st Cavalry Division at Breslau in 1932. Later that year (on November 1), he became a full colonel. He then became chief of staff of the 3rd Infantry Division in Frankfurt/Oder (1933–1934), a staff officer in the operations directorate of the Training Office (1934–1935), and chief of operations of the High Command of the Army (1935–1936). Promoted to major general on July 1, 1934, and to lieutenant general on April 1, 1936, he assumed command of the 29th Infantry Division at Erfurt on October 6, 1936. He directed its conversation into a motorized division, showed great natural talent for directing mobile operations, and made the 29th Motorized one of the best divisions in the world in the process. As a result, he was promoted to general of infantry (February 1, 1938) and was given command of the XIV Motorized (later Panzer) Corps at Magdeburg in Saxony-Anhalt on March 1.

Wietersheim led the XIV Motorized in the Polish campaign, where he fought at Radom and Warsaw. He distinguished himself in the French campaign of 1940, where he helped secure the walls of the "Panzer Corridor" as the Germans drove from the Ardennes to the English Channel. He took part in the conquest of Yugoslavia in 1941 and the invasion of Russia, where he fought at Tarnopol, Kiev, and Rostov, among other battles.

In 1938, Wietersheim had been earmarked to be the chief of staff to the commander-in-chief of the Western Front in case of a war over Czechoslovakia. He was vocal in his objections to Hitler's plans and even criticized to the dictator's face the sorry state of West Wall defenses. This apparently earned him Hitler's permanent animosity and explains why he was never given command of an army, despite his distinguished record as a corps commander in Poland, France, the Balkans, and the Soviet Union. Although not considered a first-class military genius, Wietersheim was certainly a solid, experienced, and highly competent combat officer. He would have been much more effective in command of 6th Army than the indecisive Friedrich Paulus. Wietersheim, of course, knew that too; he no doubt resented being passed over for the neophyte.

VICTOR VON SCHWEDLER, the commander of IV Corps, was also considerably senior to Friedrich Paulus. Born in St. Goarshausen, Prussia, on January 18, 1885, he was the son of a career officer in the Imperial Army. Young Schwedler followed in his father's footsteps. Educated in various cadet schools, he joined the army as a Fahnenjunker in early 1904 and was commissioned lieutenant in the 26th (1st Magdeburger) Infantry Regiment early the following year. Later, he was transferred to the 88th (2nd Nassau) Infantry Regiment. He was already a member of the General Staff when World War I broke out and served throughout the war as a General Staff officer. He was promoted to captain in November 1914.

During the era of the Weimar Republic (1918–1933), Schwedler served as a General Staff officer with the 3rd Cavalry Division at Kassel (1919), Wehrkreis V at Stuttgart (1919–1921), and Group Command 2 at Kassel (1921–1924). Promoted to major in 1923, he commanded the 13th (Mortar) Company of the 15th Infantry Regiment at Kassel (1924–1925) before joining the General Staff of Infantry Command III at Potsdam in 1925. He was transferred to the powerful Army Personnel Office (HPA) in Berlin in early 1926.

Now a lieutenant colonel, Schwedler assumed command of the II Battalion of the Prussian 9th Infantry Regiment (II/9th Infantry) in Berlin-Lichterfelde on February 1, 1929. Two years later, he became chief of staff of the 3rd Infantry Division in Frankfurt/Oder and was promoted to colonel on October 1, 1933. Ten days later, he was named chief of the Army Personnel Office; he was promoted to major general on October 10, 1934, and to lieutenant general exactly two years later.

A protégé of Baron Werner von Fritsch, the anti-Nazi commander-in-chief of the army, Schwedler was "kicked upstairs" when Hitler purged the armed forces in February 1938. He was promoted to general of infantry (effective February 1, 1938) and was named commander of Wehrkreis IV (IV Military District), headquartered in Dresden. His vital post in Berlin was filled by Bodewin Keitel, who was considerably more willing to take suggestions from the Nazis than Schwedler. When the war broke out, Schwedler's headquarters (like most of the other Wehrkreise) was split into a territorial command and a field command.[6] Schwedler took the field command (IV Corps) to the front and fought in Poland, Holland, Belgium, and France. He had served on the southern sector of the Russian Front since Operation Barbarossa began.[7]

Unlike von Wietersheim and von Schwedler, there was no hint of anti-Nazi sentiment or activity in the record of **WALTER HEITZ**. Born in Berlin on December 8, 1878, Heitz joined the army as an officer-cadet in the 36th (2nd West Prussian) Field Artillery Regiment "Hochmeister" on August 18, 1899. Commissioned second lieutenant, he became battalion adjutant in 1909 and was promoted to captain in 1913. He was regimental adjutant at the 36th at the time. He remained with his regiment during World War I, where he became a battery commander and battalion commander, and fought in East Prussia (1914), on the Russian Front (1914–1915), and on the Western Front from the fall of 1915 until the end of the war. Selected for the Reichswehr, he served on the staff of the Artillery School at Jueterbog (1919–1922) and in the Artillery Inspectorate in the Defense Ministry (1922–1927). He then commanded the 4th (Saxon) Artillery Regiment at Dresden (1927–1929), the Troop Maneuver Area at Jueterbog (1929–1930), and the Artillery School itself (1930–1931). He became commander of Fortress Koenigsberg in late 1931. Meanwhile, he had been promoted to major (1922), lieutenant colonel (1927), and colonel (1930). A harsh, right-wing career officer with a passion for fox hunting, Heitz was commandant of Koenigsberg when Hitler took power but became president of the Reich Military Court in 1936; and, partially because of his hatred for the Poles, he became armed forces commander, Danzig, on September 14, 1939, soon after the war broke out. "I am to rule the area with the mailed first," he wrote enthusiastically on September 10, 1939. "Combat troops are overinclined toward a false sense of chivalry."[8]

Heitz advanced rapidly under the Third Reich, being promoted to major general (1933), lieutenant general (1934), and general of artillery (April 1, 1937). Despite his advanced age (he was almost 61), he was given command of the VIII Corps on October 25, 1939, and led it into France (1940) and central Russia (1941) before it was sent back to Paris on occupation duty in the fall. The corps and its commander returned to the Soviet Union in the spring of 1942 and were assigned to the 6th Army in April.

KARL STRECKER was born in Radmannsdorf, West Prussia (now Kulm Trzebieluch, Poland), on September 20, 1884, the son of a retired army officer. His grandfather was a Lutheran minister and Karl wanted to follow in his footsteps, but Karl's father—suffering the effects of injuries incurred in the Franco-Prussian War—was unable to stand the constant pain any longer and committed suicide in 1893, leaving behind a widow and six children. The family was financially unable to pay for Karl's religious education, so his grandfather arranged for him to enroll in the Koeslin Cadet School, at the expense of the state. He was 12 years old.[9]

Strecker never abandoned his Christian principles and went into the military reluctantly, but he excelled once he got there. He graduated from the cadet schools with especially high marks in Russian and history, and entered the service as a second lieutenant in the 152nd Infantry Regiment at Marienburg, East Prussia (now Malbork, Poland), on May 14, 1905. He became a battalion adjutant in 1911 and regimental adjutant in June 1914. He was promoted to first lieutenant that same month.

On August 17, 1914, the Russians invaded East Prussia. Three days later, the 152nd Infantry Regiment was in combat. It took part in the huge German victories of Tannenburg and the Masurian Lakes, and in the subsequent invasions of Poland and Russia. It was sent south and was committed to the invasion of Rumania in late 1916. Strecker, meanwhile, was promoted to captain in July 1915.

Strecker was transferred to the Military Railroad Office of the General Staff in December 1916, and to the staff of the 52nd Infantry Division on the Western Front in May 1917, where he served on the artillery staff and with the 111th Infantry Regiment. He fought on the Aisne River northeast of Paris. Later, he briefly served with the 253rd Infantry Division in France, with the XXI Corps, and with the 84th Landwehr Brigade, training in the Vosges Mountains. After recovering from a serious automobile accident, he was assigned to the 30th Infantry Division, then fighting in Belgium. He was transferred to the 52nd Cavalry Division the day before the armistice and rejoined his regiment in West Prussia in early 1919. Here he fought against the Poles, in cooperation with the Freikorps. He was discharged from the army with the honorary rank of major on January 3, 1920.

Strecker joined the Prussian Security Police (*Sicherheitspolizei*) three months before he was officially discharged from the army.[10] Initially assigned to the Westphalian Headquarters in Muenster, he became a major of police and an instructor at the police academies in Muenster and Eiche. His reservation concerning democracy and socialism apparently cost him promotions. (Strecker once stated that, if he was in charge, he would "shoot whomever won't work" and referred to the socialists as the "We Want" party.[11]

Meanwhile, in 1920, at age 32, Strecker married Hedwig Born, the daughter of the mayor of Marienburg. She gave him a son in 1921 and a daughter in 1924.

Police Major Strecker was transferred to Potsdam in 1924, to Berlin in 1927, and back to Muenster (a city he did not like) in 1931. He welcomed the rise of Hitler in the early 1930s, although with some misgivings. He was nevertheless promoted to lieutenant colonel of police in 1932, during the last days of the Weimar Republic. After Hitler became chancellor, Strecker helped the Brownshirts suppress the Communists and found early favor with the Nazi regime. He was rapidly promoted to colonel of police (1933) and major general of police (1934), and was put in charge of the Stettin district. Strecker, meanwhile, became more and more nervous as Heinrich Himmler, the SS, and the Gestapo gained in strength and influence, and more and more power was concentrated in the hands of one man. He was delighted to be able to rejoin the army in June 1935, only three months after Hitler reintroduced conscription in Germany.

Initially General Strecker commanded Army Depot I in Neustettin. To thoroughly prepare him for future advancement, he was named as commander of the 4th Infantry Regiment at Kolberg, East Prussia, on April 1, 1937, despite his senior rank. This type of assignment was not particularly unusual in the 1930s. While here, he continued to visit the shops of his Jewish friends in full uniform, despite the Nazi boycotts, and supported a Lutheran clergyman who had the courage to attack the Nazis from the pulpit. Later, in Russia, he refused to pass Hitler's Commissar Order on to his subordinates. Although he was a decent man and deplored anti-Semitism, he could not bring himself to join the anti-Hitler resistance. The Prussian principle of obedience was too deeply engrained in him.

On November 10, 1938, Strecker was named Infantry Commander 34 and deputy commander of the 34th Infantry Division in Idar-Oberstein. As World War II approached, his command was upgraded and expanded into the 79th Infantry Division, a reserve unit formed at Koblenz, Idar-Oberstein, Darmstadt, and other posts in the summer of 1939. This Rhinelander division was lightly engaged on the Saar Front in the winter of 1939–1940 and saw limited action in France in 1940. Here he proved to be a very capable field commander. Called Papa by his men and praised by all of his superiors (including Field Marshal Erwin von Witzleben), he was promoted to lieutenant general on June 1, 1940. He remained in France on occupation duty until early 1942.

A veteran of the Eastern Front in the Great War, Strecker strongly opposed the invasion of the Soviet Union in 1941 and frankly stated that it would cost Germany the war.[12] He nevertheless led the 79th Infantry Division in the battles of Kiev and Kharkov, and in the conquest of the Ukraine. He fell ill during the Soviet winter offensive of 1941–1942 and was placed in Fuehrer Reserve in January 1942. When he returned to the Russian Front on April 2, it was as acting commander of the XVII Corps.[13] He had been promoted to general of infantry the day before. General Paulus, meanwhile, had been very much impressed by Strecker's handling of his unit during the Battle of Kharkov, and asked that he be assigned to 6th Army. He was named commander of the XI Corps of the 6th Army on June 1, 1942.

It would be difficult to find two officers less alike than Friedrich Paulus and **WALTER VON SEYDLITZ-KURZBACH**, commander of LI Corps, which was part of the 6th Army in 1942. Unlike Paulus, who was a "man of the people" (to use Third Reich jargon), Seydlitz was a Prussian aristocrat. Born and bred for command and war, he was well trained and highly qualified for his job, a man of considerable courage and combat experience, and an officer who did not believe in unquestioned obedience to anybody. He came by this attitude honestly. His most famous ancestor was General Friedrich Wilhelm von Seydlitz, a cavalry commander under Frederick the Great in the Seven Years' War (1756–1763) and a man who also believed in the right of a military commander to take independent action in battle if circumstances warranted it. Against the Russians in the Battle of Zorndorf (1758), Frederick the Great lost his composure and ordered a premature cavalry charge. The cavalry did not charge, however, because Seydlitz would not attack at an inappropriate moment. Frederick sent a dispatch warning Seydlitz that it would mean his head if he caused the battle to be lost. "Tell the king," Seydlitz said to the messenger, "that my head belongs to him after the battle; during the battle, if he permits, I should like to make use of it!" Upon hearing these words, the startled king decided to let his courageous general fight his own battle. Seydlitz delayed the attack until the right moment and then swept the Russians from the field. Later that evening Frederick admitted that Seydlitz had been right.[14] Nor was Friedrich Wilhelm von Seydlitz the only one of Walter's ancestors to risk his neck for disobedience. During the Napoleonic Wars, Major General Florian von Seydlitz was involved in the unauthorized negotiations that led to a truce between the Prussian and Russian armies and that eventually resulted in Prussia's defection from her forced alliance with France.

Walter von Seydlitz, the future general at Stalingrad, was born in Hamburg-Eppendorf on August 22, 1888, the third son of Captain (later Lieutenant General) Alexander von Seydlitz-Kurzbach. Even though Alexander married late in life by the standards of the time (he was 34), he still fathered 10 children, and his marriage (which lasted 52 years) was a very happy one.[15] Walter grew up in an atmosphere that stressed love of family, love of country, devotion to duty, and emulation of the virtues of his ancestors. When he reached manhood, he joined the army as a matter of course.[16] After a six-month basic training course in Danzig and a nine-month officers course at the War Academy at Hanover, he was commissioned second lieutenant in the 36th (2nd West Prussian) Field Artillery Regiment on January 27, 1910.[17]

Seydlitz was stationed with his regiment at Danzig until 1914, when the Russians invaded East Prussia. He spent virtually all of the next four years at or near the front or recuperating from various wounds. Seydlitz fought in the Tannenburg campaign and was thrice severely wounded in the Battle of Gumbinnen, during which he lost his left forefinger. Promoted to first lieutenant in January 1915, he was wounded a fourth time in July, when his left foot was shattered. After several weeks' medical leave he rejoined his regiment, which was sent to the Western Front in the fall of 1915. He fought in the Battle of the Somme in 1916, where his younger brother Wolfgang was killed on July 30. His oldest brother, Heinrich, had been killed in 1914. Walter remained at the front, taking part in the Third Battle of Ypres (1917), the Battle of Flanders (1917), the trench warfare around St. Quentin (1917–1918), and Ludendorff's Great Offensive of 1918. Promoted to captain in April 1917, Seydlitz successively served as battalion adjutant, regimental adjutant, and on the staff of the 36th Artillery Command (Arko 36) of the 36th Infantry Division. He emerged from the war with both grades of the Iron Cross, the Hohenzollern House Order with Swords, the Hanseatic Cross, and the Wounded Badge in Silver. He was selected for the 4,000-man officer corps in 1920.

Walter Seydlitz was an extremely efficient young officer whose competence was matched by his confidence. As a young man he was a passionate rider and horse racer. As he matured and became a family man (he married Ingeborg Barth on January 3, 1922, and fathered four daughters), he did not lose his ebullience, which bordered on arrogance. Indeed, even as a general officer in World War II, the word that appears most frequently in his efficiency reports is *Frisch* (fresh). Count von Brockdorff, for example, found him "impulsive and impetuous, enterprising and full of life."[18] This attitude helped sustain him during the lean years of the Weimar Republic, when professional advancement for the German officer was very slow.

After the war, Seydlitz returned to Danzig with the remnants of his old regiment. He became a battery commander in 1919 and moved with his unit (now designated the 2nd Artillery Regiment) to Schwerin in 1920, when Danzig was taken away from Germany under the terms of the Treaty of Versailles. Seydlitz remained there for nine years, serving on the staff of the 2nd Artillery and again as regimental adjutant and battery commander—this time under Baron Werner von Fritsch, the future anti-Nazi commander-in-chief of the army, whom he held in high esteem. From 1929 until 1933, he was in the Reichswehr Ministry in Berlin, where he served as adjutant of the Weapons Office. He was promoted to major in 1930.

Seydlitz's pre–World War II career was unusual in a number of respects. He was a member of the clandestine General Staff but without the usual training and probationary periods. He also spent very little time in Berlin (one four-year tour in an active career of 34 years) and a disproportionate amount of time with his regiment (20 of his first 21 years' service). Nevertheless, he returned to the artillery as soon as he finished his assignment in Berlin, this time as commander of the IV Mounted Battalion of the 6th Artillery Regiment, in the small Lower Saxony town of Verden/Aller. He remained here until the outbreak of the war, in what he later described as the happiest period of his military service. Seydlitz became a lieutenant colonel in 1934 and, on April 1, 1936, was promoted to full colonel and assumed command of his regiment, which was now designated the 22nd Artillery. When Germany invaded Poland on September 1, 1939, Seydlitz was ordered to the Dutch frontier and on September 20 was named Artillery Commander 102 (i.e., commander of Arko 102), a brigade-level command. He was promoted to major general on December 1 and was named commander of the Mecklenberger 12th Infantry Division in March 1940.

As commander of the 12th, Seydlitz saw his first combat in World War II. He took part in the breaching of the French Maginot Line east of Trelon in May and the forcing of the Somme River in June. He was awarded his Knight's Cross on August 15, and his division remained in France on occupation duty until December, when it was transferred to the Netherlands. In May 1941, it entrained for Poland and crossed into the Soviet Union on June 22, penetrating 30 miles on the first day of the invasion.

Seydlitz again distinguished himself in the first months of the Russian campaign, taking part in the encirclement of Nevel and the desperate winter battles around Kholm, in which he played a pivotal role in preventing a decisive Soviet breakthrough on the northern sector of the Eastern Front. He was summoned to Fuehrer Headquarters and promoted to lieutenant general on December 31, 1941—the same day Adolf Hitler personally decorated him with the Oak Leaves to his Knight's Cross. He was placed in Fuehrer Reserve the following day. Clearly his performance in France and Russia had impressed the dictator, who had him earmarked for greater things. Until then, however, he was on temporary duty at Supreme Headquarters. While there, he sat on the court-martial board of Lieutenant General Hans von Sponeck, a corps commander who had retreated without permission in December 1941. Seydlitz considered Sponeck's actions fully justified and was very upset when the board convicted him and the court-martial's president, Hermann Goering—acting on the instructions of the Fuehrer—pronounced the death sentence. Perhaps Seydlitz's outrage was a factor in Hitler's decision to commute the sentence to six years' imprisonment.[19] In any event, Seydlitz was quickly returned to the Russian Front, where he was charged with the task of rescuing the II Corps, now surrounded in the Demyansk sector, 30 miles behind Russian lines.

The hastily created Group von Seydlitz consisted of the 5th and 8th Jaeger and 122nd and 329th Infantry Divisions. It launched its relief attack on March 21, 1942, against stiff Soviet resistance. The men pressed on through thick forests and heavy snow, repulsing numerous counterattacks, until they reached the Demyansk perimeter and established a tenuous link on April 21. Even so, the six divisions of II Corps (originally 103,000 men but now considerably fewer) were in an exposed position, and Field Marshal Georg von Kuechler, the commander-in-chief of Army Group North, proposed that they be withdrawn from the salient—a move that would shorten his front by 120 miles. Accompanied by Seydlitz, he flew to Fuehrer Headquarters in early May to obtain permission to fall back.

Even though Franz Halder, the chief of the General Staff of the army, agreed with Kuechler, Hitler would not sanction the withdrawal. He wanted to use the area as a base for a future offensive. Seydlitz then took charge of the argument, pointing out that the swampy and wooded terrain around Demyansk would make it impossible to use tanks in an offensive role, as proposed by Hitler. All the general's arguments fell on deaf ears, however. Hitler would not even look at photographs taken by Seydlitz's cameramen, showing the deep forests and mud in the area. "Those are my orders!" Hitler finally snapped, bringing the conference to a close.

"I agree with everything you said in there," General of Artillery Alfred Jodl, the chief of operations of OKW, told Seydlitz after the conference.

"Then why didn't you back me up in the Fuehrer's presence?" Seydlitz asked. There followed a painful silence; Jodl did not reply.[20] And the men of the II Corps were condemned to nine more months of holding a useless salient against several Soviet armies. Hitler's impossible offensive never was launched, and the salient was not evacuated until February 1943, after the fall of Stalingrad.

Walter von Seydlitz-Kurzbach was given command of the LI Corps (part of Paulus's 6th Army) on May 8, 1942, and was promoted to general of artillery on June 1. He fought in the Second Battle of Kharkov, as the Soviet summer offensive of 1942 is now called. Here his corps and Karl Hollidt's XVII (six divisions in all) delayed 16 Red Army divisions and five armored and motorized brigades for several days until Colonel General Ewald von Kleist's 1st Panzer Army could strike the Soviets in the rear, forming a huge pocket south of Kharkov, between the 6th and 1st Panzer armies. When the battle ended, 239,000 Soviet soldiers had surrendered, and 1,250 tanks and 2,026 guns had been captured or destroyed.[21] For the Germans, however, this victory was only a prelude to disaster.

Hitler began his summer offensive of 1942 (Operation Blue) on June 28. Finally learning (from their previous mistakes, the Soviets retreated rapidly, thus avoiding the massive battles of encirclement that had cost them so much in the previous 12 months. On July 7, even though he had not achieved the kind of decisive success he had hoped for, Hitler divided Army Group South into Army Groups A and B and sent them off on divergent axes of advance. Army Group A (Field Marshal Wilhelm List) was sent south to capture the Caucasus oil fields, while Army Group B (Colonel General Baron Maximilian von Weichs) headed east, toward Stalingrad. Had Hitler chosen one or the other as the primary objective and concentrated his forces against it, his offensive might well have achieved some success. As it was, neither army group had the resources to accomplish its mission.

Paulus's 6th Army, later supported by Hermann Hoth's 4th Panzer, spearheaded the drive on Stalingrad. His advance was very slow, and on more than one occasion he was immobilized due to a lack of fuel and ammunition. Nevertheless he won an impressive tactical victory over the Soviets at Ostrov; by July 28 he had destroyed more than 1,000 enemy tanks and had taken more than 55,000 prisoners. Overly impressed by his success, Paulus reported the destruction of the Soviet 1st Tank and 62nd armies. Then on August 23, when his supplies were fully replenished, Paulus ordered Wietersheim's XIV Panzer Corps to push to the Volga north of Stalingrad—more than 30 miles away. This Wietersheim did, reaching the Volga the next day. However, Paulus had grossly underestimated the Soviets' strength and powers of recuperation. They promptly counterattacked in XIV Panzer's rear and cut it off completely. Wietersheim had to hedgehog (i.e., form an all-around defense) and await relief.

Paulus moved slowly and could not reestablish contact with the panzer corps until September 2—after 4th Panzer Army joined the battle and forced the Soviet 62nd Army (which Paulus had claimed he had destroyed more than two months before) to fall back into the outer defenses of Stalingrad. Paulus's drive to the Volga had already cost 6th Army 38,000 men—10 percent of its total strength. Naturally, the proportion of casualties in the infantry units was much higher than this.

General von Weichs wanted Paulus to attack the city on September 2, before the Russians had time to regroup. Already depressed by his heavy losses, however, the indecisive Hessian staff officer hesitated for five days, during which Stalin poured reinforcements into the sector. Finally, on September 7, the attack began, spearheaded by Seydlitz's LI Corps. Seydlitz's advance was very methodical because he had to clear a block at a time, and the Soviets fought fiercely for every building and launched repeated local counterattacks. Seydlitz finally captured the 300-foot Mamayev Hill in the center of the city on September 13, but this only intensified Soviet resistance. It took him another week to penetrate the remaining one-third of a mile to the Volga, thus cutting the Soviet 62nd Army in two. But the battle was far from over.

Paulus showed little tactical skill in the Battle of Stalingrad, which he fought as a series of frontal attacks, in an area that allowed no room for maneuver and in which all the advantages of terrain and position accrued to the defense. General Victor von Schwedler, the veteran commander of the IV Corps, foresaw disaster and called upon Hitler to withdraw from this costly and tactically unsound battle. He was immediately sacked and sent into retirement. The bad blood between Paulus and Gustav von Wietersheim, who also criticized 6th Army's conduct of the battle, boiled over on September 15, and Paulus relieved him of his command. Luftwaffe Colonel General Wolfram von Richthofen, nephew of the Red Baron and commander of the 4th Air Fleet in southern Russia, nevertheless called on the Army General Staff to replace Paulus with a better commander. Hitler, however, still had confidence in Paulus, who was, after all, obeying his orders; in fact, he had already earmarked Paulus to succeed Jodl as chief of operations of OKW. No action was taken against the pro-Nazi Richthofen, but no changes were made either.

As we have seen, Friedrich Paulus could be mentally dominated by people of stronger will. Prior to 1942 he had been under the influence of Field Marshal von Reichenau. Following Reichenau's death, Paulus allowed himself to be guided by the perceived infallibility of the Fuehrer. Now he was dominated by the strong will of his chief of staff, Major General ARTHUR SCHMIDT.

Schmidt, a bachelor, was born in Hamburg on October 25, 1895, the son of a merchant. Like Paulus, he did not come from a family with a military tradition, but he had been a dedicated soldier since he volunteered for the army when World War I broke out. He was commissioned second lieutenant in 1915 in the 26th (1st Magdeburger) Infantry Regiment, which fought in Belgium, on the Marne, in the Battle of the Somme, and in other bloody battles on the Western Front. Schmidt successively served as a platoon leader, battalion adjutant, company commander, and regimental adjutant. Among other decorations, he earned the Hohenzollern House Order with Swords, both grades of the Iron Cross, and the Wounded Badge in Black. He served in the Freikorps in 1919 and joined the Reichsheer's 12th Infantry Regiment at Halberstadt in Saxony in 1920 and was later assigned to the 11th Company in Magdeburg. He was promoted to first lieutenant in 1923.

Schmidt began in General Staff training in 1924 as a staff officer with the 1st Infantry Division, which headquartered in Koenigsberg. He attended the secret Reinhardt Course in Berlin (1926–1927) and returned to Halberstadt as an unofficial member of the General Staff. He was promoted to captain in 1928.

Arthur Schmidt was transferred to the Troop Office (as the clandestine General Staff was called) in Berlin in 1929 and was adjutant to General Wilhelm Adam from 1930 to 1931. Replaced by Major General Georg von Soderstern, he was transferred to the Foreign Armies Intelligence Office, was promoted to major in 1934, and posted to Headquarters, Wehrkreis VI, in Muenster. He became the corps Ia (chief of operations) in 1937. A true believer in the genius of the Fuehrer, Schmidt advanced rapidly under the Nazi regime, rising from major in 1937 to major general in 1942 and to lieutenant general in early 1943. During the previous four years he had served as chief of operations (Ia) of VI Corps (1937–1939), 5th Army (1939), and 18th Army (1939–1940) and as chief of staff of V Corps (late 1940–1942), before becoming chief of staff of 6th Army on June 20, 1942.

Like Paulus, the bug-eyed, thin-faced Schmidt was a master of detail, but there the similarity ended. Schmidt lacked Paulus's conscience, good breeding, and polished manners. He was an autocratic, overbearing bully who rudely interrupted people anytime he felt like it. Unlike Paulus, Schmidt was thoroughly disliked by most of the officers with whom he came into contact. Unfortunately, as Paulus's confidence declined and the situation deteriorated, he allowed himself (and 6th Army) to be guided more and more by the opinions of his chief of staff, until it reached the point where Schmidt was virtually conducting the battle for the German side.

Not a man of great daring or initiative, Schmidt was characterized by a stubborn optimism, tenacity, and a willingness to obey the orders of his superiors without question. He might have done well in other situations, but not under a commander like Paulus and not at Stalingrad.

While Paulus bled his army white in Stalingrad, Baron von Weichs had very few German soldiers available to guard against a Soviet offensive into his rear. Therefore he covered Paulus's northwest flank with the 8th Italian and 3rd Rumanian armies, while his southern flank was protected by the 4th Panzer and 4th Rumanian armies. Unfortunately, 4th Panzer Army had been used as a reservoir from which to send reinforcements to other sectors, including 6th Army's. By November 19, it retained only three understrength German divisions.

Meanwhile, as early as the beginning of November, Seydlitz saw a major trap in the making. He called upon Paulus to pull the 14th and 24th Panzer divisions out of the street fighting, use his reinforcements and replacements to bring them up to strength, and use them as a fire brigade, in case the Soviets penetrated into the army's rear, as he expected. Paulus and Schmidt rejected the idea.

The Soviets launched a major offensive against the Rumanian 3rd Army on November 19 and quickly scattered it to the four winds. The only German reserve in this sector was the XXXXVIII Panzer Corps, which had only one German division (the 22nd Panzer) and which had an operational strength of only 20 tanks. It also was quickly defeated. The following day the offensive began against the Rumanian 4th Army and the depleted 4th

Panzer on Paulus's southern flank. By November 21, the two massive Soviet pinchers were advancing almost unopposed into the rear of 6th Army in a huge double envelopment. By noon one armored column pushed to within sight of Paulus's headquarters at Golubinsky. The general and his staff hurriedly fled south, away from the bulk of 6th Army and the rapidly forming Stalingrad pocket. At 2 p.m. on November 22, Paulus and Schmidt flew back over enemy lines to Gumrak airfield, where they reestablished a command post and tried to regain control of the situation, although this proved to be no longer possible.

Later that day the two Soviet spearheads joined at Kalach. Sixth Army was encircled in a pocket 30 miles long (east to west) and 24 miles wide. Most of its rear-area supply depots and warehouses had been overrun or put to the torch to prevent them from falling into Soviet hands. Paulus's reserves of food, clothing, fuel, and ammunition were already dangerously low. In the meantime, on November 21, Adolf Hitler issued a fatal order. Sixth Army was to stand fast where it was, in spite of the danger of encirclement. There was to be no breakout from Stalingrad.

From the beginning, virtually every general except Schmidt favored an immediate breakout attempt. On November 21, before he received Hitler's decisive order, Paulus sent a message to Army Group B, recommending that 6th Army break out to the southwest and retreat more than 100 miles to the lower parts of the Chir and Don rivers. However, once he learned what the Fuehrer had ordered, Paulus accepted the dictator's will with an attitude of almost detached resignation. This lifeless obsequiousness characterized Paulus's attitude for the rest of the siege. The details of the battle he left to his more aggressive and energetic chief of staff, Arthur Schmidt.

On November 22, Paulus and Schmidt met with Hermann Hoth and Major General Wolfgang Pickert,[22] commander of the 9th Flak Division. Schmidt asked his old friend Pickert what they should do now. "Get the hell out of here," the Luftwaffe officer responded.[23] Hoth, a veteran panzer commander and a fine tactician, also favored a breakout attempt. Schmidt, however, replied that there was no need for panic and nothing in the local tactical situation as yet justified making decisions independent of Berlin. Paulus did not open his mouth during the entire conference, except to agree with Schmidt.

Later that afternoon Paulus and Schmidt set up a new headquarters in the northern part of the pocket, in an old, primitive Russian bunker, about 30 yards from Seydlitz's LI Corps headquarters. Perhaps they wanted to keep an eye on the independent-minded Seydlitz, who confronted them almost at once. He urged an immediate breakout and began drafting a message to be sent to Fuehrer Headquarters. At the end of almost every sentence, Paulus and Schmidt would ask, "Isn't that too sharp?" or "Can we really say that?" In the end Paulus rejected Seydlitz's plea for an unauthorized breakout, commenting, "I cannot go against Hitler or move without his approval."[24]

Perhaps Paulus could not but Seydlitz certainly could. On the nights of November 23–24, he withdrew much of his corps southward, shortening his front by seven miles. His objective was obvious: he intended to disengage units, which would then be free to take part in an unapproved breakout attempt. Unfortunately for him, the Soviets observed the move and struck before it could be completed, inflicting heavy casualties on the 94th Infantry Division. Paulus quickly hurried to Seydlitz's headquarters and demanded an explanation. Schmidt called the action "mutiny" and urged that Seydlitz be relieved of his command and court-martialed. Paulus would not go along with this idea, however; 6th Army's morale was low enough as it was. Besides, by this time Paulus had already signaled Hitler directly, urging a breakout. He had even formed a battering ram of armor, artillery, and motorized infantry for that purpose, should the Fuehrer approve his request. He was not willing to give the signal for the attack against orders from Berlin, however. Ironically, Seydlitz's standing with the Fuehrer was very high at this time. When he had earmarked Paulus to succeed Jodl after the conquest of Stalingrad, he had decided to simultaneously promote Seydlitz to the command of 6th Army. When he learned of the LI Corps withdrawal, Hitler assumed that Paulus was responsible for it and, completely misjudging his men, concluded that Paulus was planning an unauthorized breakout. To guard against this, on the evening of November 24, he ordered that the northern sector of the Stalingrad pocket be placed under Seydlitz's command, made independent of 6th Army's command, and be made directly subordinate to OKH. Paulus received this message about 6 p.m. on November 25 and personally carried it to Seydlitz. He seems to have appreciated the irony of the situation. "Now you can act on your own and break out!" he said.

In all likelihood Paulus was being facetious when he made this remark. Seydlitz, however, took it seriously and unbraided the Hessian. "That is a utopian idea!" he replied. "How can I break out with only a part of the army? For a breakout to succeed, the army has to act as a unit."[25] He continued to urge Paulus to act on his own initiative, but the 6th Army commander again refused.

Meanwhile, back at Fuehrer Headquarters, Hermann Goering calmly assured Hitler that he could supply 6th Army by air. General of Fliers

Martin Fiebig and Baron von Richthofen, the two principal Luftwaffe commanders in the sector, had already gone on record as stating that it could not be done, but their views were not solicited by the Reichsmarschall. General Kurt Zeitzler, who had recently succeeded Halder as chief of the General Staff of the army, called Goering a liar to his face, provoking a violent argument, but Hitler, in the end, sided with Goering because he *wanted* to believe the airlift could be accomplished. Back in Stalingrad, Arthur Schmidt reacted in the same manner. "It simply has to be done!" he exclaimed to Pickert and Hoth. The army could help, he said, by eating its horses first, to give the Luftwaffe time to organize the resupply operation.[26] The soft-spoken Paulus, as usual, passively agreed with his chief of staff.

The decision to hold Stalingrad and resupply the garrison by air doomed 6th Army to total destruction—unless its commander could muster enough courage to act on his own.

On November 27, the corps commanders of 6th Army met with Friedrich Paulus and his chief of staff at army headquarters and unanimously urged Paulus to break out against orders. Seydlitz urged him to "take the course of the Lion," a reference to General Karl von Litzmann, who had broken out against orders in similar circumstances in World War I and had thus saved his entire command from Russian captivity. The one-armed General Hans Hube, recently promoted commander of the XIV Panzer Corps and a favorite of the Fuehrer, exclaimed, "Breakout is our only chance!"

"We can't just remain here and die!" Karl Strecker pleaded. Even the pro-Nazi General Heitz, commander of the VIII Corps, called for an immediate breakout, regardless of casualties. General Erwin Jaenecke, a personal friend of Paulus's and commander of IV Corps, evoked the ghost of Paulus's mentor. "Reichenau would have brushed aside all doubts," he said.

"I am no Reichenau," Paulus replied.

Jaenecke put great pressure on his old friend to save the army. Seydlitz then revealed that he had already ordered LI Corps to destroy all equipment that could not be carried on a long march. He had set the example personally by burning everything except the uniform he had on. All the corps commanders enthusiastically expressed their approval. Even those who were looked upon as Nazis called for a breakout, despite Hitler's orders. Unfortunately, Schmidt had the last word. "We must obey," he said.

"I shall obey," Paulus responded.[27]

Later that month Lieutenant Colonel Hans-Juergen Dingler, the Ia of the 3rd Motorized Division, also suggested a breakout to Paulus. He replied, "I expect you as a soldier to carry out the Fuehrer's orders. In the same manner the Fuehrer, as my superior, can and must expect that I shall obey his orders."[28]

Even now, however, Walter von Seydlitz-Kurzbach refused to accept Hitler's disastrous decision. He urged Baron von Weichs, the army group commander, to give the order for a breakout. "To remain inactive," he signaled Army Group B, "is a crime from the military viewpoint, and it is a crime from the point of view of responsibility to the German people."[29]

Colonel General von Weichs did not reply. And 6th Army did not move.

Officers who saw Paulus during this time expressed great sympathy for him, for he was clearly shouldering a greater burden than he could bear. Already plagued by a recurrence of the dysentery he had contracted during World War I, he now developed a nervous facial tic as well. Still, however, he trusted in the genius of the Fuehrer. On November 30, Hitler rewarded Paulus for his loyalty by promoting him to colonel general. Paulus, meanwhile, recommended Arthur Schmidt for advancement to lieutenant general. He received this promotion on January 17, 1943.[30]

In late November 1942, the incredibly gifted Field Marshal Erich von Manstein, commander-in-chief of Army Group Don, took over operations on the southern sector of the Eastern Front. Despite overwhelming odds, in the dead of the Russian winter, he pushed a relief column (the LVII Panzer Corps) to within 40 miles of the Stalingrad perimeter and established a bridgehead across the Mishkova River on December 20. He could, however, go no further, so he sent Major Georg Eismann, his Ic, to Stalingrad, to persuade Paulus to break out. This time, even Hitler gave his conditional approval.

By now it was obvious that the airlift was failing. Virtually all the horses had been eaten, as well as all the cats and dogs and many of the slower rats in Stalingrad. Of 270,000 men originally trapped in the city, the effective infantry strength stood at 40,000. Most of the German soldiers slept in shell holes or on the frozen ground because there were only enough bunkers to accommodate one-third of them. There were no heating materials, almost all the wooden buildings had been burned, and thousands froze to death while tens of thousands contracted frostbite. Rations on December 7 consisted of one stale loaf of bread per day for every five men, but they declined after that. Men "no longer take cover from Russian shells," one soldier wrote. "They haven't the strength to walk, run away and hide."[31] Even now, however, Paulus refused to attempt a breakout until he received more supplies. He calculated that he had enough fuel to travel 18 miles—no more. Manstein's vanguards must push forward another 20 miles before an attempt could be made.

Manstein dispatched one of his staff officers, Major Hans-Georg Eismann, to Stalingrad, to attempt to reason with Paulus and Schmidt, but he experienced no success. "Sixth Army will still be in position at Easter," Schmidt said. "All you people have to do is to supply it better." Paulus agreed automatically. "What ultimately decided the attitude of 6th Army Headquarters," Manstein wrote later, "was the opinion of the chief of staff." He concluded that all Eismann's remonstrations "were like water off a duck's back."[32]

While Paulus hesitated, the Soviets concentrated against the Italian 8th Army and routed it. With almost nothing in reserve, Manstein had no choice but to withdraw the bulk of the LVII Panzer Corps to deal with this new threat, leaving only a holding force across the Mishkova. On December 27, this weak element began to give ground in the face of Soviet attacks, and the following day it retreated rapidly to avoid being surrounded. The last chance to save the Stalingrad garrison was gone.

On January 8, 1943, the Soviets issued Paulus an ultimatum. If he did not agree to surrender by 10 a.m. the following day, all the encircled Germans would be destroyed. Paulus did not even bother to answer. The final Soviet offensive began on January 10 and met extremely tenacious—indeed, desperate—resistance. Gradually, however, the weight of seven Soviet armies crushed 6th Army. Paulus had fewer than 100 tanks left, and they were almost out of fuel and ammunition. On January 22 the last airfield fell, the men could not be resupplied, and there were 12,000 unattended wounded lying in the streets. German soldiers had by now begun to desert in large numbers. The following day, the Russians broke through the western perimeter and cut the pocket in half. Paulus, however, still obeyed Hitler's order not to surrender. He directed that food be withheld from the wounded; only those who could still fight were to be given what meager rations remained.

Walter von Seydlitz, on the other hand, had had enough of this slaughter. On the morning of January 25, he asked Paulus to surrender on his own initiative. When Paulus refused, Seydlitz issued an order to his corps giving his regimental and battalion commanders permission to surrender on their own if the front collapsed and their capitulation would prevent unnecessary casualties. When Paulus heard about these instructions the next day, he considered having Seydlitz arrested. Instead, he placed him under the command of the fanatical General Heitz, who issued an order that there would be no surrender and that anyone caught negotiating with the enemy would be shot. This order was clearly aimed at von Seydlitz. In fact, almost certainly on Heitz's instructions, the command posts of VIII and LI corps now shared the same bunker, so Heitz could keep an eye on Seydlitz and prevent any unauthorized actions.

Paulus was by now on the verge of physical and mental collapse, a condition exacerbated by a head wound he suffered when a Soviet bomb exploded near him on January 25. Schmidt, however, continued to direct the remnants of the 6th Army, with no interference from Paulus.

Three days later—on January 28—the Red Army cut the southern pocket in half. Paulus was isolated in the southernmost of the three pockets, in the ruins of a large department store in Red Square. On January 30, he sent Hitler an inspirational message, congratulating the Fuehrer on the 10th anniversary of his assumption of power and saying that he hoped 6th Army's struggle would set an example for future generations never to surrender, no matter how great the odds. That same day, only a few hundred yards from Paulus's command post, the Headquarters, XIV Panzer Corps (now under Lieutenant General Helmuth Schloemer), was surrounded and forced to surrender. In the central pocket Soviet tanks penetrated to Heitz's CP and captured him, Seydlitz, and five other generals.

That night—and with misgivings—Hitler acted on one of Zeitzler's recommendations and promoted Paulus to field marshal. He also sent him a message reminding him that no German field marshal had ever been captured—a clear invitation for Paulus to commit suicide.

At 6:15 a.m. on January 31, 6th Army Headquarters signaled OKH that there were Russians outside the door. It did not inform them that Arthur Schmidt was even then negotiating the surrender of the 6th Army. The last transmission was made at 7:15 a.m. Shortly thereafter, Friedrich Paulus surrendered to the Soviets. Now, only General Strecker refused to surrender. William Craig called his prolonged resistance "a futile gesture of defiance."[33] This last island of resistance disappeared at 8:40 a.m. on February 2, when Strecker surrendered the northern pocket and the remnants of XI Corps to the Red Army. He and his chief of staff, Colonel Helmuth Groscurth, deliberately omitted the customary "Heil Hitler" from their last transmission.[34] Of the 274,000 men surrounded in Stalingrad on November 22, about 240,000 were Germans. Of these, approximately 25,000 (mostly sick and wounded) were flown out and 91,000 surrendered. The rest lay dead in the ruins of Stalingrad.

As General Strecker watched his men march off into captivity, he noted that they looked "spiritually broken. . . . Nothing [was] left to them. Death [could] not be worse."[35]

Most of them were soon dead. They were forced to make long marches through the Russian winter just to reach the POW camps on the other side of the Urals. In their weakened condition, many perished in the cold. Then, in crowded and filthy camps, typhoid spread quickly. At least 75 percent of them had died by spring. Of the perhaps 15,000 still alive in July 1943, only about 6,000 were returned to Germany in 1955.[36]

Walter von Seydlitz-Kurzbach was sent to a Communist prison camp, where he was subjected to Soviet indoctrination. Their words found fertile ground, for von Seydlitz was a thoroughly disillusioned man and was very embittered and perhaps emotionally unbalanced over the senseless slaughter he had witnessed at Stalingrad. Shortly before the end he was openly contemplating suicide. Before he had been in captivity very long he was convinced that any act that sped the fall of Hitler was good for Germany— even if it meant working for Stalin. By early September, Seydlitz had been completely persuaded and was actively cooperating with the Soviets. At Lunyovo on September 11 and 12, he and 93 other officers, including Lieutenant General Elder Alexander von Daniels, Major General Dr. Otto Korfes, and Major General Martin Lattmann (all captured at Stalingrad), formed the League of German Officers—a military correlate to the Communist National Free Germany Committee. Seydlitz was selected president of the League, and the Soviets had great hopes that its propaganda efforts would demoralize the Germans and convince officers in pocket situations to surrender more quickly. Their hopes were soon dashed. The League's first test was at Cherkassy, where the German XI and XXXXII corps were surrounded in February 1944. The pocket commander, General of Artillery Wilhelm Stemmermann, signaled OKH on February 14 that he had received letters from Seydlitz demanding his surrender but that he had refused to answer them.[37] Soviet propaganda trucks, loudspeakers, and radio broadcast facilities were all put at the disposal of the League, but to no avail. There were few desertions and no surrenders, and on the night of February 16–17 the defenders broke out of the cauldron. Of the 54,000 men who had been encircled, 32,000 eventually escaped. Most of the rest were killed.

After Cherkassy, the Soviet High Command quickly (and correctly) branded the League a miserable failure, and, although they continued to use it occasionally, they never again expected much from it and indeed derived very little benefit from it.

As soon as he joined the League, Seydlitz was shunned by Paulus and most of the other captive generals, including Heitz, Carl Rodenburg, Hans-Heinrich Sixt von Armin, Strecker, and Schmidt. The Nazis were not slow in responding to Seydlitz's actions, either. On April 26, 1944, a military tribunal in Dresden found him guilty of treason and sentenced him to death in absentia. In a typically tasteless Nazi gesture, the news of this sentence was made public on October 18, 1944, at the funeral of Field Marshal Erwin Rommel—who had been forced to commit suicide for his part in the July 20 plot to assassinate Adolf Hitler. Of course, the facts behind Rommel's death were suppressed until after the war. Meanwhile, Field Marshal Wilhelm Keitel informed Ingeborg von Seydlitz that he wanted her to divorce her husband; otherwise, her safety and that of her four daughters would be in jeopardy. She took the warning and quickly (and wisely) initiated the divorce action. The final divorce decree was signed on the morning of July 20, 1944—only a few hours before Count Claus von Stauffenberg's unsuccessful attempt on Hitler's life.

After the July 20 attempt misfired, the Gestapo arrested anyone who might be remotely connected to the plot, and often their families as well. Frau Seydlitz was taken into custody at Yerden/Aller on August 3 and was imprisoned at Bremen. Her two oldest daughters (Mechthild, age 19, and Dietlind, age 16) were picked up two days later, and Seydlitz's brother-in-law, Dr. Eberhardt Barth, was arrested about the same time. The general's two youngest daughters, 10-year-old Ingrid and 8-year-old Ute, were placed in the children's concentration camp at Bad Sachsa, under their mother's maiden name. Due to the divorce decree, and with the help of Reichsminister Albert Speer,[38] all five of the Seydlitz females were released around Christmas 1944, although they were not allowed to return home until March 1945.

After the war, Walter von Seydlitz was kept in various prisons until July 8, 1950, when he underwent a "show trial" by a Soviet military tribunal and was sentenced to death on five charges dealing with his period in command of the 12th Infantry Division. His sentence was commuted to 25 years' imprisonment, and he was sent to Rostov, where he was confined under deliberately cruel conditions—presumably his punishment for the failure of the League of German Officers. He was kept in solitary confinement and subjected to psychological torture, including an electric light that was kept burning in his cell 24 hours a day for four years. He was not allowed to communicate with his family and did not know if they were alive or dead. All of this, plus the guilt and worry about his wife and four young girls, gradually eroded his self-confidence and led to a nervous breakdown on November 26, 1954. After that he was transferred to the Butyrskaya prison near Moscow, where he marked time under less strenuous conditions.

In September 1955, West German Chancellor Conrad Adenauer visited Moscow, where he pulled a coup. He would refuse to establish diplomatic relations, he said, until the Germans still in Soviet prisons were released. The Soviets reacted with typical bad grace, but they finally pardoned and granted exit visas to all but 749 of them. The rest were turned over to the courts of East or West Germany for trial for war crimes.

Walter von Seydlitz was released on October 4, 1955, and reunited with his family two days later. Most of Germany and even many of his old comrades greeted his return with stony silence. Seydlitz seemed to accept this as his verdict and, his old arrogance gone, lived in relatively quiet retirement in Bremen until his death on April 28, 1976. The argument over whether or not he was a traitor to Germany continues to this day.

Friedrich Paulus never overcame Stalingrad, physically or psychologically. He initially refused to join the National Free Germany Committee or the League of German Officers because he disapproved of officers who had been taken prisoner engaging in political activity. He changed his views when he learned the details of the July 20, 1944, assassination attempt and its aftermath. Colonel Claus von Stauffenberg had served under him at OKH, and Paulus also had great respect for two other prominent conspirators: Field Marshal Erwin von Witzleben and Colonel General Erich Hoepner.

On August 8, 1944—the same day Witzleben and Hoepner were hanged—Paulus made his first anti-Nazi broadcast, calling on the German armies in the East to oppose Hitler. The Gestapo arrested his family that same day, except for his son Friedrich. He had been killed in action at Anzio four months before.

Unlike the Seydlitz family, the Paulus family was never reunited. Paulus appeared as a witness for the Soviet prosecution at Nuremberg in 1946 but was not released from prison until 1953. He never saw his wife again: she had been freed from a Nazi prison by the Americans at the end of the war, but she died in Baden-Baden in 1949. Professing now to believe that Communism was the best hope for Europe, the former marshal settled in Dresden, East Germany, where he worked as an inspector of People's Police and tried to defend his military reputation from the attacks of historians and former comrades alike, but with little success. Even though his only surviving son, Ernst, was allowed to visit him a few times, Paulus's last years were lonely. Also, Ernst openly disapproved of his father's conversion to Communism, which did not help matters. Plagued in his last years by ill health, Friedrich Paulus died (apparently of cancer) in Dresden on February 1, 1957—one day after the 14th anniversary of his surrender at Stalingrad. Ernst, incidentally, committed suicide in 1970.

Unlike Paulus and von Seydlitz, Arthur Schmidt refused to cooperate with the Soviets in any way and, in fact, maintained his belligerent attitude toward them throughout his captivity. He was, in fact, just as stubborn as a prisoner as he was at Stalingrad. Neither torture nor prolonged solitary confinement could convince him to work for the Communists, who were anxious to use him in their propaganda efforts against Hitler. When his captors were finally convinced that Schmidt would not break, they sentenced him to 25 years' imprisonment and hard labor. He was among those released in October 1955. Schmidt returned to his home town of Hamburg, where he repeatedly denied that he exerted undue influence on Field Marshal Paulus at Stalingrad. He also maintained a bitter hatred for the officers of the National Free Germany Committee for the rest of his life. He died at Karlsruhe on November 5, 1987.

Unlike Friedrich Paulus, the fanatical Nazi General Walter Heitz actually did try to commit suicide when Stalingrad fell; however, his chief of staff, Colonel Friedrich Schildknecht, prevented him from shooting himself. Like Paulus, Heitz received a special promotion (to colonel general) on January 30, 1943, the 10th anniversary of Hitler's rise to power. He was thus the second-highest-ranking prisoner taken at Stalingrad and third-highest-ranking German taken prisoner by the Allies at that time (behind Rudolf Hess and Paulus). Like most of those who surrendered in the ruins of the city on the Volga, he did not survive Soviet captivity, dying in Moscow of unspecified causes on February 9, 1944. He was buried in Krassnogorsk.

Like all the Luftwaffe generals, **WOLFGANG PICKERT**, the commander of the 9th Flak Division, flew out of the pocket before Stalingrad fell. He was later promoted to lieutenant general and commanded the III Flak Corps in the Normandy campaign, where his failure to cooperate with Field Marshal Rommel contributed to the German defeat. Since Goering and the Desert Fox bitterly disliked each other, this did not impede his advancement. Decorated with the Oak Leaves to the Knight's Cross, he was named general of the Flak Army at *Oberkommando der Luftwaffe* (OKL) in Berlin and on March 1, 1945, was promoted to general of flak artillery. When Hitler allowed nonessential personnel to leave Berlin as the Soviets approached in April 1945, Pickert headed south, for Bavaria. Here, in early May 1945, he helped free Hermann Goering from the SS guard that had arrested him on Hitler's orders several days before. Pickert, who was born in Posen, Prussia (now Poznan, Poland), on February 3, 1897, died in Weinheim (in the Rhine-Necker district, about six miles north of Heidelburg) on July 19, 1984.[39]

ERWIN JAENECKE was born in Freren in 1890 and joined the army as a Fahnenjunker in 1911. Commissioned in the 10th Engineer Battalion in 1912, he spent most of his career in the engineer branch, but first earned prominence as chief of staff of Special Staff "W" during the Spanish Civil War. He was named chief of staff to the inspector of fortresses in 1938. After various engineer staff assignments in Poland, Belgium, Paris, and the West in the first three years of the war, he was promoted to lieutenant general on November 1, 1941. For him, the road to Stalingrad began when he accepted command of the 389th Infantry Division at Prague in February 1942. He was assigned to the 6th Army in May and fought at Kharkov. His old friend Paulus named him commander of the IV Corps after he sacked Schwedler, and Paulus was behind Jaenecke's promotion to general of engineers on November 1, 1942. It seemed as if General Jaenecke would share the fate of so many of his comrades in Stalingrad, but he found a way out in the last days of the siege. There are two versions of his controversial departure. One is that he was hit by Soviet shrapnel and was evacuated with 16 holes in his body.[40] The other version is much less heroic. According to it, the building that Jaenecke was in was hit by a Soviet artillery shell, causing a board or piece of plaster to fall. It struck Jaenecke on the head and actually drew blood. After that, Jaenecke acted like lightning and had himself medically evacuated at almost the last possible minute. He remained in seclusion at an isolated hospital until he "recovered." It has been suggested that had Hitler or some of his cronies at Fuehrer Headquarters been aware of how minor Jaenecke's wound was, he might not have survived the Stalingrad campaign after all.[41] In any case, he was ready to return to active duty by March and on April 1 took command of the LXXXVI Corps in southwestern France.[42] On June 1, 1943, he assumed command of the 17th Army in the Crimea and was promoted to colonel general on January 30, 1944.

Understandably, Jaenecke did not want to preside over another Stalingrad. As the Soviet armies pushed toward the Crimea, Jaenecke agitated more and more fiercely for the evacuation of the peninsula and even made preparations to abandon it on his own initiative. This almost led to his being relieved of command by Field Marshal Ewald von Kleist in late October 1943. After the Crimea was isolated by Soviet advances in November, Jaenecke continued to call on army group, OKH, and Fuehrer headquarters to evacuate 17th Army by sea. As with Stalingrad, Hitler refused to do this. On April 7, 1944, three Soviet armies attacked Jaenecke's positions on the Perekop Isthmus and Kerch peninsula with 27 divisions and 200 tanks. Jaenecke, who had only five understrength German divisions and seven mediocre-to-useless Rumanian divisions, began a full-scale retreat on April 10, causing Hitler to fly into a rage, screaming that Jaenecke had lost his nerve. The 17th Army commander, however, was not able to hold his intermediate lines and continued to retreat until he reached Sevastopol, the naval fortress on the southwestern tip of the peninsula.

On April 28 Hitler summoned Jaenecke to Berchtesgaden and promised him "generous" reinforcements. When Jaenecke learned that this meant four battalions of recruits who had not yet finished their training, he attempted to place the responsibility for the impending disaster where it belonged (on Hitler) by asking that 17th Army be made directly subordinate to OKH (of which Hitler was commander-in-chief). The Fuehrer thereupon relieved Jaenecke of his command.[43]

The Soviets began their final assault on Sevastopol on May 5 and eliminated the last pockets of resistance on May 12. About 26,700 Germans were captured. The units that were evacuated had to abandon all their equipment and had to be dissolved or completely rebuilt. Meanwhile, Hitler ordered that Jaenecke not be given another command until a court-martial could determine if he had done everything possible to hold the peninsula. Apparently this court-martial never convened. In any event, Jaenecke was never reemployed.

Seeing doom on the horizon for Germany in January 1945, Erwin Jaenecke wrote Hitler a personal letter, describing the Reich's position and implying that Hitler should draw the appropriate conclusions. As a result he was dismissed from the army on January 31, 1945. A resident of eastern Germany, Jaenecke was arrested by the Soviets on June 11, 1945, and was deported to Czechoslovakia, where he was tried as a war criminal and sentenced to 25 years' imprisonment.[44] He was released in 1955 and retired to Cologne, where he died on July 3, 1960.

After Stalingrad fell, it was obvious even to Hitler that Victor von Schwedler's criticisms of the campaign had been justified. Despite his moderately anti-Nazi attitude, Schwedler was taken out of retirement on March 1, 1943, and placed in charge of Wehrkreis IV (IV Military

District), headquartered at Dresden. Here he was in charge of replacements and training in Saxony and northern Bohemia. He also was responsible for forming new divisions and rebuilding old ones. Like so many other generals, Victor von Schwedler sympathized with the anti-Hitler conspirators, but when the bomb actually went off on July 20, 1944, he adopted a wait-and-see attitude. When it became clear that the assassination attempt had failed and the coup seemed doomed, Schwedler came down solidly on the side of the Nazis.

General von Schwedler commanded Wehrkreis IV until January 31, 1945, when—with the Russians approaching the district—he retired at the age of 60. He died in Freiburg nine years later, on October 30, 1954.

Gustav von Wietersheim was also reemployed after Stalingrad, but in a capacity much different from Schwedler's. He ended the war as a private in the Volkssturm. After the fall of the Third Reich, he retired to Wallersberg/Bonn, where he died on April 25, 1974, at the age of 90.

Karl Strecker, the former pro-Nazi police officer, was imprisoned with his colleagues at Krasnogorsk and later at Camp 48 at Voikova, near Ivanovo. It was months before his family learned that he was still alive. He was treated reasonably well most of the time, but it was 1947 before he was allowed to receive mail from his family.

Like many German leaders, Strecker was subjected to a "show trial." Of the 13,500 Germans tried by Soviet tribunals, almost all were convicted and most received 25-year sentences. One officer was proven innocent of all offenses but one—he confessed that his horse had eaten Russian grass. His sentence: 25 years. Strecker was judged by a colonel and two lieutenant colonels. The general had made the mistake of taking his trial seriously, but he stopped his impassionate final defense plea in the middle because the two light colonels had fallen asleep. The colonel then woke his comrades, and the three of them convicted Strecker. He was sentenced to 25 years.[45]

In prison, the Stalingrad generals broke into four basic factions: the Communists and collaborators, the non-Communists, the anti-Communists, and the apolitical. Lattmann and Korfes joined the Reds and were soon studying Marxism. They were later joined by others, including Helmuth Schloemer; Alexander Elder von Daniels, the former commander of the 376th Infantry Division; and Colonel Wilhelm Adam, the former Ia of 6th Army who was finance minister of Saxony (then a province of East Germany) from 1949 to 1963. Seydlitz, Arno von Lenski, and Hans Wulz had intellectually broken with the Third Reich but could not as yet join the

Reds. Eventually, all three did. Schmidt, Heitz, Rodenburg, Strecker, and Sixt von Armin, the last commander of the 113th Infantry Division, were anti-Communists and would not break with Nazi Germany. Heitz and Sixt died in captivity, and Schmidt was sent elsewhere, because he influenced Paulus to be true to the Fuehrer. After he left, Paulus drifted from the apolitical to the Communist camp.[46]

Strecker refused to cooperate with the Reds to the end. In October 1955, he was one of the remaining 9,600 POWs to be released to West Germany. Joined by his wife and son, he took an extended vacation to the Alps and the island of Ischia, Italy. He then retired to the city of Idar-Oberstein in the Rhineland-Palatinate, where he was still living in the late 1950s. Sometime thereafter he moved to a small village in Austria, where he wrote a memoir. Now more mature, relaxed, and reflective, he came to accept democracy and was troubled by his failure to oppose Hitler more actively and aggressively. Philosophically, however, he emphatically agreed with Thomas Carlyle, who wrote, "Man is born to fight. He is best described as a born warrior and his life is best defined as a battle under the standard of the true Field Marshal [God]."[47]

Strecker claimed that he received a radio message from Berlin promoting him to colonel general at the end of the Battle of Stalingrad, and this appears to be true, but it cannot be confirmed.

General Karl Strecker died in Riezlern, Austria, on April 10, 1973.

Probably the best German general to fight at Stalingrad was HANS VALENTIN HUBE, commander of the 16th Panzer Division, who replaced Gustav von Wietersheim as commander of the XIV Panzer Corps on September 15, 1942. Hube was born in the garrison town of Naumburg in 1890, joined the army in 1909, and received his commission in the 26th Infantry Regiment the following year. After two years of fighting on the Western Front, he was so badly wounded in the Battle of Verdun that his right arm had to be amputated, and it seemed that his military career was over. With the same iron determination that characterized his entire career, however, young Hube rehabilitated himself, overcame his handicap, and returned to duty. He was a captain when the war ended.

When the 4,000-man officer corps was selected in 1919 and 1920, the Army Personnel Office had the pick of the best, both physically and mentally. Hans Valentin Hube was the only one-armed officer they chose to retain. Known for his determination, innovation, energy, and attention to detail, Hube strove to master every facet of his profession. Even so, promotions came slowly for officers in the Reichsheer (which was typical of a small army in this respect), and Hube did not become a major until 1929. He was promoted to lieutenant colonel in 1934, the same year he took charge of a special experimental motorized battalion, which distinguished itself in the summer maneuvers and added impetus to the demand for mechanization in the German Army. Meanwhile, Hube was named commandant of the prestigious Infantry School at Doeberitz, a suburb of Berlin. This was a choice assignment, but Hube's rise was just beginning.

In October 1935, Hube was named commandant of the Olympic Village, which was to be erected in the meadows adjoining the barracks. He was also in charge of security. Since Hitler was personally involved in all aspects of "his" Olympics, it was only natural that he conferred frequently with Hube. It was soon obvious that the one-armed officer was the master of his assignment. Hitler was so impressed that he rewarded Hube with a special promotion to full colonel in August 1936.

When World War II broke out, Hube petitioned OKH for a field command. He was given the 3rd Infantry Regiment in early October 1939, but this formation was nonmotorized and had an ultra-conservative (and almost hereditary) East Prussian officer corps. Not happy with his assignment, Hube used his contacts in Berlin (and possibly even the Fuehrer himself) to get a transfer. On May 15, 1940, he assumed command of the 16th Infantry Division, whose commander had fallen ill. This unit was already scheduled to be converted into a panzer division, and part of it was already motorized. In any case Colonel Hube led it with exceptional skill in France and was promoted to major general on June 1.

After France capitulated, Hube supervised the conversion of the 16th into a panzer unit and oversaw its armored training. It was slated to take part in the invasion of Yugoslavia, but the country fell so quickly that Hube's division was not committed to any heavy fighting. After taking part in the triumphant entry into Belgrade, Hube and his men were sent to Silesia and then into the Soviet Union.

From the first, Hans Hube proved to be an outstanding panzer commander and a master tactician, both in offensive and defensive operations. He fought at Uman, Kiev, Rostov, in the Mius River defense in the winter of 1941–1942, and at Kharkov. He was successively decorated with the Knight's Cross and the Oak Leaves and was promoted to lieutenant general on April 1, 1942. Meanwhile, he earned a reputation throughout the army as a tough, fair, no-nonsense commander, noted for his physical courage and tactical brilliance. The men of his unit—and others as well—called him *Der Mensch* (The Man) implying that no one else in the whole German Army approached his stature. And that is exactly the way that many of the men of the 6th Army felt about him.

A measure of the respect that Hube commanded was the fact that he echoed Wietersheim's objections to the way the Stalingrad campaign was being handled, including his criticisms of Hitler's meddling in the affairs of subordinate units. An outspoken officer known for his absolute honesty, Hube stood so high in the estimation of the Fuehrer that he not only got away with it, but he also received his promotion to general of panzer troops on October 1, 1942—only six months after his previous promotion.

In January 1943, as the end neared for the soldiers trapped in Stalingrad, Hitler signaled for Hube to fly out of the dying pocket. Many in the city would have given everything they owned to have received this order, but Hube categorically refused to obey it. He sent word back that he had led his men into Stalingrad and had ordered them to fight to the last bullet. Now he intended to show them how to do it. Hitler responded by sending four members of his SS bodyguard to Stalingrad in a special airplane. Hube and four members of his staff were called to 6th Army headquarters, where the SS men surprised them and flew them out of the pocket at gunpoint.[48]

In 1943, Hube rebuilt the XIV Panzer Corps and led it in the Battle of Sicily, where he held off 12 Allied divisions (including those of the redoubtable General George S. Patton) for 38 days with four understrength German divisions, in spite of the Allies' almost total command of the sea and the air. Then Hube escaped across the Straits of Messina with his entire command. The Man himself left in one of the last boats. After serving for a short time in Italy, where he fought at Salerno and was briefly acting commander of the 10th Army, Hube assumed command of the 1st Panzer Army in Russia and, much to the delight of the Fuehrer, brilliantly led it out of a Soviet encirclement in March 1944, with help from Field Marshal von Manstein. On April 20, 1944—his own birthday—Hitler promoted Hube to colonel general and decorated him with the Diamonds to his Knight's Cross with Oak Leaves and Swords. Hube was also earmarked to take charge of Army Group South Ukraine shortly thereafter; presumably it had already been decided to give its then commander, Ferdinand Schoerner, command of Army Group North. But Hans Valentin Hube was killed the very next day, when his airplane crashed a few miles from Berchtesgaden. A few weeks before his own death, Adolf Hitler was still lamenting the passing of Der Mensch, stating that he was one of the top three commanders to emerge from the Second World War.

4

THE COMMANDERS IN THE WEST

Nikolaus von Falkenhorst. Hugo Sperrle. Friedrich Dollmann. Rudolf Stegmann. Baron Hasso von Manteuffel. Baron Diepold Georg Heinrich von Luettwitz.

NIKOLAUS VON FALKENHORST, the conqueror of Norway, was born in Breslau, Silesia, on January 17, 1886. A soldier all his life, like his father before him, he was a descendant of the old Silesian military family of von Jastrzembski. This name was too bulky and too un-German for Nikolaus, however, so he changed it to Falkenhorst ("Falcon's eyrie") early in his career. After being educated in cadet schools, Nikolaus joined the Imperial Army as a Faehnrich (roughly "senior officer-cadet" or "senior officer candidate") in 1903 and was commissioned second lieutenant in the 7th Grenadier Regiment in 1904. Promoted to captain in 1914, he became a member of the General Staff and served in various staff and regimental posts during World War I, earning an excellent reputation in the process. He was chief of operations for General Count Ruediger von der Goltz's *Ostseedivision* (Baltic Sea Division) in Finland at the end of the war and remained there as a member of the Freikorps until 1919 or early 1920. Upon returning to Germany, he joined the Reichsheer and by 1925 was in the operations division of the Defense Ministry. From 1933 to 1935, Falkenhorst served as military attaché to Prague, Belgrade, and Bucharest, before becoming chief of staff of Army Group 3 in Dresden in 1935. Continuing his advancement as the army expanded, he became the first commander of the 32nd Infantry Division at Koeslin, Pomerania (now Koszalin, Poland) in 1936 and was named commander of the XXI Corps when it was formed at Allenstein, East Prussia (now Olsztyn, Poland), in 1939. His promotions came steadily: to major (early 1920s), lieutenant colonel (1930), colonel

(1932), major general (1935), lieutenant general (1937), and general of infantry (October 1, 1939).

Falkenhorst's corps played a minor role in the conquest of Poland and was in the Trier area of western Germany, preparing for the campaign against Belgium and France, when he was summoned to Berlin in February 1940. Unknown to him, OKW had been planning Operation Weser—the invasions of Denmark and Norway—since December 14, 1939. Hitler, however, did not become serious about the plan until February 19, 1940, when a British warship entered Norwegian territorial waters, captured the German auxiliary ship *Altmark*, and freed some 300 sailors who had been captured by the pocket battleship *Graf Spee* several weeks before. This incident convinced Hitler that the British would not hesitate to violate Norwegian neutrality when it suited their purposes. Therefore, to forestall a British invasion of Norway (and to secure his vital Swedish iron ore supplies, which had to be shipped through the Norwegian port of Narvik), the Fuehrer decided to strike first.

Sources differ as to whether Wilhelm Keitel or Alfred Jodl recommended Falkenhorst for command of this operation, but his service in Finland in 1918 was the decisive factor in his selection. In any case, Falkenhorst met Hitler for the first time at the Chancellery shortly before noon on February 21 and, unlike so many others, was not awed by his presence. The general was quite surprised when the Fuehrer offered him command of the invasion forces, which included five infantry divisions, but he eagerly accepted the appointment. Hitler then told him to come back at 5 p.m. to outline his plan for the campaign.

Without maps or a staff of any kind, Falkenhorst first went to a bookstore, where he purchased a Baedeker travel guide. He then retired to his hotel room, where he decided to use one division to capture each of Norway's major harbors: Oslo, Stavanger, Bergen, Trondheim, and Narvik. Although naturally not as detailed as the OKW plan, Falkenhorst's concept of the operation was very similar to it, and Hitler approved it at once. He then dismissed Falkenhorst with exhortations to get on with the detailed planning as quickly as possible. For this purpose he was allowed to retain his own headquarters, which was upgraded and redesignated Group XXI on March 1. Significantly, Brauchitsch (the commander-in-chief of the army) and Halder (the chief of the General Staff) were kept largely ignorant of the operation. The OKW operations staff acted as the coordinating agency in cases where Group XXI needed the assistance of other branches of the service, and Falkenhorst himself was directly subordinate to Adolf Hitler. When Falkenhorst asked for two mountain divisions, the Fuehrer approved the request without consulting OKH. Although this was supposed to be a joint armed forces operation, Falkenhorst actually commanded only the ground units. The air units were commanded in succession by General of Flyers Hans Geisler, Colonel General Erhard Milch, and General of Flyers Hans-Juergen Stumpff. The naval staff under Grand Admiral Erich Raeder did its own planning. The Danish phase of the operation (*Weseruebung Sued*) was to be conducted by General of Flyers Leonhard Kaupisch's XXXI Army Corps, which was to be subordinate to Group XXI until April 12, but then was to revert to OKH control. The fact that the Luftwaffe generals were ordered to cooperate with Falkenhorst earned the infantry general the undying hatred of Hermann Goering, who was furious that he had not been consulted in the initial planning. He was also extremely jealous of Falkenhorst's position as the first joint services commander in the history of Nazi Germany, despite the fact that his authority over the navy and Luftwaffe was largely nominal.

The invasions of Denmark and Norway began on April 9, 1940. Although he had captured all his major objectives by April 10, Norwegian resistance proved stiffer than expected, so Falkenhorst decided to proceed cautiously. First he built up a base of operations at Oslo, and not until April 12 and 13 did he strike out to the southeast, west, and northwest to link up with his other bridgeheads. Meanwhile, on April 13, the Royal Navy attacked the German destroyers at Narvik, which threw a bad scare into Adolf Hitler, who was already nervous and furious at the Norwegians for offering such protracted resistance. That same day he goaded Falkenhorst into signing an order providing for the taking of 20 hostages, including Bishop Berggrav, if resistance continued or sabotage was attempted. Falkenhorst did not actually carry out this order, however; in fact, the excited pessimism of Adolf Hitler was in diametric opposition to the calm optimism that prevailed at Falkenhorst's headquarters in Oslo, even after the British and French landed expeditionary forces near Narvik and at Namsos (127 miles north of Trondheim) on April 14, followed by a third landing at Andalsnes three days later. Not prone to panic, Falkenhorst methodically cleared one sector after another, despite horrendous logistical difficulties and a series of unpleasant signals from the Fuehrer. The objective of Falkenhorst's attacks was not to gain space, however, but to defeat the enemy forces and then pursue them without respite until they reembarked or surrendered. In the ensuing battles the aggressively pursued Allied forces lost many men and most of their equipment. Andalsnes fell on May 2, and Namsos was evacuated the next day. After a brilliant defense by Lieutenant General Dietl, the Allies finally captured Narvik on May 28, but by then it was an untenable position. Falkenhorst's relief columns were advancing through the roadless wilderness toward the city—the spearhead was only 85 miles away on June 1—and the Allied defeats in France made it impossible for them to send reinforcements. The British and French evacuated Narvik on June 8, and the remnants of the Norwegian Army surrendered the next day. Group XXI now controlled the entire country, and Nikolaus von Falkenhorst had reached the peak of his military career. On July 19 he was rewarded with a promotion to colonel general. It was to be his last.

Falkenhorst's nemesis was to be Josef Terboven, the former Gauleiter of Essen. A young, energetic, and fanatical Nazi, Terboven was a close personal friend of Hermann Goering, who was constantly lambasting Falkenhorst at Fuehrer Headquarters. It was Falkenhorst's failure to act energetically against the Norwegian population, Goering told Hitler, that caused the prolonged Norwegian resistance. On April 24, thanks to the influence of Goering (and over the objections of Keitel and Jodl), Adolf Hitler named Terboven Reich Commissioner of Norway and promoted him to SA *Obergruppenfuehrer*. From the moment he landed at the Oslo airport, Terboven made it clear that he did not like General von Falkenhorst and that he intended to rule Norway—permanently and alone—without the help of the German Army. His high-handed policies and summary executions soon undercut both Vidkun Quisling's puppet government and German rule in Norway. For his part, General von Falkenhorst, a gentleman and an officer of the old school, made it clear that he had no use for either Terboven or his methods. This friction between the civilian and military administrations continued almost until the end of the war.

From 1940 until late 1944, Adolf Hitler constantly feared an Allied invasion of Norway, which would sever his iron ore supply. To prevent this he named Falkenhorst Wehrmacht commander, Norway (on July 25, 1940), and reinforced him to a strength of more than 200,000 men and 212 army and navy coastal defense batteries, plus a few companies of PzKw II and III tanks (see appendix III). On December 19, 1940, Group XXI was upgraded and renamed the Army of Norway. Simultaneously, Falkenhorst was brought into Operation Barbarossa, when he was ordered to capture Murmansk, the major port in the northern Soviet Union (i.e., the "Far North"). His primary task, however, still was to defend Norway; only excess troops were to be used in this new campaign.

Operation Platinfuchs, the advance toward Murmansk, began on June 29, 1941. Army of Norway forces involved in this campaign included Dietl's Mountain Corps Norway, the XXXVI Corps, and the III Finnish Corps: 68,100 men in all. Seven divisions and several smaller units—150,000 men—were left behind to guard against a British invasion of Norway, and Hitler had issued firm orders not to weaken these defenses. This injunction severely hamstrung von Falkenhorst in the weeks ahead. The main problem, however, was the terrain. This was bare, forbidding tundra country, characterized by boulders, gravel, permafrost, rocky outcroppings, and hundreds of lakes left behind by the melting snow. There were no roads, railroads, or bridges; no food for the troops or forage for the horses; and the summers in this Arctic region were very short. Moreover, the German forces lacked training in Arctic warfare. For their part, the Soviets realized that they had to retain the port of Murmansk or lose much of their aid from the Western Allies; as a result, using the Leningrad-Murmansk railroad and the Murmansk Highway, they reinforced their forces west of the city and resisted tenaciously. In the month of July, for example, XXXVI Corps advanced only 13 miles but lost 5,500 men.

Falkenhorst did what he could to keep the advance going, but his logistical problems were simply insurmountable, and by September 12 his supply situation was critical. British submarines were sinking his supply vessels off the northern coast of Finland and Norway at an alarming rate, and his infantrymen had only 1.5 basic loads of ammunition left. By September 18 the Soviets were counterattacking continuously, and Falkenhorst had no choice but to go over to the defensive and fall back to winter positions. The campaign had been a failure.

On November 7, 1941, Hitler took the Murmansk forces away from Falkenhorst and gave them to Eduard Dietl's newly created Army of Lapland, which later became the 20th Mountain Army. Although he retained command of the Army of Norway, Falkenhorst had to a large extent acquired the dubious label of a hard-luck general. He spent the rest of his career supplying Dietl's men as best he could, feuding with Terboven, and preparing for an invasion that never came.

Ironically, Nikolaus von Falkenhorst acquired a measure of popularity and respect with the people of Norway, who naturally compared him with Terboven. The Reich commissioner lived in style and luxury in the King's summer palace, had spacious offices in the Storthing (the Parliament House), and toured the country in an armor-plated Mercedes, accompanied by a numerous bodyguard of Nazi thugs. Falkenhorst, on the other hand, did what he could to mitigate the repressive and increasingly brutal policies of Terboven, and the Norwegians appreciated his efforts. The general lived simply in two rooms at the Norwegian auto club and traveled all over the country in an ordinary car, accompanied only by his driver and adjutant. Although he moved freely among the people, he did not expect any assassination attempts, nor were there any. The Norwegians knew that, if he were killed, his replacement would be much worse than Falkenhorst! Nevertheless, he still obeyed the orders of the Fuehrer. In 1943, as ordered, he planned the invasion of Sweden, although he was personally opposed to it and was glad when it was finally cancelled. More seriously, he passed on to his units the Fuehrer Order instructing the German soldiers to refuse quarter to Allied commandos. In November 1942—again as ordered—he handed nine captured commandoes over to the SD, which shot them out of hand. Falkenhorst was appalled. He protested the order to Keitel and verbally instructed his generals not to obey such orders in the future, although he personally would keep up appearances insofar as his written orders were concerned. There were still, however, isolated incidents of Wehrmacht forces handing captured Allied sailors or downed airmen over to the Security Service, and most of these POWs were never seen again.

On September 6, 1944, as Finland prepared to quit the war, the 20th Mountain Army began to leave that country and move back to Norway. Clearly, Falkenhorst's days in his position were numbered, for Norway obviously did not need two army-level headquarters. On December 18, Falkenhorst was dismissed from his post for opposing the policies of Josef Terboven, and his army was absorbed by the 20th Mountain, now commanded by a pro-Nazi Austrian, Colonel General Dr. Lothar Rendulic. Germany surrendered on May 8, 1945, and two days later Terboven blew himself up in his bunker. Then, on July 29, 1946, Nikolaus von Falkenhorst found himself on trial before the Allied Military Court at Hamburg, charged with nine counts of war crimes. He defended himself on the grounds of "Befehl ist Befehl"—an order is an order. "I had to pass on the order," Falkenhorst pled at one point. "The only way of avoiding the order would have been to take a pistol and shoot myself!"[1] He was nevertheless forced to admit that the act of passing on the order had caused deaths.

On August 2, Colonel General von Falkenhorst was found guilty on seven of the nine charges and sentenced to death, even though the British record of the trial admits that he was a benevolent commander who did what he could to mitigate the suffering of the occupied people. It must be remembered that, at this time, the passions of the war had not died down, and the world was still rightly shocked and outraged by the Nazi atrocities. Even then, however, General Falkenhorst was separated from the other "war criminals"; he was to die a soldier's death—by firing squad; he would be spared the traditional execution of a criminal—death by hanging: the death suffered by Goering, Keitel, Jodl, Joachim von Ribbentrop, and others. Falkenhorst did not die, however. His execution was delayed, and his sentence was eventually reduced to 20 years' imprisonment. He served less than half of this, and on July 23, 1953, was released, ostensibly for reasons of health. He moved to Detmold, where he was living in retirement in 1957. He died at Holzminden on June 18, 1968. His son-in-law was Major General Erich Dethleffsen.[2]

HUGO SPERRLE, the son of a brewer, was born in Ludwigsburg, Wuerttemberg, on February 2, 1885. He joined the Imperial Army as a Fahnenjunker (officer-cadet) in 1903 and was commissioned second lieutenant in the 8th Wuerttemberg Infantry Regiment about a year later. He was promoted to first lieutenant in 1913 and became a captain in late 1914. He was in an artillery spotter training course when World War I broke out.

Sperrle did not distinguish himself in the Great War, but he did compile a solid record in that conflict, where he specialized in aerial reconnaissance. He served as an aerial observer with the 4th Field Flying Detachment (*Feldfliegerabteilung 4*). Later, after undergoing pilot training, he led the 42nd and 60th Field Flying detachments and the 13th Field Flying Wing, before assuming command of the Air Observers School at Cologne. At the end of the war he was officer-in-charge of all flying units attached to the 7th Army on the Western Front. After the Kaiser fell, Sperrle promptly joined the Luettwitz Freikorps and commanded its aviation detachment. In 1919, he was one of the 180 former aviators selected for retention in the 4,000-man Officer Corps of the Reichsheer.

Back in the infantry, Captain Sperrle served on the staff of Wehrkreis V at Stuttgart (1919–1923), in the Defense Ministry (1923–1924), and with the 4th Infantry Division at Dresden (1924–1925). He also maintained his commitment to aviation and underwent secret advanced flight training at the clandestine German air base at Lipetsk, Russia, in 1928. He made at least two trips to the United Kingdom to observe Royal Air Force displays. After he returned to Germany, Sperrle (who physically resembled a bear) continued to make steady if unspectacular progress. He spent four years on the General Staff in the Reichswehr Ministry (1925–1929), was promoted to major (1926) and lieutenant colonel (1931), and served as commander of III Battalion, 14th (Baden) Infantry Regiment in Kontanz (in extreme southwestern Germany), from 1929 to 1933. From October 1, 1933, until the end of his army career, Sperrle was commander of the 8th (Prussian) Infantry Regiment at Frankfurt/Oder. Sperrle joined Goering's Luftwaffe as a full colonel on April 1, 1934, and was placed in charge of the 1st Air Division; simultaneously he held the office of commander of Army

Aviation, and his territorial responsibilities included the city of Berlin (see appendix IV for the Luftwaffe chain of command and unit strengths). Sperrle was thus well placed to assume a prominent role in the emergence of the Luftwaffe when Hitler decided it was time to openly defy the Allies and renounce the part of the Treaty of Versailles that prohibited Germany from having an air force.

On March 9, 1935, Hitler announced the existence of the Luftwaffe to the entire world. Sperrle was among the first army officers officially transferred to the Luftwaffe. Initially in charge of flying units in II Air District (*Luftkreis II*), his previous aviation experience gave him a tremendous advantage over most of his peers. As a result he was promoted to major general and named commander of Luftkreis V, headquartered at Munich, on October 1, 1935. He was already one of the leading figures in the Luftwaffe when the Spanish Civil War erupted.

For Germany, the campaign began on July 26, 1936, when a delegation from General Francisco Franco, the commander of the rebel forces, arrived in Berlin. Prevented from crossing the Mediterranean by the Loyalist Navy, Franco urgently needed transport aircraft to ferry his troops from Morocco to the Spanish mainland. Goering was enthusiastic about the venture, and that same day Hitler agreed to provide 20 Ju-52 transports, complete with crews, to the pro-Fascist rebels. Initially, Army Lieutenant Colonel Walter Warlimont was in charge of the German military mission to Spain, but in late October Hitler decided that the situation required a separate Luftwaffe command. It was christened the Condor Legion, and Hugo Sperrle was named its first commander. Traveling under the alias of Sanders, he arrived in time for the formal activation of the Legion on October 31.[3]

Sperrle's new command initially consisted of one bomber squadron (*Staffel*), a fighter squadron, a naval air squadron, and one heavy and one light anti-aircraft battery. Although assigned to support rebel ground units, Sperrle was responsible only to General Franco and thus held rank equivalent to an air theater commander. Both by necessity and by design, he did considerable experimenting with combat tactics, formation flying and organization, and airplane models while commander of the Condor Legion. Most of the Luftwaffe tactics used in the Second World War were developed in Spain. Although his primary duty was to support rebel ground forces, Sperrle managed to distinguish himself in a number of ways. On November 15 he personally led the attack that destroyed the Republican naval base at Cartagena and forced the enemy fleet to put to sea to escape destruction. He also designed a plan for the ground battle of Madrid, which probably would have ended the war had it not been for the incompetence of the Italian corps commander, General Mario Roatta. Sperrle also pioneered the concept of the Fascist terror raid. At Guernica, for example, his bombers killed hundreds of Spanish civilians by plastering the town with high-explosives, while his fighters strafed fleeing townspeople, in clear violation of the laws of warfare. "Guernica," Fletcher wrote, has "become a synonym for Fascist brutality in Spain."[4] Sperrle, however, never received so much as a verbal reprimand for this attack.

After supporting Franco's ground forces on their drive to the Bay of Biscay and helping wipe out the last Loyalist resistance in northern Spain, Sperrle turned command of the Condor Legion over to Major General Helmuth von Volkmann on October 31, 1937, and returned to Germany a hero.[5] He had been promoted to lieutenant general on April 1 and on November 1, 1937, was advanced to the rank of general of flyers. On February 1, 1938, he assumed command of Luftwaffe Group 3, which was redesignated 3rd Air Fleet in February 1939. Sperrle led the 3rd for the rest of his career.

Headquartered in Munich, Hugo Sperrle was in charge of all Luftwaffe units, bases, and operations in southern Germany, including those in the Austrian border area. At this time Hitler was planning his Anschluss: the annexation of Austria into the Third Reich. The Fuehrer hoped to bluff and bully Austrian Prime Minister Kurt von Schuschnigg into handing over his country without a fight, so he made sure that the physically intimidating Sperrle was present throughout the negotiations. Richard Brett-Smith described him as a "huge, solid, ferocious-looking man" and Hitler described Sperrle and Army General Walter von Reichenau as "my two most brutal-looking generals."[6] Sperrle's heavy-jowled face seemed to be frozen in a permanent scowl, which, coupled with his huge bulk and numerous decorations, made him look sinister. His presence, along with Hitler's overbearing tactics, had the desired effect. On February 12, 1938, Hitler met with Schuschnigg at Berchtesgaden and extracted from him a virtual surrender of Austrian sovereignty. A month later, Hitler formally annexed Austria and entered Vienna in triumph on March 14. Sperrle took part in the occupation of Austria but soon turned over the Luftwaffe's territorial administration of the region to the newly formed 4th Air Fleet under General Alexander Loehr, the former commander-in-chief of the Austrian Air Force.

After the Anschluss, Sperrle commanded the bombing demonstrations aimed at intimidating Czechoslovakia into giving up the Sudetenland. He was unsuccessful in this effort but no doubt impressed the British and helped influence them into signing the Munich accords in September 1938. Czechoslovakia, deserted by her allies, was compelled to abandon the Sudetenland in October. This move cost Prague its border fortifications and its only real hope of preserving its independence. Six months later, Hitler occupied the rest of the country without a fight. Along with Loehr, Sperrle directed the Luftwaffe's part in the occupation of Czechoslovakia.

When Hitler invaded Poland on September 1, 1939, 3rd Air Fleet supported Colonel General Ritter Wilhelm von Leeb's Army Group C in guarding Germany's exposed western frontier. The Allies, however, failed to take advantage of the Wehrmacht's weakness here. Soon, Poland was conquered and the bulk of the victorious invasion force was on its way back to the West.

During the invasion of France in May 1940, Sperrle's 3rd and Colonel General Albert Kesselring's 2nd Air fleets controlled some 3,400 aircraft. Kesselring supported von Bock's Army Group B, while Sperrle supported the main thrust—von Rundstedt's Army Group A, which included the bulk of the panzer units and the main assault forces. When the decisive Battle of Sedan began on May 13, Sperrle controlled the lion's share of Germany's combat aviation forces: General Ulrich Grauert's I Air Corps, General Bruno Loerzer's II, Ritter Robert von Greim's V, and Major General Baron Wolfram von Richthofen's VIII, as well as General Hubert Weise's I Flak Corps. At the last minute, Sperrle attempted to change the Luftwaffe's plan of operations from a series of attacks by small formations to one massive all-out attack against the French positions near Sedan; however, General Loerzer ignored his orders and did not pass them on to the squadrons.[7] Why Sperrle wanted to throw away carefully prepared plans made over a period of weeks in favor of a single hasty attack is a mystery, but apparently he panicked at the last minute. Had he been obeyed, he might have endangered the success of the entire campaign. As it worked out, General Guderian, the commander of the panzer spearhead, could not have been more pleased with the close air support he received at Sedan.

The breakthrough at Sedan led to the drive to the English Channel, the destruction of the best French divisions in Flanders, and the forced evacuation of the British Expeditionary Force at Dunkirk. Luftwaffe support of the panzer and motorized units was superb, despite the fluid nature of the battlefield. Sperrle redeemed his near blunder at Sedan and was awarded the Knight's Cross on May 18, two days before Guderian's tanks reached the sea near Abbeville.

France surrendered on June 21, 1940. On July 19, at ceremonies in Berlin, Hitler promoted Sperrle to field marshal, along with Kesselring and

Erhard Milch and a dozen army generals. Sperrle completely bypassed the rank of colonel general.

There is no doubt that Hitler was partial toward Sperrle and solicitous of his feelings and welfare. Sperrle returned the affection, at least until 1943. Though not a party member, he supported the Nazis' aims and never waivered in his loyalty to the Fuehrer, although he occasionally objected to his strategic plans. Neither Hitler nor Goering, however, paid very much attention to the advice given by the brewer's son; that would cost them dearly in the days ahead.

Meanwhile, Hitler tried to eliminate Great Britain from the war by diplomatic means. When these efforts failed, the Battle of Britain began in earnest. Sperrle's 3rd Air Fleet was now stationed in France, south of the Seine, and included Richthofen's VIII Air Corps (mostly Stukas), von Greim's V (primarily bombers), and Kurt Plugbeil's IV (night fighters, bombers, and dive-bombers). He also received Major General Werner Junck's 1st Fighter Command,[8] which included 300 Me-109 single-engine fighters and 130 Me-110 twin-engine fighters.

The all-out effort to defeat the Royal Air Force (RAF) began on "Eagle Day," August 13, 1940. Sperrle's zone of operations was eastern England, where the RAF had its major fighter bases. Third Air Fleet suffered heavy casualties, especially in its dive-bomber squadrons. Richthofen's VIII Corps had to be withdrawn from the battle on August 19; indeed, primary responsibility for the campaign was shifted from Sperrle to Kesselring that day, as the single-engine fighter units of the 3rd Air Fleet were transferred to 2nd Air Fleet (north of the Seine). In compensation, Sperrle received the decimated Me-110 squadrons of the 5th Air Fleet, which was operating out of Norway.

The German tactics over England were costly but were having their effect on the British by early September. For the first time, the RAF was weakening. Sperrle, out of the main battle, primarily concentrated on night bombing raids, especially against Liverpool, over which he had some success. He was not allowed to attack London—yet.

One of the most fateful meetings in the history of the Luftwaffe took place between Goering and his two principal air fleet commanders at The Hague on September 3. Goering suggested that the current tactical plan of concentrating on smashing the RAF and its bases be abandoned in favor of large-scale bombing of London, the hub of the British war effort. He wanted to know if the RAF had been sufficiently weakened to allow his own air fleets to accomplish this task without undue risk to the bomber force.

Sperrle advocated the destruction of the British Fighter Command, correctly asserting that it was still a force to be reckoned with. Kesselring, optimistic as usual, believed Luftwaffe intelligence reports that the British had only a few fighters left. Sperrle, on the other hand, was not by nature an optimistic man. He estimated that the British had about a thousand fighters and strongly urged that the battle continue exactly as it was being fought. The pressure on the British must not be relieved, he shouted. The argument became heated, but Goering—under pressure from Hitler—ruled against Sperrle in the end. The first major attack on London took place two days later, and the British capital superseded the RAF as the primary target of the Luftwaffe. British Fighter Command quickly recovered and was never again threatened with annihilation, as it was in early September 1940. The decision to focus on London instead of against the RAF airfields was one of the decisive turning points of the entire air war.

Hugo Sperrle left The Hague a disgusted man. As he had foreseen, the Luftwaffe was defeated over the skies of London. In October, Goering seized on the pretext of deteriorating weather to call off daylight operations over the United Kingdom. Great Britain remained in the war, and the Luftwaffe suffered its first major defeat.

It was clear that Goering and Kesselring were wrong in changing their tactics, but was Sperrle's assessment of the situation correct? It would appear so. After the war, Churchill wrote:

> If the enemy had persisted in heavy attacks against the adjacent sectors and damaged their operations rooms or telephone communications, the whole intricate organization of the Fighter Command might have been broken down. This would have meant not merely the maltreatment of London, but the loss to us of the perfected control of our own air in the decisive area. It was therefore with a sense of relief that Fighter Command felt the German attack turn on to London on September 7, and concluded that the enemy had changed his plan. Goering should certainly have persevered against the airfields, on whose organization and combination the whole fighting power of our air force at this moment depended . . . he made a foolish mistake.[9]

Second Air Fleet left France for Poland in May 1941, and Field Marshal Sperrle became the sole air fleet commander on the Western Front. There was little left to command, however. Of the 44 bomber wings that had attacked Britain in August, only four remained. A month later, Hitler invaded the Soviet Union. Sperrle was now commanding what amounted to a backwater theater of operations.

* * *

The decline of Hugo Sperrle can be dated from July 1940, when he transferred his headquarters to Paris and took up residence at the Palais du Luxembourg, the former palace of Marie de Medici.[10] Prior to this, Lieutenant General Karl Veith described him as "very unpretentious," but now "gradually everything went to his head."[11] The brewer's son was corrupted by the debauchery of Paris. He became addicted to laziness and luxurious living. Munitions Minister Albert Speer later commented, "The Field Marshal's craving for luxury and public display ran a close second to that of his superior Goering; he was also his match in corpulence."[12]

As early as September 1, 1940, Sperrle was seen in the company of Field Marshal Milch, enjoying life in the gambling casinos of Deauville, where Sperrle had established a command post, despite its lack of military value. Field Marshal Sperrle enjoyed the life of power and luxury, neglected his duties, and allowed training to go to seed. Then on March 1, 1943, the RAF attacked Berlin. When the last bomb fell, 35,000 people in the German capital had lost their homes. Hitler immediately ordered Sperrle to raid London in reprisal. On March 3, Sperrle's bombers flew across the English Channel and dropped 100 tons of bombs, but only 12 tons fell on London. Hitler was furious. In his conference of March 5, he lambasted 3rd Air Fleet's inability to find London, a target 30 miles wide and only 90 miles from the French coast. The Fuehrer was still criticizing Sperrle six days later. Propaganda Minister Dr. Paul Joseph Goebbels recorded Hitler's views (and his own) in his diary: "Field Marshal Sperrle . . . was not equal to his tasks. Like all air force generals he had withdrawn to a castle and was there leading a sybaritic life. Air warfare against England probably didn't interest him much more than, say, an excellent luncheon or dinner. The Fuehrer wants to recall him."[13]

Hitler's attitude toward Sperrle had softened by early July 1943. Perhaps because the air fleet commander was in debt as a result of his luxurious lifestyle and gambling, the Fuehrer sent him a gift of 50,000 Reichsmarks. The field marshal was not found at his headquarters, however; he was busy vacationing on the Atlantic coast south of Biarritz at the time.

Sperrle became more and more disillusioned over Hitler and Goering's conduct of the war, and this may have accelerated his own lack of interest in the conflict. Lieutenant General Hans Speidel, the Chief of Staff of Erwin Rommel's Army Group B in France in 1944, remembered, "Sperrle was a man of unusual vitality; but the more clearly he saw the unholy disorder in Hitler's leadership, the more he expended his energies in bitter sarcasm."[14]

The 3rd Air Fleet had no chance of defeating the U.S. and British air forces, who, in April 1944, began paving the way for the Allied invasion. As of May 31, Sperrle had only 891 aircraft, of which 497 were serviceable. His few, understrength units faced a vast aerial armada of some 14,000 combat aircraft. The enemy's primary objective prior to D-Day was to seal off the battlefield and isolate 7th Army in Normandy from its supplies and reinforcements. To accomplish this task, the French railroad network had to be destroyed. Before the Allied air offensive began, the German transportation staff was running more than 100 supply trains a day to the armies in France. By the end of May only 20 trains per day were operating throughout France. All bridges over the Seine, Oise, and Meuse rivers had been destroyed or seriously damaged, and railroad traffic to Normandy had virtually ceased. By April 30, some 600 supply trains were backlogged in Germany, and the Allied air forces were destroying up to 113 locomotives per day in France. By early June, MacDonald and Blumenson wrote, "Allied air attacks had weakened the railroad transportation system in France to the point of collapse."[15]

On June 3, 1944, the Luftwaffe Operations Staff reported:

> In the area of northern France and Belgium—the zone of the invasion in the narrower sense of the word—the systematic destruction that has been carried out since March of all important junctions of the entire network—not only the main lines—has most seriously crippled the whole transport system (railway installations, including rolling stock). Similarly, Paris has been systematically cut off from long distance traffic, and the most important bridges over the lower Seine have been destroyed one after another. . . . In the "intermediate zone" between the German and French-Belgian railway system all the important through stations . . . have been put out of action for longer or shorter periods. . . . In May the first bridge over the Rhine—at Duisburg—was destroyed "according to plan" in a large-scale attack.[16]

The report concluded that the rail network had been completely wrecked and that "the Reichsbahn authorities are seriously considering whether it is not useless to attempt further repair work."[17]

On D-Day, June 6, 1944, Normandy resembled a strategic island. Field Marshal Rommel was unable to bring up his panzer reserves quickly enough to launch a counteroffensive before the Allied beachhead was firmly secured. Meanwhile, enemy fighter-bombers absolutely dominated the air space above the battle zone, destroying tanks, strongpoints, supply installations, and gun emplacements. Sperrle's units were able to operate only on the fringes of Eisenhower's air umbrella. German operations against the Allied naval forces were equally devoid of success.

When the Anglo-Americans broke out of the Normandy bridgehead in August, most of the Luftwaffe ground service and signal units simply turned tail and headed east as rapidly as they could. Hitler (with considerable justification) charged them with running away and held Sperrle responsible. This was the last straw. On August 19 the Fuehrer relieved Sperrle of his 3rd Air Fleet command and replaced him with Colonel General Otto Dessloch. A month later, on September 22, 3rd Air Fleet was downgraded and redesignated Luftwaffe Command West.

Very much embittered after the fall of France, Sperrle was no longer considered fit for important assignments and was unemployed for the rest of the war. After the collapse of Nazi Germany, Field Marshal Milch and General Speidel, among others, charged that Sperrle was a scapegoat for Goering's failures in the West.[18] However, it is significant that Sperrle hardly raised a voice in his own defense. Also, Field Marshal Rommel had expressed disappointment about the Luftwaffe in France as early as the end of 1943, and Milch biographer David Irving described Sperrle as "indolent and harmful"[19] to the Luftwaffe's war effort in the West.

Richard Suchenwirth noted that in 1944 Sperrle was unaccustomed to the rigors of war and attributed at least part of his failure in France to that fact.[20] Major Lionel F. Ellis, the official British historian, summed it up well when he wrote of the Luftwaffe's battle in Normandy:

> Greatly outnumbered by the Allied air forces, they had perhaps been as active as their strength and supremacy of Allied air forces allowed, but their resulting effort was of little account to the Allied armies. Their most effective operations were the dropping of mines in the shipping-infested waters of the assault area. The commander of the Third Air Fleet, Field Marshal Hugo Sperrle, had held that appointment during the whole of the German occupation of France, "living soft" in Paris. He does not seem to have had any lively reaction when the Allies landed and none of his subordinates is distinguishable in the air fighting in Normandy. The war diaries of the army commands in the West have few references of the Luftwaffe that are not critical and they give no indication that Sperrle had any voice in shaping the conduct of operations.[21]

Sperrle was captured by the British on May 1, 1945.[22] He was tried at Nuremberg for war crimes but was acquitted of all charges on October

27, 1948. Officially de-Nazified in June 1949, he moved to Munich. Here he lived quietly (although bitter and depressed) until his death on April 2, 1953.²³ He was buried in Munich on April 7.²⁴

FRIEDRICH DOLLMANN, a large, physically impressive officer who showed great adaptability throughout his career, was born at Wuerzburg, Bavaria, on February 2, 1882. He joined the army as a Fahnenjunker in 1899 and was commissioned second lieutenant in the 7th Bavarian Field Artillery Regiment in 1901. Despite his junior rank he attended the School of Artillery and Engineering at Charlottenburg from 1903 to 1905, did a stint as a battalion adjutant (1905–1909), and was sent to the War Academy for General Staff training in 1909. Promoted to first lieutenant in 1910 and to captain in 1913, he served briefly as a brigade adjutant in early 1913, before becoming an aerial observer—an unusual post for a General Staff officer. Moreover, he served in this capacity for the first two years of the Great War, before assuming command of an artillery battalion in late 1916. He did not take up his first wartime General Staff assignment until November 1917, when he became the intelligence officer of the 6th Infantry Division on the Western Front, a post he held at the end of the war.²⁵

Dollmann did not win any promotions during World War I, nor did he achieve any particular distinction; nevertheless he was selected for the Reichswehr and was appointed to the administrative section of the Peace Commission in 1919, no doubt largely because he could speak both French and English and because he had a talent for making himself acceptable. There is little in his personnel file to explain why he advanced to the top rungs of the army in the next 20 years, except that he was an expert in long-range artillery, was a good administrator, and knew how to play the political angles that exist in any army but proliferated in those of the Weimar Republic and the Third Reich. The fact that he was stationed in Munich (the cradle of Nazism) almost continuously from 1923 to 1933 no doubt gave him some early contacts with the Nazis and may have accelerated his later advancement; in any event, by February 1930, he was a colonel and chief of staff of Wehrkreis VII (Munich) and on February 1, 1931, assumed command of the 6th Artillery Regiment. Eighteen months later, he was promoted to Artillery Commander VII and deputy commander of the 7th Infantry Division in Munich, and on February 1, 1933, he was named inspector of artillery in the Defense Ministry in Berlin. Dollmann was promoted to major general on October 1, 1932, and to lieutenant general exactly one year later.

Although not a Nazi, Friedrich Dollmann saw which way the political winds were blowing and made himself very prominent in fostering good relations between the army and the party in the early years of Hitler's regime. Partially as a result, he was named commander of Wehrkreis IX at Kassel on May 1, 1935. From this corps-level military district headquarters he issued directives criticizing those members of the officer corps who opposed the concept and outlook of the Nazi Party. He openly and officially blamed the officer corps for the mistrust that existed between the party and the army and wrote that "the Officer Corps must have confidence in the representatives of the Party. Party opinions should not be examined or rejected."[26] He demanded that "worthy" pictures of the Fuehrer be hung in officers' messes and that those of the Kaiser be removed or hung only in tradition rooms; furthermore, officers' wives should play active roles in the National Socialist League of Women, and the only civilian guest speakers who should be invited to address service functions were the politically nonbiased National Socialists.[27]

Dollmann went even further in 1937, when he called in his Catholic chaplains and harangued them for not having a sufficiently positive attitude toward the Nazis. Although he was a Catholic himself, he told the padres, "The Oath which [the soldier] has taken to the Fuehrer and supreme Commander of the Wehrmacht binds him unto the sacrifice of his own life to National Socialism, the concept of the new Reich. . . . No doubts may be permitted to arise out of your [the padres'] attitudes towards National Socialism. The Wehrmacht, as one of the bearers of the National Socialist State, demands of you as chaplains at all times a clear and unreserved acknowledgement of the Fuehrer, State and People!"[28]

Largely because of his pro-Nazi attitudes and orders, Friedrich Dollmann was promoted to general of artillery on April 1, 1936, and on August 25, 1939, he was elevated to the command of 7th Army. This last advancement seems to have been engineered by Bodewin Keitel, the chief of the Army Personnel Office, who had worked for Dollmann for years and was his chief of staff at Kassel until 1938. Six days after Dollmann took charge of his new command, the German Army crossed the Polish frontier, starting the Second World War.

Dollmann's army, which consisted of nonmotorized divisions made up primarily of inadequately trained, older-age reservists, remained in Germany while Hitler conquered Poland. In the invasion of France (1940), it had the unspectacular mission of manning the southern end of the Westwall (the Siegfried Line), opposite the Maginot Line. Only after the best of the French divisions had been destroyed and the end of the campaign was clearly in sight did the 7th Army go over to the offensive, breaking through the Maginot north of Belford. Demoralized French resistance collapsed quickly, and on June 19, Dollmann linked up with the 1st Panzer Division of Panzer Group Guderian, completing the encirclement of 400,000 French soldiers in the Vosges Mountains. The French formally surrendered at Compiègne two days later. On July 19, 1940, a jubilant Adolf Hitler rewarded his generals with an outpouring of medals and promotions. Among those to benefit was Friedrich Dollmann, who was promoted to colonel general. He then returned to occupation duty in France, where he remained for the next four years.

From 1940 until 1944, while most of the Wehrmacht was fighting on the Eastern Front, Colonel General Dollmann and his 7th Army vegetated in France. During this period Dollmann—to his credit—began to have serious second thoughts about the Nazi regime he had previously supported. As the months went by and the war dragged on, and as the Nazis became more and more repressive and vicious in the occupied areas, the directives exhorting his troops to cooperate with the party ceased to flow from Dollmann's headquarters. He was, in fact, a deeply troubled man; his health began to deteriorate, and he apparently felt guilty and ashamed of his previous support for the Nazis and was deeply concerned about the future of his country and his command. However, he did very little about either. Headquartered comfortably in LeMans, Dollmann grew fat and followed the lead of his superior, Field Marshal Gerd von Rundstedt, and neglected the coastal defenses of his sector. He did not see any active campaigning of any kind and, more debilitating, did not keep abreast of developments in his profession. Indeed, he had little or no grasp of panzer tactics and no understanding of the implications of Allied air superiority. By 1944, Dollmann was almost an anachronism; he simply was not prepared to deal with what he would soon be called upon to face: the D-Day invasion of June 6, 1944. Before Eisenhower's forces landed, however, Dollmann faced another threat to his position when Field Marshal Rommel arrived in France in December 1943.

Erwin Rommel, the famous Desert Fox, was the commander-in-chief of Army Group B, a headquarters that was interjected between Rundstedt's *Oberbefehlshaber West* (OB West)[29] and Dollmann's 7th Army Headquarters. Rundstedt, like Dollmann, had vegetated in a static command and was living in the past. He believed that the proper strategy for Germany was to let the Allies land, build up, and advance inland. Here they could be engaged and perhaps destroyed in a blitzkrieg-like tank battle, well out of range of their big naval guns. Rommel, however, had experienced firsthand the devastating effects of Allied aerial supremacy in North Africa and realized that a battle of the kind envisioned by Rundstedt and his chief armored adviser, General of Panzer Troops Baron Leo Geyr von Schweppenburg, was no longer possible. The dynamic Rommel now insisted that the invaders be halted on the beaches and immediately counterattacked to throw them back into the sea. These tactics would require the laying of tens of thousands of mines, the construction of dozens of bunkers and anti-tank traps, and the erection of countless anti-glider and anti-parachute obstacles.

For almost four years, Friedrich Dollmann had done little to improve his coastal defenses. But Erwin Rommel had a reputation for replacing subordinate commanders who did not enthusiastically support his concept of operations. Suddenly, therefore, the 7th Army commander became a firm advocate of coastal obstacles and offshore barriers. "Dollmann was now absolutely for Rommel's ideas," Rommel's naval adviser recorded in February 1944.[30] However, four months of feverish activity could not make good four years of inactivity. When the Allies landed on D-Day, 7th Army was not ready.

Friedrich Dollmann was not only ill-prepared for D-Day—he was unlucky as well. Field Marshal Rommel was in Germany, away from his post, and Dollmann had scheduled a war game at Rennes for the morning of June 6. As a result, most of the key divisional and corps commanders of the 7th Army were also absent when the Anglo-American paratroopers began to land. Shortly thereafter, the assault forces stormed ashore. Acting in Rommel's absence, Dollmann tried to restore the situation via an immediate armored counterattack with his only available armored division, but he experienced little success, and the 21st Panzer Division was devastated in the process. Furthermore, when Lieutenant General Fritz Bayerlein, the commander of the elite Panzer Lehr Division, turned up at 7th Army Headquarters in LeMans, Dollmann ordered him to move up his division at 5 p.m.—in broad daylight.

Bayerlein objected immediately. Having served with Rommel in the Afrika Korps, he realized the risks involved in a daylight move, but Dollmann refused to listen. He was more concerned with his invasion front, which was being hammered by vastly superior Allied forces and would soon be on the verge of collapse. Summer days are long in France; to comply with Bayerlein's request would have meant a delay of more than three hours, and Dollmann did not think he could spare the time. He insisted that the division begin its move at 5 p.m. and even proposed a change in the preselected approach routes, but on this point Bayerlein held firm—any modification at this point certainly would have resulted in chaos, as Doll-mann surely should have known. To make matters even worse, Dollmann imposed radio silence on the division. "As if radio silence could have stopped the fighter-bombers and reconnaissance planes from spotting us!" a disgusted and angry Bayerlein snapped later.[31]

As Fritz Bayerlein foresaw, the Allies quickly spotted the move, and Panzer Lehr's approach to contact quickly became a nightmare. The fighter-bombers were soon everywhere, shooting up the long columns of vehicles and blasting bridges, crossroads, and towns along the division's five routes of advance. Night brought no relief, because Allied airplanes now knew the approximate location of the division's columns, so they illuminated the countryside with flares until they found a suitable target. All the while the columns became more and more spread out, scattered, disorganized, and fragmented. The tanks were relatively safe from the bombardment (only five were knocked out), but the rest of the division suffered terribly. During the night of June 6–7, Bayerlein lost 40 loaded fuel trucks; 84 half-tracks, prime-movers, and self-propelled guns; and dozens of other vehicles. Perhaps more important, the elite but now depleted Panzer Lehr Division arrived at its assembly areas in dribs and drabs. Field Marshal Rommel once predicted that the invasion must be thrown back into the sea within 48 hours or the war would be lost. Partially as a result of the Panzer Lehr debacle, the Desert Fox could not launch his armored counterattack until June 9—at least two days too late. It was repulsed. The war was lost.

Significantly, almost as soon as he returned to France (he was in Germany, en route to see Hitler, when the invasion struck), Rommel took the panzer divisions away from the control of Friedrich Dollmann and placed them under Headquarters, Panzer Group West (later 5th Panzer Army) under Geyr von Schweppenburg. Seventh Army now had responsibility only for the left wing of the invasion front—which was quite enough. For the next three weeks an increasingly distressed Dollmann slowed, but could not halt, the progress of the Allied invasion, and the units of the 7th Army were slowly ground to bits in the hedgerow country of Normandy. The French port of Cherbourg, Eisenhower's initial strategic objective, was cut off from the rest of the army on June 18. Despite the fact that it had enough food and ammunition to hold out for eight weeks, the defenses of Cherbourg collapsed with incredible speed. Lieutenant General Karl Wilhelm von Schlieben, the fortress commander, surrendered at 1:30 p.m. on June 26. Although isolated resistance would continue for several days, the fall of the critical port was now just a matter of time.

Hitler, naturally, was furious, and Keitel ordered a court-martial investigation of the fall of the fortress. Dollmann was questioned, of course, and not too politely. He was accused of negligence in connection with the disaster—and probably rightfully so. In any event, Hitler summoned Rommel and von Rundstedt to Berchtesgaden and, on the afternoon of June 29, demanded that Dollmann be court-martialed for losing Cherbourg. Rundstedt, however, refused to listen to such talk. (Dollmann, after all, had been no more negligent in the pre-invasion years than Rundstedt himself had been.) Hitler then turned to Rommel and demanded that Dollmann at least be relieved of his command. Dollmann, however, had obeyed Rommel's orders to the best of his ability and the field marshal was personally fond of the fat general; furthermore, the Desert Fox was not accustomed to sacking commanders who had served him loyally.

Like Rundstedt, he stood up for Dollmann and then changed the subject.[32] It was only after the marshals left that Hitler sent the order to Le-Mans, personally relieving Dollmann of his command. He was replaced by SS Obergruppenfuehrer Paul Hausser (see chapter 8). Friedrich Dollmann, however, never knew that he had been sacked. At 10 a.m. on June 28, overworked, stressed out, and very worried about the ongoing investigation that Hitler had ordered, he suffered a heart attack at his forward command post.[33] Sources differ as to whether he succumbed on June 28 or 29, and word of his death did not reach LeMans for hours; however, it seems certain that while Hitler, Rommel, and von Rundstedt were arguing about his fate, Dollmann was already dead. In any case he was buried in France on July 2. Perhaps remembering better days, or perhaps feeling a twinge of guilt for sacking him (if that were possible), Adolf Hitler authorized a laudatory obituary for Colonel General Dollmann.

RUDOLF STEGMANN, one of the few German heroes of the Cherbourg debacle, is a good example of the typical German divisional commander—tough, resourceful, courageous, and innovative. Having this caliber of officer at the divisional level and below was a major contributing factor in the successes the Wehrmacht enjoyed during its glory days and one reason it managed to stay in the field as long as it did, once the tide of war had turned irrevocably against it.

Born at Nikolaiken, East Prussia, on August 6, 1894, Stegmann entered the Imperial Army as a Fahnenjunker in 1912 (at age 18) and was commissioned second lieutenant in the 141st Infantry Regiment in May 1914. This unit remained in East Prussia when the Russians invaded that province later that year, and it helped scatter the czar's armies at Gumbinnen and Tannenberg—a defeat from which Imperial Russia never recovered. After taking part in the invasions of Poland and Russia, young Stegmann's regiment was transferred to France in September 1915 and spent the rest of the war on the Western Front. When the war ended, Lieutenant Stegmann was selected for the Reichsheer and was a major when Adolf Hitler became ruler of Germany.

Apparently never a member of the General Staff, Stegmann was associated with the infantry and motorized infantry throughout the Nazi era. He was promoted to lieutenant colonel on January 1, 1938, and was named commander of the II Battalion, 14th Motorized Infantry Regiment at Oppeln, Silesia (now Opole, Poland), later that year. After fighting in Poland, he was promoted to the command of his regiment (part of the 5th Panzer Division), which he led in the Western campaign of 1940, fighting in the Ardennes breakthrough and in the battles around Cambrai, Lille, Rouen, and Brest. Promoted to colonel in late 1940, Stegmann directed the refitting of his regiment in Germany in the summer of 1940, serving on occupation duty and participating in maneuvers in Poland in the winter of 1940–1941. He then took part in the conquests of Yugoslavia and Greece, before being sent to the Russian Front in time to take part in the final drive on Moscow and the subsequent retreat, during which Army Group Center was almost destroyed.

It is unclear from the few available records whether Rudolf Stegmann collapsed from exhaustion or from wounds, but he was forced to give up command of the 14th Motorized Infantry on February 5, 1942, and was without an assignment for several months. When he did regain his health and returned to the front in September 1942, it was with a promotion: he was now commander of the 2nd Panzer Grenadier Brigade (part of the 2nd Panzer Division) in the Rzhev salient of the Moscow sector. For Stegmann, this command was destined to be extremely brief, because he was sent back to Germany in late 1942 to attend a divisional commanders' training course. He returned to Russia in April 1943, where he assumed command of the remnants of the 36th Panzer Grenadier Division, which had been mauled in the Rzhev battles of 1942–1943. Stegmann was given the dubious task of rebuilding the 36th as a nonmotorized infantry division. This task he successfully completed by September, when his division took part in the battles around Smolensk, in the retreat to Mogilev, and in the successful defensive battles around Bobruisk, during which he was seriously wounded. Sent back to Germany, Stegmann did not fully recover until spring. By then the prospect of the Anglo-American invasion loomed large in the minds of the generals of the German High Command, and

OB West needed every experienced divisional commander it could get; consequently, Stegmann was sent to France, where he officially assumed command of the 77th Infantry Division on May 1, 1944.

Stegmann's new command hardly fit the definition of an elite unit. It had been created in January 1944, when the 364th Infantry Division had been combined with the remnants of the 355th Infantry Division to form the 77th. The 355th Infantry—a unit composed mainly of Wuerttemberger reservists—had been smashed in the Kharkov and Krivoy Rog battles on the Russian Front. The 364th Infantry was formed in Poland in late 1943 but never saw combat. The new division was understrength and had only two infantry regiments (the 1049th and 1050th Grenadiers); its artillery regiment (the 177th) was very weak; it had no engineer battalion, few reconnaissance forces, and only two anti-tank companies (instead of the normal battalion); and it was short on trained officers and equipment of every description. The human factor was no more promising. A high proportion of the men were Volksdeutsche, Polish, or Soviet citizens, mainly Tartars from the Volga region, whose loyalty to the Third Reich was questionable at best. In short, General Stegmann had very little to work with in May 1944. A highly dissatisfied Field Marshal Rommel had come to the same conclusion somewhat earlier. In April he had inspected the 77th Infantry Division, which was charged with the defense of the Caen area. Deciding that this unit was too poor to defend such a potentially important sector, he replaced it with the 21st Panzer Division, which is why the 77th Infantry was not involved in the initial D-Day landings. He sent the 77th to the less threatened St. Malo–St. Brieuc sector in Brittany and sent its original divisional commander to find employment elsewhere. This is how Stegmann came to command the 77th in the first place.

Colonel General Dollmann alerted the 77th Infantry Division for a possible movement to Normandy on the morning of D-Day, but Rommel's headquarters delayed this move, based on erroneous reports of possible Allied paratroop landings in Brittany. (Rommel himself was on his way back from a trip to Germany at this time and could not be reached.) On the morning of June 7, however, the Desert Fox was back and trying to gain control of the battle. He immediately realized that the port of Cherbourg was the initial strategic objective of the landings. He understood that the weak left flank of the Normandy sector must be reinforced or the Americans would drive west from their invasion beachheads, cut across the Cotentin peninsula to the sea, and isolate Cherbourg to the north from the rest of 7th Army, in the St. Lô sector to the south. Consequently, he ordered the 77th Infantry to reinforce Group von Schlieben, which was assigned the task of holding the southern approaches to Cherbourg. Stegmann received this order at 10:15 a.m., but his division did not move out until 3 p.m. Once it began, the march was to be rapid—or relatively so under the circumstances. Since there were no motorized transportation units available, the entire distance had to be covered on foot, and the division was constantly harassed by Allied fighter-bombers. General Dollmann was very much concerned that it would not arrive in time to prevent the collapse of von Schlieben's line, but the vanguard of the division arrived on June 10, and by the next day much of the 77th was on the front line, defending in the hedgerow country on both sides of the Merderet River, where it prevented much stronger elements of the U.S. VII Corps from outflanking the critical position of Montebourg, a major junction on the road to Cherbourg. A much-relieved Friedrich Dollmann signaled Rommel on June 11 that he was satisfied that the situation had been restored on his part of the front. The following day the rest of Stegmann's division arrived and went into the line.[34]

General Dollmann's sense of relief was short-lived. South of Stegmann's positions lay the 100th Panzer Replacement Battalion, which consisted mainly of foreign personnel. On the morning of June 12, it broke and ran away upon first contact with the enemy. U.S. Lieutenant General Joseph "Lightning Joe" Collins, the commander of the VII Corps, was quick to take advantage of this gap in the German line. Living up to his nickname, he committed the U.S. 9th Infantry and 82nd Airborne divisions into an attack along the Pont-l'Abbe–St. Sauveur–le Vicomte road, which was now defended only by the few surviving remnants of the 91st Air Landing Division, a battle-weary unit that had been in action since D-Day and was now at regimental strength. It was here that Collins achieved the decisive breakthrough that Stegmann had foiled the day before. The American spearheads reached the sea near the little port of Barneville at 5:05 a.m. on June 18, isolating Group von Schlieben in the northern part of the Cotentin peninsula and trapping what was left of four German divisions: the 91st Air Landing and the 77th, 243rd, and 709th Infantry Divisions.

While Collins pushed to the sea, the 77th Infantry Division engaged the U.S. 90th Infantry Division in bitter fighting. It took the U.S. 357th Infantry Regiment two full days of fighting to capture the village of Gourbesville, while the 358th and 359th Infantry regiments (also of the 90th Division) accomplished even less. The road to Montebourg, Valognes, and Cherbourg remained blocked, the 77th continued to resist tenaciously, and Rudolf Stegmann was proving that he could get the maximum combat effort from a division that previously had been considered unreliable.

The American breakthrough, however, had left his right flank completely exposed, and even a retreat to Cherbourg could only end in the sacrifice of the division—if it could even make it to the "fortress." Since the 77th was nonmotorized and the Americans were fully motorized and had several tank battalions, even an escape to the north was highly doubtful. Rommel, therefore, authorized the division to disengage and break out to the south, where the German forces in the thinly manned St. Lô sector would soon need every rifle they could muster. This sensible order, however, was countermanded by Adolf Hitler. The 77th Infantry, he decreed, was to hold its present positions at all costs. The American breakthrough was to be dealt with by ignoring it. What good this would accomplish, with a gaping hole in the German line, the Fuehrer did not explain.

While Stegmann held firm, General Collins's VII Corps turned north and began to work its way behind the 77th. Meanwhile, a new U.S. corps—Major General Troy H. Middleton's VIII—was committed to hold the corridor across the Cotentin, in the unlikely event that Dollmann's battered 7th Army tried to relieve Cherbourg. On June 18, the Americans at last began to close in on the 77th Infantry. By now Hitler had relaxed his original order somewhat. Limited withdrawals toward Cherbourg were permitted, he said, but only under enemy pressure. Any breakout to the south was still forbidden. Nevertheless, General Stegmann led a breakout attempt to the south, taking whatever he could with him—right through American lines. Whether this move was initiated or even authorized by Colonel General Dollmann is still the subject of debate. Naturally enough Dollmann denied it at the time, and it is true beyond question that his chief of staff denied permission for just such an action as late as the evening of June 16. In any case, Stegmann was the man who finally acted. He began thinning out his line on the afternoon of June 17, arranged elements of his division into a five-column formation during the night of June 17–18, and attempted to find a hole in and/or break through the U.S. line on June 18.

It was already too late for most of the division. While Hitler delayed, the veteran U.S. 9th Infantry joined the battle against the 77th and much of the German division was not able to disengage. The column consisting of the bulk of the 177th Artillery Regiment (and most of the division's motorized vehicles) successfully made its way through the American front line but was caught on the road west of Hill 145 and destroyed by the U.S. 60th Field Artillery Battalion, with the aid of a few infantry and anti-tank units. Meanwhile, other columns were spotted by the Allied fighter-bombers, which seemed to be everywhere. Grenadiers dove for cover as the airplanes struck, but the horse-drawn wagons could not do so. The slaughter was terrible, and confusion and disorganization soon seized the columns, which threatened to disintegrate. In the middle of all this, Rudolf Stegmann raced from place to place in his camouflaged command car, restoring order out of chaos and keeping the columns moving south, toward the main German lines. Then, near the village of Bricquebec, his car was spotted by an American pilot, who dived to almost ground level and opened up on Stegmann's car at close range. The general's body was riddled with 20mm shells, one of which hit him in the head. He was dead before his body reached the floorboard.

Command of the division now devolved on the senior regimental commander, Colonel of Reserves Bernard Bacherer of the 1049th Grenadier. He ignored advice to surrender or to turn back toward Cherbourg and instead kept trying to find a way through the American line. He found one and, accompanied by about 1,700 men, marched deep into the corridor between the U.S. VII and VIII corps during the night of June 18–19. Colonel Bacherer was lucky. He marched south all night long, and when dawn broke on June 19, a heavy cloud cover and drizzle kept the enemy fighter-bombers on the ground, enabling the division to continue pushing south undetected. About 11 a.m. his forward patrols reported that a strong American force was encamped less than 500 yards away. Bacherer ordered his men to hide in a sunken lane and go to sleep. With no rest for more than 30 hours, they did not have to be told twice: they slept where they fell. Late that afternoon they moved on, still unspotted by the enemy. That night they reached the Ollande River but found all the crossings blocked by strong American detachments. Bacherer then pulled a last, desperate maneuver: he launched an old-fashioned bayonet charge against one of the bridges. The American defenders (part of the 2nd Battalion, 47th Infantry Regiment) were taken completely by surprise and were quickly overwhelmed. The 77th Infantry had breached the last obstacle to safety. Colonel Bacherer reached German lines without further incident, carrying with him about 1,500 soldiers (including all his wounded), plus 250 prisoners and 12 captured jeeps. As small as it now was, the 77th was a welcome addition to the German defenders, who would continue to hold up the Allies in the hedgerow country of Normandy for more than another month.[35]

Ironically, General Stegmann's career was not ended by his death. He was credited with saving the remnants of the 77th Infantry Division and—even though he had acted against the Fuehrer's orders—he was posthumously promoted to lieutenant general, effective June 1, 1944. Hitler's empire was indeed a strange and lethal place to be in the last year of the war.

★ ★ ★

I have vivid memories of my meeting with **BARON HASSO VON MANTEUFFEL** in 1973, when I visited him at his home in Bavaria, near Ammersee, a large glacial lake in Upper Bavaria. He was very polite, energetic, and extroverted. Although he was thin and small in stature, about five foot two, I could understand how he commanded respect by his obvious self-confidence and his knowledge of military affairs. He was a gracious host, and when I told him I was staying with a brother-in-law who was stationed in Wurzburg with the American army, Manteuffel remarked that one of his ancestors took the famous castle there for the Hohenzollerns in the 1850s. Indeed, his family had served the Hohenzollerns of Prussia faithfully and with distinction for several generations. Otto von Manteuffel, for example, served as prime minister of Prussia from 1850 to 1858, and General Edwin von Manteuffel was once chief of the military cabinet of Kaiser Wilhelm I, until he was pushed aside by Otto von Bismarck.[36]

Hasso von Manteuffel was born in Potsdam on January 14, 1897. He and his three sisters were raised primarily by his mother, for his father died when Hasso was seven years old. The family was well off and lived on a well-groomed estate in a villa that was exquisitely furnished. Young Manteuffel received an excellent education in an expensive preparatory school operated by his cousin. (Young Manteuffel was an exemplary student who always put his studies first.) Continuing in the family tradition, he entered the Prussian cadet school at Naumburg/Saale in 1908. This school was one of the most modern in Germany, and its curriculum centered on the classical model, with heavy emphasis on sports and military instruction.

Upon leaving the school in Naumburg/Saale, Manteuffel entered the main cadet school in Berlin-Lichterfelde. One of a thousand cadets, he lived in a plainly furnished apartment with seven others. In January 1916, Manteuffel passed his finals and received his Certificate of Maturity and the next month he was promoted to officer candidate (Faehnrich). At the request of Manteuffel's stepfather, Crown Prince Wilhelm intervened on his behalf and Manteuffel was transferred to the replacement squadron of the Hussar Regiment von Zieten (Brandenburger) Number 3.[37] Later that year, Manteuffel was promoted to second lieutenant and was transferred to the 5th Squadron of the 6th Prussian Infantry Division, stationed on the Western Front.

While carrying out a reconnaissance mission near Bapaume, France, in October 1916, Baron von Manteuffel was wounded when a piece of shrapnel struck him in the leg. He was sent to a rearward hospital for medical attention and to recover; however, he desperately wanted to return to his unit and, in January 1917, left the hospital without authorization and returned to the front. Although he was later sentenced to three days arrest in his quarters, he never served the sentence. Manteuffel was transferred to the 6th Infantry's divisional staff in February and remained with the division as it fought the Russians in East Galicia in July 1917 and when it returned to the Western Front in March 1918.

After the war ended, Manteuffel joined Freikorps von Oven as second adjutant and fought the Spartacists in Berlin, as well as other Communist revolutionaries in Munich and Leipzig. He was selected to remain in the 100,000-man army and, in May 1919, was assigned to the 25A Cavalry Regiment at Rathenow. In 1921, he married a beautiful, blue-eyed blonde named Armgard von Kleist, whose uncle was future Field Marshal Ewald von Kleist. The von Manteuffels were to have two children. From 1925 to 1930, Hasso served as the regimental adjutant of the 25A Cavalry and then became commander of the experimental mechanical squadron—a position normally reserved for a captain. In 1932, he became a squadron leader in the 17th Cavalry Regiment at Bamberg and in October 1934 was promoted to Rittmeister (captain of cavalry). Later that same year he was transferred to the 2nd Motorcycle Battalion, along with two squadrons of the 17th Cavalry. Although Manteuffel was an excellent horseman, he was literally drafted into the motorized battalion by Major General Viktor von Schwedler, the chief of the Army Personnel Office. In 1935, Colonel Heinz Guderian of the panzer branch convinced Manteuffel to transfer to one of the newly created tank divisions. Manteuffel responded by joining Guderian's own 2nd Panzer Division as a squadron leader in the 3rd Motorcycle Battalion. Guderian developed such confidence in Manteuffel that he put him in charge of all cadet training for the division in 1936, shortly after Manteuffel received his promotion to major.

The close relationship between the two men continued, and, as Guderian's fortunes rose, so did Manteuffel's. Early in 1937 Manteuffel served as official adviser to the Inspectorate of Panzer Troops (part of OKH), directly under Guderian. On February 1, 1939, Manteuffel was named commandant of Officer Training School Number 2, located at Potsdam-Krampnitz, and was promoted to lieutenant colonel two months later. "Manteuffel somehow left the stamp of his own personality on his trainees, and he taught them independent action within the framework of an integrated team effort," General Frederick Wilhelm von Mellenthin wrote later.[38] He believed that tank crews needed to be very much aware of battlefield tactics, so that if necessary each crew could make independent decisions during the heat of battle to positively affect the outcome. He stressed the concepts of mobility and maneuverability and the use of ground cover, all of which may give a particular panzer force a decisive advantage. He remained at the school during both the Polish and French campaigns. Upon hearing of the impending invasion of the Soviet Union, Manteuffel asked for a field command and, as a result, was named commander of the I Battalion of the 7th Rifle Regiment of the 7th Panzer Division in June 1941. During that same month his battalion saw heavy fighting on the Russian Front; among other things it spearheaded a bridgehead across the Memel River in Lithuania. The 7th Panzer Division continued to engage in intensive combat as it penetrated deep into Soviet lines, becoming the first German force to reach the highway between Minsk, Smolensk, and Moscow.

In August 1941, Colonel Erich von Unger, commander of the 6th Rifle Regiment, was killed in action and Manteuffel was named as his replacement. The baron's energy and indomitable will filtered throughout his new command as the 6th Rifle Regiment became the first unit to breach the Stalin Line as the spearhead of General Hermann Hoth's 3rd Panzer Group; indeed, Manteuffel's troops were always out in front, in the "thick of the action," and were constantly carrying out daring, bold maneuvers. Clearly Manteuffel put into practice what he had taught at the academy. In October he was promoted to colonel, and his regiment participated in the assault on Moscow, crossing the Moscow-Volga Canal at Jakhroma, on the outskirts of the Soviet capital, under extremely heavy enemy fire. Once again, his forces acted as the spearhead for the panzer group. For his courage and leadership, Manteuffel was awarded the Knight's Cross in December 1941.

Meanwhile, the German juggernaut stalled due to the onset of a severe Russian winter and stiffer Russian resistance. On December 6, 1941, Stalin launched a major winter counteroffensive all along the front, but Army Group Center in the Moscow sector was especially hard hit. In temperatures hovering around 40–42 degrees below zero, Manteuffel's regiment fell back to defensive positions between Vyazma and Rzhev and held its line despite repeated Soviet attacks. General of Panzer Troops Walter Model, the commander of the 9th Army, ordered Manteuffel's regiment, which was already under heavy attack, to launch a major counterattack. Manteuffel refused, pointing out the lack of food, fuel, supplies, and camouflage uniforms (without which the German soldiers would be easy targets for Soviet snipers). In response, Model demanded that Manteuffel's troops attack on skis, noting that the division was from Thuringia, where all children learn to ski at an early age. Once again Manteuffel refused, and this time Model threatened a court-martial. The confrontation ended when the 7th Panzer Division was transferred to France for reorganization, and the divisional commander saw to it that Manteuffel left early, with the advance party, perhaps thereby saving him from a court-martial. Later, on the Western Front, Manteuffel and Model forgot their differences and worked well together. After the war, Manteuffel told the famous British military historian B. H. Liddell Hart that "Model was a very good tactician, and better in defense than in attack. He had a knack of gauging, what troops could do, and what they could not do."[39]

Back in France, Manteuffel supervised the rebuilding of his regiment and in July 1942 was named commander of the 7th Panzer Grenadier Brigade (of the 7th Panzer Division). His next combat assignment, however, was in North Africa, where he arrived in early 1943. Assigned the task of holding the right (coastal) flank of the 5th Panzer Army in Tunisia, Baron von Manteuffel in effect created his own division from an assortment of units, including the Italian 10th Bersaglieri Regiment, the 11th (Witzig) Parachute Engineer Battalion, and the Barenthin Parachute Regiment, among others. With this odd mixture (labeled the Manteuffel Division), he once again achieved stunning successes over his vastly superior opponents and held his thin line in the Tunisian hills for weeks against repeated attacks by French and Anglo-American forces. These battles took their toll, and on April 28, 1943, an exhausted Manteuffel collapsed on the front line. He was rushed to a military hospital in Bizerta and, while under medical attention, was promoted to major general on May 1, 1943. A few days later he was placed on the last Italian ship heading for Sicily and safety, as the Tunisian Bridgehead collapsed.

From Sicily, Manteuffel traveled to Rome and then to Berlin, where his family lived. Shortly before Manteuffel was to be discharged from the hospital, Adolf Hitler ordered him to appear at Fuehrer Headquarters in East Prussia. A surprised Manteuffel responded and appeared before his Fuehrer, who asked the general what were his wishes. Manteuffel replied that he would like to command the 7th Panzer Division, to which Hitler agreed. In August 1943, Manteuffel joined the 7th Panzer and, within three days of his return to the front, incurred shrapnel wounds from a grenade. Although in great pain, he refused to return to the hospital and, temporarily bandaged at the front, remained in command of the division and led it through some brilliant defensive fighting over the next four weeks. Manteuffel also participated in Field Marshal Erich von Manstein's offensive against Kiev in November 1943, during which his 7th Panzer Division led the attack that overpowered Zhitomir and recaptured an important German supply depot. For this accomplishment, Manteuffel was awarded the Oak Leaves to the Knight's Cross.[40] He succeeded at Zhitomir by dividing his forces into small mobile units that were self-contained and that penetrated between Russian columns, striking them from the rear. Such tactics completely confused the enemy. Hitler heard of Manteuffel's exploits and invited him to Fuehrer Headquarters for Christmas. Hitler congratulated the general and gave him a present of 50 tanks. Hitler further rewarded Manteuffel with command of the Grossdeutschland, an elite, all-volunteer, specially reinforced panzer grenadier division. To complete the accolades, Manteuffel was promoted to lieutenant general in February 1944 and was awarded the Swords to his Knight's Cross with Oak Leaves that same month.

Manteuffel saw Hitler several times throughout 1944, as the Fuehrer was obviously taken with the small Prussian general's uncanny successes. The general was impressed by Hitler's magnetic personality and, as Albert Speer also told this writer, by Hitler's ability to disarm one with his eyes and fluid discourse.[41] Although Manteuffel was impressed with Hitler's grasp of combat from the field soldier's point of view, as well as the Fuehrer's knowledge of military literature, he recognized Hitler's weaknesses concerning grand strategy and tactical awareness, even though the Fuehrer had a flair for originality and daring. Although he was always respectful, Manteuffel always expressed his own views, regardless of how they might be received by Hitler.

The Grossdeutschland put forth a heroic effort in the Rumanian theater of the Eastern Front in early 1944, escaping from a Russian encirclement in March without losing a single tank. The Red Army kept coming, however, and in April the division halted a major Soviet advance in the Jassy area of Rumania and annihilated the enemy spearhead. Farther to the north, however, the Soviets were successfully advancing into East Prussia, and consequently the Grossdeutschland was hurriedly transferred and assembled near Trakehnen, approximately 25 miles behind the front lines. Berlin ordered the division to attack immediately, forsaking artillery support and adequate reconnaissance reports. Manteuffel's attack took the Soviets completely by surprise, and his success managed to stabilize the German front. Still, the Grossdeutschland lost more than 80 tanks, and a furious Hitler called Manteuffel to Fuehrer Headquarters to explain the horrible losses. Momentarily taken aback, Manteuffel blurted out that he was ordered to attack and that the order—which he showed Hitler—compelled him to attack prematurely. After reading the order, Hitler called for Keitel and demanded that the field marshal tell him where the order had come from. Apparently Keitel had issued the order on his own, carrying out what he believed to be the Fuehrer's will when Hitler had mentioned that the Grossdeutschland could stop the Soviet advance by taking the offensive. Consequently, Hitler turned his wrath on his despondent chief of OKW berating him for improperly issuing an order based simply on Hitler's offhand remark. According to Manteuffel, there were other occasions when Keitel and Jodl, the chief of operations at OKW, issued orders on their own.[42]

In September 1944, the baron was again summoned to Fuehrer Headquarters. This time, however, Hitler greeted him with open arms, promoted him to general of panzer troops, and gave him command of the 5th Panzer Army. Moved to the Western Front, Manteuffel had a new mission: counterattack and halt the drive by General George Patton's 3rd U.S. Army. He halted Patton's attack on Metz and recaptured Luneville on September 17. He was then ordered to attack Patton's forces north of the Marne-Rhine Canal, which Manteuffel did under protest, realizing the hopelessness of such an attack. As usual, the panzer general proved correct: he lost 50 tanks and gained very little.

Manteuffel attended an important briefing conference in November, along with Field Marshal Gerd von Rundstedt, Field Marshal Model, and Colonel General Jodl. Jodl presented Hitler's plan for an Ardennes offensive to the other officers. This offensive, which had as its principal objective the rapid seizure of the port of Antwerp, is now popularly known as the Battle of the Bulge. The operation aimed at splitting the British and American forces and possibly forcing a second Dunkirk and potential British withdrawal from the war. If successful, Hitler reasoned, it would allow him time to recoup his defenses to better withstand the continued Soviet offensive toward Germany. The officers, however, were very skeptical and suggested a modified plan, to which Jodl curtly replied that there would be no changes to Hitler's orders. Consequently, the attack would take place in December, with Manteuffel's 5th Panzer Army and SS General Sepp Dietrich's 6th Panzer Army making the major German thrusts toward Antwerp. Manteuffel agreed with B. H. Liddell Hart in an interview immediately after the war that airborne troops would have been very useful to the attack; however, following the Crete invasion of 1941, during which the German paratroopers suffered tremendous losses in taking the island, Manteuffel told the British historian that there was a great reluctance on the part of Hitler to use parachute troops.[43]

Although Hitler's plan remained intact, Manteuffel did at least convince the Fuehrer to allow him to begin the attack during nighttime hours, thus foregoing an artillery barrage that Hitler had originally planned and allowing the general additional daylight hours once his tanks reached clearings in the Ardennes. Although Dietrich's army was supposed to be the main assault force, it was 5th Panzer Army that enjoyed the most success. Once again, Manteuffel's strategy of creating self-sustaining mobile fighting units proved successful, as they penetrated deep into the American lines, racing toward Bastogne. At the same time, Dietrich, who opted to advance on a narrow front, bogged down and, rather than assisting Manteuffel's rapidly advancing spearheads, stuck to the Fuehrer's order and vainly attempted to drive his stalled regiments forward. Ultimately, mud, lack of fuel, the lifting of the foggy weather (allowing Allied air power to inflict tremendous damage on the panzer armies), and a rapid American recovery doomed the Ardennes offensive. Manteuffel was particularly accusatory toward General Jodl, who had assured both Manteuffel and Dietrich that adequate fuel reserves were available for the offensive. Manteuffel argued that Jodl had no idea of the amount of fuel necessary for such an operation. Even though the offensive failed, Hitler summoned his brilliant panzer commander to Fuehrer Headquarters in February 1945 and awarded Baron von Manteuffel the Diamonds to his Knight's Cross and offered him an endowment of 200,000 marks. Manteuffel refused the cash, because he felt it was not fitting for a soldier to accept a "reward" for doing what was expected of him.[44]

In March 1945, Manteuffel was given command of the 3rd Panzer Army, which was stationed on the Eastern Front. He tenaciously held his positions on the Oder River, although toward the end of April he ordered a retreat; recognizing that the end was near and again thinking of his men, he moved westward to surrender to the British. On May 3, General Hasso von Manteuffel surrendered his panzer army to the representatives of Field Marshal Sir Bernard Law Montgomery at Hagenow. Manteuffel's retreat was another noteworthy accomplishment, as he kept his units together during those hectic days when millions of refugees (along with soldiers from disbanded units) were streaming westward to escape the Soviets.

Manteuffel was placed under arrest and initially taken to an internment camp with other generals, where he was interviewed by Liddell Hart. When the historian remarked about the unpleasantness of the camp, Manteuffel replied "with a smile, 'Oh, it might be worse. I expect we shall be spending next winter on a barren island, or else in a ship anchored in the mid-Atlantic.'"[45] It was this marvelous sense of humor that aided Manteuffel in difficult situations and endeared him to the men who served under him. Indeed, those who served with the highly decorated baron did so with loyal admiration for the general who, in turn, treated everyone with respect and courtesy.[46] Above all, he kept his calm demeanor in the most difficult situations and consistently carried out what he believed to be an officer's obligation: duty to the welfare of the men under his command. Such characteristics were clearly displayed during an event that occurred during Manteuffel's retreat, as part of Colonel General Gotthard Heinrici's Army Group Vistula, to British lines. Having heard of the unauthorized retreat, an angry Field Marshal Keitel drove to the front and confronted Manteuffel and Heinrici. Both Manteuffel and his chief of staff, Major General Burkhart Mueller-Hillebrand, related the following to this writer: Manteuffel, aware of Keitel's desire for attack, prepared for the worst. Before meeting the chief of OKW, the panzer general made certain his pistol was loaded and kept his hand near the revolver. Further, Mueller-Hillebrand ordered several officers armed with machine-pistols to hide behind some trees at the crossroads. Keitel arrived and, pounding his baton into his gloved hand, angrily reproached Manteuffel and Heinrici. The generals explained the folly of holding fast and emphasized the desperate need for reinforcements. Keitel exploded and shot back, "There are no reserves left!" Hitting his hand with the baton, he ordered them to turn the army around immediately. Both Heinrici and Manteuffel refused.

Having lost control, Keitel shouted, "You will have to take responsibility of this action before history!"

Manteuffel angrily replied, "The von Manteuffels have worked for Prussia for two hundred years and have always taken the responsibility for their actions. I, Hasso von Manteuffel, gladly accept this responsibility."

Keitel was unable to face down Manteuffel and turned his wrath on Heinrici, relieved him of his command, and then drove away in his staff car.[47] Manteuffel and Heinrici merely shrugged their shoulders and continued the retreat westward. Once again, Manteuffel demonstrated that he was a man of convictions who would not yield.

General von Manteuffel remained in British custody at various sites in England throughout 1945 and into 1946. In March, 1946, he returned to Germany to testify before the Nuremberg tribunal in the trial against OKW. Finally, shortly before Christmas 1946, he was released and went to work for the Oppenheim Bank in Cologne. He was soon rejoined by his wife, who had been in a refugee camp near Hamburg.[48]

Respect and admiration followed Manteuffel into civilian life. He was elected to the town council of Neuss-on-the-Rhine in 1947 (he was working for a manufacturing firm at the time), and from 1953 to 1957 he served in the West German *Bundestag* (Parliament). He was also a guest of several foreign military commands, including the Pentagon in Washington, and lectured at the U.S. Military Academy at West Point. He passed away at home, Diessen-on-the-Ammersee, on September 24, 1978.

BARON DIEPOLD GEORG HEINRICH VON LUETTWITZ, called Heinrich, was born on his family's estate at Krumpach in East Prussia on December 6, 1896.[49] His ancestors had been soldiers since the reign of Duke Heinrich I of Silesia (1321–1388), when one of them was knighted for service against the Poles. Thus a tradition of military service was deeply ingrained in the Luettwitz family over a period of centuries; in fact, Heinrich's first cousin, Baron Smilo von Luettwitz, also became a general of panzer troops, commanded the 9th Army on the Eastern Front, and ended up as a corps commander in the West German Army.[50] Heinrich's grandfather, a lieutenant colonel, had been killed in the Battle of Gravelotte in 1870, during the Franco-Prussian War. Baron Friedrich Karl von Luettwitz, Heinrich's father, also fought in that war, after which he retired from the army as a captain, returned to Krumpach, and lived the life of a Prussian Junker until he passed away in 1919.

Meanwhile, young Heinrich entered the regular German school system, in which he excelled. An avid horseman from the age of eight, he wanted to join the Imperial cavalry when World War I broke out but apparently was unable to get the permission of his father. Undeterred, Heinrich volunteered for the army and, at the age of 17, was rushed to the Western Front as a private. Heinrich's mother, Klara, sprang from another Prussian military family, the von Unruhs, who had considerable influence in the Imperial Army. In late 1914, her brother intervened on Heinrich's behalf and had him brevetted second lieutenant on December 4, 1914, two days before his 18th birthday. Luettwitz completed a quick officers training course and was given a Royal Prussian patent as a second lieutenant on June 18, 1915. He was immediately posted to the 48th Infantry Regiment, where he was given a rear-area assignment. (Friedrich von Stauffenberg speculated that the elder von Luettwitz used his influence to keep his son out of danger, and this seems very likely, but cannot be confirmed.) In any case, Second Lieutenant von Luettwitz was not satisfied with his new position and besieged higher headquarters with numerous written requests for a frontline assignment. This letter-writing campaign did not bear fruit until 1917, when Heinrich was given command of a platoon, which he led in the bloody trench fighting in northern France that summer. Here Luettwitz distinguished himself, earning the Iron Cross, First and Second classes, before being severely wounded. He was sent back to Germany to recover and did not leave the hospital until the spring of 1918. By this time his family had decided to use a little more influence on his behalf, and on May 2, 1918, Heinrich was transferred to the 3rd Troop of the 1st Uhlan, an elite cavalry regiment, as a troop leader.

General Ludendorff planned to use the 3rd Uhlan as a pursuit force, once his assault troops achieved their decisive breakthrough in the summer offensive of 1918. This breakthrough never took place, so the Uhlans were never used. Then the armistice came, and Luettwitz and his squadron returned to their garrison post at Brieg/Oels, in Silesia, and engaged in peace-keeping duties on the Polish frontier. Luettwitz was accepted into the Reichswehr as a second lieutenant in the 8th Cavalry (as his regiment was renamed) in late 1919. During this first period of garrison duty, Heinrich met and paid court to Jutta von Engelmann, the attractive sister of a fellow officer. They were married at the von Engelmann estate of Pzybor, East Prussia, in the fall of 1920. After a brief honeymoon they returned to the Luettwitz estate of Krumpach, before Heinrich rejoined his regiment. It was not destined to be a good marriage. Jutta gave birth to a son, Hans, on January 18, 1922, but she was unhappy living with her in-laws. She returned to her family in the spring, effectively ending the marriage.

Meanwhile, Heinrich von Luettwitz continued to serve in the backwater garrison post, finally receiving his promotion to first lieutenant on April 1, 1925. Then, in 1926, Lieutenant Colonel Baron Hans von Stein zu Kochberg assumed command of the regiment. He and the young officer liked each other very much, and Luettwitz spent a great deal of time with Stein and his daughter, also named Jutta, a beautiful 19-year-old noted for her ability as a pianist and equestrienne. Heinrich soon fell in love with her.

Just before his retirement in 1927 Stein arranged to have Heinrich enrolled in the senior regimental staff course of Wehrkreis Officers Training School. During the Christmas season Luettwitz went to Breslau and filed for a divorce, which was easy to obtain under the Weimar Republic. He received the final decree within a few days, and he and Jutta von Stein were married on December 11, 1928, at Ober Naundorf near Dresden. Their first child, a daughter named Christa, was born on July 21, 1929. A second (and final) child, a son named Hans-Jürgen, would be born in 1932. In the meantime, Luettwitz graduated from his staff course in early 1928 and remained at the school as an administrative officer. Then, in April 1929, the cavalry lieutenant enrolled in a special course aimed at training officers to control motorized formations via the radio. Although his love for horses never diminished, Luettwitz was converted to the revolutionary concept of motorized warfare from that time on. It was the turning point of his career. He became an enthusiastic disciple of Colonel Oswald Lutz, Germany's first inspector of motor troops. With the approval of his superiors, Luettwitz took part in various motorized training exercises at the school and was highly successful. For most of the next year (1929–1930), he traveled throughout Germany, conducting a series of lectures on mechanized warfare in the training centers of the other military districts. Few senior commanders, however, were ready to accept the new ideas, and the tour was generally a failure.

Luettwitz did not give up. On February 1, 1931, he was promoted to Rittmeister (captain of cavalry) and three weeks later took over a course in artillery fire control for motorized formations. Then he was sent back to Oels/Brieg, where he assumed command of the I Battalion of his old 8th Cavalry Regiment. By this time, however, the decision had been made to motorize the I Battalion, a process that von Luettwitz oversaw, along with the training of the battalion in the new tactics. He excelled in this difficult task and was rewarded by being given command of the 3rd Motorized Battalion, which was armed with the new PzKw I infantry tanks. He was promoted to major on January 1, 1936—the same day he officially transferred to the panzer branch.

In spite of his transfer to the tank arm, Major von Luettwitz continued to be an enthusiastic and outstanding horseman, and in 1936, he was named leader of the German Olympic Equestrian Team. His squad performed credibly in the autumn games and won several medals, but in Hitler's Germany the Olympic Games were no longer games. When Luettwitz did not capture the elusive gold medal, he was abruptly transferred to the staff of the 4th Cavalry Regiment at Insterburg, East Prussia, as a supernumerary. He was in unofficial exile for a full year, and someone in power in Berlin obviously held this failure against him for some time, as we shall see. However, Luettwitz did have something working in his favor: Hitler's rapid expansion and motorization of the Wehrmacht required a large number of trained motorized and panzer officers, and there were few available. In the summer of 1937, Berlin decided to motorize the 4th Cavalry, and on October 12, Baron von Luettwitz was given command of the regiment (which was part of the 1st Cavalry Brigade), to supervise this process. Once this program was well under way, however, the Panzer Inspectorate decided that an officer with more seniority should command it, and Luettwitz was demoted to the command of the I Battalion. He was nevertheless promoted to lieutenant colonel on March 1, 1939, and took command of the 1st Reconnaissance Battalion of the 1st Cavalry the day World War II broke out. This battalion spent most of the campaign in reserve in the East Prussian capital at Koenigsberg. It did not catch up to the rest of the brigade until September 14, when it rejoined the 1st Cavalry outside Warsaw. Two days later, Lieutenant Colonel von Luettwitz was wounded and had to be evacuated back to Koenigsberg for treatment. His World War II career had gotten off to an inauspicious beginning, to say the least.

Luettwitz was not able to resume command of his battalion until early 1940. There was not much satisfaction in this assignment, however, because the 1st Reconnaissance had been left behind in the east. While the rest of the panzer forces were gaining glory during the six-week conquest of France, Luettwitz cooled his heels in Prussia, fox hunting and going on long rides in the countryside. He felt utterly frustrated, for Luettwitz was an ambitious and partriotic soldier who wanted nothing more than to lead his command in action.

It was Major General Walter Nehring, the commander of the 18th Panzer Division, who rescued Lieutenant Colonel von Luettwitz from this professional limbo. The creation of the 18th Panzer was decreed by OKH in the fall of 1940, in response to Hitler's illogical desire to create more panzer divisions by weakening the existing ones. During this process the 101st Infantry Regiment was transferred from the 14th Infantry Division to the 18th Panzer, with orders that it be equipped and trained as a motorized formation. Nehring then asked for von Luettwitz specifically, because he realized the Prussian baron knew how to train men who had no experience in trucks and half-tracks. Luettwitz arrived at the 101st's home base at Chemnitz and immediately threw himself into his task. Then on January 3, 1941, despite the fact that he had achieved commendable results, he was abruptly ordered back to Koenigsberg as a reserve officer for armor under General of Artillery Gunther von Vollard-Bockelberg, the Wehrkreis commander. Walter Nehring was outraged enough to write a letter of protest to the Army Personnel Office, as did generals of panzer troops Erich Hoepner and Heinz Guderian. Although they were unable to get Luettwitz another command, they were at least successful in getting him transferred to the 1st Panzer Division as a supernumerary.

Heinrich von Luettwitz spent the first week of Operation Barbarossa as an observer with Army Group North. Then he got his third chance at a regimental command on June 29, 1941, when the commander of the 59th Rifle Regiment of the 20th Panzer Division was killed in action. Luettwitz was rushed to the Nieman River area (on the central sector of the front), where he assumed command of the 59th Rifle the following day. Now Luettwitz was to justify his years of hard work and training.

On July 6, the 20th Panzer began its advance to the Dvina. The following day Luettwitz took Ulla by storm and broke the Soviet line. Continuing in close pursuit of the enemy, Luettwitz outran his division and captured the key city of Vitebsk by coup de main on July 10. The Soviets realized that they could not leave this important city in German hands, so they threw their reserves against it in a series of fierce counterattacks. Luettwitz hedgehogged his regiment and held his positions until the rest of the division arrived two days later. Then the Soviets retreated toward Velizh, closely pursued by the 59th Rifle. After that the regiment was in more or less constant combat, driving to within 60 miles of Moscow in the process. Meanwhile, on October 1, Luettwitz was promoted to full colonel, to rank from November 1, 1940. He was awarded the German Cross in Gold on December 20, 1941.

Meanwhile, Stalin launched his winter offensive of 1941–1942. In terrible weather the 59th Rifle was slowly pushed back to a line east of Desna-Oka, which it held until the spring thaws effectively halted all operations. The 20th Panzer Division was then pulled back to Bryansk, to rest and refit. Baron von Luettwitz and his surviving officers worked diligently to integrate raw replacements into the regiment and were overjoyed at being able to equip the I Battalion with some of the new half-track personnel carriers. The refitting was completed at the end of April, at which time the division was transferred to the Orel sector, where its mission was to pin down Soviet reserves and help convince the Soviet High Command that the German summer offensive of 1942 would be launched against Moscow instead of toward its true objectives: the Caucasus oil fields and Stalingrad. Luettwitz performed exceptionally well in this secondary mission, during which he led a battle group and captured the town of Livny in heavy fighting. For this success he was awarded the Knight's Cross on May 27, and on June 8 was given command of the 20th Rifle Brigade, which consisted of the 59th and 101st Rifle regiments. His divisional commander, Major General Ritter Wilhelm von Thoma, the future commander of the Afrika Korps at the Second Battle of El Alamein, wrote of Luettwitz at this time, "passionate soldier, ambitious, sometimes more critical than necessary. With much combat experience he joined the front line fight himself. A professional soldier capable of improvising. Socially courteous, he leads men by his personality and handles them well, both in theory and in practice."[51]

Three weeks after Luettwitz received his brigade command, von Thoma was called to Berlin for another assignment. He was replaced by Major General Walter Duevert, who himself had just recovered from a case of nervous exhaustion, suffered in the winter battles as commander of the 13th Panzer Division.

The aggressive German attacks provoked the desired Soviet reaction—the commitment of reserves into counterattacks in the Orel-Oka-Livny sector and elsewhere. These were turned back in heavy fighting. In late July, Colonel von Luettwitz was touring his forward positions east of Livny when he was caught up in a sharp firefight. During this skirmish, he was severely wounded and spent the next three weeks in a forward hospital at Bryansk. He returned to duty on August 20, by which time the Soviet command had realized that the real heart of the German offensive was to the south. Luettwitz spent the rest of 1942 in the relatively inactive Voronezh-Livny sector.

In the meantime, the unfortunate General Duevert proved that he had not fully recovered from his nervous condition and had to be returned to Germany for further medical treatment.[52] On October 10, Luettwitz was named acting commander of the division. As the winter deepened and the German 6th Army was encircled at Stalingrad, it became obvious that Duevert would not be able to return to his post. As a result, Heinrich von Luettwitz was promoted to major general on December 1 and was confirmed as permanent commander of the 20th Panzer Division.

On January 5, 1943, the division was rapidly transferred to Orel, where it was given the mission of covering this important supply center. This Luettwitz accomplished despite heavy Soviet attacks. After the March thaw again brought operations to a halt, the 20th Panzer was once more withdrawn to Bryansk for another quick refit. On May 4, as the division was preparing to move back to the front lines, Luettwitz was ordered to turn command of the 20th Panzer over to Major General Mortimer von Kessel and to report to Berlin. The chief of staff of the High Command of the Army, Colonel General Kurt Zeitzler, assigned him to a special staff being formed to supervise the testing of new panzers being readied to go to Russia. By this time Colonel General Heinz Guderian had been named inspector general of panzer forces, a post Hitler had made virtually independent of OKH. Luettwitz and the other specialists on the staff felt that their mission was useless, as they were duplicating the efforts of Guderian's people, but they nevertheless made a serious effort at warning Zeitzler—and through him Hitler—that the new Panther and Ferdinand tanks were full of defects and should not be relied upon in the upcoming Kursk offensive. Both Guderian and Field Marshal von Manstein endorsed these reports, but to no avail. Meanwhile, Luettwitz was promoted to lieutenant general on June 1.

In July 1943, the German summer offensive was defeated at Kursk, largely because of the failure of their new tanks. Luettwitz went to the front to observe the battle and then returned to Berlin to write his report, which was filed and promptly forgotten. Luettwitz was then placed in Fuehrer Reserve, where he remained from September 25 to January 1, 1944. During this period he went home to Neuburg, the estate in northern Bavaria he had recently purchased, to spend some accumulated leave time with the family of his second, happier marriage. In January he again reported to OKH in Berlin, which sent him on an inspection tour of the panzer divisions in France. Upon returning to Berlin on January 25, he was summoned to the office of the chief of army personnel, Lieutenant General Rudolf Schmundt.

At Guderian's suggestion, Schmundt ordered Luettwitz back to Russia, to relieve the terribly depressed and exhausted Major General Vollrath Luebbe, the commander of the decimated 2nd Panzer Division.[53] After a quick visit to his family (January 27–28), he took an airplane for the southern part of White Russia, arriving at the railhead at Bobruisk on February 1, 1944. As General Luebbe went off for an extended rest leave at Bad Tolz, Luettwitz supervised the entraining of the remnants of the 2nd Panzer for transfer to the West, leaving what equipment survived for other panzer divisions still in Russia. On February 17 he set up his new headquarters in a spacious chateau on the outskirts of Amiens and began the monumental task of rebuilding his battered division, which included the 3rd Panzer Regiment, the 2nd and 304th Panzer Grenadier regiments, the 74th Panzer Artillery Regiment, and the 2nd Panzer Reconnaissance and 38th *Panzer-jaeger* (anti-tank) battalions.

The new replacements for the 2nd Panzer were mostly boys of 17 and 18, formerly exempted factory workers, and a few veterans of the Russian Front, returning from the hospital. Luettwitz was very careful to establish a good mix in the various regiments and battalions, so that no unit had too many "green" troops. He was even more careful with officers. He transferred or sent home no fewer than 20 prospective platoon leaders and company commanders who did not measure up to his standards of leadership qualifications. He also sent the veterans home on leave (on a rotational basis) and carefully screened the records, promoting many Iron Cross and German Cross holders to higher ranks. Luettwitz also made sure his charges got plenty of practice in the art of camouflage, night movement without headlights, and other skills they would need in the upcoming battles. The 2nd Panzer developed rapidly into an excellent division, and Luettwitz was commended by General Baron Leo Geyr von Schweppenburg, the commander of Panzer Group West.

In the fifth year of the war, however, Luettwitz could not make up all the division's deficiencies. The regimental commanders, for example, were all highly decorated veterans of the Eastern Front, but they had never exercised command at their present levels. Luettwitz devised a special series of exercises for these men and even gave them training at the next higher level. His four regimental commanders, for example, periodically rotated as divisional commander, and all the battalion commanders got the opportunity to act as a regimental commander, and the various company commanders got to practice as battalion commanders. Luettwitz showed considerable foresight in adopting this method of officer training, because many of the young commanders would, in fact, exercise command at the next higher level, due to the high officer casualties the 2nd Panzer Division would suffer in the days ahead.

The Allied D-Day avalanche hit the beaches in Normandy on June 6, but due to the paralysis in the German higher commands it was June 10 before the 2nd Panzer was ordered to the battlefield. Now the extensive training and practice in road movements under conditions of extreme enemy air supremacy paid dividends. Debouching from its camouflaged positions in and around Amiens and Abbeville, the columns of the 2nd Panzer Division made a series of advances by night and under cloudbursts and morning fogs. By June 14 its vanguards were in position along the Odon, ready to counterattack. The rest of the division was up by the following day. It had made a truly exceptional daily average of 60 miles per 24 hours. Even more importantly, the Allies did not know it was coming. This rapid advance enabled Luettwitz to launch a surprise combined arms attack against the veteran British 7th Armoured Division on June 14. At that time a British corps was attempting to work its way around the left flank of the vital city of Caen, and Luettwitz's mission was to stop and then throw back this dangerous offensive. Luettwitz was to distinguish himself in this operation and confirm what he had already proven in Russia: that he was an exceptionally good panzer division commander. Before the day was over the 2nd Panzer had succeeded in recapturing the critical Hill 174. At dawn on June 15, the Allied artillery laid down a heavy barrage on the German forward positions in order to disrupt any further advances, but the canny Luettwitz had pulled back his armor for just such an eventuality, and the bombardment was ineffective. By noon the 2nd Panzer, pushing forward again, captured the villages of Launay and St. Germaine d'Ector in heavy fighting.

June 16 was a day of regrouping for both sides. The battle resumed in earnest the next day, with a fierce battle developing at Le Quesnay. Colonel Siegfried Koehn's 304th Panzer Grenadier Regiment stormed this village on June 18, and a vanguard pushed the British back toward Briquessard. Simultaneously, the 3rd Panzer Regiment smashed a British armored force near Villers-Bocage and forced another Allied withdrawal. The night, however, the stubborn and tenacious British dug in around Briquessard, and Luettwitz was unable to dislodge them the next day, despite the fierceness of his attack; nevertheless, he could be well pleased with his results. Enemy losses had been heavy and Montgomery had to discontinue his attack at Caen for an extended period. Luettwitz's own casualties had not been light, however, and his calls for replacements went unanswered, due to Allied air strikes on the roads, bridges, and supply centers and Hitler's stubborn insistence that the Normandy landings were a diversion. He still averred that the main attack would come in the Pas de Calais area and kept the strong 15th Army there. Because of this, no infantry units were available to relieve the 2nd Panzer Division for more than a week, and the valuable mobile formations of Luettwitz's division suffered further attrition as a result.

Near the end of June, the 2nd Panzer was finally relieved and again successfully moved by night, this time to the southwest, toward Mortain and St. Lô, where an American offensive was expected. Luettwitz's division dug in along the Vire River and held its positions there on July 22, when it was pulled out of the line and placed in reserve. On July 29, it was sent back into the attack, with the mission of closing the gap in German lines between Notre Dame de Chenilly and the Vireo. Luettwitz gained some ground, but Allied fighter-bombers intervened and halted the attack before it could accomplish its objective. The Americans counterattacked Luettwitz's bridgehead in turn but were repulsed at Tessey and Beaucouvray in sharp fighting on June 29 and 30. Heavy fighting in this sector, however, continued for days.

On August 2, the Americans finally broke through the 352nd Infantry Division and overran its command post, killing its commander, Lieutenant General Dietrich Kraiss, and capturing most of his staff. Later that day, Baron von Luettwitz assumed command of the remnants of the 352nd, even though there wasn't much left of it, as it had been in action almost continuously since D-Day. These were the first reinforcements Luettwitz had received since May—and even this entailed assuming responsibility for a larger sector. Three days later his battered 3rd Panzer Regiment received its first reinforcements: a company-size battalion of 12 Czech-built Skoda tanks on loan from the Panzer Lehr Division. By now the 2nd Panzer Division was at half its original strength. All four of Luettwitz's original regimental commanders had been killed, and four majors were in acting command. Of these, Major Ferdinand Schneider-Kostalski of the 304th Panzer Grenadier would be killed in the first hour of the attack of August 7.

Meanwhile, the Americans had broken out of Normandy, and George Patton's U.S. 3rd Army was driving rapidly into the German rear. In East

Prussia, Adolf Hitler had a brainstorm and ordered XXXXVII Panzer Corps to attack due west and break through the U.S. 1st Army to the sea, thus cutting off Patton and forcing his surrender. The 2nd Panzer Division took part in this forlorn attack, along with the remnants of several other panzer divisions. Even though it penetrated the U.S. lines at two points, the 2nd never really had a chance of reaching the coast and suffered very heavy casualties to the American fighter-bombers in the process. On August 15, it was down to 1,874 officers and men, five self-propelled guns, and only seven tanks. Most of the division nevertheless managed to break out of the Falaise Pocket on August 20–21 in very confused fighting. During this battle the 2nd Panzer came under heavy American artillery fire, and control of the division was generally lost as men and vehicles made a frantic drive to get across the Dives River Bridge. Baron von Luettwitz was severely wounded as he tried to steady his men. He refused to hand over his command and go to the rear for medical treatment but instead restored order to the main body of his division and rallied it at Orville early on August 21. Here he was joined by his rearguard (the much-reduced 304th Panzer Grenadier Regiment under the gallant Major Ernst von Cochenhausen) later that day. Unlike the rest of the division, this unit had not panicked at the Dives River Bridge.

The confusion on the Dives did not repeat itself during the next several days, as Luettwitz helped cover the withdrawal of the shattered 5th Panzer and 7th armies. In this operation he fought a number of rearguard battles east of the Seine from August 22 to 25. Then the 2nd Panzer fell back to the vicinity of Spa, Luxembourg, where Luettwitz set up his headquarters on August 28–29. On September 1, General of Panzer Troops Baron Hans von Funck, the commander of the XXXXVII Panzer Corps, took matters out of Luettwitz's hands by giving him a direct order to go to the hospital. He was flown to Wiesbaden, where doctors found that his wound (which medics had treated with sulfa a week before) was healing well. Here, on September 3, Lieutenant General von Luettwitz received the Oak Leaves to his Knight's Cross. He was en route back to Spa the following day when he received a counterorder sending him to Metz, where he was to assume command of the XXXXVII Panzer Corps, because Baron von Funck had been summarily relieved as the result of one of Hitler's whims.

Luettwitz spent most of September rebuilding his depleted command behind the Moselle. On September 21, he directed a counterattack along the Marne-Rhine Canal toward Nancy, against Patton's aggressive forces. Striking in fog and under cloud cover, he achieved a temporary victory at Juwelize, but that afternoon the sun came out and with it the fighter-bombers. His spearhead, the 111th Panzer Brigade, was virtually destroyed. It lost its gallant commander, Colonel Heinrich Karl Bronsart von Schellendorff, and all but seven tanks and 80 men. Fuehrer Headquarters ordered that the attack be resumed the next day, but Luettwitz decided to regroup instead, and he was backed by his superiors (Generals Hasso von Manteuffel and Hermann Balck, commanders of the 5th Panzer Army and Army Group G, respectively). Luettwitz struck again on September 24, this time using the 559th Volksgrenadier Division and the recently arrived l06th Panzer Brigade. Again he initially achieved success, but the fighter-bombers (called *Jabos* by the Germans) appeared again and put an end to the advance. That evening, new orders arrived from Rastenburg. The XXXXVII Panzer Corps was to attack again the following day, this time using the 11th Panzer Division. The generals stared at each other in total disbelief. The 11th had been so badly mauled in the retreat from the Mediterranean that it had little combat strength left. Luettwitz was so furious with this order that he reportedly became almost hysterical, and Manteuffel thought it better to send him away. Much to Luettwitz's chagrin, headquarters, XXXXVII Panzer Corps, was sent north, to a quieter sector, and LVIII Panzer Corps (under the phlegmatic Walter Krueger) was ordered to direct the new attacks, which came to nothing. Later, after he calmed down, Luettwitz sent a letter to Manteuffel, apologizing for his behavior, and the army commander sent him a gracious reply.

In mid-October, the XXXXVII Panzer was pulled out of Alsace and sent north of the Rhine, where it assumed control of the 9th Panzer and 15th Panzer Grenadier divisions. These it directed in some limited-objective attacks in the Peel Marshes. It was pulling back to its reserve positions on November 9, when von Luettwitz was formally promoted to general of panzer troops, to rank from November 1. He again launched a series of spoiling attacks against the Americans from November 16 to 21, during which he halted the advance of the U.S. 2nd Armored Division and relieved the hard-pressed German infantry. Casualties were fairly heavy on both sides, and XXXXVII Panzer was again sent into reserve on November 24, but these orders were quickly countermanded when the Americans seized the town of Lindern. Luettwitz's forces were again thrown into the counterattack and even managed to surround the town, but their lack of infantry and the prompt Allied reaction doomed the operation to failure. On December 2, the corps was again pulled back into reserve. Six days later, Luettwitz and Walter Krueger were let in on a closely guarded secret: Hitler planned to launch a massive, surprise offensive in the Ardennes later that month. On December 12, Luettwitz and his two divisional commanders were among those taken by indirect routes from von Rundstedt's head-quarters at Ziegenberg Castle to the elaborately camouflaged Fuehrer Bunker at Adlershorst. Here they listened in grim silence to Hitler's rambling oration on his hopes and plans for the campaign. No one was particularly pleased with his exaggerated expectations, but naturally no one dared contradict him.

Upon his return to his own headquarters at Gerolstein, Luettwitz summoned his own divisional commanders and their operations officers to a special planning conference. For this offensive, Luettwitz was to have his old 2nd Panzer Division (under recently promoted Major General Henning Schoenfeld), as well as the 26th Volksgrenadier Division (Major General Heinz Kokott) and the Panzer Lehr Division (lieutenant General Fritz Bayerlein). The plan called for the 2nd Panzer to cross the Our River over bridges laid by his engineers and to push on to Houffalize by evening. On his left, Kokott would also cross the Our and then the Gerf, whereupon Bayerlein's armor would dash through the gap and drive for Bastogne.

Schoenfeld doubted the ability of his division's engineers to achieve its initial objectives and asked that the Fuehrer Begleit Brigade be released from reserve to support his attack. Luettwitz said that he would check into the state of his old division himself and get back to Schoenfeld, although he doubted if it were feasible to commit the Fuehrer Begleit so early, even if Field Marshal Model (the army group commander) agreed, which he also doubted. In fact, Luettwitz arrived in the 2nd Panzer Division's assembly area before Schoenfeld returned and found that his old subordinates disagreed with Schoenfeld's estimates of the division's capabilities. Luettwitz then went to Manteuffel's headquarters and asked permission to relieve Schoenfeld of his command. Manteuffel concurred and recommended that he be replaced by one of his own former subordinates from the Grossdeutschland Panzer Grenadier Division—44-year-old Colonel Meinrad von Lauchert, a holder of the Knight's Cross with Oak Leaves. Lauchert was already at Manteuffel's headquarters so the two were quickly introduced, and Luettwitz liked what he saw. At 9 a.m. on December 15, Luettwitz sacked Schoenfeld and replaced him with Lauchert, who immediately began an inspection of his new command.[54] He soon assured the corps commander that his division could accomplish its missions. Famous last words!

Lauchert had not been a divisional commander two days before Hitler's last major offensive of the war began on the morning of December 16. Luettwitz's corps struck along an 11-mile line against a single U.S. infantry regiment. Colonel von Lauchert succeeded in getting his 2nd Panzer across the Ourthe and was well on the way to Clervaux during the first 24 hours, but Kokott's grenadiers had less luck and thus delayed Bayerlein's forces, which were supposed to follow them across the river. By late on December 17, however, Bayerlein's tanks and grenadiers were finally on the move, making for the central town of Bastogne, which Luettwitz believed to be the corps' most important objective. Hitler, however, had directed that if Bastogne could not be taken quickly and easily, it was to be bypassed and left for the following infantry to deal with. As late as the night of December 18–19, Luettwitz was still appealing for permission to envelope Bastogne and attack it with his entire corps. Manteuffel turned down this request (he had no choice, given Hitler's orders) but did give Luettwitz authorization to launch a limited attack.[55]

Meanwhile, five miles north of Bastogne, the 2nd Panzer (which had swung north instead of attacking the heavily defended hamlet of Longvilly) ran into what Lauchert believed was a powerful defensive force at Noville. Since the defenders of Noville effectively blocked the advance to the west, Lauchert awaited the arrival of his badly strung-out main body—that is, until Luettwitz arrived. The panzer general, however, believed that the Noville positions were only lightly held and at once ordered an attack with tank support, which he proceeded to direct himself.

For once, the corps commander was wrong. Not only was Noville strongly held, but it was defended by brave and determined U.S. troops who delayed the entire 2nd Panzer Division a full 48 hours and inflicted disproportionate losses on von Lauchert's forces in the process. It was not until the evening of Wednesday, December 20, that the young colonel and von Luettwitz met on the gutted main street of Noville.

"I propose to drive south in pursuit of the enemy and capture Bastogne," Colonel von Lauchert suggested.

But, as we have seen, the commander of the XXXXVII Panzer Corps already had his orders. "Forget Bastogne and head for the Meuse," Luettwitz snapped.[56]

By this time Luettwitz was a full three days behind schedule. None of his divisions had done what they should have, and, at higher headquarters, Manteuffel and Model (the commander of Army Group B) were becoming more and more annoyed. Nor had things gone any better with his other two divisions.

Luettwitz's affinity for his own former command led him to habitually travel with the 2nd Panzer. Left to his own devices, Fritz Bayerlein of the Panzer Lehr developed his own ideas of how the offensive should proceed, and Kokott, his junior in rank, was dragged along with him. Having crossed the Clerf River during the night of December 17–18, Bayerlein split his forces and drove on Bastogne from two directions. He sent half his force toward Longvilly and headed down a back road via Niederwampach to Mageret with the rest (including most of the panzers). By 2 a.m. on December 19 he had secured Mageret, capturing an American hospital in the process. Badly informed of U.S. strength, he wasted almost four hours here, apparently trying to seduce an American nurse. Finally, about 5:30 a.m., he moved toward Neffe and again halted, this time for the better part of the day.[57]

Kokott's slower-moving infantry got involved in a two-day battle with the American defenders at Longvilly, thus frustrating any hope of a quick capture of Bastogne, which was heavily reinforced during these delays.

Although he did not have orders to defend Bastogne, the American commander in this sector, Lieutenant General Troy Middleton, was convinced that it had to be held even if its defenders had to accept temporary encirclement. The seven roads radiating from this modest town of 3,500 made it the hub of the road network for all of the southern Ardennes, and Middleton firmly believed that the Allies could not afford to abandon it to the Germans. Consequently, on December 19, he posted the bulk of his reserves here—18,000 men in all, including dozens of tanks and guns and the elite U.S. 101st Airborne Division.

By nightfall on the 20th, when Luettwitz at last turned his attention to his other two divisions, he discovered that the U.S. perimeter around the junction town was fiercely held and neither Bayerlein nor Kokott seemed to be making much headway. He read their reports with considerable annoyance—particularly the part about Panzer Lehr's taking to almost impossible back roads. "If Bayerlein can't read a map," he growled at Colonel Albrecht Kleinschmidt, his chief of staff, "then he should have let one of his staff officers do it!"[58]

Although he now had 45,000 men in the vicinity of Bastogne, Luettwitz, in conformance with his instructions, ordered the 2nd Panzer Division to bypass it to the north, while most of the Panzer Lehr bypassed it to the south. Kokott's 26th Volksgrenadier, reinforced with a regiment from Panzer Lehr, was left to handle the isolated American garrison.

During the next few days, Bastogne was completely sealed off by the Volksgrenadiers and the accompanying motorized infantry. The Neufchateau road, the last supply line into the town, was cut off only minutes after Brigadier General Anthony C. McAuliffe (the acting commander of the 101st Airborne) returned from a conference at the corps headquarters (General Middleton's VIII) in Neufchateau.

On December 21 and 22 the Germans pressed their attacks only desultorily, which incensed Baron von Manteuffel when he visited Luettwitz's headquarters at noon on the 22nd. Somewhat earlier, General von Luettwitz had ventured a maneuver that was to annoy his fellow commanders, amuse his enemies, and win for him a dubious place in the history of the Second World War.

Since the departure of the 2nd Panzer Division and the bulk of Panzer Lehr, the capture of Bastogne by attack would be both costly and time-consuming, and Luettwitz doubted if it could be accomplished at all with the forces at hand. He therefore decided to take by bluff what he could not take by force. Selecting a major and a lieutenant from his staff, Luettwitz directed them to bear a surrender ultimatum to the American commander in Bastogne. They reached the forward U.S. outposts about 11:30 a.m., where an American captain took their message to General McAuliffe's headquarters. Luettwitz's note informed McAuliffe that he was surrounded by strong armored forces, which would soon be reinforced by his own corps artillery and six heavy anti-aircraft battalions. If he wanted to avoid useless loss of life, Luettwitz stated, McAuliffe's only alternative was an honorable surrender. McAuliffe made the classic monosyllabic retort, "Nuts!" This he soon put in writing:

"To the German Commander: Nuts! From the American Commander."

When Hasso von Manteuffel was informed of this unauthorized ultimatum, he was furious. According to postwar interviews, this was the almost unanimous reaction of all the German commanders when they heard about the incident. When the two staff officers returned with the short but sharp refusal, the commander of the 5th Panzer Army was even more outraged. Luettwitz's bluff had been called. In fact, XXXXVII Panzer Corps could not even get its own artillery over the frozen roads to Bastogne, much less six heavy flak battalions, which it did not have.

Desperately, Manteuffel informed Army Group B headquarters of the situation at Bastogne and called for as much artillery as Model could spare. Failing that, he asked for Luftwaffe bombing attacks.

Model was unable to send the artillery; in fact, much of the divisional artillery of Luettwitz's three divisions had failed to get up to the front after six days. The air force, however, managed to mount a series of ineffective strikes against the town over the next four days, but these were far from the overwhelming punishment Luettwitz had so unwisely promised.

The unfortunate corps commander was not allowed to forget his rash act for some time, either. Manteuffel, who had lost faith in him, spent as much time as he could breathing down Luettwitz's neck, and when he was forced to absent himself to 5th Panzer Army Headquarters, he delegated Major General Carl Gustav Wagener, his chief of staff, to oversee the operations of his disgraced subordinate. Indeed, it is difficult to explain why Manteuffel left Luettwitz in command at all, unless it was because he considered the senior divisional commander, Lieutenant General Fritz Bayerlein, even less trustworthy.

Despite the urgent need for a rapid advance to the Meuse (as specified in Hitler's original plan), the encircled garrison of Bastogne took on an almost exaggerated importance in the minds of the commanders in Army Group B after it had been bypassed. Though von Lauchert's division was making fairly steady progress in the right direction, Manteuffel ordered it to divert one of its two grenadier regiments, plus artillery support, for employment against the pocket. By Christmas Eve, the crack Fuehrer Begleit Brigade—that legion of heroes specially chosen for their bravery to guard the Fuehrer—was committed to the attack, following in succession (as December turned into January) by the 9th Panzer Division, the 15th Panzer Grenadier Division, and part of the 116th Panzer Division.

All their efforts produced nothing. Not only was the inimitable General Patton able to break the siege on December 26 and open a supply route to McAuliffe's courageous defenders, but the westward drive of the 2nd Panzer Division came to a halt in the vicinity of Celles, about four miles from the Meuse, because it had run out of fuel. Then, on December 25 and 26, it fell victim to a rapidly developing Allied counterattack, spearheaded by the strong and relatively fresh U.S. 2nd Armored Division. The weather had now cleared and Allied Jabos were once again everywhere, pinpointing German positions, paving the way for the attacks of the ground forces, and blasting every German vehicle that moved.

In the ensuing carnage, the 304th Panzer Grenadier Regiment, the II Battalion of the 3rd Panzer Regiment, and two-thirds of the 273rd Panzer Anti-Aircraft Battalion were wiped out. About 2,500 German soldiers were killed or wounded and 1,200 captured. Some 450 trucks and 81 artillery pieces were also lost. Only about 600 men, led by the indomitable Major von Cochenhausen, managed to break out of the pocket. They eventually succeeded in reaching German lines—on foot. No vehicles or tanks escaped the American encirclement.

At the same time the 304th Panzer Grenadier Regiment was being annihilated, the 2nd Panzer Reconnaissance Battalion was attacked by the U.S. 82nd Reconnaissance Battalion and the British 29th Armoured Brigade at Foy-Notre Dame, less than two miles to the northeast. It also was destroyed.

As soon as he learned that a substantial part of his old division had been encircled, Luettwitz ordered Bayerlein to attack to the north and relieve the pocket. It was already too late, however; Bayerlein had barely started his move when Panzer Lehr found itself under heavy aerial attack. It then ran into strong forces from the U.S. VII Corps, which was just arriving on the battlefield. Soon Baron von Luettwitz ordered Bayerlein to go over to the defensive. There was no reason for him to go on to Celles, for the bulk of the 2nd Panzer Division had already been destroyed.

After Celles, all roads led back to Germany for the XXXXVII Panzer Corps. By January 28, 1945, the surviving German forces had their backs to the West Wall and the Roer River, almost where they had started from. The last great offensive had blundered to an ignominious defeat at great loss and expense—and with virtually nothing to show for it all.

By now, von Luettwitz's corps headquarters, with the battered remnants of the 2nd Panzer and Panzer Lehr divisions, had been switched south, to the Vianden area of the Our River, in the zone of General of Panzer Troops Erich Brandenburger's 7th Army, where the hard-pressed infantry divisions were being chopped to pieces by Patton's powerful forces.

Luettwitz was now thoroughly despondent. After a frightening series of air attacks on January 22, his troop strength was down to pitiful levels. Model, therefore, pulled his headquarters out of the area and sent it northward to Terborg, on the Issel River. At first the staff had no troop units attached, but toward the end of February the 15th Panzer Grenadier and 116th Panzers (under Colonel Wolfgang Mauch and Major General Siegfried von Waldenburg, respectively) were assigned to it. Between them, however, these two divisions could muster only 35 tanks. They were both seriously understrength in infantry, and most of their units had few veterans left. To make matters worse, the XXXXVII Panzer Corps now comprised the entire reserve of the recently formed Army Group H, commanded by the overworked and underpromoted Colonel General Johannes Blaskowitz.

Opposed to Blaskowitz's makeshift formations was a massive concentration of guns, tanks, and infantry under British Field Marshal Bernard Montgomery, who, in typical "Monty style," was preparing for a set-piece crossing of the Rhine. On March 24 this huge force was at last ready, and it began to cross the river at Rees and near Wesel in such strength that it was impossible to resist. Blaskowitz threw Mauch's grenadiers into a counterattack at Rees but with negligible results. The British were across the river in strength by the following morning.

Luettwitz's headquarters with the 116th Panzer was sent into battle south of Lippe against the American wing of the huge 21st Army Group, and by nightfall much of the 60th Panzer Grenadier Regiment had been killed or captured. Nevertheless this area east of the Rhine became Luettwitz's responsibility. He was given the newly arrived 190th Infantry Division, which had rushed south from Holland. Its commander, Lieutenant General Ernst Hammer, was a recuperee from the Russian Front and an ardent Nazi.

During the next three days, the irresistible mass of Montgomery's armies rumbled forward, pushing back or crushing everything in its path. The XXXXVII Panzer and LXIII corps were relentlessly driven back into the Ruhr industrial area, where a huge pocket was forming. Their last connection with Army Group H was severed by March 31, whereupon Field Marshal Model, still commanding Army Group B and in charge of the pocket, gave Luettwitz overall command of both corps as Group von Luettwitz. The group was holding from north and east of Lippstadt in an arc down the Lippe to the Moehne reservoir. Under him, for the first few days of April, were Special Division "Hamburg" and the 2nd Parachute, 116th Panzer, and 190th Infantry divisions (north to south). By now, Luettwitz shared the general opinion within the pocket that the war was over and that further resistance would be useless. As a result, the situation in the Ruhr Pocket deteriorated rapidly; however, it was April 15 before Model conceded defeat by dissolving the army group. It was now every man for himself. Some continued to resist, and some tried to make their way out of the pocket. Most, however, simply surrendered. The day following Model's order, Baron von Luettwitz and his staff joined Lieutenant General Bayerlein of the LIII Corps in capitulating to the Americans. General of Infantry Erich Abraham, lately the commander of the LXIII Corps and now acting as Luettwitz's deputy, also gave himself up.

Now Luettwitz and his associates began an extended period of imprisonment. As is evident from the interrogation records of the period, many of the German generals did not care for each other—and several had it in for the unfortunate von Luettwitz because of the Bastogne affair. This appears to have been particularly true of Bayerlein, whose own conduct during that battle is hardly above reproach, as we have seen. Certainly the U.S. historian Brigadier General S. L. A. Marshall was unimpressed with General Baron von Luettwitz. He wrote:

> Luettwitz is an old-time cavalryman. Now past 58, he is large, gross and paunchy. His monocle and his semi-belligerent manner of speech would

suggest that he is the typical arrogant Prussian, but among other German commanders he had the reputation of being especially kind to troops. He would talk only when he had a map before him; then he liked to lay pencils on the map to represent the movements of his regiments. What was most remarkable about him was that in battle he seemed to have concerned himself more with the movements of squads and companies than with the employment of divisions. He was frequently hazy about how his regiments had been disposed but he could invariably say what had been done by a particular patrol or outpost.[59]

Released from the POW camps in 1946, the now-retired General von Luettwitz finally reached his home at Neuberg in Bavaria, a bone-tired man, considerably overweight from months of forced inactivity, and with no real place in the world as it now was. He began once more to cultivate his horsemanship—so long forcibly neglected—and, with funds saved from the von Luettwitz's lands in the occupied East, again acquired a stable.

In this manner he passed the rest of his life. General of Panzer Troops Baron Heinrich von Luettwitz died at Neuburg on October 9, 1969, at the age of 73. He was survived by his two sons and his daughter, as well as by his wife.

5

THE PANZER COMMANDERS

Heinz Guderian. Hermann Balck. Walter Wenck. Traugott Herr. Wolfgang Fischer. Karl Decker. Dr. Heinz Goering.

No chapter on the German panzer commanders would be complete without at least a brief discussion of the life and career of HEINZ GUDERIAN, the "father" of the blitzkrieg. Since many of the details of his career are well known, this discussion will be somewhat abbreviated.

Guderian was born in Kulm, West Prussia (now Chelmno, Poland), on June 17, 1888. His father was Friedrich Guderian, a future Prussian general who died of natural causes as a brigade commander during the advance of 1914. Heinz was educated in the cadet school system and entered the service as a Faehnrich (senior officer-cadet) in the Hanoverian 10th Jaeger Battalion in 1907. At the time, his father was the battalion commander.

Heinz attended the War School at Metz (then part of Germany) in 1907, underwent officer training, and was commissioned second lieutenant on January 27, 1908. He remained with the 10th Jaeger until 1913, when he was transferred to the War Academy in Berlin, to attend General Staff training. This class never graduated, however, because World War I began in August 1914. Guderian was named commander of the 3rd Heavy Radio Section of the 5th Cavalry Division on the Western Front. Later he commanded the 14th Heavy Radio Section of the 4th Army in France (1914–1917) and was briefly attached to the Army High Command, again as a signals officer (1915–1916). He was promoted to first lieutenant in November 1914 and to captain in late 1915.

In the spring of 1917, Guderian had a series of orientation assignments as a supply officer (Ib) and intelligence officer (Ic) with various commands, including the 4th Infantry Division and X Reserve Corps, as well as a tour with the operations staff of Army Detachment C. In early 1918, he attended the abbreviated General Staff course at Sedan and, on what he later declared to be the happiest day of his life, graduated and became a General Staff officer. Guderian spent the rest of the war on the General Staff of the XXXVIII Reserve Corps and as Ia to the German commander in occupied Italy.

In the chaos after the armistice—what the Germans called "the war after the war"—Captain Guderian headed east, serving with border protection units in Silesia and with the Iron Division in the Baltic States (1919–1920). A right-wing officer and strong German nationalist, Guderian was very upset when General Hans von Seeckt, the de facto commander of the army, recalled the German forces from the Baltic. Guderian never forgave Seeckt, but the general was right—and was certainly more politically astute than Guderian.

After he returned to Germany, Guderian commanded a company in the 10th Jaeger, which was now stationed at Goslar in Lower Saxony. (Later it became part of the III Battalion, 17th Infantry.) Guderian commanded his company until 1922, when he was transferred to the 7th Motor Transport Battalion in Munich and then to the Department of Motor Transport Troops in the Defense Ministry. Here Guderian found his cause. He became the "Apostle Paul" on the idea of motorized and armored warfare, which he saw as the future. Collectively, they revolved around the word *blitzkrieg*, or lightning warfare. Despite opposition from certain senior generals and virtually the entire cavalry branch, Guderian advocated his ideas to anyone who would listen. He wrote articles for professional military journals, translated others, and even wrote a book on the subject. He also gained a great many converts—and made a great many enemies. He nevertheless continued to advance professionally, receiving promotions to major (1927), lieutenant colonel (1931), and colonel (1933).

Guderian's cause received a major boost in 1933, when Adolf Hitler became chancellor of Germany. Hitler considered himself to be a revolutionary and his party to be a revolutionary party. Naturally, he was favorably disposed toward revolutionary military ideas, such as the concept of the blitzkrieg, as advocated by Heinz Guderian. With the support of the Fuehrer, Guderian and his mentor and protector, General Oswald Lutz, the chief of the Motor Transport Inspectorate, Germany began to create panzer units. On October 15, 1935, the first three panzer divisions were activated. Colonel Guderian received command of the 2nd Panzer at Wuerzburg. He was promoted to major general in 1936.

Guderian led the 2nd Panzer until February 1938, when Adolf Hitler purged the army of many of its anti-Nazi leaders. Among those to go was General Lutz, who learned over the public radio that he had been involuntarily retired. Guderian was offered Lutz's job: chief of the Panzer Troops Command, along with a promotion to lieutenant general. He was delighted to accept and did not lift a finger to help his former protector.[1]

In 1938, Guderian led the XVI Motorized Corps in the occupation of Austria, after which he was promoted to general of panzer troops. The following year, he distinguished himself as commander of the XIX Motorized (later Panzer) Corps in the conquest of Poland. His greatest campaign, however, was in the conquest of France, in which he commanded seven of Germany's ten tank divisions. His corps was upgraded to 2nd Panzer Group in November 1940, and he was promoted to colonel general on July 19, 1940.

The German Wehrmacht invaded the Soviet Union on June 22, 1941. Guderian's panzers led the way from the very beginning and took part in some of Nazi Germany's greatest tactical victories: Bialystok-Minsk (290,000 Russians captured; 3,332 tanks and 1,809 guns captured or destroyed), Smolensk (310,000 Russians captured; 3,205 tanks and 3,120 guns captured or destroyed), Gomel (84,000 Russians captured; 144 tanks and 848 guns captured or destroyed), Kiev (667,000 Russians captured; 884 tanks and 3,718 guns captured or destroyed), and Vyazma-Bryansk (663,000 Russians captured; 1,242 tanks and 5,412 guns captured or destroyed).[2] As a reward for Guderian's victories, the 2nd Panzer Group was upgraded to 2nd Panzer Army on October 5, 1941, but after Vyazma-Bryansk, with the Russian winter fast approaching, Guderian took part in Army Group Center's last thrusts on Moscow and then faced Stalin's winter offensive with seriously depleted forces.

As mentioned earlier, Guderian had made enemies. Perhaps the worst of them was Field Marshal Guenther Hans von Kluge. He and Guderian hated each other so badly that they had almost fought a duel before it was forbidden by Hitler. Guderian had been scathing in his criticism of Kluge's conduct of operations as commander of the 4th Army in Russia, to which 2nd Panzer Group had briefly been attached. Nevertheless, on December 18, 1941, Kluge replaced Field Marshal Fedor von Bock as commander-in-chief of Army Group Center. His command included Guderian's 2nd Panzer Army.

Meanwhile, Adolf Hitler began issuing his tactically irrational hold-at-all-costs orders. Guderian ignored them. Kluge promptly reported his disobedience to Fuehrer Headquarters. Heinz Guderian was relieved of his command on December 26. He held no further assignments until after the fall of Stalingrad.[3]

The destruction of Friedrich Paulus's 6th Army shocked Hitler to the point that he recalled Guderian from disgrace. On February 28, 1943, he named "Fast Heinz" the inspector general of Panzer Troops. He placed Guderian in charge of all replacement panzer, motorized, and mechanized forces and equipment, including the formation of new units.[4] His authority encompassed such broad powers that he rivaled the chief of the General Staff as the leading officer within the army. Despite the opinion of some historians, Hitler's decision to create this post was a poor one, because it further divided the army command. Meanwhile, Guderian attempted to rebuild Germany's motorized forces, while he took part in the political infighting that characterized the Third Reich.

On July 20, 1944, Colonel Claus von Stauffenberg, Colonel General Ludwig Beck, and their colleagues launched a coup against the Nazi regime. Heinz Guderian came down solidly on the side of the Nazis and helped suppress the revolt. Afterward, suspension fell on many generals, among them Kurt Zeitzler, the chief of the General Staff of the army. The next day, Hitler replaced him with Heinz Guderian.[5]

After the war, Guderian wrote the World War II classic *Panzer Leader*. It is an extremely valuable historical work, but should be handled with care by the layman. Certainly Guderian presents himself in the best possible light and emphasizes his opposition to Hitler and the Nazis. Reality is somewhat different. He sat on the "Court of Honor," which expelled dozens of officers from the army, so that they could be tried and executed by the Nazis' People's Court. Although he later spoke of the Court of Honor with great disdain, he voted with the rest. Also, within 48 hours of taking charge, he replaced the traditional army salute with the Nazi (Hitler) salute. He also aided in the spread of Nazi propaganda within the forces. On the other hand, he did oppose Hitler's irrational tactical decisions at every opportunity. This led to a number of fierce altercations, which eventually resulted in Guderian's dismissal on March 28, 1945. Berlin fell less than five weeks later.

By this time, Guderian's estate had been overrun by the Soviets, and his wife had escaped one step ahead of the Red Army. Officially on leave, Guderian joined the staff of the inspector of panzer troops in Tyrol, Italy. He surrendered to the American army on May 10, 1945, and remained in POW camps until June 1948. He died of congestive heart failure at Schwangau in southern Bavaria on May 14, 1954. Guderian is buried in the Friedhof Hildesheimer Strasse in Goslar. His son Heinz (1914–2004), who was chief of operations of the 116th Panzer Division during the war, later became a general and headed the panzer inspectorate of the West German Army.

Born in Danzig-Langfuhr, East Prussia, on December 7, 1893, HERMANN BALCK joined the German Army in 1913 as an officer-cadet in the Hanoverian 10th Jaeger Battalion, a light infantry unit. He became a platoon leader on August 1, 1914, when World War I began, and was promoted to second lieutenant on August 10. By 1916, he was commanding a machine gun company. Balck saw action on the Western, Italian (Alpine), Balkan, and Eastern fronts. He was wounded five times and was nominated for the Pour le Merite in October 1918, but did not receive the award, probably because the Second Reich collapsed the following month.

Following the armistice, Balck joined a volunteer jaeger battalion. Selected for the Reichswehr, he remained in the infantry, initially as a battalion adjutant in the 20th Infantry. He was adjutant of the West Prussian–Brunwickian III (Jaeger) Battalion of the 17th Infantry Regiment at Celle (1920–1921), and a company and later staff and training officer with the 17th Infantry (1921–1925). He was promoted to *Obeleutnant* (first lieutenant) in 1924. Later that year he transferred to the 18th Cavalry Regiment at Cannstatt (near Stuttgart), where he led a machine gun platoon (1925–1928) and commanded a cavalry squadron (1928–1933). He was promoted to Rittmeister captain of cavalry on February 1, 1929. Even then, he strongly believed in the merits of mechanized warfare and the principles that would distinguish him as panzer commander in World War II.

Balck was square jawed with fiery eyes that signified his zeal and full commitment to duty. As a commander, he assumed all of his officers would obey his orders with the intensity that Balck himself brought to the battle. During the first six years of the Hitler regime, Balck advanced to the rank of major (1935) and lieutenant colonel (1938). In the meantime, he held staff positions at Frankfurt/Oder (1933–1938) and commanded the 1st Bicycle Battalion at Tilsit, East Prussia (now Sovetsk, Russia). He joined the staff of the Heinz Guderian's Inspectorate of Motorized Troops Directorate at OKH in 1938 and was here when World War II began.

After the fall of Warsaw, Balck was given command of the 1st Rifle Regiment of the 1st Panzer Division, and established the first bridgehead over the Meuse River during the Western campaign of 1940. Following the fall of France, Balck recommended that infantry and tank forces be more fully combined, which was later approved and strengthened German combat units' combat capabilities.

Promoted to colonel on August 1, 1940, Balck's next assignment took him to Greece in 1941, where he commanded *Panzerregiment 3* and afterward 2nd Panzer Brigade. It was Balck's panzer group that outmaneuvered the British at Mount Olympus, thus assuring Germany of victory in the Balkans. He was appointed to the Inspectorate of Armored Forces in July of 1941, an assignment that lasted until May 16, 1942, when Balck was given command of the 11th Panzer Division on the Eastern Front.

The 11th Panzer Division had a remarkable, successful combat record under the aggressive leadership of Hermann Balck. Colonel Balck often moved his division on night marches to strike the enemy at his most vulnerable positions at daybreak. Frequently, Balck would visit his regiments to make certain the officers were carrying out his battle plans. He also kept in constant contact with his officers by radio, even during the heat of the battle. Balck demanded a great deal from his officers and would not tolerate anyone who could not meet his standards. He sacked more than one officer during his career.

Balck was promoted to major general on August 1, 1942, and led his 11th Panzer Division in brilliant counterattacks against a Soviet thrust aside the Chir River near Stalingrad. Field Marshal Erich von Manstein, the commander-in-chief of Army Group Don, had held the 11th Panzer Division (one of the best equipped German panzer divisions) as a mobile combat reserve unit in his attempt to break through the Soviet encirclement of Paulus's 6th Army at Stalingrad. The Soviet commander, Marshal Georgi K. Zhukov, decided to punch holes in the German offensive that was threatening the Russian encirclement of Stalingrad.[6] On December 7, 1942, Zhukov sent two tank brigades from the 1st Soviet Tank Corps deep into the flank of the German 336th Infantry Division, stationed near the Chir River (a tributary to the River Don). The Soviet tanks reached State Farm No. 79, where they paused, awaiting arrival of Russian infantry the next day. Sensing an opportunity, Balck ordered regiments from the 11th Panzer Division to swing around State Farm No. 79 and take up a position on a hill overlooking the rear entrance to the agricultural complex, leaving a screen of 88mm guns and personnel at the forward end of State Farm No. 79. At day break, Russian infantry were moving toward State Farm No. 79 in a long column of trucks.

The German panzer battalions attacked and decimated the infantry column, while the 88mm fire confused the Soviet tanks in the agricultural complex. The Soviet tanks rolled out of State Farm No. 79, and were met by Balck's panzers, which appeared in small groups of three or four tanks and totally annihilated the Soviet armor. The Russians lost some 53 tanks against a German loss of less than 4. This engagement, and others to follow, was a prime example of Balck's combat philosophy: separate the tanks from the infantry for quick armored attacks in small groups, thus not exposing the entire armor of the division in a single engagement. Sometimes, Balck would also combine some of the grenadier regiments' anti-tank weapons and personnel with the tanks to deliver a stronger blow to the enemy. During the series of engagements in 1942, Balck destroyed the Soviet 5th Shock Army, thus preventing the Soviets from establishing a bridgehead on the Chir River. However, the intense fighting took its toll on men and machines of the 11th Panzer Division, while the Soviets continued to increase their firepower. The die was soon cast; Stalingrad would fall next month.

Balck was promoted to lieutenant general on January 21, 1943, and was later assigned to command the XIV Panzer Corps at Salerno. Unfortunately, while stationed there he was injured in an airplane crash, broke several bones, and was sidelined for a few months. He returned to combat duty as commander of the XXXXVIII Panzer Corps, following his promotion to *General der Panzertruppen* on November 12, 1943. His chief of staff, Colonel Friedrich Wilhelm von Mellinthin, praised Balck as the best panzer field commander of the war.[7] Balck's panzer corps saw combat in several major engagements on the Eastern Front, including the battles of Kiev and Tarnopol, in early 1944. Balck successfully destroyed three Russian armies, adding more hard-fought victories to his record, employing his usual night march strategy and concentration of mobile firepower at key points. His ability to move his tanks to the enemy's flank was achieved by his constant communications with his field officers, even during the heat of battle.

Recognizing the abilities of General Balck, the German High Command assigned him the command of 4th Panzer Army in 1944. Once again, Balck demonstrated his combat leadership by completely halting a Soviet offensive on the Vistula, near Baranov. He received the Knight's Cross with Oak Leaves, Swords, and Diamonds for his successful actions.[8]

Balck was transferred to command Army Group G in the West on September 21, 1944, replacing General Blaskowitz.[9] General Balck was told to halt General George S. Patton's U.S. 3rd Army Offensive in the Lorraine area of France. Balck soon found he had more of a "paper" army than a full-fledged fighting force. Several units were withdrawn from Army Group G for the upcoming Ardennes Offensive Hitler was planning. Balck had only one truly veteran division, the 361st Volksgrenadier, numbering 7,000 men. The other divisions either had no combat experience or were a mixture of veterans and recruits (including older men and 16–18-year-olds) who had no combat experience.

Still, Balck tried to set up an elastic defense, with the Metz Fortress as the lynchpin. Metz proved to be a formidable fortress for Patton, who assigned Walton Walker, commander of XX Corps, the task of taking the historic military fort.[10] With a significant number of Patton's forces engaged at Metz, Balck attempted to create mobile panzer forces to disrupt, and if possible, stop Patton's forward movement toward the German West Wall. Accordingly, Balck established *Panzerkampftruppen* (tank battle teams) consisting of two tank platoons and two panzer grenadier platoons.[11] These formations deflected Patton's offensive in 1944. However, Patton received additional supplies and replacements, and after Metz fell in late November, Balck had no choice but to retreat toward the Sarre River.

Angry that Balck was unable to stop Patton, and at Heinrich Himmler's urging, Hitler removed Balck from command of Army Group G in December 1944. General Heinz Guderian, Hitler's latest chief of General Staff, managed to convince Hitler to assign Balck a new command rather than simply cashier him. Consequently, Balck was given command of the reconstituted 6th Army, stationed in Hungary. The 6th Army was composed of both German and Hungarian troops. The onslaught of the Russian offensive in the spring of 1945 proved too much for Balck's men. He recognized that Russia would overwhelm his forces and, therefore, moved his troops to Austria so they could surrender to the U.S. Army's XX Corps.

After the end of the war, Balck remained in captivity until 1947. In 1948, he was arrested and convicted of murder for the execution of Lieutenant Colonel Johann Schottke, an artillery commander he found drunk on duty near Saarbruecken in late November 1944. The court found that Balck had had Schottke shot without a proper trial. He served half of a three-year sentence. After he was released, he found employment as a depot worker. Although Balck refused to be interviewed by the U.S. Army's Historical Division after the war, he did join his former chief of staff Mellinthin on panel discussions and in seminars with senior NATO officers in the late 1970s. Balck's own autobiography, *Ordnung im Chaos*, was published in 1981. General Hermann Balck passed away in Erbenbach-Rockenan, Wuerttemberg, West Germany, on November 29, 1982, and was buried in Asperg, near Ludwigsburg.

On the night of April 29–30, 1945, Field Marshal Wilhelm Keitel, the chief of the High Command of the Armed Forces, received an anxious message from Adolf Hitler, part of which read, "Where are Wenck's spearheads?"[12] The reference was to General **WALTER WENCK**'s 12th Army, which Hitler believed was the only hope for saving both himself and Berlin—a hope that ignored reality, as General Wenck had no tanks and very little artillery. Although Wenck had proven himself to be a brilliant improviser earlier in the war, the task of saving Berlin was an impossible one.

Walter Wenck was a handsome individual of medium height who always beamed with self-confidence. Born in Wittenberg on September 18, 1900, he entered the Cadet Corps at Naumberg (on the Saale River in Saxony-Anhalt) in 1911 and the senior cadet school at Gross-Lichterfelde in 1918. Following service in two Freikorps units, he was accepted into the Reichswehr as an enlisted man on May 1, 1920. He began active duty with the 5th Infantry Regiment at Stettin, Pomerania, but soon transferred to the elite 9th Infantry Regiment in Potsdam, with which he served until 1933. He received his commission as a second lieutenant on February 1, 1923.

In May 1933, Wenck (now a first lieutenant) was transferred to the 3rd Motorized Reconnaissance Battalion. After his promotion to captain in 1934, he underwent General Staff training and in 1936 was transferred to the staff of the panzer corps in Berlin. On March 1, 1939, he was promoted to major and joined the 1st Panzer Division at Weimar as its operations officer.

Wenck served with the 1st Panzer during the attack on Poland and in the Western campaign of 1940. During the German blitzkrieg through the Low Countries and France, Major Wenck was wounded in the foot but refused to leave his post. Late on June 17, the 1st Panzer Division reached its day's objective of Montbeliard and still had plenty of fuel. Wenck was unable to reach his divisional commander (Lieutenant General Friedrich Kirchner), so he signaled General Heinz Guderian (the commander of the XIX Panzer Corps), telling him that he had ordered an attack on Belfort on his own initiative. Guderian approved this bold move, which completely surprised the French.[13] Wenck was rewarded for his aggressive action and competent performance with a promotion to lieutenant colonel on December 1, 1940.

The 1st Panzer Division crossed into the Soviet Union on June 22, 1941, with Wenck still serving as operations officer. After pushing to within sight of Leningrad, the 1st Panzer was transferred to Army Group Center to take part in the final drive on Moscow. Like the other panzer divisions, it bogged down on the muddy Russian roads and could not reach the Soviet capital; it was surrounded by strong Soviet forces during their counteroffensive of December 1941. It broke out (according to plans drawn up by Wenck) and successfully made its way back to German lines. Wenck received the German Cross in Gold for his efforts and, two months later, was assigned to the War Academy to train General Staff officers, utilizing his own experiences as model lessons.

On June 1, 1942, Walter Wenck was promoted to colonel and in September was posted as chief of staff of the LVII Panzer Corps on the Eastern Front. At that time the corps was driving east in the Rostov-on-Don area of southern Russia.[14] He took part in the drive on the Caucasus, and in November, during the dramatic battle for Stalingrad, Wenck was attached to the Rumanian 3rd Army as its chief of staff. The Rumanians had just been mauled by the Soviets and most of them were in full flight, leaving behind only scattered remnants of various German forces. Wenck then "rode the highways and dragooned stragglers into ad hoc units. He played movies at intersections and when exhausted soldiers stopped to watch, Wenck brusquely marched them back to war."[15]

Soldiers pressed into Wenck's new army included remnants from the XXXXVIII Panzer Corps, emergency Luftwaffe formations, rear-area units of the encircled 6th Army, and men of the 4th Panzer and 6th armies returning from leave in Germany. Field Marshal Erich von Manstein, commander of newly created Army Group Don, met Wenck at Novocherkask and told the colonel, "You'll answer with your head if you allow the Russians to break through toward Rostov in your sector. The Don-Chir line must hold. If it does not, then not only the 6th Army in Stalingrad but also Army Group A in the Caucasus will be lost."[16] Wenck kept his head, and Manstein did not lose his army; the colonel stopped all the Soviet attempts to penetrate his line. For his valiant efforts Wenck was awarded the Knight's Cross on December 28, 1942, the day after he became chief of staff of Army Detachment Hollidt.

On February 1 of the following year, Walter Wenck was promoted to major general and on March 11 became chief of staff of the 1st Panzer Army. The 1st saw considerable action in 1943 and in March 1944 found itself encircled in the Kamenets-Podolsky Pocket near the Dneister River. Once again Wenck (called Pappi by the troops) played a major role in a German breakout. As a result, he moved up again (to chief of staff of Army Group South Ukraine) and was promoted to lieutenant general on April 1, 1944. He remained in this post for only four months, before being named chief of operations and deputy chief of staff of the High Command of the army (OKH). He now reported directly to Hitler and in his first briefing told the dictator that the Eastern Front was like Swiss cheese— "full of holes." Although Field Marshal Keitel was concerned with that kind of language (and direct honesty?), Hitler appreciated it and seemed to admire Wenck's intelligence and directness.

By the middle of February 1945, the Russians had reached the Oder River between Schwedt and Grunberg, leaving their flanks vulnerable.

The General Staff planned a counterattack by Army Group Vistula, commanded by Reichsfuehrer-SS Heinrich Himmler. In a heated argument, Heinz Guderian—now chief of the General Staff of the army—convinced the Fuehrer to appoint General Wenck chief of staff of the army group, in order to assure that the counterattack had at least some hope of success. Wenck's coordinated attack was initially successful; however, Hitler also required him to continue to attend Fuehrer briefings each evening—requiring him to make a round-trip of nearly 200 miles. On February 14, 1945, on the way back to the front, an extremely tired Wenck took the wheel of the car from his driver, Hermann Dorn, who had collapsed. Wenck fell asleep at the wheel, and the car went off the road, crashing into the parapet of a bridge on the Berlin-Stettin Autobahn.[17] Dorn dragged Wenck from the fiery wreck, pulled off the general's coat and doused out his burning clothes. Wenck suffered a fractured skull, five broken ribs, and numerous contusions. With Wenck in the hospital, the German attack failed.

While still recovering from the accident, Wenck was promoted to general of panzer troops on April 1, 1945. Early that same month Hitler created the 12th Army and put General Wenck (who was wearing a corset due to his injuries) in command. Wenck's army had no panzer units and only one anti-tank battalion. Originally positioned to defend against the Americans, Wenck was ordered to turn east on April 20 and attack the Russians. Wenck's goal, however, was to rescue General Theodor Busse's 9th Army, as opposed to saving Berlin (which was already virtually encircled by Soviet troops).

Shortly before midnight on April 22, a frustrated Field Marshal Keitel arrived at Wenck's headquarters.[18] Wenck was somewhat amazed to be receiving Keitel. The field marshal appeared in full dress uniform, saluted formally (touching his cap with his baton), and excitedly pointed to the map, telling Wenck that they must save Hitler.[19] Keitel told Wenck that the situation was absolutely desperate and that both Busse's 9th Army and Wenck's 12th must immediately drive toward Berlin. Wenck, realizing it was hopeless to argue with the agitated and irrational Keitel, merely said okay.

Walter Wenck, however, knew that time was running out for the 12th Army. Although he maintained his position and even launched a spearhead toward Potsdam, he did so only to give the encircled 9th Army an opportunity to link up with his forces. Furthermore, Wenck wanted to hold on as long as possible to allow refugees fleeing west from the Russians to seek refuge with his forces. At the last possible moment he intended to move westward and surrender to the Americans.[20] Field Marshal Keitel returned on the 24th and 25th of April, exhorting Wenck to liberate Potsdam and establish contact with Berlin. Although Wenck, surprisingly, managed to reach Potsdam on a narrow front, he simply did not have the resources to accomplish anything more. Hitler still hoped to be rescued, and on the night of April 29–30 signaled Keitel, demanding to know where Wenck was. For his part, Wenck managed to hang on until May 1, when a few remnants of Busse's army managed to break out and link up with the 12th Army. Wenck then gathered his forces together and, along with thousands of German civilians, hurried to the west, crossed the Elbe River, and surrendered to the Americans on May 7, 1945.

After the war, Wenck assumed a middle management position for a commercial firm in Dalhausen. He proved to be as successful in the business world as he was in the military. In 1950, he became a member of the management team of a large industrial firm, was appointed a member of the board of directors in 1953, and became chairman of the board in 1955. He retired from business in the late 1960s, although he continued to maintain an office in Bonn. He died in Bad Rothenfelde, Lower Saxony, on May 1, 1982, as the result of an automobile accident. He was 81 years old.

TRAUGOTT HERR was a good-looking, six-foot, 150-pound, blonde-haired, blue-eyed professional soldier who looked something like a model on a Nazi recruiting poster. He was born in Weferlingen, in Prussian Saxony, on September 16, 1890. He entered the service as a Fahnenjunker in the 35th (1st Brandenburger) Fuesilier Regiment at Brandenburg/Havel in April 1911, and attended the War School at Glogau. Commissioned second lieutenant in 1912, he went to the field with his regiment when World War I began and became a battalion adjutant in October 1914. He took part in the drive on the Marne and was severely wounded in late 1914 and again in the fall of 1916. After recovering from his second wound, Herr took a short course to be a machine gun company commander. He returned to the Western Front as a machine gun company commander in the newly formed 451st Infantry Regiment of the 234th Infantry Division. Promoted to first lieutenant in 1917, he remained with this division for the rest of the war, eventually becoming a deputy battalion commander.

Herr joined the Transition Army after the war and was selected for retention in the Reichsheer. He spent most of the 1919–1929 period in the 9th (Prussian) Infantry Regiment at Potsdam, although he did undergo training with the 3rd (Prussian) Motorized Battalion. He was promoted to captain in 1926. He was a tactics instructor at the War School at Dresden from 1933 to 1937, and was promoted to major in 1935 and to lieutenant colonel the following year.

Traugott Herr's career took a major step forward in 1937, when he was named commander of the III Battalion, 13th Motorized Regiment (III/13th Motorized) at Zerbst in 1937. He would be associated with motorized or panzer units for the rest of his career. Promoted to colonel on August 1, 1939, he was named commander of the 13th Motorized Replacement Regiment at Madgeburg when Germany mobilized on August 26. He was sent to Poland near the end of the campaign, assuming command of the 66th Motorized Regiment of the 13th Motorized Division on September 18. Herr led the 66th in the invasion of France the following year. He continued to impress his superiors and was named commander of the 13th Rifle Brigade of the 13th Panzer Division, when it was formed from the 13th Motorized in October 1940.

Herr's brigade took part in the invasion of the Soviet Union as part of Colonel General Ewald von Kleist's 1st Panzer Group (of Army Group South) in 1941, and saw heavy fighting at Uman, Kiev, and Rostov. His division commander, Major General Walter Duevert, collapsed under the strain of these operations, and Herr was named acting commander of the 13th Panzer on December 1. Duevert never fully recovered from his breakdown, and Herr was named permanent commander and was promoted to major general on April 1, 1942.[21]

General Herr continued to fight on the southern sector of the Eastern Front and took part in the drive across the Terek River and into the Caucasus Mountains. On October 31, 1942, however, he was seriously wounded when a piece of shrapnel struck him in the skull. He did not return to active duty until June 29, 1943, when he was named commander of the LXXVI Panzer Corps in Italy. Even then, he was not fully recovered and suffered from severe headaches. Germany, however, badly needed experienced panzer commanders, and Herr was an excellent one. He fought delaying actions against Montgomery's British 8th Army in Calabria (the "toe" of Italy) and launched a counterattack against the U.S. 5th Army at Salerno. Later, he fought the 8th Army in the Adriatic sector of Italy and took part in the Battle of Anzio. He also fought in the battles of the Gustav Line (Cassino) and in the retreat from Rome to the Arno and the Gothic Line. He directed all of his operations with an undeniable skill and was promoted to general of panzer troops on September 1, 1943.

Herr became acting commander of the 14th Army in Italy on November 24, 1944, but only held it three weeks. He stepped down for medical reasons on December 16 and underwent a brain operation (a result of his wound in Russia). He returned to Italy on February 15, 1945, as commander of the 10th Army. He defended the Adriatic sector against the British 8th Army in the final battles, but was severely hamstrung by Hitler's hold-at-all-costs orders. He was, however, not one of those officers who wanted to surrender against the Fuehrer's orders. As a result, 10th Army was overrun by the British. On May 2, 1945, he surrendered the remnants of his command to the 8th Army. He was a prisoner of war for the next three years.

Herr's former home was now in the Eastern Zone, so he relocated to Achterwehr, Schleswig-Holstein. Never accused of war crimes, he lived his final years in peaceful retirement and died on April 13, 1976.

WOLFGANG FISCHER was born on December 11, 1888 in Carolath, Upper Silesia. He entered the service as a Fahnenjunker in the 154th (5th Lower Silesian) Infantry Regiment on March 18, 1910. A career infantry officer, he was transferred to the 7th Landwehr Infantry Regiment as a platoon leader when World War I broke out, but was soon promoted to company commander. He was named adjutant of the 3rd Landwehr Division in late 1915 and became adjutant of the 22nd Landwehr Infantry Brigade in the fall of 1917, serving on the Western Front. He emerged from the war as a captain.

During "the war after the war," as the civil unrest of 1918–1920 was called, Fischer joined a battalion of volunteers. He was accepted into the Reichswehr in 1919 and was posted to the 3rd (Prussian) Infantry Regiment at Deutsch Eylau, East Prussia (now Ilawa, Poland), in 1920. He remained with the regiment until 1929, working as a regimental adjutant and as a company commander. In 1929, he assumed command of a company in the 6th Infantry Regiment at Luebeck and remained there until 1934. Promoted to major in 1932 and to lieutenant colonel in 1935, Fischer directed a battalion of the 46th Infantry Regiment at Neumuenster from 1934 to 1937, when he was promoted to colonel and joined the staff of the 69th Infantry Regiment at Hamburg. He assumed command of the 69th on February 4, 1938, during the Blomberg-Fritsch purge, when Hitler removed many anti-Nazi or non-Nazi officers and sent them into forced retirement.

Fischer's new unit consisted mainly of former *Landespolizei* (provincial policemen). They made good soldiers and fought well in Poland in 1939. Then, on October 27, 1939, for reasons not made clear by the records, Fischer was given command of the 10th Rifle Brigade of the 10th Panzer Division, which was then in the process of forming. Fischer led it in France (where he earned the Knight's Cross) and in the early stages of the Russian campaign, where he fought in the battles of encirclement of Minsk and Smolensk as part of Guderian's 2nd Panzer Group.

Fischer was promoted to major general effective August 1, 1941. The next day, he assumed command of the division. (His former commander, Ferdinand Schaal, had been picked to command a corps in France.)[22] Fischer distinguished himself as a divisional commander during the drive on Moscow, although his division suffered heavy casualties.

In the spring of 1942, the 10th Panzer was one of the divisions selected for a return to France, this time to rest, rebuild, and reequip. When the armies of Vichy France failed to offer more than token resistance to the Allied invasion of North Africa, however, Hitler ordered it occupied in November 1942. As the main German armored force available, 10th Panzer spearheaded one of the main columns, but experienced no resistance.

Meanwhile, the Allies drove on Tunis and threatened the rear of Rommel's Panzer Army Afrika in Egypt and Libya. To meet this threat, Hitler created Headquarters, 5th Panzer Army, and rushed reinforcements to the endangered sector. The most significant of the reinforcements was the 10th Panzer Division. Fischer (a lieutenant general since November 1) directed and led a series of brilliant counterattacks against the Anglo-American spearheads and pushed them back, thus saving the Tunisian Bridgehead. Then, on February 1, 1943, during the Battle of the Mareth Line, Fischer's command vehicle drove into a poorly marked Italian minefield. Wolfgang Fischer lost both of his legs and an arm in the ensuing exploration. He was fully conscious but in great pain and knew that he would soon bleed to death. With iron self-control, he ordered that some paper be brought to him, so he could write a farewell letter to his wife. He had written a page and a half when death overtook him. In recognition of his courage and undeniable skill as a panzer leader, he was posthumously promoted to general of panzer troops and was awarded the Oak Leaves to the Knight's Cross.

KARL DECKER was another in Germany's seemingly endless list of outstanding panzer commanders. Like virtually all of the tank generals, he began his service in another branch.

Decker was born in Boratin, near Neustettin, Pomerania (now Szczecinek, Poland) on November 30, 1897, the son of an army officer. He joined the army on August 3, 1914, just as World War I began, as a Fahnenjunker in the 54th Infantry Regiment of the West Prussian–Pomeranian 36th Reserve Division. He first saw action in East Prussia in 1914, and was then part of General Mackensen's pursuit to the Vistula. In 1915, he fought in Poland, Russia, and Courland (in present-day Latvia) and was commissioned second lieutenant on July 12. He would not be promoted again for 10 years and 13 days. He remained with his regiment as a platoon leader in a machine gun company and as a battalion adjutant, fighting in Galicia (1916). Along with his division, he was transferred to the Western Front in the spring of 1917 and fought in Lorraine, the Artois sector, Flanders, and the Battle of the Lys in 1918, where his division suffered very heavy casualties. It was holding a defensive position in a relatively quiet part of Belgium when the war ended.

Second Lieutenant Decker was accepted into the Reichsheer in 1920 and joined the 5th Infantry Regiment at Stettin. In 1921, he became adjutant of the II/5th Infantry at Prenzlau, but transferred to the 6th Cavalry Regiment at Pasewalk, Mecklenburg-Vorpomerania, in 1923. He spent a dozen years with the 6th, rising to the rank of Rittmeister (captain of cavalry) in 1931. He commanded a squadron in 1934 and 1935. After a year on the staff of the 15th Cavalry at Paderborn, Westphalia, Decker was promoted to major and named commander of the 38th Anti-Tank Battalion at Troop Maneuver Area Ohrdruf in Hessen in October 1936. Thus did Decker join the armored branch, because the 38th was part of Guderian's famous 2nd Panzer Division. He quickly learned about motorized warfare, was promoted to lieutenant colonel on April 1, 1939, and led his battalion with some success in Poland. In April 1940, he was given command of the I/3rd Panzer Regiment, which he led with great success in the battles of Sedan, St. Quentin, and Abbeville. He was wounded near the end of the French campaign, but was back in command of his battalion shortly thereafter, and led it in the conquests of Yugoslavia and Greece. For his role in the capture of the Balkans, he was awarded the Knight's Cross.

Karl Decker was accepted as a talented tank officer by May 15, 1941, when he succeeded Hermann Balck as commander of the 3rd Panzer Regiment. Part of the 2nd Panzer Division, Decker's regiment was part of OKH's reserve in the summer of 1941 and missed the early part of the invasion of Russia. It was, however, part of the 3rd Panzer Army during the last part of Barbarossa and the winter battles of 1941–1942. Decker, meanwhile, was promoted to full colonel on February 1, 1942.

Karl Decker continued to command the 3rd Panzer Regiment on the Eastern Front until January 1943, when he took charge of the 35th Panzer Regiment of the 4th Panzer Division for a month. Then he was sent home for a well-deserved leave, and, in April 1943, temporarily joined the staff of Guderian's panzer inspectorate. On June 20, 1943, he was named commander of the 21st Panzer Brigade of the 20th Panzer Division, on the central sector of the Eastern Front. Finally, on September 7, 1943, he was named commander of the 5th Panzer Division, also on the central sector. He was promoted to lieutenant general on June 1, 1944.

The 5th Panzer was arguably the best division in the German Army. Under Decker's command, the Soviet High Command paid it a huge left-handed compliment when it advised its generals that, if they ran into the 5th Panzer, the best way to deal with it was to try to go around it. When the Soviets launched Operation Bagration, which smashed Army Group Center in June and July 1944, the 5th Panzer managed to fight its way out, despite heavy odds against it. The division, however, suffered heavy losses in the battles around Bobruisk. Decker performed so well as division commander that he was awarded the Oak Leaves to his Knight's Cross and was given command of the XXXIX Panzer Corps on October 16.

Decker's new command was a rebuilt headquarters, replacing one largely destroyed in Bagration. Decker commanded it in Courland and East Prussia as part of the 3rd Panzer Army. Promoted to general of panzer troops on December 27, he was sent west at the end of the year and fought in the final stages of the Battle of the Bulge in January 1945. Serving as a fire brigade, the XXXIX Panzer fought in Pomerania in February, in Silesia in March, and on the Western Front in April. When Army Group B was surrounded in the Ruhr Pocket, however, General Decker realized that the war was hopelessly lost—as was his Pomeranian homeland, which had been overrun by the Red Army. In despair, and probably suffering from combat fatigue, Hans Decker took his own life at his headquarters in Gross-Brunsrode, Brunswick, on April 21. He was 46 years old. In an almost unprecedented gesture, he was posthumously awarded the Swords to his Knight's Cross on April 26—only four days before Adolf Hitler also committed suicide.

DR. HEINZ GOERING was the eldest nephew of Hermann Goering, the Reichsmarschall and commander-in-chief of the Luftwaffe—which also had its panzer units.

Heinz was born in Wiesbaden on September 4, 1907, the son of Heinrich Goering. Heinz attended college and received his doctorate in law from Wiesbaden in 1936. He was called up for active duty late that year and initially served as a gunner in the 9th Flak Regiment in Muenster. Heinz made no attempt to evade service, as he easily could have done. He was promoted to corporal in 1937, sergeant in 1938, and second lieutenant on August 1, 1940. Meanwhile, he became a platoon leader in the 141st Reserve Flak Battalion, which was stationed at Duesseldorf.

Heinz volunteered for duty with the Motorized Flak Regiment "General Goering" in the fall of 1940 and served as a platoon leader on the Eastern Front. He returned to Germany the following spring, married Charlotte Seelhof, and was assigned to the replacement (Ersatz) battalion of the Brigade "Hermann Goering." Eventually, he became a platoon leader in its panzer engineer replacement company. In late 1942, he became a company commander in the Hermann Goering Replacement Training Regiment. He was promoted to first lieutenant on July 1, 1942.

Heinz joined the Hermann Goering Panzer Regiment of the Hermann Goering Panzer Division in Italy in October 1943, and became the IIa (chief personnel officer) of that unit. He fought in the Italian campaign, where he was wounded and temporarily blinded by an exploding bomb. He nevertheless transferred to the III Battalion of the Hermann Goering Panzer Regiment, a *Stug* (assault gun) unit. He was advanced to company commander in March 1944.

Meanwhile, Army Group Center was overrun in June 1944, and the Hermann Goering Panzer Division was transferred to Poland, to help stem the tide, which it succeeded in doing. On July 29, Heinz Goering left his *Jagdpanzer IV* (a very modern assault gun) when the Reds launched an attack and a Russian shell exploded in the trees above him. Badly wounded, he was put aboard another Jagdpanzer IV and was about to be transported to the rear when three Soviet T-34 appeared and knocked out the assault gun. It is not clear whether Heinz Goering was already dead when his body fell into Russian hands, but, if not, he died shortly thereafter.

Despite a certain physical resemblance, Heinz Goering was nothing like his uncle. He was not corrupt, he was not lazy, he was not addicted to luxury or drugs, and he did not attempt to evade his responsibilities. He was, in fact, a credit to his family. He was promoted to captain posthumously.

6

THE LORDS OF THE AIR

**Hermann Goering. Erhard Milch. Walter Wever. Ernst Udet.
Wilhelm Balthasar. Hans "Fips" Philipp. Otto "Bruni" Kittel.
Prince Heinrich zu Sayn-Wittgenstein. Erich Hartmann.
Hans-Joachim "Jochen" Marseille. Kurt Andersen.**

From January 30, 1933—the day the Nazis came to power in Berlin—the leader of the German Air Force was HERMANN GOERING. Born in the Marienbad Sanitarium at Rosenheim, Bavaria, on January 12, 1893, he had a most interesting and exciting career. Assisted by Ritter Hermann von Epenstein, a rich and powerful half-Jewish aristocrat who was his godfather and his mother's lover, Goering was educated in the Karlsruhe Military Academy and the prestigious Gross-Lichterfelde Cadet Academy in Berlin. Commissioned second lieutenant in the Prince Wilhelm (112th Infantry) Regiment at Muelhausen in 1912, he fought on the Western Front in 1914. That winter, however, he became bored with trench warfare and transferred himself (!) to the 25th Air Detachment at Ostend, Belgium, as an aerial observer. When the commander of the Prince Wilhelm Regiment learned of this impertinence, he instituted court-martial proceedings against Goering, but these were quietly quashed by his godfather's friends at the Imperial Court, and Goering's transfer to the air service was soon given official sanction.

From the beginning, Lieutenant Goering proved to be an incredibly brave aviator, largely, it seems, because he did not believe he could be killed. In the Battle of Verdun (1915) he and his pilot, Bruno Loerzer,[1] performed so courageously that both won the Iron Cross, First Class, and were personally decorated by Crown Prince Friedrich Wilhelm. Goering's adventures were just beginning, however. By the end of the war he was a captain, a fighter pilot with 22 kills, a holder of the Pour le Merite, and was the last commander of the famous 1st Fighter Wing "Richthofen," whose original leader had been the Red Baron himself.

After the war, an embittered Hermann Goering briefly joined the Freikorps and then went into self-imposed exile in Sweden, where he seduced Karin von Kantzow (nee von Fock), the beautiful wife of a Swedish army officer. Karin soon left her husband and moved in with Goering, whom she would eventually marry after her divorce became final in 1923. Meanwhile, Goering—supported by his mistress and her husband's money—returned to Germany and, in 1922, enrolled in the University of Munich as a history and political science student. Here he met Adolf Hitler, the second and last hero of his life (his half-Jewish godfather had been the first). Hermann Goering served his Fuehrer and the Nazi Party in a variety of important jobs and assignments from 1922 to 1933, but only one is germane here: on November 9, 1923, during the so-called Beer Hall Putsch, Goering was in the front ranks when the police opened fire on the right-wing revolutionaries. A high-velocity 7.9mm slug hit him in the upper right thigh, just inches from the groin. He fell to the pavement and got dirt in the wound, causing serious medical complications. Given morphine to relieve the terrible pain, his metabolism was permanently altered. Besides becoming a drug addict, he quickly doubled his weight, ballooning to more than 320 pounds.

When Adolf Hitler took power, Hermann Goering assumed a multitude of offices. He was Hitler's chief deputy, president of the Reichstag, minister of the interior of Prussia, and minister without portfolio in the national cabinet. Soon he would add the posts of prime minister of Prussia, Reichs forest master, Reichs game warden, minister of aviation, and chief plenipotentiary of Hitler's Four Year (economic) Plan. He was also (unofficially) the commander-in-chief of the Luftwaffe. (The German Air Force was officially banned by the Treaty of Versailles; it was not until March 9, 1935, that Hitler officially announced its existence.) However, he had neither the time nor the inclination to personally direct the development of the Luftwaffe. This he left to his state secretary for aviation, Erhard Milch, and Lieutenant General Walter Wever, the chief of the Air Command Office and (unofficially) the first chief of the General Staff of the Luftwaffe.

ERHARD ALFRED RICHARD OSKAR MILCH was born on March 30, 1892, in Wilhelmshaven, the son of a naval pharmacist named Anton, who happened to be a Jew. Anton Milch left the navy in the 1890s and moved to the Ruhr, where he established his own pharmacy in Gelsenkirchen. His wife, the former Klara Vetter, left him in the 1900s and returned to her native Berlin, where she saw to it that her children received good educations. Erhard matriculated in 1910 and promptly volunteered for duty with the Imperial Navy, which turned him down, allegedly because of his Jewish ancestry.[2] Undeterred, he joined the 1st Foot Artillery Regiment at Koenigsberg and, after attending the Anklam War Academy, was commissioned second lieutenant in 1911. He was back with his regiment when World War I broke out.

Lieutenant Milch served on the Eastern and Western fronts as a battalion adjutant, aerial observer, intelligence officer, and (briefly) the commander of the 6th Fighter Group (*Jagdgruppe 6*), even though he could not yet fly himself. Promoted to captain in 1918, he was chosen to attend the all-important War Academy in Berlin, but the war ended before he could undergo his General Staff training. Then the Treaty of Versailles outlawed the General Staff and the air service and reduced the Officer Corps to 4,000 men. In 1920, a 27-year-old Milch found himself unemployed in a Germany rocked by revolution.

Erhard Milch returned home a disillusioned and embittered man. The Imperial Germany he had fought for no longer existed, and idealism in him was extinguished forever. From this point on, Milch had no guiding star except his own ruthless ambition. After briefly serving in the Freikorps and in the police, he went to work for Professor Hugo Junkers, the aviation pioneer, in 1922. Through ruthless corporate maneuvering he became chief executive officer of Lufthansa, the German national airlines, in 1929, at the age of 36. Later he turned on his mentor. As a result Hugo Junkers—a pacifist and the father of 12 children—escaped conviction on trumped-up charges of high treason only by dying in 1935.

Like his corporate life, Milch's home life was not above reproach. In 1927, he married Kaethe Patschke, the daughter of a landowner from Schoeneck, possibly because she was pregnant. Their first daughter was born later that year, and a second daughter was born in 1928. Milch, however, loved luxury, good food, fine wines, excellent cigars, and other pleasures of the flesh. He and his wife were separated by the late 1930s.

In 1929, the Nazi Party became a serious factor in German politics. Milch, very much aware of his Jewish ancestry, quickly ingratiated himself with the future Fuehrer and his lieutenants—especially Reichstag President Hermann Goering. By 1932, Milch had placed a Lufthansa airplane at Hitler's disposal (free of charge) and was depositing Lufthansa funds of 1,000 Reichsmarks a month into Goering's personal bank account. Milch was named Goering's deputy and state secretary for aviation in 1933. At the same time he was given the rank of colonel in the secret air force. Eventually he would be rapidly promoted: to major general (1934), lieutenant general (1936), general of flyers (1936), colonel general (1938), and field marshal (July 19, 1940). First, however, Goering had to conduct a cover-up of Milch's racial background. An "investigation" revealed that Milch's mother had carried on an adulterous affair with Baron Hermann von Bier for years, while still living with her husband but not having marital relations with him. None of her several children, therefore, were Jewish. ("If we're going to make Milch a bastard, the least we can do is to make him an aristocratic bastard," Goering is alleged to have quipped.) Based upon this incredibly thin tale, Goering had Milch's birth certificate reissued with Bier listed as the father. "Fat Hermann" then had Milch officially declared an Aryan and had his background file sealed, ordering that it never be re-opened. It was not, either, but whispers about Milch's ancestry continued until the end of the Third Reich.

Milch repaid Goering's generosity by attempting to use his influence with Hitler to ease Goering out as head of the growing air ministry and Luftwaffe, so that he could take his place. By now, Milch was too deeply entrenched in the Fuehrer's trust to be overtly sacked. Hitler had even presented Milch with the Golden Party Badge—a special mark of favor and distinction. Goering, therefore, employed the age-old political principle of divide and rule. He decided to pit Erhard Milch against the Luftwaffe General Staff, reasoning that if these two factions were at each other's throats, neither could challenge his own position. Hermann Goering knew less about how to set up and run an air force than either side, and although this ploy worked, it did irreparable damage to the Luftwaffe in the process.

None of this political intrigue mattered while **WALTER WEVER** was alive. Although he never officially held the title, Wever was the first chief of the General Staff of the Luftwaffe, from September 1933 to June 3, 1936. He was remembered by all who knew him as a man of incredible foresight, tact, diplomatic skill, and military ability. He was an officer in the finest professional traditions of the German General Staff and was arguably the only senior officer in the history of the Luftwaffe to consistently exhibit real strategic genius.

Wever was born in the eastern province of Posen (now Poznan, Poland) in 1887 and joined the Kaiser's army as a Fahnenjunker in 1905. In 1914, he served as a platoon leader on the Western Front. Promoted to captain in 1915, he became a member of the General Staff and in early 1917 was assigned to the staff of Field Marshal Paul von Hindenburg and General

Erich Ludendorff. Here his brilliance was fully recognized; for example, he was partially responsible for originating the concept of the elastic defense, which broke the back of the French offensive in the Chemin des Dames sector—a remarkable achievement for a company-grade officer. Continuing to exert influence far beyond his rank, Wever became Ludendorff's adjutant but broke with him professionally after the war, when the former quartermaster general began to demonstrate unstable and unrealistic right-wing political tendencies.

Walter Wever joined the Truppenamt (the clandestine General Staff) after the armistice and was held in high esteem by Colonel General Hans von Seeckt, the commander of the Reichsheer. He was promoted to major in 1926 and to lieutenant colonel in 1930; he was chief of the Training Branch of the army in 1933, when the Luftwaffe began its secret expansion.

General Werner von Blomberg, Hitler's defense (and later war) minister from 1933 until early 1938, was not a selfish man. Realizing that the embryonic air force was in desperate need of competent General Staff officers, he assigned some of his best men to the new branch. Foremost of these was Walter Wever, who was named chief of the Air Command Office and, in reality, chief of the General Staff of the Luftwaffe. When he transferred Wever, Blomberg remarked that he was losing a future chief of the General Staff of the army.

Colonel Wever quickly immersed himself in his new duties and in a remarkably short period of time grasped the fundamentals of how the Luftwaffe should develop. A firm and enthusiastic believer in National Socialism, he read Hitler's book, *Mein Kampf*, from cover to cover (a remarkable achievement in itself), and it became his strategic Bible. Unlike most of his peers, Wever learned that Hitler wanted no war of revenge against France and/or Britain; instead, the Fuehrer believed that Germany's principal strategic enemy in its struggle for German *Lebensraum* (living space) was Russia. Wever, therefore, designed and began to build the Luftwaffe for a strategic air war against the Soviet Union.

Wever believed that it was far more economical to destroy the enemy's weapons at their sources—the factories—than on the battlefield. He therefore demanded a heavy bomber that had sufficient range to reach Russia's industrial heartland and beyond—even as far as the Ural Mountains, which were 1,500 miles east of the Reich's nearest airfield. The result was the so-called Ural Bomber, a four-engine strategic airplane. By 1936, two promising prototypes were ready for test-flying—the Junkers 89 and Dornier 19. Wever—by now a lieutenant general—was not satisfied with their speed, so he instructed the German aircraft industry to develop additional bombers with greater horsepower. Guided by the inspired leadership and clearly stated, firm requirements of the brilliant chief, research and development work on the German strategic bomber accelerated and intensified in the first half of 1936.

In addition to General Wever's many other talents, he was also a master of the vital art of handling people. He made his way through the jungle of political intrigue that was the government of the Third Reich without resorting to intrigue himself but nevertheless having his way on all critical issues concerning the development of the Luftwaffe. For example, neither Goering nor Milch appreciated the need for a long-range strategic bomber, and both opposed its development. Then Wever—the consummate diplomat—went to work on them one at a time. Soon they were wavering, doubting their own previously held opinions, while the Luftwaffe continued to develop along the lines envisioned by the chief of the Air Command Office.

Lieutenant General Wever was a unique character in the history of Nazi Germany. In the context of a regime noted for its backbiting and political infighting, one searches the literature of the Third Reich in vain for negative references aimed at Walter Wever. Had this gifted officer lived, the outcome of the entire war might have been different. His skills as an aviator, however, were marginal at best. He was not a natural flyer and did not become a pilot until after he was transferred to the Luftwaffe in 1933. He had less than 200 hours of flight time in his logbook on June 3, 1936, when he flew to Dresden to address the cadets of the Air War Academy. He returned to the nearby airfield angry and upset because his co-pilot had disappeared. In a hurry to return to Berlin (to attend the funeral of General Karl von Litzman, a hero of World War I), Wever impetuously decided to skip the preflight inspection of his aircraft. This decision has killed many people who were far better pilots than Wever, before and since. When the unfortunate co-pilot at last returned from his unauthorized excursion, the general hustled him into the awaiting He-70—a type of airplane Wever had flown only once or twice before. In his haste, the general did not notice that the aileron lock was still engaged. As a result, his last flight was extremely short. The fully fueled Heinkel barely became airborne before it stalled, plunged to earth just beyond the runway, and exploded. Lieutenant General Walter Wever was killed instantly.

Hermann Goering cried like a baby at Wever's funeral. He then appointed Lieutenant General (later Field Marshal) Albert Kesselring to succeed him. Kesselring was the first in a series of chiefs of the General Staff Goering named to counterbalance the influence and ambition of Erhard

Milch. About all Kesselring and Milch could agree on was that the four-engine bomber was too costly in terms of raw materials and fuel consumption to produce. Goering duly acted upon their recommendations and, on April 29, 1937, ordered the heavy bomber scrapped, despite the objections of Colonels Paul Deichmann and Kurt Pflugbeil, the chief of the operations branch of the Luftwaffe and the inspector of bomber forces, respectively. As a result of this decision, Germany had no true strategic bomber in World War II. The Luftwaffe was not able to support the U-boats in the Battle of the Atlantic or to launch effective attacks against many of the factories of the United Kingdom in the Battle of Britain in 1940. The principal production facilities of the Soviet Union were also beyond the reach of the Luftwaffe throughout the war, while the Allies devastated the cities of Germany—with their own four-engine bombers.

Continuing his policy of divide and rule, Goering fragmented the Luftwaffe command apparatus in 1937 by making three offices independent of both the Air Ministry (Milch) and the General Staff. These were the Personnel Office, the Office of the Chief of Air Defense, and the Technical Office. By making them directly subordinate to himself, Goering had, in reality, made them independent agencies, since he was far too lazy to pay more than perfunctory attention to them. In the case of the first two offices, this made little difference, since they were directed by competent General Staff officers who needed no supervision. In the case of the Technical Office, however, it made a world of difference, because this vital agency was under the inept direction of Ernst Udet.

ERNST UDET was a World War I flying ace, barnstormer pilot, womanizer, drug abuser, adventurer, Hollywood stuntman, and borderline alcoholic. Had he been born two centuries earlier, he might have been a successful pirate. Born when he was, he was destined for tragedy, and he took the Luftwaffe with him.

The fun-loving Udet was born in Frankfurt-am-Main on April 26, 1896. After an unremarkable education in Munich, he entered Imperial service as a motorcycle dispatch rider for the 26th Infantry Division on the Western Front when World War I broke out. A war volunteer rather than a regular soldier, he managed to secure a discharge in the fall of 1914 and immediately volunteered for pilot training. He was turned down because he was too young, but this did not deter Ernst Udet. He returned to Munich and took private flying lessons, paid for by his father. He rejoined he service on June 15, 1915, as an enlisted man in the 9th Reserve Flying Detachment and was soon sent back to the Western Front.

Private Udet was initially assigned to the 206th Artillery Flying Detachment as an aerial observer in the Vosges sector. He quickly won a promotion to corporal (1915) and was awarded the Iron Cross, Second Class, for bravery. He also spent seven days in the stockade for needlessly destroying an airplane due to his own carelessness. Shortly after his release, he was promoted to sergeant and, in late 1915, was transferred to the 68th Field Flying Detachment in Flanders as a fighter pilot.

During his first aerial combat, Udet froze for the first time in his life and was almost shot down as a result. He soon mastered his fear and managed to shoot down his first enemy airplane (a French Farman) on March 18, 1916. He still had not fully developed his skills, however, and did not score another victory until October. He did not become an ace (i.e., did not score his fifth kill) until April 24, 1917. He was nevertheless promoted to second lieutenant of reserves in January 1917.

After he was named commander of the 37th Fighter Squadron on August 5, 1917, Udet came into his own. Just after he shot down his 20th victim (a Sopwith Camel) on February 18, 1918, Captain Manfred von Richthofen offered him command of the 11th Fighter Squadron, part of his celebrated 1st Fighter Wing. Udet took the Red Baron up on his offer and led the 11th for the rest of the war. Richthofen (a close friend of Udet's) was killed in action on April 21, 1918, and was succeeded by Captain Wilhelm Reinhardt, who died in an air accident a few weeks later. Almost everyone expected Udet to succeed him, and they were surprised when the choice fell to an outsider: Captain Hermann Goering.

Udet was initially suspicious of the future Reichsmarschall, but the two soon became good friends. Udet went on to shoot down a great many more enemy airplanes and was awarded the Pour le Merite. When the armistice was signed, Udet had 62 victories to his credit and was the leading surviving German ace.

When the war ended, Udet smashed his airplane and joined the anonymous ranks of job-seekers in the Weimar Republic. Initially employed as an automobile mechanic in Munich, he flew on Sundays as a stunt pilot for a POW relief organization, putting on exhibition dogfights against Ritter Robert von Greim, another former ace.[3] Then Greim flew into a high-power line and destroyed his airplane. Since no replacement could be found, Udet was grounded for a time, until he went to work for the Rumpler Works. He flew a regular route from Vienna to Munich for this firm until the Allied Control Commission confiscated his airplane, allegedly because it violated the Treaty of Versailles. After this, Udet went to work constructing sports airplanes.

Unhappy in the democratic Weimar Republic, former lieutenant Udet left for Buenos Aires in 1925 and began a prolonged period as an international wanderer. Finding employment as a charter pilot and barnstormer, he hopped all over the globe, from South America to East Africa, from the Arctic Ocean to Hollywood, California, where he was a stunt pilot in some American movies. He did not return to Germany until the advent of Adolf Hitler.

Udet's old friend Goering greeted him warmly when he returned to the Fatherland. The aging stunt pilot did not care for the idea of joining the new air force, but Goering insisted, so Udet relented and was commissioned colonel (on special assignment) on June 1, 1935. He became inspector of fighters and dive-bombers on February 10, 1936, and on June 9 of that same year became head of the Technical Office, which was expanded and renamed the Office of Supply and Procurement in 1938. In addition, Udet was named *Generalluftzeugmeister* (roughly translated as chief of air armaments) of the Luftwaffe on February 1, 1939. His promotions came rapidly: major general (April 20, 1937), lieutenant general (November 1, 1938), general of flyers (April 1, 1940), and colonel general (July 19, 1940).

It is hard to imagine a man less qualified for a high-level technical/managerial position than Ernst Udet. He had no advanced education and no industrial management experience, no military experience above the rank of lieutenant, no technological or General Staff training, and he did not have the shrewd ability to judge character that Sepp Dietrich used to partially overcome the deficiencies in his background in a somewhat related situation. Indeed, in Udet's case, quite the opposite was true. The new chief of air armaments had a talent for creating large, unworkable bureaucracies and picking the wrong man for the wrong job. Also, he was no match for the tricks of the German industrial and aviation magnates, who hoodwinked him almost daily. Even if he had possessed the mental qualities necessary to succeed in this exceedingly complex and demanding post, Udet probably would not have had time to do so. Mentally undisciplined, he hated desk work but proved to be psychologically unable to delegate authority. As a result, no fewer than 26 department heads were responsible directly to him. Udet, however, was seldom in his office. Usually he was too busy chasing women, smoking, throwing or attending wild parties that often lasted until dawn, and drinking until he could barely stand up. He also took drugs with depressing side effects and periodically went on diets in which he ate only meat. (And, judging from his photos, the diets did not work.) As a result of this regimen, department heads were unable to see him for weeks at a time, and critical decisions were often made by default or by Udet's chief of staff, Major General August Ploch, or his chief engineer, 34-year-old *Generalstabsingenieur* (lieutenant general of engineers) Rulof Lucht. Both these men had been promoted above their abilities.

A good example of the effect of the disastrous impact that Udet's office had on the Luftwaffe's war effort is the Ju-88 bomber. The standard bomber in 1937 was the He-111 medium bomber, which had a maximum speed of about 250 miles per hour, a range of only 740 miles, and a payload of only 2.2 tons. The prototypes of the twin-engine Ju-88, which was designed to replace it, were ready for test flying in March 1938. Unfortunately, Udet and the Air General Staff had been overly impressed with the concept of dive-bombing and with the success the Ju-87 "Stuka" dive-bomber had enjoyed during the Spanish Civil War against limited aerial opposition. With the concurrence of the General Staff, Udet added the design requirement that the Ju-88 be able to dive. As a result the airplane had to be greatly modified. Air brakes had to be added and the airframe strengthened, which reduced speed, range, climbing ability, and payload. Eventually the weight of the Ju-88 was increased from 6 tons to more than 12. The first model (Ju-88-A-1) was even slower than the He-111, which it was designed to replace. Although it was used in a variety of roles throughout the war, the Ju-88 never did perform well enough to replace the obsolete He-111 as the standard German bomber.

If the Ju-88 was a disappointment, the He-177s and Me-210s were disasters. In early 1938, Udet apparently decided that the Luftwaffe might need a long-range bomber after all. He initially wanted a four-engine bomber (as had Wever before him), but aircraft designer Ernst Heinkel convinced him to allow the development of the He-177, which featured four engines joined to two propellers by a coupling arrangement. A few months later, Udet issued the requirement that it be able to dive at a 60-degree angle. Heinkel was horrified and protested to Udet that an airplane of this weight (30,000 pounds) could not be made to dive, but the chief of air armaments brushed aside his objections. Heinkel had no choice but to try. By late 1938, when the He-177 prototype first flew at Rechlin, it weighed 32 tons.

In the Battle of Britain, the weaknesses of the He-111 and Ju-88 were exposed for all the world to see. Largely because of Udet's ineptitude, the German Air Force had clearly lost its previous superiority in military aviation technology, and the Luftwaffe lost its first battle. Udet's star, of course, began to fade. To restore his position with Goering and Hitler, and to quickly regain the technological edge, Udet gambled. In October 1940, he ordered the He-177 put into mass production despite unfavorable test

Hitler shakes hands with an officer while Field Marshal Wilhelm Keitel (right), the commander-in-chief of the High Command of the Armed Forces, looks on. The officer on the far left is Colonel Count Claus von Stauffenberg, who attempted to assassinate Hitler a few days later. *Source:* United States National Archives

Adolf Hitler in his Brownshirts uniform. *Source:* Nazi Party photo album from 1933, loaned to the author by former Captain Waldo Dalstead

Colonel General Alfred Jodl, the chief of operations at OKW, talks with Minister of Propaganda Dr. Joseph Goebbels. This photo was taken on July 20, 1944, only a few hours after the Stauffenberg assassination attempt. Jodl was slightly wounded in the explosion. *Source:* United States National Archives

Werner von Blomberg, minister of war and Hitler's first field marshal. He was forced to retire after marrying a prostitute in 1938. *Source:* U.S. Army War College

General of Artillery Bodewin Keitel, the brother of Wilhelm Keitel. *Source:* United States Army Institute of Military History

Colonel General Alfred Jodl, chief of operations of the High Command of the Armed Forces, en route to surrender the German Wehrmacht to General Eisenhower. *Source:* United States National Archives

Field Marshal Wilhelm Keitel signs the instrument of surrender to the Soviet Army in Berlin, May 9, 1945. *Source:* United States National Archives

Field Marshal Ritter Wilhelm von Leeb, who commanded Army Group C and North, 1939–1942. *Source:* Courtesy of John Angolia

Baron Wolfram von Richthofen (left) and Kurt Student, the "father" of the parachute branch. *Source:* United States National Archives

General of Flak Artillery Wolfgang Pickert (1897–1984), commander of the 19th Flak Division in Stalingrad and the III Flak Corps in Normandy. *Source:* Courtesy of Col. Ed Marino

Field Marshal Baron Wolfram von Richthofen, commander of the 4th Air Fleet. *Source:* United States National Archives

Field Marshal Friedrich Wilhelm Paulus, who surrendered the German 6th Army at Stalingrad. *Source:* United States National Archives

Hugo Sperrle, the first commander of the Condor Legion and later commander-in-chief of the 3rd Air Fleet (1940–1944). Although he performed well until 1940, he grew lazy and indolent as Luftwaffe commander in France and was sent into involuntary retirement after the German defeat in Normandy. *Source: United States National Archives*

Field Marshal Ritter Robert von Greim, veteran air fleet commander who succeeded Goering as commander-in-chief of the Luftwaffe in the last days of the war. *Source: Imperial War Museum*

A German 88mm anti-aircraft gun, destroyed in Normandy. *Source: United States National Archives*

Colonel General Alexander Loehr, commander of the Austrian Air Force (1934–1938) and later commander of the 4th Air Fleet on the Eastern Front (1941–1942). He later commanded the 12th Army (late 1942) and Army Group E (1943–1945). He was executed by the Yugoslavs after a show trial in 1947. *Source: United States National Archives*

The German Army on parade in the late 1930s. *Source: United States Army Institute of Military History*

Colonel General Heinz Guderian, father of the Blitzkrieg. *Source:* United States National Archives

A German panzer during German Army maneuvers, 1920s. *Source:* United States Army Institute of Military History

A Jadgpanzer self-propelled anti-tank gun. *Source:* U.S. Army War College

Lieutenant General Walter Wever, the first chief of the General Staff of the Luftwaffe—and a military genius. He died in an air accident in 1935. *Source:* Courtesy of John Angolia

Erich Hartmann (right), the highest scoring ace of all time. *Source:* Author's personal collection

Wilhelm Balthasar, the highest scoring German ace during the battle of France. A gallant gentleman who believed in chivalry, he was a throwback to an earlier era. He was killed when one of his wings collapsed during a dogfight in 1941. *Source:* Courtesy of John Angolia

Army Field Marshal Walter von Reichenau and Luftwaffe Field Marshal Erhard Milch, two military officers who were very friendly to the Nazis. *Source:* United States Archives

A Dornier Do-217 bomber, night fighter and high-altitude reconnaissance aircraft. Too mechanically complex and suffering from structural strain, it was an inadequate airplane and was typical of the poor models produced during the Udet era. *Source:* United States National Archives

Reichsmarschall Hermann Goering, the Supreme Commander of the Luftwaffe. *Source: Courtesy of Col. Ed Marino*

Ernst Udet, seen here as a lieutenant in Baron von Richthofen's "Flying Circus." The leading ace to survive World War I, he was over his head as chief of air armaments and played a significant role in the decline of the Luftwaffe. He committed suicide in November 1941. *Source:* U.S. Army War College

Colonel Johannes "Macki" Steinhoff (1913–1994), an ace who had 180 kills during World War II. He was severely burned at the end of the war. Later he became chief of staff of the Luftwaffe and a high-ranking NATO officer. His daughter married a former Colorado state senator. *Source:* Bundesarchiv

Prince Heinrich zu Sayn-Wittgenstein, the inventor of the "Dark Trains" on the Eastern Front. A top night fighter, he had 83 kills when he was shot down and killed in early 1944. *Source:* United States National Archives

Adolf Galland (1912–1996), the general of fighter pilots. *Source:* United States National Archives

Major Walter Nowotny (1920–1944), an Austrian-born fighter pilot, had 258 aerial victories when he was killed in action in November 1944. *Source:* United States Army Institute of Military History

Field Marshal Erhard Milch (right), state secretary for aviation and chief deputy to Hermann Goering, the commander-in-chief of the Luftwaffe. A ruthless political general, he attempted to maneuver the Reichsmarschall out of his post and become commander of the air force himself. He is seen here talking with Major General (later General of Fliers) Martin Harlinghausen, an anti-shipping expert. Harlinghausen later commanded the II Air Corps in Tunisia. *Source:* Author's personal collection

Hermann Goering visiting some of this troops during the Battle of Britain. *Source:* United States National Archives

Erich Hartmann (1922–1993), shown here as an officer-cadet. The leading ace in military history, he shot down 352 enemy aircraft in four years. The Soviets called him the "Black Devil of the Ukraine." *Source:* United States Army Institute of Military History

Allied air support over the hedgerows of Normandy, June 7, 1944. The aircraft on the ground are discarded gliders. *Source:* United States National Archives

Grand Admiral Erich Raeder, the commander-in-chief of the German Navy (1928–1943). *Source:* United States Army Institute of Military History

Naval Captain Wolfgang Lueth, a native of Estonia, became the number two U-Boat ace of World War II. As commander of the Naval School at Muerwik/Flensburg, he was killed by a German sentry on May 14, 1945, after he gave the wrong password. The sentry was acquitted by a court-martial. *Source:* Courtesy of John Angolia

Naval Lieutenant Guenther Prien, the commander of *U-47* and the first major naval hero in the history of the Third Reich. In early October 1939, Prien worked his way through the defenses of the major British naval base of Scapa Flow, where he sank the British battleship *Royal Oak*. Prien and the entire crew were killed in action on March 8, 1941 *Source:* Courtesy of John Angolia

German assault troops cross a river under enemy artillery fire, Western Front, 1940. *Source:* United States National Archives

Captain Erich Topp, the number three U-Boat ace of World War II. He later became a West German admiral and an architect. *Source:* Author's personal collection

SS Colonel General Paul Hausser, the father of the Waffen-SS. A former army lieutenant general, he did well as an SS panzer division commander, but was not as successful in higher commands. *Source:* United States National Archives

SS-Brigadefuehrer and Generalmajor der Waffen-SS Helmut Becker, a former concentration camp guard and the last commander of the 3rd SS Panzer Division "Totenkopf." Captured by the Soviets at the end of the war, he was executed for sabotage in 1953. *Source:* United States National Archives

SS Colonel General "Sepp" Dietrich, the former commander of Hitler's bodyguard regiment who rose to the command of the 6th (later 6th SS) Panzer Army. *Source:* United States National Archives

Right to left: Dr. Paul Joseph Goebbels, SS General Sepp Dietrich, and Adolf Hitler attend the funeral of a Nazi killed in the street fighting of the early 1930s. *Source:* Nazi Party photo album from 1933, loaned to the author by former Captain Waldo Dalstead

Left to right: Colonel General Bruno Loerzer and Hermann Goering confer with
Reichsfuehrer-SS Heinrich Himmler and Albert Bormann (the brother of Martin Bormann) outside Fuehrer Headquarters in 1944.
Loerzer, former commander of the II Air
Corps (1940–1943), was chief of personnel
armament at the time. *Source:* United States
National Archives

Utah Beach during the Allied build-up, June
9, 1944. *Source:* United States National Archives

A dead German infantryman killed in the
Battle of Cherbourg. He is still clutching a
live hand grenade, which is why no one had
removed his body. *Source:* United States National Archives

Luftwaffe officers go for a walk near Fuehrer
Headquarters in East Prussia. Left to right:
Field Marshal Baron Wolfram von Richthofen,
Colonel Nicholaus von Below (Hitler's Luft-
waffe adjutant), Colonel General Hans Je-
schonnek (chief of the General Staff of the
Luftwaffe) and General of Paratroopers Kurt
Student, commander of the XI Air Corps.
Source: United States National Archives

The German High Command. Left to right: Goering, Hitler, Keitel, Doenitz and Heinrich Himmler, the chief of the SS. *Source:* U.S. Army War College

The German surrender delegation in Berin, May 9, 1945. They capitulated to the Soviets because Stalin wanted a separate surrender. Left to right: Luftwaffe Colonel General Hans-Juergen Stumpff (1889–1968), the commander of Air Fleet Reich; Field Marshal Wilhelm Keitel; and Admiral Hans-Georg Friedeburg, the commander of the High Seas Fleet. Friedeburg committed suicide on May 23. *Source:* United States National Archives results. This disastrous directive started a time-consuming reorganization of the German air industry. The He-111 was taken out of production, numerous factories had to be closed and almost completely retooled, and mass production of the new bomber began. All of this took several months. When the new bombers rolled off the assembly lines they were found to have a number of critical problems—the most serious of which was the tendency to explode in straight and level flight for no apparent reason. (Apparently the fuel line dripped highly explosive aviation fuel on the hot manifolds.) They also broke apart during dives and had severe engine defects. Because so many of the new heavy bombers destroyed themselves during test flights (killing at least 60 veteran bomber crews), only 33 of the 1,446 He-177s that were manufactured during the war ever reached the front-line squadrons. Only two of these were still operational a few weeks later. As a result of the He-177 project, tens of thousands of industrial man-hours and huge amounts of raw materials were wasted.

The Me-210 was another one of Udet's disasters. Designed by Professor Willi Messerschmitt as a multipurpose reconnaissance/dive-bomber/twin-engine fighter, it was ordered into mass production by Udet solely on the basis of the reputation and skilled sales pitch of its designer. The result was a death trap: the Me-210 was an unstable and dangerously unpredictable airplane that whipped into spins at high angles of attack, killing a number of crews. Like the He-177, it was a total failure.

In February 1940, as the Luftwaffe's technological problems mounted and aircraft production lagged far behind schedules, Adolf Hitler sharply criticized Hermann Goering for the first time; Goering, in turn, lashed out at Ernst Udet for the first time. His criticisms became more and more pointed and vicious after the Battle of Britain, when the Luftwaffe's aerial supremacy ebbed. The happy-go-lucky Udet could not stand this kind of pressure and began to deteriorate both mentally and physically. In October 1940, Heinkel ran into him unexpectedly and almost did not recognize him. The aircraft designer recalled that Udet looked "bloated and sallow . . . as if he were heading for a nervous breakdown. He was suffering from irremedial buzzing in his ears and bleeding from his lungs and gums."[4]

Udet's condition worsened as Goering continued to berate him and Milch plotted to replace him. Formerly close friends (Udet had even taught Milch how to fly), the two were now bitter enemies. The state secretary did not let it escape anyone's attention that the best of the German airplanes (including the Me-109 single-engine fighter) were developed when the Technical Office was part of his domain, and Milch was not slow in taking advantage of the chaotic situation in the air armaments realm to regain some of the power he had lost in 1937. Goering, after all, really had no one else to whom he could turn in this area. Continuing his policy of divide and rule, however, the Reichsmarschall refused to replace Udet or subordinate him to Milch, but he did give the state secretary full powers to requisition or shut down aircraft factories, to requisition or reallocate workers and raw materials, and to sack or transfer key personnel within the air armaments industry. The result of this arrangement was more friction, for the ruthless Milch was not satisfied with half a loaf. He continued to lobby for full control of the air armaments industry and waged a war of nerves against the well-meaning but incompetent ex-ace. Before long, all of Udet's principal assistants had been replaced by Milch's yes-men, and the state secretary (with Goering's permission) had reorganized the Technical Office and the Office of Supply and Procurement in accordance with his more rational ideas. Meanwhile, as the war dragged on and air force casualties mounted, Udet's depression continued to deepen. On November 15, 1941, Major General Ploch (whom Milch had sent to the Russian Front) visited his former chief while home on leave. He told Udet about the mass murders of Jews and others taking place in the East.[5] Udet was horrified and very upset; he may have been incompetent, but Ernst Udet was not a monster. Two days later he drank two bottles of cognac and telephoned his mistress. "I can't stand it any longer!" he cried. "I'm going to shoot myself. I wanted to say goodbye to you. They're after me!" A few moments later, as she tried to talk him out of it, Ernst Udet pulled the trigger. He left behind a suicide note, asking Goering why he had surrendered to "those Jews" Milch and Major General Baron Karl-August von Gablenz, a principal Milch assistant.[6]

For propaganda reasons Udet was reported as having been killed in a crash while testing a new airplane. Goering wept at his funeral but later said of Udet, "He made a complete chaos out of our entire Luftwaffe program. If he were alive today, I would have no choice but to say to him: 'You are responsible for the destruction of the German Luftwaffe!'"[7] Goering's own responsibility in this destruction, of course, was not insignificant.

As the tide of the air war turned against Germany, Hermann Goering devoted more and more of his time to pleasure-loving pursuits. He lived "the life of Riley" with his second wife (a former actress) in a huge palace (which he tastelessly dubbed Karinhall after his first wife) on his massive estate in the Schoenheide, north of Berlin. On this 10,000-acre fiefdom (which he seized from the public domain at little or no cost to himself), he set up a private game reserve stocked with elk, deer, bison, and other animals, which he frequently hunted. He also acquired a castle in Austria and other properties and spent much of his time ransacking Europe for art treasures. In fact, he was probably the greatest art thief in history, for he considered himself the last Renaissance man, and his gigantic greed matched his corpulence. The bloated Reichsmarschall ballooned to around 320 pounds and went back on drugs again in the late 1930s; he was soon taking pills by the handful. Busy acting as Reichs Hunting Master and playing dress-up with an incredible number of uniforms and decorations, he pretended to be the hard-working master of the Luftwaffe, but in fact he had long ago given in to laziness, indifference, and indolence. In reality he had very little interest in the air force, as long as no one challenged his position as its undisputed leader.

With Goering preoccupied with luxurious living and Udet out of the way, Milch succeeded the late air armaments chieftain in all his offices. Reasoning that obsolete airplanes were better than no airplanes at all, he cancelled the Me-210, He-177, and Ju-288 (B-Bomber) projects and ordered that the obsolete Me-110s and He-111s be returned to mass production. Under his ruthless but capable direction, German aircraft production figures began to rise again in 1942. However, he could not make good five years lost to incompetence and neglect. He also continued to feud with the chiefs of the General Staff (Colonel General Hans Jeschonnek and others),[8] did his best to throttle the development of the jet airplane, and continued to plot to replace Hermann Goering—even to the point of suggesting to Adolf Hitler (shortly after Stalingrad) that the Reichsmarschall be relieved of his air force duties. Goering, his power and influence at a low ebb, could do nothing toward ridding himself of his deputy at this point, but neither did he forget the incident.

Erhard Milch was very slow in recognizing the potential of the jet airplane. He first saw a jet prototype fly in August 1939 (before the war began), but, like Udet, was not impressed. In 1941, however, when Professor Messerschmitt enthusiastically reported on the fine performance of his Me-262 jet prototype, Udet came out in favor of its speedy development. Milch refused to allow it, and Udet (now in decline) could do nothing about this decision. (Perhaps Milch had had enough of revolutionary aircraft types after the He-177.) A disappointed Messerschmitt continued to develop the turbojet clandestinely via a secret arrangement with BMW and Junkers. Milch did not even become marginally interested in the jet until 1943, when Lieutenant General Adolf Galland, the chief of the fighter arm, flew one and was deeply impressed. Milch respected Galland and allowed the

Me-262 to be put into production, albeit at a very low priority. In August 1943, Milch announced a production goal of 4,000 fighters per month and recoiled in shock and horror when Galland recommended that 25 percent of these be jets. This reaction, Trevor Constable and Raymond Toliver wrote, "exemplified, even as it reinforced, the Technical Office climate of hesitancy and irresolution."[9]

Unfortunately for Milch, he was unable to meet his ambitious production goals, and his prestige began to decline at Fuehrer Headquarters. Sensing this, Milch—like Udet before him—gambled. He ordered Volkswagen to begin mass production of the Fi-103 flying bomb even though severe technological problems had been reported in the prototypes. Two hundred defective Fi-103s were manufactured before it was discovered that their structures were too weak. More precious man-hours and resources had been wasted at a time when Germany was struggling against the combined industrial might of the United States, Great Britain, and the Soviet Union. Also, Milch now faced a new threat to his position: Minister of Armaments and War Production Albert Speer, a favorite of Adolf Hitler and a good political infighter in his own right. Taking advantage of the weakness of the Luftwaffe, Speer was making inroads into Milch's territory—the air armaments industry—by 1943. Goering, of course, refused to try to intervene on Milch's behalf, and Speer continued to raid the aircraft factories for skilled laborers; Milch continued to undershoot his production goals; and his stock continued to fall at Fuehrer Headquarters.

When Hitler became interested in developing the jet as a fighter-bomber, Willi Messerschmitt told him (on November 26, 1943) that the Me-262 could be modified to carry two 550-pound bombs or a single 1,100-pound bomb. Milch, fearing that his standing with the Fuehrer would be further diminished and ever mindful that Goering was only waiting for an opportunity to sack his would-be usurper, was afraid to tell the dictator that it was not possible to make these modifications; instead, he continued to develop the Me-262 as a fighter. Hitler, who had been led to believe that he was going to get a sizable number of jet fighter-bombers by D-Day, did not learn of Milch's duplicity until May 23, 1944—only two weeks before the Allies landed in France. Justifiably furious, Hitler withdrew his protection from Milch. Goering wasted little time in stripping his deputy of his power. On May 27, the entire air armaments industry was transferred to Speer's jurisdiction. Milch should have taken the hint and resigned at once, but he did not; therefore, on June 20, with Hitler present, Goering ordered him to submit his resignation as chief of air armaments and state secretary for aviation. This he did the following day.

Milch was allowed to retain the figurehead post of inspector general of the Luftwaffe. No doubt to the surprise and annoyance of Goering and others, Milch actually made a number of inspection trips; then, on October 1, his car skidded off the road near Arnhem and struck a tree. Milch, who woke up in the hospital, suffered three broken ribs and lung damage. He lay immobilized at his luxurious hunting lodge until early 1945.

With typical brashness, Milch showed up at Goering's palatial home, Karinhall, uninvited, on Goering's birthday in January 1945. He found the Reichsmarschall's attitude toward him was most unpleasant. Three days later he found out why: a week-old letter arrived from Goering, dismissing Milch as inspector general—his last remaining post. He was transferred to the Fuehrer Reserve and not reemployed.

Hitler's attitude toward Milch softened toward the end, and the Fuehrer even decided to put him in charge of a special staff to repair the German transportation system, but then changed his mind three days later. At the end of March 1945, Hitler sent Milch his usual birthday greetings, and the two met for the last time in the Fuehrer Bunker on April 21, nine days before the dictator committed suicide. Once again, even this late in the war, Milch was impressed with the Fuehrer's behavior.

In the early morning hours of April 26, Milch left his hunting lodge for the last time and headed north. He had really waited too long, for he passed Soviet tanks on the road, but the field marshal drove with his lights off and was lucky enough not to be halted. He drove to Sierhagen Castle (at Neustadt, on the Baltic coast), where the British arrested him at noon on May 4. Before the day was over, a British commando ripped his marshal's baton out of his hand and beat him to the floor with it. Like so many others on both sides, Milch was abused and tortured while in prison. Such acts were counterproductive in this case, however, because they turned Milch from a potentially friendly witness for the prosecution into a fervent defender of Hermann Goering—to spite his captors, if for no other reason.

Goering put up an excellent defense in his own behalf at Nuremberg and is praised even by his worst detractors for the mental skill he exhibited while making a certain U.S. Supreme Court Justice look foolish. This made little difference, as the end was a foregone conclusion and Goering was sentenced to death by hanging. The former World War I flying ace had one more trick up his sleeve, however; outwitting his opponents one last time, he committed suicide by taking poison at 10:40 p.m. on October 15, 1946—two hours before he would have been hanged.

Milch, meanwhile, was confined to a cell at Dachau called "the bunker." Designed for one person, its occupants included Milch, his old enemy

Kesselring, Field Marshal Walter von Brauchitsch (who was seriously ill and who died shortly thereafter of heart failure), Colonel General Nikolaus von Falkenhorst, and General of Infantry Alexander von Falkenhausen, the former military governor of Northern France and Belgium. Eventually tried at Nuremberg as a minor war criminal, Milch was convicted of deporting foreign labor to Germany, which resulted in enslavement, torture, and murder. The fact that he called the conspirators of July 20 "vermin" on the witness stand did not help his case. He was sentenced to life imprisonment and was incarcerated in the penal facility at Rehdorf. His sentence was commuted to 15 years' imprisonment in 1951, and he was released in 1955. The former state secretary settled in Duesseldorf, where he lived with relatives and worked as an industrial consultant for the aviation division of Fiat and for the Thyssen steel combine. His taste for power politics had apparently been cured, and he never attempted to return to the limelight or hold public office again. The last surviving Luftwaffe field marshal, Erhard Milch was much more genial in his later years than he had been in the days of his power. Hospitalized in late 1971, he died at Wuppertal-Barmen on January 25, 1972.

Due to Udet's incompetence, Goering's laziness, and Milch's combination of ruthless ambition, lack of foresight, and timidity in developing the new jet technology, German pilots spent most of the war flying obsolete airplanes. This makes their achievements even more remarkable.

WILHELM BALTHASAR was one of the earliest heroes of the Luftwaffe and an outstanding junior commander. Born in Fulda on February 2, 1914, he followed in the footsteps of his father, a captain and World War I aviator who was killed in Flanders only 10 months after the birth of his son.

Tall and thin, Balthasar was a throwback to an earlier era. He believed in chivalry and insisted that captured pilots whom he had shot down be brought to his headquarters so he could treat them to a meal and some wine and/or schnapps before they began their confinement in the POW camps. Balthasar was also known for taking care of his own young pilots (who were not much younger than he), and he had a reputation as an excellent flight instructor.

Balthasar joined the Luftwaffe in 1935 and, as a second lieutenant, first saw action in Spain in 1937, where he flew He-70 reconnaissance airplanes, obsolete He-51 fighters, and the new Me-109 fighters. He shot down his first victim, a Soviet-built Rata, on January 20, 1938. Then, in an incredible free-for-all dogfight, he shot down four adversaries in six minutes on February 7. He added two more victims to his list before he returned to Germany a short time later. There, Balthasar served as a squadron commander in the 131st Fighter Wing and in the 2nd Fighter Wing Richthofen. Shortly thereafter he first earned an international reputation as an aviator by flying around Africa (25,000 miles) in early 1939.

Balthasar did not see action in the Polish campaign but distinguished himself in France as commander of the 7th Squadron, JG 27 (see appendix V for a table of Luftwaffe unit abbreviations and designations at the wing level and below). On June 6 alone he shot down nine French airplanes, and on June 14 (the day Paris fell) he became the second member of the Air Force to receive the Knight's Cross. Balthasar (now a captain) was Germany's highest-scoring pilot in the Battle of France, accounting for 23 French and British airplanes in aerial combats, not counting another 13 he destroyed on the ground.

During the Battle of Britain, Balthasar was elevated to the command of III Group, JG 27. He was seriously wounded in the battles of September 4—an experience from which he never fully recovered psychologically. Nevertheless he was further elevated to wing commander on February 16, 1941, succeeding Major Helmut Wick as commander of JG Richthofen after the latter was shot down over the English Channel on November 28, 1940.[10] When most of the Luftwaffe moved east in May 1941, in preparation for the invasion of Russia, the Richthofen Wing was left behind to oppose the Royal Air Force in the skies over France. Despite the increasing odds and the lingering effects of his wound, the gallant Balthasar shot down his 39th and 40th enemy airplanes on June 27.[11] Meanwhile, some new Me-109F-4s arrived in France to replace the older Me-109E models. Noted for his technological expertise as well as his flying ability, the young wing commander did not like the new version of the standard German fighter because of its weak wings and aileron flutterings, among other things. Characteristically, Balthasar decided to test-fly the new airplanes himself. On July 3 he was making lazy turns and rolls near Hazebrouck (a town not far from Aire) when he was jumped by several British Spitfires. Balthasar immediately took evasive actions and engaged them in aerial combat, but suddenly his Messerschmitt plunged to the ground, killing him instantly. A subsequent investigation found that there were no bullet holes in his airplane; one of his wings had collapsed during the stress of combat.

At the time of his death, Wilhelm Balthasar had shot down 40 enemy aircraft (excluding the seven in the Spanish Civil War). He had already been awarded (but had not yet received) the Oak Leaves to his Knight's Cross. Shortly thereafter he was posthumously promoted to the rank of major. Honoring one of his last wishes, his men (after some searching) buried him in a cemetery near Abbeville, in the plot next to his father—a man he never knew but in whose footsteps he had followed—all the way to the grave.

HANS "FIPS" PHILIPP, the son of a Saxon physician, was born in Meissen on March 17, 1917. He first took an interest in flying as a member of the Hitler Youth, which offered its members glider training, with an eye toward sparking an interest in aviation among Germany's young men. This idea was quite successful and certainly worked in the case of Hans Philipp, who grew up to be one of Germany's most feared aces. He volunteered for the Luftwaffe as an officer candidate in 1936 and, as a lieutenant in the Polish campaign, scored the first of his 206 victories.

According to his commander, General Hannes Trautloft, "Fips" Philipp "took full part in all the joys of life"[12] and certainly enjoyed his role as a hero of the Third Reich. In aerial combat he was often compared to a duelist because of his uncanny marksmanship and his ability to take advantage of the slightest opening to inflict a fatal wound. Rising rapidly, he was promoted to first lieutenant and squadron commander (in JG 54) during the Battle of Britain and to captain and group commander (I/JG 54) in early 1942. He was the fourth pilot in the Luftwaffe to shoot down 100 airplanes and the second to shoot down 200. The eighth recipient of the Knight's Cross with Oak Leaves and Swords, he was also instrumental in training other high-scoring aces, including Walter Nowotny, who would eventually shoot down 258 enemy airplanes and would be the first commander of the first jet fighter wing in history.[13] Philipp was promoted to lieutenant colonel in 1943 and given command of the 1st Fighter Wing (JG 1) in Holland, where his mission was to defend the Reich against American heavy-bomber raids. Here he knew fear for perhaps the first time in his life. He once wrote that fighting 20 Soviet fighters or British Spitfires was a joy, but to attack a formation of Flying Fortresses "lets all the sins of one's life pass before one's eyes."[14]

Colonel Philipp led his wing against these monsters for six months, with some success. Then, on October 8, 1943, as he was leading an attack against a U.S. bomber formation over Nordheim, he was jumped by its fighter escorts and was shot down by a Thunderbolt. He was 26 years old.

OTTO "BRUNI" KITTEL was nothing like the extroverted Hans Philipp and certainly nothing like the propaganda version or public image of a German ace. He was a physically small, quiet, unselfish little man who spoke with a slight hesitation. Born in Kronsdorf (Komotau) in the Sudetenland on

February 17, 1917, "Bruni" Kittel began his career as an enlisted man and, in the fall of 1941, joined I/JG 54 as an NCO (noncommissioned officer) pilot. A late bloomer, Sergeant Kittel displayed deplorable aerial marksmanship at first, so he was tutored by Hannes Trautloft (then the wing commander), Hans Philipp, Walter Nowotny, and other members of the *Gruenherz* (Green Heart) Wing. These men never gave up on him, and their patience was rewarded in 1943, when Kittel found his shooting eye and started blasting Soviet airplanes out of the sky with remarkable frequency. Awarded the Knight's Cross in October 1943, Master Sergeant Kittel was given a battlefield commission and command of the 2nd Squadron of JG 54 in April 1944, and he led it with great success against overwhelming odds.

As the German armies in the East reeled under the sledgehammer-like blows of the Red Army, Lieutenant Kittel became a symbol and an inspiration for the air and ground forces alike. Once he was shot down and captured, but he managed to escape and make his way back to German lines after being missing in action for two weeks. He was later promoted to first lieutenant and decorated with the Knight's Cross with Oak Leaves and Swords—one of Germany's highest decorations, presented by the Fuehrer himself. Through all the excitement, however, success never went to his head; Bruni Kittel remained a modest, unassuming man to the end.

Kittel's squadron was isolated in the Courland Pocket in western Latvia in late 1944. On February 14, 1945, while flying his 583rd combat mission, Otto Kittel attacked a formation of low-flying Shturmoviks. While engaged in this low-altitude battle he was shot down, apparently by a Soviet anti-aircraft gun. When he died, Otto Kittel had 267 confirmed aerial victories, ranking him fourth among the leading fighter aces in the history of the world.

PRINCE HEINRICH ZU SAYN-WITTGENSTEIN was born in Copenhagen, Denmark, on August 14, 1916, the descendant of a Russian field marshal and the son of a German diplomat. Unlike Kittel, Prince Heinrich was an arrogant, highly intense, deeply patriotic, and extremely abrasive and ambitious young aristocrat. Military service was a tradition with his family, and he cared for very little other than personal glory and serving his country. His strong and humorless sense of self-discipline led him to demand the highest standards of himself and his men. He was respected, but certainly not loved, by his contemporaries. To his girlfriend, a White Russian émigrée, however, he showed an entirely different side of his personality. Initially an enthusiastic Hitler Youth, he was profoundly disappointed with Hitler and the Nazis. Unlike many of his contemporaries, he was sensitive to what was happening to Germany and, in 1943, even discussed personally assassinating Hitler when he received his next decoration, because he had access to the Fuehrer and considered himself expendable. Unfortunately, he would receive that decoration posthumously.

Wittgenstein (as he called himself) entered the Luftwaffe about the time Hitler declared its existence in 1935. He began his combat career flying bombers in 1939 and took part in the Battle of Britain as a captain in 1940. After more than 150 missions as a bomber pilot, he transferred to the night fighters in August 1941. (Prince Heinrich flew the Ju-88 bomber, an aircraft that was being used extensively as a night fighter in 1941.) In his new role, the prince proved to be a courageous warrior and an excellent air-to-air marksman with a sixth sense for danger. By 1943, he was Germany's leading night fighting ace. He also proved to be a highly competitive and envious young man; his wing commander, for example, had a difficult time making him take leave or go to Rastenburg to receive a decoration from the Fuehrer, because Captain Prince zu Sayn-Wittgenstein was afraid that Helmut Lent or Werner Streib might exceed his night kill total during his absence.[15]

Prince Heinrich was too concerned with his own personal victory totals to be a good junior commander; nevertheless, he was successively promoted to squadron leader (in the 2nd Night Fighter Wing [NJG 2]), group commander (I/NJG 100), and wing commander of NJG 2. In late 1942, he was sent to Russia to help devise tactics against Red Air Force night attacks. Here he commanded one of the first "Dark Trains"—self-contained air units that could be moved by rail to various sectors of the front and deployed rapidly on dirt fields, allowing the German pilots to surprise their Soviet counterparts on successive nights and to inflict heavy casualties on them. Sayn-Wittgenstein personally shot down 29 Soviet airplanes using these deployment tactics, including three in 15 minutes.

Sent back to the Western Front in 1943, he celebrated New Year's Day 1944 by shooting down six RAF heavy bombers. On January 21, 1944, Prince Heinrich (now a major) attacked a large formation of British bombers over Schoenhausen and shot down five of them. As the last bomber exploded, a Mosquito fighter (flying escort for the bombers) spotted him in the flames of the dying bomber and shot him down. Two members of his crew managed to bail out, but not Sayn-Wittgenstein. At the time of his death, Prince Heinrich zu Sayn-Wittgenstein had 83 victories—all at night. Fifty-four of these were scored against the British, and most of these were four-engine bombers. On January 23 he was posthumously awarded the Swords to his Knight's Cross with Oak Leaves. Initially buried in the cemetery at Deelen Air Base, he was later reinterred at the Prince Egmont zur Lippe-Weissenfeld Cemetery at Ysselsteyn, the Netherlands.

ERICH HARTMANN, the greatest fighter ace of all time, was born in Weissach on April 19, 1922. He spent part of his childhood in China, where his father was a practicing physician. Erich, however, took after his mother, Elisabeth Machtholf, who was a pioneer airwoman and sports flyer. In 1936, she helped establish a glider club at Weil im Schoenbuch, near Stuttgart, where her son learned to fly gliders. By 1938—at age 16—he was a fully qualified glider instructor, and his mother was teaching him how to fly powered aircraft. Hartmann, who was nicknamed "Bubi" ("boy" or "lad"), grew into a ruggedly handsome young man with blond hair and Nordic features. He joined the Luftwaffe on October 15, 1940 (at age 18) and was assigned to the 10th Luftwaffe Military Training Regiment at Neukuhren, near Koenigsberg, East Prussia. After completing basic training he began pilot training at the Air Academy School at Berlin-Gatow and in early 1942 was posted to the 2nd Fighter Pilots School at Zerbst, Anhalt, where he underwent training in the Me-109. In August 1942, after a very thorough and excellent education for aerial combat, he was posted to the 52nd Fighter Wing, then serving on the Caucasus sector of the Eastern Front.

Lieutenant Hartmann was in trouble almost from the beginning. He first saw combat on his third mission, during which he did everything wrong: he failed to keep his position, he flew into his leader's firing position (instead of protecting him), got separated from his leader, got lost, ran out of gas, and crashed into a sunflower field, destroying his airplane. Fortunately for him, he was only 20 miles from his base—and behind German lines. When he returned to his home airfield, Hartmann was given a severe reprimand and was grounded for three days as punishment. He resolved never to make the same mistakes again.

Back on flight status, Hartmann scored his first kill (an IL-2 fighter-bomber) on November 5, 1942. Apparently too excited by his victory to pay attention to his rear, he was promptly shot down himself a few minutes later, probably by a Lagg-3 fighter. He bailed out and his luck held: he was picked up by a German army vehicle. Hartmann did not score his second kill (a MIG fighter) until January 27, 1943.

The German fighter pilots said that slow starters had "buck fever." Erich Hartmann cured his buck fever in April 1943, when he had the first of many multiple-kill days. On July 7, during the Battle of Kursk, he shot down seven Soviet fighters. His tactics were a throwback to the days of the Red Baron: he tried to get as close as possible to his opponent before opening fire. He recalled that he normally pulled the trigger "only when the whole windshield was black with the enemy [aircraft]." He emphasized that a fighter pilot had to learn not to fear a mid-air collision.[16]

Hartmann's tactics were dangerous in the extreme. He was forced down 16 times—and at least three times his airplane was so badly damaged by flying debris from his victim that he had to crash-land. Remarkably, he was never wounded. His narrowest escape came in August 1943, when he was shot down behind Soviet lines and was captured. The quick-thinking Hartmann, however, faked an injury, so he would not be guarded too closely. He was thrown into the back of a truck with two guards but managed to escape four hours later, when the truck was buzzed by a Stuka dive-bomber. The driver ran the truck into a ditch and rapidly headed for cover, along with the guards. Hartmann also ran—in the opposite direction. Then he walked by night and hid by day until he reached German lines, where he was fired on by a nervous sentry. The bullet tore through his trouser leg but did not touch his body.

Meanwhile, Hartmann's reputation grew on both sides of the line. To Joseph Goebbels's propaganda machine, he was "the Blond Knight of Germany"—one of the Nordic supermen of the air. To the Soviets, and especially to the Red Air Force, he was "the Black Devil of the Ukraine." Stalin went so far as to place a price on his head.

In early 1944, Erich Hartmann became commander of the 7th Squadron/JG 52, and a few weeks later he was named operations officer of the III Group, 52nd Fighter Wing. Meanwhile, his victory total mounted. During one four-week period in the summer of 1944, he shot down 78 Soviet airplanes—including 19 in two days (August 23 and 24).

Near the end of August 1944, Adolf Hitler decorated Bubi Hartmann with the Knight's Cross with Oak Leaves, Swords, and Diamonds, in recognition of his unprecedented 301st victory—62 of which he had shot down in the previous six weeks. Then he went on leave and on September 10 married Ursula Paetsch, the only woman he ever loved. They had been steadies since he was 17 and she was 15. Hartmann then returned to the Eastern Front, where both the German Army and Luftwaffe were in danger of being overwhelmed. Hartmann received an accelerated promotion to major (he was only 22) and, in February 1945, was named commander of I Group/JG 52, which he led until the bitter end. Major Hartmann scored his 352nd and final victory over Bruenn, Germany (in Thuringia), on May 8, 1945—the last day of the war. When he landed from this, his 1,425th and final mission, his airfield was already under Soviet artillery fire; however, an American armored unit had been spotted 10 miles away.

Hartmann gave the order to burn the remaining airplanes, and he and his group headed for American lines, accompanied by dozens of women and children who were fleeing the Russians. Two hours later, at 1 p.m., they surrendered to the U.S. 90th Infantry Division at Pisek, Czechoslovakia. Their respite was short-lived, however. On May 16, the entire group was handed over to the Soviets, along with the women and children.

That night was the worst of Hartmann's life. The men and boys were separated from the women and girls and forced to watch as the Soviets raped the females repeatedly—including grandmothers and girls who had not yet reached their teens. Many were carried off in Red Army vehicles and were never seen again. The rest were returned to their fathers and husbands. Several families committed suicide that night, but, for Erich Hartmann, the ordeal was just beginning. When the Soviets found out that they had the Black Devil, they decided to break his spirit. They tortured him repeatedly, frequently kept him in solitary confinement in total darkness, and periodically denied him his mail. His three-year-old son, Peter Erich, whom Hartmann never saw, died in 1948. Major Hartmann did not learn of this until two years later. Nevertheless, despite all their efforts, Hartmann refused to endorse Communism, refused to cooperate with his captors, sabotaged work projects, and deliberately provoked his guards, possibly in hopes that they would kill him. When he was finally released in 1955, after ten and a half years in prison, both of his parents were dead, but Ursula was still waiting for him. Perhaps surprisingly, Erich Hartmann never hated the Russians. The emaciated ex-officer quickly regained his health and rebuilt his life with the help of his loyal wife. Their second child, a daughter named Ursula (and called "Little Usch" or "Boots"), was born in 1958.

In 1956, Hartmann joined the new West German Air Force and became commander of the 71st Fighter Wing "Richthofen" based at Fliegerhorst Ahlhorn in Oldenburg. Here he vocally objected to the adoption of the Lockheed F-104 Starfighter, which he considered a poor aircraft. Later, almost 300 crashes and the deaths of 115 pilots seems to have proven his opinion was correct. He had nevertheless offended several of the "powers that be," including former General of Night Fighters Joseph Kammhuber, who was now commander of the West German Air Force. Hartmann was forced to retire as a lieutenant colonel in 1970. He died in Weil im Schoenbuch, a town near Stuttgart, on September 20, 1993, at age 71.

Hartmann's younger brother, Alfred, also joined the Luftwaffe and served as a gunner in a Ju-87 in North Africa. He was captured by the British and spent the last years of the war in POW camps.

★   ★   ★

HANS-JOACHIM "JOCHEN" MARSEILLE was one of the most unusual of Hitler's junior commanders. Constable and Toliver wrote that he "was an anachronism. He was a knight born a few centuries too late, a beatnik born 15 years too soon."[16] A unique cross between a relentless killing machine and a hippie, Marseille had a brief career that was one of the most exciting and interesting in the history of the Wehrmacht—both on and off the battlefield.

He was born in Berlin-Charlottenburg on December 13, 1919, the descendant of French refugees who fled to Brandenburg because of their Lutheran religion. Hans-Joachim was the son of Siegfried Marseille, a World War I pilot and a police colonel in the interwar years who would later rise to the rank of major general in Hitler's army before being killed in action near Novoselki on the Russian Front on January 29, 1944. Jochen's father and mother permanently separated when he was a small child, which may partially explain the son's lifelong aversion to military ideas, attitudes, and appearance, including the dress code. He did love flying, however, which is why he enlisted in the Luftwaffe at the age of 18.

Marseille began flight training in November 1938, and showed great ability as an aviator, even though he was reckless and collected several reprimands for stunt flying in training aircraft and for other minor offenses. Even so, Master Sergeant Marseille was posted to Second Lieutenant Johannes "Macki" Steinhoff's squadron of the 52nd Fighter Wing (JG 52). Here he did quite poorly. Marseille claimed seven kills during the Battle of Britain, but only three were confirmed—indicating poor flying discipline, since he was so far separated from his comrades that there were no witnesses to confirm his claims. Marseille did, in fact, have a lone-wolf attitude. He was himself shot down or had to crash-land because he ran out of fuel at least four times (some sources say as many as six), but each time he managed to get his crippled Me-109 as far as the French coast before he bailed out or bellied into a beach or field. Meanwhile, his personnel file bulged with negative reports concerning his unmilitary behavior, his long hair, and/or his overly casual, bad attitude. Indeed, Marseille was more a lover than a fighter during this period. He was very good looking and had a manner that women seemed to find irresistible. Marseille, for his part, made no attempt to resist the females, who were attracted to him like a magnet. A genuine playboy, he would sometimes be so exhausted from a night of lovemaking with one or more women that he could not fly the next day.

Although Lieutenant Steinhoff showed great patience in dealing with this immature young man, the situation did not improve with the passage of time, and eventually the lieutenant had enough. "Marseille was extremely handsome," he recalled years later. "He was a gifted pilot and fighter—but he was unreliable. He had girlfriends everywhere, and they kept him so busy that he was sometimes so worn out he had to be grounded. His sometimes irresponsible way of conducting his duties was the main reason I fired him. But he had irresistible charm."[17]

Steinhoff went on to become a general and commander of the West German Air Force; Marseille returned to Germany in disgrace. In January 1941, however, the Luftwaffe Personnel Office assigned him to I Group, 27th Fighter Wing, which was the best move it could possibly have made, for I/JG 27 was earmarked to reinforce the battered Italian Air Force (the Regia Aeronautica) in Libya.

In North Africa, Hans-Joachim Marseille came into his own as a fighter pilot. Here, in the Luftwaffe's desert bases, there were no women to distract him and he was patiently tutored by a true expert: Major (later Major General) Edmund Neumann, the group commander. Before long, Marseille proved to be probably the best aerial marksman in the air force. He would sometimes return to base with as many as six kills and less than half his ammunition expended. In fact, he averaged only 15 bullets per kill—an amazing statistic! As a result, he was commissioned second lieutenant in 1941 (despite his personnel file) and, in December, was decorated with the German Cross in Gold by Field Marshal Kesselring. He had 33 victories at the time.

The handsome and sophisticated young officer from Berlin was extremely popular in the Third Reich, which idolized heroes of his type. Naturally Goebbels's propaganda ministry took full advantage of his story to bolster morale on the German home front, and Marseille received fan mail by the bagful—especially from women. Some of them were quite hysterical, others quite explicit—some with accompanying photographs. He was dubbed the African Eagle and the Star of Africa by the Italians, who were also crazy about him. Mussolini, for example, awarded him the Italian Gold Medal for Bravery, a decoration not even granted to Erwin Rommel, the Desert Fox. (But then, Marseille never told Mussolini what he thought of him; Rommel did.)

Meanwhile, Jochen Marseille was awarded the Knight's Cross following his 48th victory on February 24, 1942. That April he was promoted to first lieutenant and in June was made commander of the 3rd Squadron of JG 27. However, he was still too impetuous and individualistic to be a good squadron commander. His tactics were still those of the lone wolf, as was his entire outlook on life. His tent, for example, resembled a cross between Paris and something out of *The Arabian Nights*. Once he was visited by Lieutenant General Adolf Galland, the general of the fighter arm. After a few libations, Galland asked for directions to the latrine. Marseille handed him a shovel and told him to walk exactly 20 paces in a certain direction. Galland was surprised, but did as he was told. The next day, the amazed general found that Marseille had erected a small monument, complete with a sign and the date, to certify for future pilgrims that the general of fighters had indeed answered the "call of nature" on this particular spot.

In the wider theater, Field Marshal Erwin Rommel began his summer offensive of 1942 on May 31, determined that it would be decisive, one way or the other. Flying in support of it, Marseille attacked the Curtiss Kittyhawks of the South African Number 5 Squadron over Gazala on June 3. He shot down six of them in 11 minutes. Three days later he was awarded the Oak Leaves for achieving 75 victories. The fighting in North Africa was so intense, however, that he scored his 100th kill only 11 days later (on June 17), when he shot down 10 opponents—6 of which he cut down in only seven minutes! The next day he was promoted to captain and sent on leave to Germany, where Hitler decorated him with the Knight's Cross with Oak Leaves and Swords. Although he naturally enjoyed his leave (one wonders how many fan letters he answered), by now even Hans-Joachim Marseille was beginning to show the strain of the relentless air war over the harsh desert of North Africa, and he looked tired and drained.

Marseille rejoined JG 27 at Sidi Barrani on August 23. By this time Rommel's advance had been halted at El Alamein, and stalemate was setting in on the North African Front. The Desert Fox decided to make one more effort to break the deadlock—an advance that led to the Battle of Alam Halfa Ridge. Marseille and his squadron flew in support of this advance, and on September 1 he made history by downing 17 British aircraft in one day—a record against the RAF that still stands. (Only Luftwaffe Major Emil Lang shot down more airplanes on a single day, when he claimed 18 victories against the Red Air Force.) Captain Marseille, however, did no celebrating. He slept very little that night but lay in bed with his eyes wide open. He got up very early the next morning, sweating profusely. During September he did not have a single day's rest—there was too much RAF activity for that. This did not affect his performance behind the controls, however. "His fast reaction is incredible," Heinz Joachim Nowarra wrote. "He knows automatically what are his opponent's intentions, which he counters. He is absolutely sure that his burst of fire is lethal and attacks the next aircraft without waiting to observe results. Thus he is able to take every opportunity to shoot down one plane after the other."[18]

Marseille reached his peak in September 1942, when he shot down the incredible total of 61 British airplanes in a single month. He had shot down more British aircraft than anyone else in history, including Baron von Richthofen. In the middle of the month, Field Marshal Rommel summoned him to Panzer Army Afrika Headquarters and thanked him for his efforts. It was the only time they ever met. Meanwhile, in Rastenburg, Adolf Hitler awarded him the Diamonds to his Knight's Cross, Germany's highest combat decoration at that time, and an investiture ceremony was planned for later that year. By September 30 he had 158 victories against the British or their Western allies. That morning he led a sweep over the Cairo area but did not make contact with the enemy. On the way back, his cockpit suddenly filled with black smoke. Marseille was soon suffocating, but he kept on flying until he was over Axis lines. Near El Alamein, he dumped his canopy and bailed out, but, weakened by near-asphyxiation and probably nearly blinded by the smoke, he undoubtedly failed to notice that his airplane was in a shallow dive. Traveling at 400 miles an hour, he was caught in the airplane's slipstream and hurled into the tail fin, a blow that probably killed him. In any event, as his horrified comrades watched, he fell to the desert floor. His parachute never opened.

His body was found four miles south of Sidi Abdel Raman and was buried on the spot. Captain Hans-Joachim Marseille had crammed a great deal of living into the short span allotted to him. Had he lived another two months he would have reached his 23rd birthday.

KURT ANDERSEN was a member of an underappreciated branch of the German Luftwaffe: the flak artillery branch.

He was born in Hohenrade, near Koenigsberg, East Prussia (now Kaliningrad, Russia), on October 2, 1898. He joined the army as a war volunteer in the replacement machine gun company of the 3rd (2nd East Prussian) Grenadier Regiment of the 1st Infantry Division. He fought in France (including the Battle of Verdun) and on the Eastern Front, and was wounded at least once. In late 1916, he transferred to the signals branch and served in telegraph and telephone construction units until the armistice. After the fall of the Second Reich, he fought with General Count Ruediger von der Goltz's Iron Division in the Baltic States.

Andersen was discharged from the army in the fall of 1919 and joined the Landespolizei (land police), where he served in Elbing-Marienburg, Dortmund, and Duesseldorf. He was commissioned second lieutenant of police in late 1925 and promoted to first lieutenant in 1928 and captain in

1934. Given the chance to transfer to the Luftwaffe in 1935, he joined immediately. After a brief training course, Andersen became a battery officer in the 23rd Flak Regiment at Duesseldorf. He became a battalion commander in the Flak Lehr Regiment in 1938 and saw action in Poland and France. From June 1940 to November 1942, Andersen was commander of the Flak Artillery School at Stolpmuende, Pomerania (now Ustka, Poland), and was promoted to major (1938), lieutenant colonel (1941), and colonel (1942).

Kurt Andersen was named commander of the 153rd Motorized Flak Regiment on the Eastern Front in November 1942, during the week Stalingrad was surrounded. Here he distinguished himself in ground combat, where his regiment destroyed dozens of Soviet tanks on the Don River sector. (The German flak artillery was responsible for knocking out hundreds of Allied tanks on all fronts. The 88mm guns were especially deadly.) For his heroism, Andersen was awarded the Knight's Cross.

Transferred back to the Reich in June 1943, Colonel Andersen served as commandant of Air War School 6, where he was involved in training flak artillery troops. He returned to the Eastern Front in the spring of 1944, as flak artillery inspector, east. On January 30, 1945, he was named commander of the 23rd Flak Division, which he led in heavy ground fighting at Frankfurt/Oder, Kuestrin, and other battles east of Berlin. Promoted to major general on February 17, 1945, he surrendered the remnants of his division to the British at Tangemuende on May 8, 1945.

Andersen was a POW until 1948, when he rejoined his family at Wittlaer, near Duesseldorf. Three years later he joined the *Bundesgrenschutz* (West German Border Guard) as a *Brigadegeneral* (brigadier general). He retired 10 years later at the same rank.

General Andersen enjoyed a long retirement and died in Bonn on January 9, 2003, at the age of 104.[19] He is believed by this author to have lived longer than any of Hitler's generals.

Despite his age, Kurt Andersen was not the last of Hitler's generals to pass away. That distinction fell to Heinrich Trettner, who was born on September 19, 1907, in Minden, Westphalia. He died at Moenchengladbach-Rheydt, Westphalia, on September 18, 2006—one day short of his 99th birthday. During World War II, Trettner was chief of operations of Kurt Student's celebrated 7th Air Division—the world's first parachute division. Later he was chief of staff of Student's XI Air Corps, another parachute unit. He assumed command of the 4th Parachute Division in 1943 and led it on the Italian Front for the rest of the war, with considerable distinction. He was a lieutenant general when he was captured by American troops on May 3, 1945.

After the war, Trettner became a full general in the West German Army, directed logistics for NATO, and became inspector general of the armed forces. He retired rather than face court-martial in 1966, because he had so forcefully opposed the unionization of the German military—despite the opinion of the defense minister. He was the last surviving general of the Wehrmacht.

7

THE NAVAL OFFICERS

Erich Raeder. Hermann Boehm. Wilhelm Marschall. Gunther Luetjens. Karl Doenitz. Guenther Prien. Joachim Schepke. Otto Kretschmer. Wolfgang Lueth. Erich Topp. Engelbert Endrass. Lothar von Arnauld de la Periere.

ERICH RAEDER was born on April 24, 1876, at the small seaside resort of Wandsbeck (near Hamburg), where his father, Hans Raeder, was a teacher of French and English at a public school. His mother's father was Albert Hartmann, a musician at the royal court, and she instilled in him a love for music that stayed with him his entire life.[1] In the spring of 1889, Dr. Raeder was transferred to the small town of Gruenberg, Silesia, where his son matriculated with honors in March 1894. Young Erich immediately applied to join the Imperial German Navy, a decision he had taken only two weeks before.

Unlike the army, the Imperial Navy did not place a premium on a young man's Prussian Junker background, so Raeder's middle-class origins would not be held against him. He was accepted at once and ordered to report to Kiel on April 1 to begin his training.[2] Perhaps because of his lack of athletic ability, his initial homesickness, and his relatively small stature (he was only five foot six), Raeder was at first seemingly overlooked by his superiors. However, his academic achievement was such that he graduated first in the class of 1895, becoming a *Faehnrich zur See* (midshipman). By that time he had already made training cruises in the Baltic Sea and to the West Indies. Further training followed in navigation, gunnery, torpedoes, mines, tactics, sports, and sailing. He again excelled and in the fall of 1897 was commissioned ensign and assigned to SMS *Sachsen* as the signals officer. Undoubtedly he made a good impression, for shortly thereafter he was made signals officer for the battleship *Deutschland*, the flagship of Prince Heinrich, the brother of the Kaiser and commander of the Eastern Squadron. Young Ensign Raeder was thus a member of the admiral's staff as well and, as an additional duty, was in charge of the ship's band.

The *Deutschland* sailed for China in late 1897. Prince Heinrich soon took his young communications officer under his wing and Raeder accompanied him to Tsingtao, Peking, Port Arthur, Vladivostok, Japan, Korea, the Philippines, Saigon, and other stations. Promoted to lieutenant in 1901, Raeder returned to Kiel as a training officer. Later that year, however, he was transferred to the battleship *Kaiser Wilhelm der Grosse*, the new flagship of his mentor, Prince Heinrich, who was now the commander of the 1st Battleship Squadron. From 1903 to 1905 he attended the Naval Academy at Kiel, a sure sign that he had impressed his superiors and was marked for distinction. During this period he was sent to Russia for three months of advanced language training. (He chose Russian because he was already fluent in French and English and was studying Spanish on his own time.) After graduating from the academy in 1905, he served as navigation officer for the coastal defense armored ship *Frithjof* and on April 1, 1906, was posted to the Naval Information Office in Berlin, where he dealt with the foreign press and edited the naval journal *Marine Rundschau* (*Naval Review*) and *Nauticus*, the German naval annual. "Clear-headed and responsive to another point of view, he was exactly the man to deal with foreign press questions and to present an acceptable exterior to the many anxious inquirers from other countries," a former officer wrote of him later.[3] He also proved to be an excellent writer and was calm and composed, without being eloquent, when being interrogated by foreign journalists. All of this combined to create a very favorable impression. He also attracted the attention of the Imperial Navy's leading benefactor, Kaiser Wilhelm II, who, in 1910, named him navigation officer for his personal yacht, the *Hohenzollern*. This was quite an honor for Raeder, who remained something of a monarchist his entire life. Even as the commander-in-chief of Hitler's navy, his personal flag carried the colors and emblems of the Imperial Navy, rather than the swastika.

Raeder was promoted to commander in 1911 and the following year became senior staff officer (and in 1917 chief of staff) to Vice Admiral Ritter Franz von Hipper, the commander-in-chief of the reconnaissance forces of the German High Seas Fleet. In 1914 and 1915, he took part in mining operations and hit-and-run attacks against the British coast and in support operations for the German Army in the Baltic area. He also fought in the battles of the Dogger Bank (April 24, 1915) and Jutland (May 21, 1916), called the Battle of the Skaggerak by the Germans. Here he was in the navigation room of the *Luetzow* when it was battered to pieces by British warships. Somehow Raeder escaped the inferno and ended the battle aboard a cruiser.

In January 1918, Raeder left Hipper's staff and took command of the light cruiser *Koeln II*, a post he held until October. Shortly before the war ended, Captain Raeder became chief of the Central Bureau of the German Naval Command.

In late October and early November 1918, the German High Seas Fleet mutinied, an event that sparked the revolution that swept away the House of Hohenzollern. Wilhelm II fled into exile in Holland on November 9, and the Weimar Republic was proclaimed in Berlin a few hours later. From the beginning, Captain Raeder was deeply involved in the political maneuvering that accompanied the birth of the republic. With the admirals of the old naval command in disgrace and retiring in droves, the conservative Raeder wanted to make sure that the new commander of the navy was not someone from the political left. He therefore visited the new defense minister, Gustav Noske, almost as soon as he arrived in Berlin. During this meeting, Raeder emphasized that the new head of the navy should be an active officer who had the confidence of the Officer Corps. He added that Admiral Adolf von Trotha, the then chief of the Personnel Office (and former chief of staff of the High Seas Fleet), was just such a man. Noske was receptive and sent Raeder to discuss the matter with Friedrich Ebert, the new president of the republic. It is impossible to tell if Raeder's actions were decisive, but von Trotha was eventually appointed.[4]

Naturally, Erich Raeder was selected for retention in the 15,000-man navy of the Weimar Republic, where he did what he could to circumvent the harsh Treaty of Versailles, later telling the judges at Nuremberg that he did so "as a matter of honor."[5] In the spring of 1920, he backed Wolfgang Kapp's Putsch against the republic.[6] When this East Prussian monarchist was defeated by a general strike and fled into exile in Sweden, Raeder's continued presence in the Central Bureau was unacceptable to the government; indeed, he was fortunate to have been allowed to remain in the service at all. He was assigned to the Naval Archives—a backwater post, true enough, but much more significant than one might think. Here Raeder had the chance to study the development of the naval tactics and strategy of World War I as they affected Germany. He was also assigned the task of preparing a two-volume history of German cruiser warfare in foreign waters and in the process became a noted naval historian and strategic theorist, especially on the subject of cruiser warfare. His books included *Die Kreuzerkrieg in den Auslandischen Gewaessern* (published in 1922), *Das Kreuzergeschwader* (1922),

Die Taetigkeit der Kleinen Kreuzer Emden und Karlsruhe (1923), and *Der Krieg zur See*. In his spare time he attended the University of Berlin and was on the verge of earning his Ph.D. in political science when he was promoted to *Konteradmiral* (rear admiral) and became inspector of naval education in July 1922.

By this time Raeder was a professed democrat and a strong believer in the Weimar Republic, or so he said. In reality his views had not changed. One officer referred to his attitude as "stage-prop liberalism."[7] Nevertheless his politically adaptable attitude fooled most of the politicians and parliamentarians. His participation in the Kapp Putsch was forgiven, and he was no longer disqualified from rising to the top posts of the navy. In October 1924, he became commander of Light Reconnaissance Forces, North Sea, and in January 1925, was promoted to vice admiral and made commander of the Baltic Naval District. He became noted for his strict (if fussy) moral code and his strong sense of duty.

In August 1927, the "Lohmann Scandal" rocked the navy. A Berlin newspaper exposed the fact that secret naval rearmament funds existed and were being administered by *Kapitaen zur See* (Captain) Walter Lohmann of the Naval Transport Department and Captain Gottfried Hansen of the Weapons Department. Among other things, it was revealed that German-designed submarines were being constructed at a Krupp-controlled shipyard in Turkey. A Reichstag investigation followed and, naturally, heads rolled, chief among which were the defense minister and Admiral Hans Adolf Zenker, the chief of the Naval Command. What was needed now was a good republican flag officer to replace the disgraced Zenker. Erich Raeder suited the bill admirably. The fact that President Paul von Hindenburg liked him did not hurt his cause at all. On October 1, 1928, after some unpleasant Reichstag hearings, he was promoted to *Admiral* (equivalent to U.S. vice admiral) and became chief of the Naval Command—the highest post in the German Navy at that time.

The first item on Raeder's agenda was to set an authoritarian tone for his administration of the navy. He ordered, among other things, that once he made a decision all officers were to support it, no matter what. He then carried out what the junior officers called the "great seal hunt," in which several senior officers were forced to retire, supposedly so that bright, young officers could be promoted. However, as Charles Thomas, the noted historian of the German Navy, wrote, "Raeder was clearly taking no chances that his authority might be challenged by one of his more charismatic subordinates, and throughout Raeder's tenure of office one criticized the commander at one's peril."[8]

In his new post Raeder pursued the policy of a balanced fleet—a policy he continued into World War II and one that was disastrous to the German Navy and, indeed, to the entire German war effort.

Basically Raeder was a "big ship" man. He wanted some of every type of naval vessel, but his main reliance was on the *Panzerschiff*, the so-called pocket battleship—light battle cruisers that could "outrun anything that could defeat it and could defeat anything that could overtake it."[9] He also authorized the construction of a flotilla of freighters that could double as auxiliary cruisers and a flotilla of trawlers that could quickly be converted into minesweepers. Secretly, but more carefully than Zenker, he continued to support submarine development abroad.

Raeder wanted a navy of highly trained and disciplined men divorced from political activity of any kind. Straitlaced, taciturn, and almost devoid of humor, he was old-fashioned and considered himself the guardian of the morality of the naval officers corps—which included their wives. He once issued an order that officers' wives could not bob their hair, wear any type of cosmetics or short skirts, or put lacquer on their fingernails! He also had an unpleasant knack for showing up unannounced at isolated bases, poking his nose into crew's quarters and galleys, and generally making a pest of himself. He was particularly concerned with the appearance of uniforms and flower boxes in barracks' windows. Such fussiness, plus his regulations prohibiting naval personnel from visiting bars in uniform, or from smoking when driving, walking on the streets, or riding in public vehicles, did not make him particularly popular with his men. Once, a submarine returned after a patrol of several weeks. As soon as it docked, according to one German officer, Admiral Raeder jumped abroad, inspected the men, and reprimanded the crew for its slovenly appearance.

Although fastidious, he was somewhat different at home. Married, with a son, he purchased a modest villa in Charlottenburg (a suburb of Berlin) and enjoyed playing with his dachshund and listening to music. He liked to attend musical concerts (especially if Beethoven or Brahms was being played), enjoyed yachting, and went to every soccer game he could find.

Despite some misgivings, Admiral Raeder welcomed the rise of National Socialism because he could now press on with his naval expansion program without interference—although he was careful not to alienate any possible future governments until after the Nazis came to power on January 30, 1933. He first met Hitler on February 2, 1933, and soon was describing him as "an extraordinary man who was born to lead."[10] Hitler also was glad to have Raeder in charge of the navy, because the admiral confined his ambition to his own branch of the service, was not a danger to the regime, and seemed to be an excellent adviser on naval affairs, about which Hitler admitted he knew nothing.

The Raeder naval construction program began in earnest in March 1935, when Hitler unilaterally renounced the Treaty of Versailles. On June 18, 1935, German special envoy Joachim von Ribbentrop signed the Anglo-German Naval Treaty in London. Under the terms of this treaty, Germany agreed to restrict the size of its naval forces to 35 percent of those of Great Britain and her Commonwealth—except in the area of U-boats, where Germany was allowed parity. Hitler and Raeder were delighted, for the treaty seemed to rule out the possibility of Britain as a naval adversary. Raeder went so far as to forbid any references to a possible naval war with Britain—even in contingency plans or theoretical studies by his staff. Hitler had told him as early as February 3, 1933, that he wanted peaceful coexistence with Great Britain, and the admiral stubbornly insisted on believing him, to the exclusion of all other possibilities. Raeder continued to maintain this dangerously unrealistic position until May 1938.

It takes much longer to build a navy than an army and, to a much greater degree than with ground forces, a navy must be modeled after that of its most likely enemy. Hitler told Raeder to pattern his navy after those of Russia and France—the most likely enemies. Raeder did so without a backward glance. Neither wanted a war with Great Britain; therefore, they assumed that there would be no war with Great Britain. Apparently it never occurred to either of them that, whatever the provocation, Britain might declare war on Germany in 1939, just as she had done in 1914.

The honeymoon period between Raeder and the Fuehrer continued into 1937. In 1935, Raeder's title was changed to commander-in-chief of the navy, and on April 20, 1936, Hitler used the occasion of his own 47th birthday to promote Raeder to *Generaladmiral* (full admiral). The straitlaced officer was made an honorary member of the Nazi Party in 1937. Meanwhile, in 1936, the keels were laid for the giant battleships *Bismarck* (41,700 tons) and *Tirpitz* (42,900 tons). In the following two years the battle cruisers *Scharnhorst* and *Gneisenau* joined the fleet, as did the light cruisers *Leipzig* and *Nuremberg*. The heavy cruisers *Admiral Hipper* and *Bluecher* followed soon after. Numerous destroyers, submarines, and other vessels were also built during this period, and the 1st U-boat Flotilla was created under Captain Karl Doenitz (see later discussion).

Cracks began to appear in Raeder's relationship with the Nazi Party in 1938.[11] As early as January, Hitler was clearly putting pressure on him, saying that Germany needed a bigger battle fleet and criticizing Raeder for not moving fast enough. The admiral caustically pointed out that his naval construction program was in competition with Hitler's public works programs, such as the Munich subway system, the huge Volkswagen Works, the autobahns, the reconstruction programs in Berlin and Hamburg, and others. As a result, the shipyards lacked skilled laborers, welders, and raw materials. Hitler ignored the protest but brought up the matter again on May 27; when he demanded, among other things, that the *Bismarck* and *Tirpitz* be completed by early 1940, that shipyard capacity be increased, that an artillery U-boat be developed, and that the Type VII U-boat go into mass production. No doubt on Raeder's instructions, the German Supreme Naval Staff (*Seekriegsleitung*, or SKL; also referred to as the German Admiralty) responded by asking that all nonmilitary construction projects be shut down to release skilled labor for the military. Hitler refused to do this, so the naval construction program struggled slowly forward—well behind Hitler's schedule for it.

A major part of the problem was that Hermann Goering, the commander-in-chief of the Luftwaffe, was also head of the Four Year Economic Plan, which was in charge of resource allocation to industry and to the various branches of the armed forces. He and the puritanical admiral despised each other. Raeder hated Goering because he blocked all the admiral's attempts to secure a Fleet Air Arm and because of Goering's disgraceful part in the Blomberg-Fritsch affair. Goering, on the other hand, undermined Raeder's standing with Hitler by questioning his political beliefs, by pointing out that he went to church suspiciously often, and by giving the Fuehrer false or misleading information about the navy. Unwilling or unable to curry favor, or to persuade Hitler to overrule Goering on matters of allocation, the admiral saw his program languish. He did not seem overly concerned about it, however. The Fuehrer had told him that he would not need the navy until 1944 at the earliest, and Raeder believed him and acted accordingly.

Raeder was also having trouble from another enemy at court: SS-Gruppenfuehrer Reinhard Heydrich, head of the notorious State Secret Police (*Geheimes Staatspolizeiamt*, or Gestapo) and the Security Service (the SD). As a young naval officer Heydrich had broken off a marriage engagement in such a "peculiarly tasteless manner" that the young woman subsequently suffered a nervous breakdown. The puritanical Raeder—always the unbending guardian of naval morality—had him hauled before a court of honor and dismissed from the service for "impropriety."[12] Heydrich retaliated in the late 1930s by trying to "get something" on Raeder. He never did (because there was nothing to get), but having the vengeful chief of the Gestapo as an implacable enemy would be enough to play on anybody's nerves. Because of the backbiting political infighting, Raeder was considering resigning in 1938.

Erich Raeder viewed the Nazi persecution of Jews and other groups as a nasty business of which he did not approve, but, as it was not a naval matter, he considered it basically none of his concern. When such persecution touched on his navy, however, he sprang into action like an angry rooster. In the late 1930s, for example, the Nazis began to harass retired Rear Admiral Karl Kuehlenthal because he was half-Jewish and his wife and children were Jews. As soon as Raeder got word of it, he took the matter straight to Adolf Hitler himself. The first time Raeder brought up the matter, the Fuehrer sharply refused the naval commander-in-chief's request to exempt the Kuehlenthals from the Nuremberg Laws (which set the framework for the Jewish persecution), but if Hitler thought the matter was ended here, he was seriously mistaken. Like a bulldog that has been kicked off once, Raeder simply kept coming back to it. These people were navy! Stinging verbal reprimands to the sailor's face did the Fuehrer no good. The diminutive admiral brought up the request at the next encounter, and the one after that, and the one after that, until Hitler finally realized that the only way he would ever lay the matter to rest was to replace Raeder or give him his way. At last worn down, he personally signed the exemption. With this document, the Kuehlenthals not only avoided the death camps—they got to keep their property and Admiral Kuehlenthal continued to draw his pension until the end of the war.[13] This was not the only case of Raeder protecting naval people who happened to be Jewish; in fact, the Nazis succeeded in forcing only two non-Aryan officers out of the navy under the Nuremberg Laws. When the war broke out, however, Raeder quickly recalled them to active duty, where they received the same treatment as other officers.[14] Raeder even went so far as to intercede (successfully) for a few Jewish families he knew as a child in Gruenberg, even to the point of securing their release from the concentration camps, which he later swore he knew nothing about. This was as far as he would go, however; he did nothing to try to halt the persecution of non-naval Jews or other groups that the Nazis hated.

Jews were not the only people Raeder protected—provided, of course, they were navy people or personal friends. Christian Science Church members (with navy connections, of course) benefited from his intercessions, and at least one was released from a concentration camp because of him.

Raeder also had a more or less continuous running battle with Propaganda Minister Joseph Goebbels and the Gestapo over the naval chaplains, who Raeder firmly supported on every occasion. A 1942 incident is typical. A naval officer (who doubled as a Gestapo stool pigeon) accused a naval chaplain of making derogatory remarks about some leading Nazis. The Gestapo attempted to have the case tried in a civil (i.e., Nazi) court, but Raeder would not stand for it. The chaplain was quickly brought before a naval court-martial (the members of which were appointed by Raeder) and was promptly acquitted. The admiral personally confirmed the verdict and then gave the Gestapo agent a dishonorable discharge from the navy for perjury!

Raeder's relationship with Hitler became strained on November 1, 1938, when Hitler lost his temper with the admiral for the first time. Hitler tore the naval construction program plans to pieces and ordered Raeder to submit a new one. The Fuehrer was especially critical of the weak armament and armor on the *Bismarck* and *Tirpitz* and demanded that the U-boat fleet be rapidly expanded to reach parity with the British submarine fleet. He also ordered that the British be notified of his intentions immediately, in accordance with the terms of the 1935 treaty.

There were several more meetings between Hitler and Raeder in the winter of 1938–1939. And Raeder warned, "If war breaks out in the next year or two, our fleet won't be ready." Hitler loftily replied, "For my political aims I shall not need the Fleet before 1946!"[15]

Once again Raeder believed him, just as he had when he had promised that there would be no war with Great Britain. Now the talk was of war with Britain and her allies, but not before 1946, and still Raeder believed— even though the Sudetenland crisis had brought the world to the brink of war barely three months before. The results of all of this was the famous Z-Plan (*Z* for *Ziel*, or "target"), which Raeder submitted to the Fuehrer on January 17, 1939. Although its final target date was not until 1947, the new naval construction plan called for Germany to have six Type H battleships (of more than 56,000 tons displacement and armed with 420mm guns) by the beginning of 1944, in addition to four *Bismarck* class battleships. It was also to have four aircraft carriers, 15 surface raiders (Panzerschiffe, or pocket battleships), five heavy cruisers, 44 smaller cruisers, 68 destroyers, and 249 U-boats. Hitler approved the plan on January 27 and assigned it absolute priority over both other services, while at the same time assuring Raeder that he would not need the fleet for several more years.

After the approval of the Z-Plan, Raeder was back in the Fuehrer's good graces in the first half of 1939. On April 1, 1939, Hitler promoted him to grand admiral (*Grossadmiral*), the fifth in German history.[16] This era of good feeling was short-lived, however, and the reason was Hitler's defense of a woman he had not even met.

In June 1938, Commander Karl-Jesso von Puttkamer, Hitler's naval adjutant, returned to the destroyers for a tour of sea duty. He was replaced by 35-year-old Lieutenant Commander Alwin Albrecht. In 1939, Albrecht married a young schoolmistress from Kiel, with Erich Raeder acting as one of the witnesses. A few weeks later, in June 1939, the grand admiral received some anonymous letters revealing that she had been living in sin with a wealthy man. It turned out that she was well known to the local naval garrison at Kiel—in the biblical sense. Naturally, tales of Frau Albrecht's past reached the ears of the navy wives, who quickly made their indignation known. Commander Albrecht sued one agitator—and lost. At this point the puritanical Raeder sent the adjutant on leave and showed up unexpectedly at the Berghof (Hitler's residence on the Obersalzburg) and insisted that the commander be dismissed for entering into a dishonorable marriage. Hitler, however, refused to sack Albrecht or allow the grand admiral to do so.

The ensuing argument lasted two hours. Hitler screamed at Raeder—and Raeder screamed back. Their shouts could be heard all over the house. "How many of the navy wives now flaunting their virtue have had affairs in the past?" yelled the outraged Fuehrer. "Frau Albrecht's past is the concern of nobody but herself!" Finally Raeder announced that he would resign unless Albrecht were dismissed.

The grand admiral could do as he pleased, Hitler replied. Raeder returned to Berlin in a huff. Shortly thereafter, Hitler invited Frau Grete Albrecht to the Obersalzburg. She was taken to the Bechstein guest house, an isolated villa near the Berghof, where Hitler visited with her for an hour and a half. Grete Albrecht was a tall blonde—just the type of woman Hitler liked. He found her charming and left the guest house furious with what he considered the double standard of the officer corps.

After this the incident took on overtones of a comic opera. Instead of resigning, Raeder dismissed Albrecht as naval adjutant on his own authority as commander-in-chief of the navy. Hitler retaliated by making Albrecht a personal adjutant. Albrecht was discharged from the navy on June 30, 1939, and was commissioned Obetfuehrer in the National Socialist Motor Corps the next day. (In effect, he had been promoted three grades in rank.) Raeder then refused to appoint a new naval adjutant. With war on the horizon, however, this important post could not remain vacant, so Puttkamer was recalled from the destroyer branch to reassume his old duties (although he was officially referred to as Alfred Jodl's adjutant until October, to save Raeder's face). Meanwhile, the navy invited Hitler to a launching at Bremen on July 1, but the dictator declined. The navy wives, meanwhile, rallied around Raeder, bombarding Albrecht with social invitations but not inviting his wife. For his part, Admiral Raeder never forgave Hitler's insults and refused to confer with him again—a resolution he did not break until the start of the war.

Meanwhile, as if to complete the comedy, Grete Albrecht left her husband and moved back in with her former lover. Oberfuehrer Albrecht divorced her in 1940 and remarried the following year—more fortunately, this time. As a footnote, Albrecht never forgot the way Hitler defended him. He became a fervent Nazi and was reportedly killed fighting Russians in the streets of Berlin in 1945.[17]

On the afternoon of September 3, 1939, two days after the invasion of Poland began, Grand Admiral Erich Raeder put his personal feelings aside and met with Adolf Hitler. Even now Hitler expressed the opinion that Britain would not fight. For the first time, Erich Raeder did not believe him. But now it was too late. The United Kingdom declared war on Nazi Germany that same day.

The German Navy went to war five years ahead of schedule and only four years after the post-Versailles expansion began. It had the wrong kinds of vessels and was in no way ready. "The surface forces . . . can do no more than show that they know how to die gallantly," Admiral Raeder wrote gloomily in the SKL war diary. The German Navy's total strength in surface vessels stood at two battleships, three pocket battleships, one heavy cruiser, six light cruisers, and 34 destroyers and torpedo boats. Of this total, however, very little was at sea, except for the pocket battleships *Deutschland* and *Graf Spee*, and the U-boats, which were under tight restrictions. Gradually Raeder persuaded the dictator to relax these restrictions until, in November 1939, with the main armies home from Poland and western Germany no longer exposed to invasion, Hitler agreed to declare unrestricted submarine warfare.

Germany's most effective naval weapon in 1939, however, was not the U-boat but the magnetic mine. Deposited off the east coast of Britain by destroyers and minelayers, and off the southern and western coasts by U-boats and naval floatplanes, they were unsweepable by the technology of the day. By December they had sunk 67 Allied and neutral ships (252,237 gross registered tons), and by March 1940, they had sunk 128 merchant ships, three destroyers, and six auxiliary ships. Unfortunately for

Germany, Grand Admiral Raeder, with his multiplicity of prewar armaments plans and his obsession that Germany would not fight England, had
all but ignored this as yet undefeatable weapon. Nor was Hermann Goering
any help. He refused to use his Luftwaffe to drop mines until his stockpile
reached 5,000—and by then the British had discovered a magnetic mine
accidentally dropped in a mud-flat by a floatplane and had devised effective countermeasures. Meanwhile, the *Graf Spee* had been destroyed, and
Hitler was sending mixed signals to OKM (*Oberkommando der Kriegsmarine*,
or High Command of the Navy). In one breath he wanted aggressive naval
action, but in the next he advised caution and restraint. Raeder took the
same approach: he wanted his surface units to achieve major victories but
not to risk their capital ships in doing so. Just how a surface commander
was supposed to win a major victory over the Royal Navy without risk to
his own forces was never specified. But any surface commander who did
not conduct operations exactly as Admiral Raeder and his staff thought he
should (after the fact!) forfeited his job. The first to go was Admiral Hermann Boehm, the fleet commander.

HERMANN BOEHM was born in Rybnik/Upper Silesia (now Poland) on
January 18, 1884, and entered the Imperial Navy as a sea cadet in 1903.
Commissioned ensign in 1906, he served as the commander of various
torpedo boats from 1911 to 1918. Discharged from the navy as a *Kapitaenleutnant* (lieutenant) in 1919, he reentered the service the following year
and went on to distinguish himself in a number of assignments, including
commander of the 2nd Torpedo Boat Flotilla (1926–1928), chief of staff
of the Fleet Command (1932–1933), commander of the battleship *Hessen*
(1933–1934), and commander of the Reconnaissance Forces (1934–1937),
while simultaneously commanding German naval forces in Spanish waters
during the first year of the Spanish Civil War (1936–1937). Upon returning
to Germany, he was named commander of the North Sea Naval District
(on October 4, 1937). Boehm was promoted rapidly by the standards of the
day, to lieutenant commander (1922), commander (1928), captain (1930),
rear admiral (1934), vice admiral (1937), and admiral (1938). He was made
fleet commander on November 1, 1938. His tenure in this important post,
however, was destined to be brief. Admiral Boehm was not relieved of his
command because he was incapable, or because of any tactical mistakes on
his part, or due to any operational considerations whatsoever. Rather, he
was sacked because Raeder took exception to the wording of an order that
Boehm's operations officer had issued. The grand admiral thought there
was an implied criticism of one of his decisions in an operational recom-

mendation, and Erich Raeder did not take criticism (real or imagined) very well. Boehm was replaced by Vice Admiral Wilhelm Marschall, the former commander of surface raiders, on October 21, 1939.

Despite the fact that he had been sacked, Admiral Boehm's abilities were never questioned at SKL. After Raeder's temper cooled he recalled Boehm and appointed him commanding admiral, Norway (and later commander-in-chief, Naval Command Norway), and even promoted him to Generaladmiral on April 1, 1941. He remained at this post until the rise of Grand Admiral Doenitz, who sent him back into retirement in early 1943 because of Boehm's lack of faith in National Socialism, because of his opposition to the measures imposed on the people of Norway by Reichs-commissioner Josef Terboven, and because the relatively junior Doenitz felt threatened and (like Raeder before him) replaced any senior officer he thought might challenge him.

Hermann Boehm was in retirement a full year. Then, on March 1, 1944, Doenitz (again like Raeder before him) recalled Boehm to active duty as chief of inspectors for naval education. Boehm remained in this office until the end of the Reich was in sight. He retired from active duty on March 31, 1945, and moved to Kiel, where he died on April 11, 1972, at the age of 88.[18]

The Hermann Boehm case was just one example of Grand Admiral Raeder's inability to make proper use of a potentially gifted subordinate. Raeder's unsure hand was also seen in the odd command structure he set up. The fleet commander was not directly subordinate to the grand admiral, at least theoretically. Instead, Raeder set up two naval group headquarters (formerly naval districts Baltic and North Sea), which were directly subordinate to him, and the fleet commander was directly subordinate to one of these. (If the fleet was operating in the Baltic, he reported to Naval Group East; otherwise, Naval Group West. Conceivably, if the fleet was split, he could be subordinate to both. Later other naval groups were established.) However, Raeder himself often issued orders directly to the fleet commander, bypassing group headquarters: a direct and flagrant violation of the chain of command. It was not uncommon for a commander at sea to receive contradictory orders from Berlin and from group command. To make matters worse, Raeder's orders were frequently vague. But heads would roll if an admiral did not act exactly as Raeder thought he should—every step of the way.

A good example of Raeder's fractiousness is the case of Fleet Commander Admiral WILHELM MARSCHALL, a talented (and perhaps brilliant) officer who had a thorough grasp of naval tactics. Born in Augsburg, Bavaria, on September 30, 1886, he entered the navy as a sea cadet (*Seekadett*) in 1906. Commissioned in 1909, he served in several types of vessels, from battleships to hulks. Then, in 1916, he volunteered for U-boat school. In the last two years of the Great War he commanded *UC-74* (a mine-laying submarine) and later *UB-105* and sent a number of Allied ships to the bottom. Consequently, on July 4, 1918, he was decorated with Imperial Germany's highest medal, the Pour le Merite. Marschall's postwar career was also conspicuous and included tours as commander of the survey ship *Panther* (1924–1926), first officer of the battleships *Schleswig-Holstein* (1929–1930) and *Hanover* (1930–1931), chief of staff of the Baltic Sea Naval Station (1931–1934), commander of the battleship *Hessen* (1934) and the pocket battleship *Admiral Scheer* (1934–1936), chief of operations of OKM (1936–1937), and commander of German Sea Forces in Spain during the Spanish Civil War (1937–1938). He was commander of pocket battleships (Panzerschiffen) when the war broke out.[19]

Marschall first ran afoul of Grand Admiral Raeder in November 1939, when he took the *Scharnhorst* and *Gneisenau* out into the North Sea. His objective was to create a diversion in favor of the *Deutschland*, which was attempting to return home after a disappointing raid into the Atlantic. Just as he hoped, the British Home Fleet came after the two battleships, allowing the *Deutschland* to reenter German waters safely. Then Marschall not only eluded the British trap, he isolated and sank the British armed merchant cruiser *Rawalpindi* in the process. However, he received no thanks from the German Admiralty—only unfair and savage attacks and a clear implication that his job was in jeopardy. It seems that the German battleship had withdrawn after seeing the silhouette of a darkened ship at nightfall on November 23. Raeder, ever the chairborne critic, was furious that Marschall had not attacked and sunk the second British ship—whatever it was. Marschall should have attacked an unknown ship at night, in the middle of the British fleet, when any damage that slowed his speed even slightly could cost Germany one of her two operational battleships? This from Raeder, the man who had previously ordered that capital ships should not be risked? "Till now," Marschall commented, "no one has ever questioned the naval axiom that capital ships should avoid all contact at night with torpedo craft and reconnaissance vessels."[20] Marschall was quite right, of course: the potential prize was simply not worth the risks. Raeder, however, continued to launch scathing attacks, but never officially and never face-to-face. He never gave Marschall a chance to defend himself. Instead, he made his bit-ing remarks behind Marschall's back but in places where he could be sure that word of them would get back to the fleet commander.

From the beginning of the war both Admiral Raeder and Winston Churchill wanted the same thing: Norway. Raeder wanted it to prevent the British from cutting off Germany's supply of Swedish iron ore, which was shipped through the northern Norwegian port of Narvik, and to prevent the British from blocking the German exit to the North Sea, as they had done in World War I. Churchill wanted it for the opposite reasons. In addition, Raeder wanted the excellent ports Norway offered.

Hitler was initially opposed to the idea of invading Norway because he did not believe the British would violate Norwegian neutrality. On December 24, 1939, Raeder arranged a meeting between Hitler and Vidkun Quisling, the head of the Norwegian version of the Nazi Party, in an attempt to change Hitler's mind, but it did no good. Only in February 1940, when a British warship attacked an unarmed German ship in Norwegian waters (to rescue some British prisoners) did Hitler draw the correct conclusions: the United Kingdom would violate Norwegian neutrality, and he had better act quickly to prevent the loss of his vital iron ore supply.

He was right.

Urged on by Churchill, the Allied Supreme War Council decided on February 5 to seize Narvik and the Swedish iron mines at Gaellivare, on the pretext of sending aid to the Finns, who were fighting the Soviets in the Winter War of 1939–1940. The Allied plan was thwarted only because Finland sued for an armistice. First Lord of the Admiralty Churchill did not give up, however. In fact, the British began laying mines in Norwegian waters on April 8, while in the Scottish ports British soldiers were already on the troop ships, awaiting the German reaction that Churchill and his cronies hoped the mine-laying would provoke. They were then to put Plan R 4—the Allied occupation of Narvik, Trondheim, Bergen, and Stavanger—into immediate execution. They were too late: the German Fleet had already sailed.

Operation *Weserueburg Nord*, the occupation of Norway, was the only major action conducted by the German surface fleet in World War II. It was also Erich Raeder's major contribution to the German war effort. It was an extremely bold and daring plan, taken in the face of nearly overwhelming odds. Even though virtually the entire German fleet was committed, it was no match for the Home Fleet of the Royal Navy; therefore a British intervention while the fleet was at sea would result in the failure of the operation and the virtual annihilation of the German Navy. Everything depended on speed, surprise, and accurate timing. The detailed planning was done by a staff under the direction of Captain Theodor Krancke and was modified by the Supreme Naval Staff under Raeder. It consisted primarily of a warship echelon of 11 groups (to clear minefields and conduct the landings); a tanker and export echelon (carrying military equipment and fuel for the destroyers' trip back to German waters); and a sea transport echelon of eight groups, which formed the main troop and supply movement. Despite Doenitz's objections (see later discussion), 42 submarines were stationed off the Norwegian coast, to attack the Royal Navy if it tried to intervene. As Raeder saw it, the most dangerous part of the operation would be the return of the warships to their home bases. They would be exposed to attack by superior British forces most of the way back. However, if everything went according to plan, only the submarines would engage the enemy's naval forces.

The main German forces departed for Norway in serials between March 31 and April 6—only two days before the British mine-laying operation began. The British spotted the move at 9:50 a.m. on April 7, but it was late afternoon before the Home Fleet sailed—in the wrong direction. Thinking the German Fleet was trying to break out into the Atlantic, they sailed to block this move, leaving the central North Sea uncovered.

The landings took place on April 9 and were successful except for that of Naval Group 5, which was charged with depositing the assault elements of the 163rd Infantry Division at Oslo. It was spearheaded by the heavy cruiser *Bluecher*, which was severely damaged by the 280mm guns at Fort Oscarsborg, 10 miles south of the Norwegian capital, and then was hit by two torpedoes. The crew was unable to control the ensuing fires, which set off a magazine. The captain gave the command to abandon ship at 7 a.m., and the heavy cruiser sank 30 minutes later. Due to the strong currents at this spot of the fjord, many soldiers and sailors drowned, including most of the staff of the infantry division. Oslo did not fall until the next day.

German naval costs began to mount as the Norwegian campaign progressed. The *Hipper* was rammed by a mortally wounded British destroyer (which sank in the collision), and the German cruiser was severely damaged. The light cruiser *Karlsruhe* was sunk by a British submarine after providing covering fire for the landings at Kristiansand and Arendal. During the Bergen landings the light cruiser *Koenigsberg* was crippled by Norwegian coastal gunfire and, unable to put to sea, was sunk at her moorings by British aircraft on April 11. Early that same morning the *Luetzow* (formerly the *Deutschland*) was torpedoed by a British submarine and lost her entire stern. By superhuman effort her crew somehow kept her afloat until she could be towed to Kiel, but her operational usefulness was over. After this, she could be used for training purposes only. For Admiral Raeder this was perhaps the bitterest blow of the campaign, for he had not wanted either the *Luetzow* or the *Bluecher* used in the Norwegian operation, preferring instead to use them as ocean raiders. Sending them to Oslo was Hitler's idea. But the grand admiral had only himself to blame, because neither he nor the Admiralty staff offered serious objections to the Fuehrer's decision on this issue. And at this point of the war, Hitler still listened to the advice of his military experts, especially on air force and naval matters.

The biggest defeat for the German Navy in the Norwegian campaign took place in Narvik and adjacent fjords, where Naval Group 1 under the command of Rear Admiral Friedrich Bonte, the commander-in-chief of destroyers, landed Major General Eduard Dietl's 3rd Mountain Division on April 9. The city fell the same day, as planned, but only one of the eight ships in Bonte's export echelon arrived. (Three had been sunk or forced to scuttle, and the others, dispersed by a storm, put in at Bergen.) With his fuel tanks nearly empty, Bonte could not leave the port. Instead, he relied on four U-boats to cover the harbor entrance and was taken by surprise when the British 2nd Destroyer Flotilla sailed into the harbor under the cover of a snowstorm. Two German destroyers were sunk in the ensuing battle and three damaged, while one British destroyer was sunk, one beached, and a third was badly damaged. Admiral Bonte was among the dead.

What had happened to the U-boats? They had done what they were supposed to have done. They fired torpedo after torpedo into the British vessels, but all of them had been duds. Once again, as with the magnetic mine, a major German weapon had been neglected. Three days later the pattern was repeated when the British battleship *Warspite* and nine destroyers entered Narvik harbor and sank the remaining German destroyers. The *Warspite* and some of the destroyers had been hit by torpedoes from at least three different U-boats, but again they all were duds. The 10 destroyers lost at Narvik represented almost half the German prewar destroyer strength.

These were not the first incidents of German torpedo failure. In October 1939, when Guenther Prien entered Scapa Flow and sank the *Royal Oak* (see later discussion), four of the seven "fish" he fired failed to explode. Later that month Lieutenant Herbert Schulze (*U-48*) returned from patrol after sinking five ships, and reported five torpedo failures. And Lieutenant Commander Victor Schuetze of *U-25* signaled U-boat Command hopping mad. He had halted a steamer, ordered its crew off, and fired four torpedoes into it at close range, one after the other—every one a dud!

The most important non-sinking occurred (or did not occur) in the North Sea on October 30, 1939, when Lieutenant Wilhelm Zahn of *U-56* fired a fan of three torpedoes into the British battleship *Nelson*.[21] The range was only 800 meters, and there was no way Zahn could miss. All three torpedoes were duds. The *Nelson* sailed away, all its passengers safe. These included Admiral Sir Charles Forbes, the commander-in-chief of the Home Fleet; the First Sea Lord, Admiral of the Fleet Sir Dudley Pound; and the First Lord of the Admiralty, Mr. Winston Churchill.

By early November 1939, Karl Doenitz was reporting to OKM that at least 30 percent of his torpedoes were duds. Yet it was not until April 20, 1940, after Naval Group 1 had been wiped out and a frustrated Doenitz had recalled the entire submarine force on the grounds that he could not fight with blunted weapons did Grand Admiral Raeder belatedly appoint a special commission to investigate the "torpedo crisis." The resulting scandal shook what was left of the German Navy. Among other things it was discovered that the percussion pistol in the German *Aufschlagzuendung* (percussion detonating device) had been test-fired only twice (in 1928) before it was labeled "indispensable" by the Torpedo Experimental Institute and, without further testing, was incorporated into all German torpedoes. The magnetically operated detonating device (*Magnetzuendung*) on the magnetic torpedoes had been developed and tested with a similar lack of thoroughness and had also failed under wartime conditions. The U-boats investigation also uncovered the shocking fact that Vice Admiral Friedrich Goetting, the chief of the Torpedo Inspectorate at OKM, had discovered that the German torpedoes were defective and had twice sent urgent warnings to Admiral Raeder and his SKL staff before the start of the war. His warnings had been ignored. And at Narvik, Admiral Bonte and his men paid the full price for the lethargy of their High Command. Eventually Rear Admiral Oskar Wehr, chief of the Torpedo Trials Command and long-time head of the Torpedo Testing Institute (*Torpedo-Versuchs-Anstalt*, or TVA), was court-martialed and sentenced, along with two of his principal associates. TVA alone bore the blame for the torpedo crisis, in what one officer called "a travesty of justice."[22] Grand Admiral Raeder and his staff should have been called to account for ignoring Admiral Goetting's warnings, but no such action was ever taken.

With the destruction of the German destroyers at Narvik, the way was paved for Allied ground forces to land in northern Norway, which they did on April 24, 1940. Meanwhile, beginning on May 10, Hitler's Western offensive swept across France and Belgium and trapped the main Anglo-

French armies in the Dunkirk pocket, with their backs to the sea. At this point Admiral Raeder informed Hitler that the *Scharnhorst* and *Hipper* would be repaired and ready for new missions about May 27 and the *Gneisenau* a few days later. Raeder wanted to commit them in the area between Norway and the Shetland Islands, to attack Allied supply convoys which, of course, would be protected by Royal Navy warships. Earl F. Ziemke wrote, "During the following days a wide divergence of opinion developed between the Naval Staff [Raeder] on one hand and the operating commands, Naval Group West and Fleet Command, on the other. The operating commands wanted to conserve their forces and believed the chances of success too small to warrant risking the few German heavy ships. But Admiral Raeder and the Naval Staff, probably believing the war was drawing to a close, insisted on adopting aggressive methods to prove the worth of the navy and assure its future development."[23]

By the time the warships sailed out of Kiel on June 4, the main Allied armies in France had been destroyed or forced off the mainland, and the situation for Dietl's mountain troops was desperate. They had been forced out of Narvik, were nearly out of ammunition, and were in danger of being destroyed altogether. Meanwhile, at Trondheim, miles south of Narvik, Lieutenant General Valentin Feurstein had organized a relief force and was pushing north toward Narvik. By now Admiral Marschall, the fleet commander and officer in charge of the task force, had been given instructions to provide direct relief for the hard-pressed ground forces at Narvik by attacking British warships and transports at their nearby base of Harstad. But then Admiral Raeder, acting on the orders of Adolf Hitler, commanded him to provide flank protection for General Feurstein. Which mission had priority? Marschall asked. Raeder, in effect, refused to make a decision. "Equal priority" was his answer.

As Marschall steamed toward Narvik with the battleships *Scharnhorst* and *Gneisenau*, the cruiser *Hipper*, four destroyers, and the naval tanker *Dithmarschen*, he still did not know what was expected of him. Specific orders from Generaladmiral Alfred Saalwaechter, his direct superior at Naval Group West, did not help, because Admiral Otto Schniewind, Raeder's chief of staff, signaled him that the Supreme Naval Staff's order contained no such precise instructions. Schniewind did not, however, actually revoke Saalwaechter's orders. This was typical of the confusion fleet and task force commanders had to deal with under Admiral Raeder.

On the night of June 7, Marschall received an aerial reconnaissance report that three naval convoys had left Narvik and concluded that the British were evacuating the place. He signaled that he intended to attack these valuable prizes. Raeder and Saalwaechter, however, did not agree with Marschall's conclusions and signaled back at 5 a.m. on June 8 that his primary mission was still (?!) to strike at Harstad.

Marschall was right: the British were evacuating Narvik. Between June 4 and 8, they pulled out 24,500 men, and Marschall had stumbled right across their line of retreat. Furthermore, they did not yet know he was there. So Admiral Marschall, furious at his superiors' meddling with the operations of a commander on the spot, took matters into his own hands and went out searching for convoys. The battleships had no luck, but the *Hipper* sank the British escort trawler *Juniper*, the Norwegian tanker *Old Pioneer*, and the 20,000-ton troopship *Orama* (which was empty). Meanwhile, about 1 p.m., Marschall dispatched his destroyers to assist Feurstein's advance (as ordered by Hitler) and headed north, where intercepted radio signals indicated he would find the aircraft carriers *Ark Royal* and *Glorious* and the cruiser *Southampton*.

The *Scharnhorst* found the 22,500-ton *Glorious* at 5:10 p.m. and opened up on her from 26 kilometers away. The *Gneisenau* opened up a few minutes later with her big guns, while her mediums engaged the British destroyer *Ardent*. The German battleships pounded the *Glorious* until she sank at 7 p.m. There were only 43 survivors. Meanwhile, the *Ardent* went down, and the British destroyer *Acasta*, a burning wreck, fired four torpedoes at an extreme range of 14 kilometers. Nine minutes later one of them struck the *Scharnhorst*, tearing a 12-by-4-meter hole in its side. A few minutes later the *Acasta* disappeared below the waves. Only one man survived.

The *Acasta*'s lucky shot no doubt saved a great many other British ships, for Admiral Marschall now broke off the pursuit and the *Scharnhorst* limped into Trondheim for repairs. Admiral Marschall had won a victory even though it had not been a one-sided one. The British had lost more than 1,500 men in the *Glorious* alone, plus a troopship, a tanker, an armed trawler, and two destroyers. Had Marschall not been saddled with the requirement of supporting Feurstein, his victory would have been even more convincing, and, with the evacuation of Narvik in progress, Feurstein did not need support. But once again the fleet commander received no thanks for his actions, for Admiral Raeder now decided that Harstad had been the primary objective all along and bitterly denounced Marschall for his failure to achieve even greater success. Once again, however, he did not do it officially or to Marschall's face, but in such a manner that he would be sure to hear about it through third parties. Raeder would not permit a man-to-man confrontation. Nevertheless, he continued to urge Marschall to make another foray (of the type he was simultaneously mercilessly criticizing), this time with the *Gneisenau* and the *Hipper*. The fleet commander, however, felt very strongly that Germany should conserve her few remaining capital ships. This elicited new unofficial scorn from Berlin.

On June 18, Fleet Commander Wilhelm Marschall reported himself ill, and indeed he was sick—sick of his chairborne grand admiral. Raeder quickly replaced him with a more pliable man. Now freed of his responsibilities, Marschall began a campaign to have a court of inquiry examine his conduct during Operation Juno, as his Norwegian sortie was called. He made several such attempts, but always in vain. Raeder never gave the former fleet commander a chance to state his case or justify his actions.

Perhaps to shut him up, Raeder recalled Marschall to active duty as an inspector of naval education in late August 1940. From late 1941 until May 1942, he was on special assignments, first at Naval Group South and then with Naval Group Baltic, but still with no real responsibility commensurate with his rank. After that he was again unemployed and went into semi-retirement.[24]

Marschall was replaced as fleet commander on June 18 by Vice Admiral Gunther Luetjens, the former commander-in-chief of Reconnaissance Forces. At SKL's urging, he sailed out of Trondheim at 4 p.m. on June 20 with the *Gneisenau*, *Hipper*, *Nuremberg*, and one destroyer. Seven hours later the *Gneisenau* was rocked by an explosion: a torpedo from a British submarine had ripped through her bows, leaving a hole as big as a house in both sides of the ship. The task force headed back for Trondheim, its mission a failure.

The Norwegian campaign had cost the German Navy dearly. In the summer of 1940, it had only one heavy cruiser, two light cruisers, and four destroyers fit for action. Norway was the high point for the German surface fleet, which had virtually expended itself. This was no small comfort to the British in the dangerous months ahead.

For Operation Sea Lion, Hitler's proposed invasion of Britain, Raeder was charged with the task of transporting the German Army across the English Channel. However, the German Navy had never developed any landing craft. Raeder therefore collected more than 3,000 vessels of all kinds, including tugboats, river barges, motorboats, steam trawlers, and other dubious vessels, for the assault. If a single British warship had broken into the channel when this fleet attempted to cross, thousands of soldiers would have been slaughtered. Many men looked at these boats and said that they would prefer to swim, and they were only half joking. A great many generals were very happy when the operation was cancelled and not because they were afraid of the British Army.

After Norway, the German naval war became primarily a U-boat war. Raeder had neglected this arm in his quest for a balanced fleet, but on October 10, 1939, after the Z-Plan was scrapped, he called on Hitler to authorize an increase in U-boat production from 2 per month to 29 per month. This was unrealistic—well beyond the capabilities of the German shipyards, which were, in the meantime, supposed to continue with battleships, cruisers, an aircraft carrier, and other vessels already on the stocks. Hitler nodded to Raeder and turned the matter over to Wilhelm Keitel, who informed Raeder that Hermann Goering was in charge of the armaments program. The grand admiral, of course, knew he would get very little help from this enemy. He basically had a choice: continue using his dock capacity for capital ships or for U-boats. This effectively ended the accelerated U-boat construction program, at least for the time being. "Raeder," Cajus Bekker wrote, "though he supported the U-boat construction programme, refused to do so at the expense of his heavy surface ships, from which he promised himself great strategic results."[25]

Except for the U-boat war, 1941 was not a good year for the German Navy. The battleship *Bismarck* was sunk, the few German commerce raiders were run down, and the German battleships found their new French bases vulnerable to RAF attacks. The grand admiral and his staff had underestimated the value of aircraft against naval targets—one reason why Germany never did have an aircraft carrier. They did have one under construction, but it had a low priority and was an on-again, off-again affair.

Also in 1941, Adolf Hitler began to interfere more and more in naval matters at the operational level.

Hitler opposed the idea of sending the *Bismarck* on its fateful raid into the Atlantic, but Raeder insisted, backed by his yes-man fleet commander, Luetjens. Despite his personal misgivings, Hitler let them have their way. The huge 42,000-ton battleship was sunk off the French coast on May 27, 1941, taking more than 2,000 officers and men to their deaths.

After this disaster, Hitler became more and more critical of Raeder and the surface fleet, and less and less inclined to give him a free hand. On November 13, 1941, Raeder asked permission to send the battleships out on a fresh foray into the North Atlantic in February 1942. Hitler rejected the idea and asked if it were possible to bring the ships home (to German waters) via a surprise breakout through the English Channel. Raeder and his staff doubted it, but on January 12, 1942, Hitler ordered it done nevertheless. And it worked. Raeder's stock dropped even lower in the Fuehrer's eyes.

In late December 1942, Vice Admiral Oskar Kummetz led a task force consisting of the *Hippel*, the *Luetzow*, and six destroyers in a raid from Trondheim into the Arctic Ocean and Barents Sea. Its object was to intercept and destroy Allied Convoy PQ-17; which was heading for Russia with every conceivable type of war material. Unfortunately, bound by SKL orders not to take any major risks, Kummetz accomplished very little. His force was superior to the screen of British destroyers that blocked his path to the convoy, but he could not penetrate it without risk. Even so, as he withdrew from the battle he was surprised by two British cruisers, which had come up unseen from the opposite direction. The *Hipper* was damaged and a destroyer was lost with all hands.

Meanwhile, back at his Rastenburg headquarters in East Prussia, Adolf Hitler anxiously awaited news of the foray for three days. He was so nervous that he could not sleep. On January 1, 1943, he finally heard what had happened and flew into a rage. He decided on the spot to pay off the heavy ships and reduce them to scrap. Their guns, he said, could be used as coastal defense artillery. He demanded that Grand Admiral Raeder appear before him at once.

Back in Berlin, however, Raeder feigned illness. This bought him five days. He hoped that Hitler would calm down in that amount of time. The Fuehrer did not. When he saw Raeder on January 6, he launched into a roaring monologue that lasted two hours. The grand admiral never said a word as Hitler recited the list of failures of the German surface fleet, damning it every way he could think of. He ended his tirade by repeating his order to disband the surface fleet. When Hitler finally finished, Erich Raeder resigned his post as commander-in-chief of the navy. The Fuehrer immediately softened his attitude and tried to dissuade him from quitting, but Raeder insisted. He had heard too much. To preserve the fiction of harmony within the High Command, Raeder retired on January 30, 1943—the 10th anniversary of Hitler's assumption of power. He was also given the honorary title of inspector general of the navy—a strictly ceremonial position. Ironically it was his successor, U-boat Fuehrer Karl Doenitz, who convinced Hitler not to disband the remnants of the surface fleet.

Erich Raeder's resignation came too late to help the German Navy. One by one the remaining ships of the surface fleet were destroyed by Allied submarines or air attacks, and the U-boat offensives were smashed by an enemy that was both quantitatively and technologically superior. Meanwhile, the Allied ground forces closed in, and in May 1945, Erich Raeder and his wife were captured by the Russians. The former admiral suffered a near-fatal heart attack on May 20, but as soon as he had recovered enough to travel, he and his spouse were flown to Moscow. That fall he was indicted as a war criminal and brought to Nuremberg to stand trial. On the stand he spoke of how Hitler deceived him many times and how he found the dictator impossible to get along with. In general, he tried to disassociate himself from the regime and minimized his own involvement as much as possible. On the issue of the invasion of Norway, he merely told the truth: all he did was beat the British to the punch. However, his attorney's efforts to get the official British directives and plans introduced as evidence were rejected. Raeder's conviction on the Norwegian charge is widely considered a travesty of justice, considering that the Allies were planning to do the same thing, but the tribunal was very selective about the evidence it would allow to be presented. On the other hand, however, Admiral Raeder could not dodge the fact that he passed on Hitler's Commando Order of October 18, 1942, which ordered that Allied commandoes and paratroopers captured behind German lines were to be executed, whether they were in uniform or not.

Karl Doenitz, for one, was furious with Raeder's testimony. "I cannot stand it when people turn their coats because the wind is blowing the other way," he remarked. "I know how Raeder talked when he was the big chief and I was just a little man in the navy. It was altogether different then, I can tell you that. It gives me a pain to hear them change their tune now and say they always opposed Hitler."[26]

Despite Raeder's evasions he was convicted and sentenced to life imprisonment. When he heard the sentence, he implored the court to change it to death by firing squad. His request was denied. Raeder was sent to Spandau while his wife, who was never accused of committing any crime, remained a Soviet prisoner until September 1949. The couple was finally allowed to see each other again in March 1950, when they got to spend 15 minutes together. Raeder requested to be released long enough to attend the funeral of his only son, Hans, who died in Lippstadt on January 17, 1953, but this was denied him.

Much to his surprise, Erich Raeder was released due to his ill health on September 17, 1955, at the age of 80. He retired to Kiel, where he wrote his memoirs, *Mein lben* (*My Life*), a book that makes very interesting reading even though, in places, the author's recollections are highly selective. Plagued by ill health in the last years of his life, Grand Admiral Raeder died in Kiel on November 6, 1960, at the age of 84.

★　★　★

GUNTHER LUETJENS, who succeeded Wilhelm Marschall as commander of the German fleet, was born in Wiesbaden on May 25, 1889, the son of a merchant. Enthralled from childhood by stories about the sea, he decided to make the navy his career and joined as an officer-cadet in 1907. In 1910, he graduated from the Naval Academy, ranking 20th in a class of 160. As befitted his high standing, he was assigned to a battleship. Ironically, Luetjens was uncomfortable on large ships. As soon as the opportunity arose, he transferred to the torpedo boats and served on them throughout World War I. In the Weimar days, he alternated between training and staff assignments (mainly involving transport vessels) and was considered an outstanding instructor. He served as commander of the 1st Torpedo Boat Flotilla (1929–1931) and, after a staff tour as chief of the naval officer personnel department (1932–1934), Luetjens was given command of the cruiser *Karlsruhe* in 1934 and spent the first half of 1935 in South American waters, showing the German flag. When he returned to Germany, he was named chief of staff of Naval District North Sea, serving in that capacity until March 16, 1936, when Erich Raeder named him head of the naval personnel office. The grand admiral needed a staff officer of proven ability for the rapidly expanding navy, and the experienced and dependable Captain Luetjens was his man.

Gunther Luetjens was a taciturn officer with a monk-like devotion to his calling. His friends considered him quite charming once they got beyond his stoic exterior. A confirmed monarchist, he never used the Nazi salute or carried an admiral's dagger with a swastika on it, preferring instead to wear his old Imperial Navy dirk. He even lodged a protest against Hitler's treatment of the Jews, but it was buried by Hermann Boehm, the fleet commander at the time.

In 1938 Raeder named Luetjens commander-in-chief of Reconnaissance Forces, and in late 1939, as a rear admiral, he took part in the mining operations off the English coast. He was promoted to vice admiral effective January 1, 1940. After Luetjens's cruisers took part in the Norwegian campaign, Erich Raeder appointed him fleet commander (*Flottenchef*) on June 18, 1940. In him, the grand admiral found exactly the man he wanted to command the surface fleet: an officer of the old school he could trust to obey every order SKL gave him without too many questions or objections. The fact that Luetjens had spent the bulk of his career in the torpedo boat and cruiser arms did not make him particularly well qualified to command the fleet, but this did not seem to bother Raeder, who had Luetjens promoted to full admiral on September 1, 1940.

Meanwhile, at Raeder's urging, Luetjens attempted to take the *Gneisenau* and the *Hipper* out on a raid into the Atlantic on June 20, 1940, but (as we have seen) his flagship *Gneisenau* was torpedoed the same day and out of action for months. Meanwhile, Admiral Luetjens was in charge of the naval portion of Operation Sea Lion, under the overall supervision of Admiral Raeder.

Repairs on the *Gneisenau* were completed by December, when Luetjens went out to sea again with it and the *Scharnhorst*. However, he ran into a gale, and both ships were damaged by heavy seas, forcing him to return to base again. On his third attempt, in early 1941, Admiral Luetjens finally succeeded in breaking out into the North Atlantic and fell on the British shipping lanes with the *Scharnhorst* and the *Gneisenau*. They sank 13 British merchant ships and tankers before being confronted by the British battleship *Rodney* and its escorts. In accordance with the take-no-risks orders of Raeder and Hitler, Luetjens felt obliged to retire rather than engage in a surface battle. On the morning of March 23, 1941, he entered the port of Brest, France. He was then summoned to Berlin.

On Saturday, April 26, 1941, Gunther Luetjens took his leave of Grand Admiral Raeder after having been briefed on his next mission: he was to conduct a raid in the Atlantic with the heavy cruiser *Prinz Eugen* and the *Bismarck*. It would be the maiden voyage of Germany's monstrous 42,000-ton battleship.

Luetjens voiced some valid objections to this plan. The difference between the endurance of the two ships would prevent them from operating together as a homogeneous force, he pointed out. Luetjens wanted to wait until the *Scharnhorst* was repaired and the *Tirpitz*, the sister ship of the *Bismarck*, completed her crew training period, which would be in about four months. As a combined force, these three ships would be very difficult indeed to defeat. Otherwise, the German Navy would be committing its forces piecemeal. Raeder, however, argued the opposite case. Each pause in the Battle of the Atlantic helped the enemy; also, it was essential to create a diversion in the Atlantic, to force the British to withdraw naval forces from the Mediterranean, thus reducing pressure on the Italian-German supply routes to North Africa.

Although he had by far the stronger argument, Luetjens let himself be persuaded. He would obey the grand admiral's wishes. When Adolf Hitler visited Gotenhafen (now the Polish port of Gydnia) on May 5, to inspect both the *Tirpitz* and the *Bismarck*, he also expressed doubts about the advisability of this operation; Luetjens, however, strongly supported Raeder's point of view. Had Luetjens said what he really thought and agreed with

Hitler, it is quite likely that the tragedy of the *Bismarck* would have been avoided. However, faced with the united front of his naval experts, Hitler decided not to interfere with Raeder's plans, despite his personal reservations. The stage was set for yet another naval disaster.

Once again, as with Marschall, the fleet commander was cautioned again and again against taking unnecessary risks. Raeder told him to use "prudence and care" and not to stake too much for the sake of a limited success of dubious value. At his SKL briefing, Luetjens was told that "the primary objective is the destruction of the enemy's carrying capacity. Enemy warships will be engaged only in furtherance of this objective, and provided such engagements can take place without excessive risks."[27]

After leaving Berlin, Gunther Luetjens paid a visit to his friend and predecessor Wilhelm Marschall, a champion of the right of freedom of action for a commander at sea. Marschall, now in retirement, warned him not to feel too closely bound by the Supreme Naval Staff's instructions.

"No, thank you," Luetjens said as he rejected Marschall's advice. "There have already been two Fleet Commanders who have lost their jobs owing to friction with the Admiralty, and I don't want to be the third. I know what they want, and shall carry out their orders."[28]

The *Bismarck* and the *Prinz Eugen* left port on May 18 and were spotted by British reconnaissance aircraft on May 22. The Home Fleet tried to prevent them from breaking out into the Atlantic, and on the morning of May 24, a classic naval battle took place in the Denmark Straits, between Iceland and Greenland. Firing from 10 miles away, the *Bismarck* sank the British *Hood*. One of the German 15-inch (380mm) shells hit her aft magazine, setting off 112 tons of high explosives. The 42,000-ton battle cruiser went down only six minutes after the *Bismarck* opened fire, taking 1,416 officers and men with her, including Vice Admiral Sir Lancelot Holland. Only three men survived.

One minute later, at 6:01 a.m., the *Bismarck* turned its guns on the British battleship *Prince of Wales*. By 6:13 a.m. this opponent had sustained several hits and was laying a smoke screen, trying to escape the German task force. Ernst Lindemann, the captain of the *Bismarck*, wanted to pursue the crippled British battleship and finish her off, but Luetjens—ever mindful of SKL orders—refused to do so. A violent argument ensued, but Luetjens held firm, and the *Prince of Wales* escaped.

The *Bismarck* headed for the open Atlantic, where the British lost her. Luetjens, however, broke radio silence and transmitted a long report to Berlin, enabling the British to re-fix his position. Even so, the bearings were misinterpreted and the pursuing force went off in the wrong direction. The *Bismarck* was re-sighted by a Catalina flying boat two days later, and a wave of Swordfish dive-bombers from Vice Admiral Somerville's Force H attacked the German battleship with torpedoes late in the afternoon of May 26. One of these struck aft, jamming the rudder and making the battleship unmaneuverable. Efforts at repairing her proved futile. Nor could the *Bismarck* be towed, for Luetjens had already detached the *Prinz Eugen*. As he had predicted, it did not have the endurance to operate with the *Bismarck*.

On May 27, the British closed in on the *Bismarck* in overwhelming force. The last anyone ever saw of Admiral Luetjens was early that morning, as he and his staff walked across the deck of the *Bismarck* and headed for the bridge. He was unusually quiet and did not bother to return the salutes of the crew. About 9 a.m. the bridge suddenly became an inferno of flames, and this is probably when Gunther Luetjens perished, but this is impossible to confirm. Only 110 of the *Bismarck*'s crew survived, while some 2,100 (including the entire fleet staff) perished. Many of them drowned after the battleship sank at 10:40 a.m. The British made very little effort to save them. Some have suggested that had the situation been reversed, there would probably have been another "war crimes" trial in 1946 or 1947.

Luetjens made several serious mistakes in his last campaign. There is little doubt but that he should have sunk the *Prince of Wales* when he had the chance. Adolf Hitler was right when he dressed down Grand Admiral Raeder for this failure, which was at least as much Raeder's as Luetjens's. Hitler showed a rare flash of strategic judgment when he recognized this fact—although he seems to have forgotten that he himself had urged caution from time to time. In any event, after the *Bismarck* debacle, Hitler never fully trusted Erich Raeder's judgment again. "Whereas up till then he had generally allowed me a free hand, he now became much more critical and clung more than previously to his own views," Raeder wrote later.[29] This was not necessarily bad for the German Navy. Raeder had exhibited questionable judgment since before the war began and since 1939 had shown a tendency to dissipate the navy's strength on raids of dubious value. Hitler's biggest mistake as a naval leader—other than not building enough U-boats and going to war too soon—was not replacing Erich Raeder much sooner.

Although from all accounts a good person, Luetjens must go down in history as a failure as a fleet commander. Certainly he was an unlucky one. His fatal flaws included an underestimation of the potential threat of aircraft to capital ships, a gross violation of the most elementary principles of radio security, and a slavelike obedience to the poor strategic thinking of the Supreme Naval Staff—even to the point of allowing it to cloud his own, sounder judgment. "Luetjens," one former German naval officer wrote, "personifies the tragedy of a commander whose personal ability was sacrificed on the altar of dutiful obedience."[30]

And what happened to Wilhelm Marschall, who had warned Luetjens not to listen too closely to the instructions of Raeder and his Supreme Naval Staff? His career seemed to be over until Admiral Raeder suddenly called him out of retirement on August 12, 1942, and named him commanding admiral, France. Six weeks later he was promoted to commander-in-chief of Naval Group West, then headquartered in Paris. Raeder had thus promoted the fleet commander he had previously dubbed a failure and worse, and whom he had forced into retirement in semi-official disgrace. Even so, when Marschall tried to bring up the subject of his actions in Norway, Raeder refused to discuss it. Did this mean that Raeder had realized the validity of Marschall's concept of tactical freedom of action for commanders at sea and thus recognized his own errors? Marschall thought so but also believed that Raeder "would rather have bitten his tongue out than admit it."[31]

Generaladmiral Marschall was among those senior officers retired in the first weeks of the Doenitz regime in 1943. He was again recalled in June 1944, to head a special authority staff for the Danube River. Retired again in November 1944, he was reappointed commander-in-chief of Naval Command West on April 19, 1945. He held this post until the end of the war. After being released from Allied captivity in mid-1947, Wilhelm Marschall wrote a number of articles on naval history and strategy. He died at Moelln (in Schleswig-Holstein) on March 20, 1976, at the age of 89.[32]

KARL DOENITZ was born in Gruenau-bei-Berlin on September 16, 1891, the second (and last) child of Emil Doenitz, an optical engineer working for the famous Karl Zeiss firm of Jena. His wife, Anna, died in 1895, so Karl and his older brother Friedrich were raised by their father in a thoroughly Prussian mold, with one exception: not being of the nobility, Emil realized that the key to his sons' futures lay in having a good education. As a result, Karl was sent to the Gymnasium at Zerbst and the Realschulen in Jena and Weimar. Brought up in the Prussian tradition of selfless service to the state, young Doenitz joined the Imperial Navy as an officer-cadet at the Naval School at Kiel on April 1, 1910.

Cadet Doenitz was a hard-working, reserved, stern, and silent young man who believed that "duty fulfillment was the highest moral value."[33] He was not an outstanding officer candidate (Doenitz proved to be something of a late bloomer) nor a particularly popular one, but he nevertheless passed his intensive training. He was promoted to midshipman in 1912 (the year his father died) and was transferred to the Navy School at Muerwik (on the coast of Schleswig-Holstein) for further training. To complete his apprenticeship he was sent to the light cruiser *Breslau*, where he was named signals officer—an unusually responsible post for a Faehnrich. He was appointed *Leutnant zur See* (equivalent to ensign, U.S. Navy) in the fall of 1913.

Aboard the *Breslau*, Doenitz was part of the international squadron blockading Montenegro during the Balkan crisis of 1913. Caught in the Mediterranean when World War I broke out in 1914, the *Breslau* evaded the Royal Navy and escaped to Turkey, where it, in effect, joined the Ottoman Navy and fought against the Russians in the Black Sea. On one raid it sank every ship in the Russian oil port of Novorossisk and destroyed the petroleum storage facilities there.

Meanwhile, Doenitz met and became engaged to Ingeborg Weber, the independent-minded daughter of a general. At the time the slim, outgoing, and energetic Ingeborg was a 21-year-old nurse at the General Embassy Hospital in Constantinople. She and Ensign Doenitz exchanged vows in May 1916, and it was to be a good marriage despite their different personalities. Both their sons were killed in action as naval officers in World War II.[34]

In July 1915, the *Breslau* hit a Russian mine off the entrance to the Bosporus and was out of action for months. While the cruiser was being repaired, Doenitz joined the Air Service and fought at Gallipoli as a gunner and aerial observer. When the *Breslau* came out of dock in February 1916, he was named adjutant, and in March he was promoted to *Oberleutnant sur See* (lieutenant in the U.S. Navy). By now Doenitz was marked as a superior junior officer. In the summer of 1916 he was recalled to Germany and transferred to the U-boats—a branch on which the German Navy now pinned all its hopes.

Oberleutnant Doenitz reported to the U-boat school in Flensburg-Muerwik on October 1 and, after intensive and difficult training, graduated with distinction as a qualified submarine officer in January 1917. Leaving his wife (who was six months pregnant with their only daughter, Ursula), Doenitz was posted to the Adriatic port of Pola, where he joined Kapitaenleutnant (lieutenant, senior grade) Walter Forstmann's *U-39* as the torpedo officer. Here he received invaluable on-the-job training under one of the outstanding U-boat "aces" of World War I, a Pour le Merite holder who was credited with sinking 400,000 tons of enemy shipping by 1917.[35]

Doenitz performed well aboard *U-39* and, after almost a year, was recalled to Kiel, where he attended a four-week U-boat commanders' course. In January 1918, he was given his first command: the 417-ton *UC-25*, a combination minelayer and torpedo attack boat based at Pola. He was ordered to operate in the Mediterranean. By the time Doenitz went out on his first independent patrol in the spring of 1918, the German unrestricted submarine warfare campaign was clearly being defeated by the British convoy system and its improved depth charges. Doenitz nevertheless excelled, sinking a steamer, and then, boldly entering the Sicilian port of Augusta, he torpedoed a 5,000-ton Italian coaling vessel, which he mistook for the British repair ship *Cyclops*. For this daring raid the Kaiser ordered him decorated with the prestigious Hohenzollern House Order, even though on the way back to home port, while attempting to negotiate a minefield at night, he ran his boat aground and caused significant damage to it. To add to his humiliation, he had to be rescued by an Austrian destroyer, which towed him off the bar the next day.

UC-25 was repaired in July, and Doenitz took her out again, laying mines in the Corfu area before attacking four ships. One was forced to beach at Malta, and the others apparently sank—but Doenitz could not wait around to watch because they were heavily escorted. This cruise was an outstanding success, since the obsolete *UC-25* could carry only five torpedoes. As a reward, Karl Doenitz was given command of the larger and faster *UB-68*. Unfortunately for him, this boat had an inexperienced crew and lacked stability in dives. On October 4, 1918, Doenitz attacked a convoy, sank the 3,883-ton British steamer *Oopack*, and dived. The inexperienced engineer immediately lost control, and the U-boat fell like a rock, almost literally standing on its head. Justifiably concerned that the hull of the submarine would collapse under the pressure, Doenitz ordered compressed air into all tanks, both engines full astern and rudder hard aport. This maneuver terminated the dive at 102 meters—32 meters below the maximum allowable depth rating for this boat. (The deck was, in fact, cracked, and the buoyancy tanks caved in under the pressure of the water.) *UB-68* did not collapse, but it was still out of control. It shot to the surface with such force that one-third of the boat actually left the water. Opening the hatch, Doenitz found himself in the middle of the convoy, with British destroyers racing toward him, their guns blazing. He quickly closed the hatch and ordered another dive. There was no compressed air left, however, so diving was impossible. By now British fire was hitting the boat, and Doenitz had no choice but to order abandon ship. The inexperienced engineer opened the sea cocks to scuttle the boat but could not get out before she went down. His death haunted Doenitz for years. Two other crewmen also drowned. The rest were picked up by the British. A depressed Karl Doenitz was aboard a British cruiser at Gibraltar, awaiting transport to a POW camp, when the High Seas Fleet mutinied at Kiel. A few days later the entire country was in revolt, the Kaiser had fled to Holland, and Germany was asking for an armistice.

Meanwhile, Doenitz was sent to an officers' prison camp at Redmires, near Sheffield. He naturally wanted an early repatriation, for a number of reasons. Professionally, his chances of getting a responsible job were much better than if he came back with hundreds of other officers. Doenitz went to unusual lengths to get sent home, however: he faked insanity. According to Wolfgang Frank, he played child's games with tin cans and small china dogs "until even his first lieutenant thought he was crazy."[36] In fact, years later, many of his former prison mates shook their heads in dismay as Doenitz, whom they remembered as a lunatic, climbed to the highest ranks in the navy. His insanity was instantly cured, of course, when he returned to Germany in July 1919, as one of the first POWs released.

Doenitz returned to duty as a staff officer at the Kiel Naval Station. His ambition, almost from the beginning, was to rejoin the U-boat branch—an arm that he was certain would be reformed someday in spite of the fact that Germany was denied submarines under the terms of the Treaty of Versailles. The following year (1920) he transferred to the torpedo boats, and by May 1920, was commander of *T-157*, operating out of Swinemuende on the Pomeranian coast. Promoted to Kapitaenleutnant in early 1921, he returned to Kiel in 1923 as an expert (*Referent*) in the Torpedo, Mine, and Intelligence Inspectorate, where he worked on the development of a new depth charge. In the fall of 1924, following a short staff officers training course conducted by Rear Admiral Erich Raeder, Doenitz was posted to the *Marineleitung*—the Naval Command in Berlin. Here he worked on writing new service regulations and a new military penal code, and on combating Bolshevik subversion in the navy. The political nature of this job forced the apolitical Doenitz to come into close contact with the Reichstag and reinforced his dislike for party politics.

As a staff officer in the 1920s, Doenitz proved to be a painstaking and self-critical perfectionist and very much a workaholic. He pushed himself and his subordinates to their limits—and sometimes beyond. He also dabbled in the navy's circumvention of the Treaty of Versailles. In August 1927, the navy's secret violations were exposed in the newspapers, in the so-called Lohmann Scandal. How much Doenitz knew about them or was involved in them was never made clear: the tight-lipped Doenitz would never say. In any event, he was sent back to sea duty in the Baltic as the navigator of the cruiser *Nymphe* in 1928. The scandal did not retard his advancement, however. He was promoted to *Korvettenkaepitan* (lieutenant commander) in November and simultaneously named commander of the 4th Torpedo Boat Half-Flotilla, which included four boats, 20 officers, and 600 men. Here Doenitz worked harder than ever, practicing maneuvers that would later be strongly resembled by the U-boat night surface attacks of World War II. He distinguished himself by "destroying" an enemy convoy in the 1929 autumn maneuvers, and his activities were monitored by Rear Admiral Walter Gladisch, the officer in charge of secret U-boat preparations.

From the fall of 1930 until 1934, he was assigned to the staff of the North Sea Naval District in Wilhelmshaven, where his duties again dealt with inner-service security—especially suppressing Communist activities. Considered a brilliant up-and-coming officer, he was rewarded in early 1933 with a special grant to allow him to travel and widen his knowledge of the outside world. He sailed to the Dutch and British colonies in the east, traveling to Malta, the Red Sea, southern India, Ceylon, Batavia, Java, Bali, and Singapore. He returned to duty in June 1933 and was promoted to *Fregattenkapitaen* (commander) in October. In 1934, he took a "language leave" to England and, in the fall, assumed command of the light cruiser *Emden*.

Meanwhile, Adolf Hitler had become chancellor of Germany. On February 1, 1935, he ordered the secret construction of the first U-boats to begin and six weeks later renounced the military restrictions of the Treaty of Versailles. Not surprisingly, on June 6, 1935, Commander Karl Doenitz was appointed *Fuehrer der U-boote* (FdU) and commander of the 1st U-boat Flotilla. By the time he took charge at the end of September, Germany had 11 small (250-ton) U-boats. On October 1 Doenitz was promoted to Kapitaen zur See. Karl Doenitz was in the position destiny had created for him. The High Command in Berlin was dominated by "big ship" men who thought that the U-boat (defeated in World War I) was obsolete or at least of marginal value. Doenitz, who realized how much submarine technology had changed since 1918, was allowed to develop "his" branch with little interference (or help) from OKM. He quickly won over his men with his enthusiasm, dedication, and total commitment. By 1938 he was practicing group attack tactics and calling for 626-ton (Type VII) U-boats, which could operate in the Atlantic. The German Admiralty was thinking more in terms of 2,000-ton submarines, which would have greater endurance. Doenitz, however, wanted smaller boats, because they would be easier to handle, would be less vulnerable to detection and depth charges, and would require fewer raw materials per boat to construct—which meant more of them could be built. Despite his junior rank, the dedicated and hard-driving Doenitz was allowed to have his way on this issue. During World War II, he was proven right beyond a shadow of a doubt.

Admiral Rolf Carls, the fleet commander in the mid-1930s, was both impressed by and supportive of the U-boat Fuehrer. Unfortunately for Doenitz, Admiral Raeder planned to wage a "cruiser war" against Great Britain and gave U-boat development and construction a low priority. Doenitz, in turn, bombarded Raeder with memoranda and requests for more U-boats. Three hundred of them, he said, could win a war against Britain for Germany. Raeder always listened politely, as if to humor the FdU, but his answer was always no.

Unlike Raeder, Doenitz believed that war would come before 1944. Unlike Raeder and Hitler, he did not believe that the Polish campaign would be a limited one. When Great Britain and France declared war on Nazi Germany on September 3, 1939, Karl Doenitz was already at his command post—a collection of wooden huts built on the outskirts of Wilhelmshaven. He greeted the announcement with a profane oath. At that time he had only 56 U-boats. Of these, only 22 were large enough to operate in the Atlantic—and he needed 300. Nevertheless, thanks to Doenitz, these were already on patrol and/or laying mines around Britain, and on September 4th Lieutenant Herbert Schultze of *U-48* reported sinking the *Royal Sceptre* off the coast of Scotland.[37] It was the first of 2,603 Allied ships to be destroyed by U-boats during the war. By the end of the month, Doenitz's boats had sunk 175,000 tons of enemy shipping—proving that the U-boat was definitely not an obsolete weapon. All the same, German U-boat production remained stable at two new boats per month.

Doenitz planned and ordered the Scapa Flow operation, which was executed by *U-47* under Lieutenant Guenther Prien on the night of October 13–14 (see later discussion). When it was over, the British battleship *Royal Oak* was gone, along with 832 of her crew. When *U-47* returned, Raeder was there to greet it. He also promoted Doenitz to Konteradmiral on the spot.

The new rear admiral was unable to keep up the pace of sinkings, however. When his Atlantic U-boats came back from their first patrols, he had nothing with which to replace them. Also, November brought the usual winter storms to the North Atlantic, making hunting very difficult.

Tonnage sunk by U-boats declined from 175,000 in September to 125,000 in October; just over 80,000 in November; and 125,000 in December. From January 1 to March 31, 1940, U-boats sank only 108 merchantmen, totaling 343,610 tons. For Great Britain, these losses were well within the tolerance range. She had some 24 million tons of shipping when the war began, and new construction (200,000 tons per month) easily exceeded losses.

Karl Doenitz hoped to have his submarines back on the Atlantic shipping lanes in the spring of 1940, but instead Raeder ordered them committed to supporting the invasion of Norway. The FdU protested but was overruled, as usual. For Doenitz, April 1940, was probably the most frustrating month of the war. He committed 42 U-boats to Norwegian waters, and they fired tube after tube into Allied vessels, but almost all their torpedoes were duds. Worse, some exploded prematurely, revealing the U-boat's position to the enemy. When Prien fired two torpedoes into the battleship *Warspite* on April 19 and both bounced off without detonating, a furious Doenitz recalled the entire pack and called for an investigation, which grew into a scandal (as discussed earlier). According to Doenitz, the defective torpedoes cost Germany the sinking of the *Warspite*, seven cruisers, seven destroyers, and five troop transports. The U-boats sank only 20 ships, totaling a little more than 80,00) tons—the lowest losses to submarines since the war began.

The torpedo crisis was partially mastered by June 1940, when the fall of France gave Doenitz new bases that were much closer to the Allied shipping lanes, extending the time the U-boats could stay on patrol. It was the first "happy time" for the submarine arm, the day of the U-boat ace. Britain lost 58 ships (284,113 tons) to U-boats alone in June, 38 more in July (195,825 tons), 56 in August (267,618 tons), 59 in September (295,335 tons), and 63 in October (352,407 tons). Due to weather, sinkings leveled off in November and December (32 ships/146,613 tons, and 37 ships/212,590 tons, respectively), but the figures were nevertheless disastrous for Great Britain. In seven months, she had lost 343 ships, totaling 1,754,501 tons. Sinkings were exceeding production despite the aid sent from Churchill's "cousin" in the White House. October was a particularly alarming month, when U-boats sank an average of 920 tons of shipping every day. Churchill said after the war that the Battle of the Atlantic was the only time he felt that Great Britain was truly threatened.

What is truly remarkable about these German successes is the small number of U-boats that Doenitz deployed in these operations. On September 1, 1940, he had 57 U-boats—exactly the same number he'd had at the start of the war. Operational strength had declined from 39 to 27, however, due to necessary maintenance, damage repair (especially from ice and depth charges), and the necessity to transfer several boats to training duties. Only toward the end of 1940 did U-boat construction rise from two per month to six. Although Admiral Raeder had at least increased the allocation of raw materials to the U-boat construction sites, the submarine construction program was handicapped by bottlenecks in skilled labor and materials (especially copper), by continued construction of capital ships, and by the fact that Hermann Goering was in charge of resource allocation for the German war effort. Karl Doenitz and his crews were fighting a "poor man's war" during the critical phases of the Battle of the Atlantic.

In August 1940, Doenitz moved his command post to Paris, but this was still too far from his boats, so he relocated to a chateau at Kerneval, on the French coast outside Lorient, in September. (Later he moved back to Paris, due to the danger of raids by Allied commandoes.) Even in the French capital his headquarters was noted for its lack of ostentation—Doenitz's Spartan sense of self-discipline would not permit anything else. He never ate or drank too much and went to bed by 10 p.m. (unless duty intervened), although he did not mind if his men drank all night and painted the town red, which they frequently did. He still met almost every boat that came back, attended the graduation parade from every training course, set up special rest camps (commandeered holiday resorts) for U-boat men not on patrol or leave, and made sure his camps were well stocked with fine food and wine, which were sold well below cost. He did everything he could to relieve the enormous strain involved in underwater combat service, and his submariners loved him for it. There was not one who did not feel that he knew Doenitz, for they all had seen him at close quarters. Behind his back they called him "Vater Karl" or "Der Loewe" (the lion). Undoubtedly he had the respect and admiration of his branch, at least at this point of the war.

As Doenitz (recently promoted to vice admiral) expected they would, the British gradually improved their convoy procedures and submarine detection and attack techniques. In March 1941 alone he lost five boats, and with them some of his best commanders. Also, the RAF Coastal Command now had longer-range bombers that could attack U-boats far out to sea. Doenitz reacted by moving the operational zone farther west. Between the RAF bases in Iceland, Britain, and Canada there was a "gap" that could not yet be covered by aircraft. When this gap was eliminated, the days of the U-boat's successes would be over.

Doenitz's strategy in the U-boat war was simple: sink as much enemy tonnage as possible, as rapidly as possible. This could best be done in the North Atlantic. If his submarines could sink merchant ships more rapidly than the British could construct them, Britain could be brought to her knees. He was extremely annoyed and frustrated in August 1941, when Hitler decided to send 20 U-boats to the Mediterranean to help break the stranglehold the British had on the Axis supply lines to North Africa. Doenitz knew that once a submarine entered the Mediterranean it could never come back, due to the strong westerly Gibraltar currents. He had managed to talk Hitler out of similar decisions in April and June, but this time the Fuehrer's mind was made up. Doenitz did manage to get the number reduced, but he had no choice but to dispatch a dozen U-boats to the Mediterranean in September and October. This constituted a loss of 50 percent of his oceangoing operational capabilities and forced Doenitz to virtually give up the battle in the North Atlantic, at least temporarily. Nevertheless, until December 7, Doenitz could not view the year 1941 as a bad one. The Allies had lost 1,299 ships, displacing 4,328,558 tons— that was 240 ships and 340,000 tons more than in 1940—and about half these had been sunk by submarines. Admiral Raeder's staff estimated that British and Canadian shipyards alone produced 1,600,000 tons annually. Thus it was clear that Germany was winning the Battle of the North Atlantic.

The Japanese attack on Pearl Harbor changed all that. Hitler foolishly followed his ally's lead and declared war on the United States on December 11. Now the huge production capacity of the American shipyards was fully thrown into the balance against Germany, and they, according to OKM estimates, could produce more than 5,000,000 tons per year. Roosevelt wanted more, however, and announced that America would produce 8,000,000 tons of shipping in 1942 and 10,000,000 in 1943. The American entry into the war doomed the U-boats to eventual defeat.

Unlike Hitler, Goering, and most of the admirals, Karl Doenitz was not one who underestimated the vast potential of the American war machine or America's ability to project power overseas. Still, the Americans were unprepared and inexperienced, and their home front was basically still at peace. Also, the U.S. Navy under the anti-British Admiral Ernest J. King was extremely slow at taking advantage of the experience the British had acquired in fighting U-boats. As a result, American ships sailed singly, with all lights blazing, without escort, and there were virtually no sea or air patrols out looking for U-boats.

The second and final "happy time" for the U-boats began on January 15, 1942, when Doenitz unleashed them against shipping off the American coast. In January alone, 62 ships totaling 327,357 tons were sunk. By May 10 the German submarines had sunk 303 ships—a total of 2,015,252 tons. Even so, it would be July before the Americans began to travel in escorted convoys, and the second "happy time" came to an end.

The American losses would have been even greater had not Hitler and Raeder interfered—again. On January 22, the Fuehrer and OKM decided Norway was in danger of invasion and ordered all U-boats to this sector to act as a reconnaissance force against the expected invasion. Doenitz was beside himself with fury. Fortunately for him, he was able to point to the first reports of successes from U.S. waters and convince Hitler to suspend this order; however, on February 1, OKM ordered 20 boats posted to the sector between Iceland and Norway. This left an average of only 10 to 12 operational U-boats in American waters at any one time.[38] Doenitz was filled with a feeling of impotence and frustration, but there was nothing he could do about it. Perhaps to partially console him, Hitler had Doenitz promoted to full admiral in March 1942.

Meanwhile, U-boat strength continued to increase, ever so slowly. In the first six months of 1941, there had been an average of 18 boats at sea at any one time. In the second half of the year this average increased to 33. Twenty new U-boats were supposed to join the fleet each month in 1942, but actual production lagged well behind schedule.

When the "happy time" off the American coast ended in the summer of 1942, Doenitz's men returned to the convoy battle of the North Atlantic. The fight was much more difficult than before, however, because the Allies were using better tactics and new technology. Radar-equipped aircraft, catapult-launched airplanes, new radar that could not be picked up by German detection devices, H/FD/F (the High Frequency Direction Finder, or "Huff Duff"), the Hedgehog depth-charge projector, and the new U.S. and RAF anti-submarine patrol and reconnaissance aircraft all combined to crush the U-boat offensive in May 1943.

Meanwhile, as we have seen, an angry Hitler ordered Grand Admiral Raeder to scrap all the big ships and mount their heavy guns ashore. Raeder resigned, effective January 30, 1943. At Hitler's request he nominated two suitable successors: Generaladmiral Rolf Carls and Admiral Karl Doenitz. Predictably Hitler chose Doenitz, for several reasons. Primary, of course, was his success as FdU. Also, he found Doenitz's optimism to his liking; his attitude was more sympathetic to National Socialism than the older Carls'; and Doenitz now had friends at court, most notably Albert Speer, the minister of munitions, and Admiral Puttkamer, Hitler's naval adjutant. In any event, Karl Doenitz was promoted to grand admiral (Grossadmiral) and commander-in-chief of the German Navy on January 30, 1943. He also received a personal grant of 300,000 marks. One of his first acts was to sack Carls, who, as fleet commander in the 1930s, had been one of his biggest supporters but now was a potential rival. He also cleared the SKL staff of many former Raeder appointees. Clearly, Doenitz intended to have nothing but complete obedience and unquestioning loyalty from below.[39]

Karl Doenitz had risen from the rank of captain to grand admiral in less than three and a half years and was now at the height of his power. Ironically, he was also on the verge of his decisive defeat. First, however, he dissuaded Hitler from disbanding the surface fleet, correctly and effectively arguing that a fleet "in being" would tie up a disproportionate number of Allied warships, which could otherwise be used to protect convoys or to fight Japan.

Doenitz moved his headquarters to Berlin but retained effective command of the U-boat branch himself (although his long-time chief of staff, Admiral Eberhard Godt, officially became FdU). From here, Doenitz energetically pursued the Battle of the North Atlantic. In March 1943, his U-boats, now operating in teams called wolf packs, sank 627,300 tons of shipping (120 ships), and a delighted Fuehrer decorated him with the Oak Leaves to the Knight's Cross. Unfortunately for Doenitz, his losses were also high: 11 submarines did not come home. U-boats returning to their bases on the Bay of Biscay, formerly considered a safe haven, were now being attacked by Liberators, Fortresses, Boeings, and Beau-fighters, launched from the Allies' new "escort carriers"—converted cargo ships or mini-carriers that could catapult-launch about 20 airplanes. For the first time, the previously exemplary morale of the German submariner began to fall. Doenitz responded by hurling more U-boats into the battle. In April, the Allies lost 64 ships (344,680 tons), but 15 submarines failed to return. U-boat losses now exceeded production, but Doenitz still escalated the battle. In May, however, Allied technology was finally brought fully to bear on the U-boats, and the German submarine arm suffered its decisive defeat. Fifty-eight Allied vessels (299,428 tons) were sunk, but a shocking total of 41 U-boats were destroyed.

Karl Doenitz had no choice but to admit defeat, and on May 24, 1943, he withdrew the depleted wolf packs from the North Atlantic. It is a measure of his influence with Hitler that the dictator accepted this decision without protest or reproach. Nevertheless, the U-boat weapon was finally blunted.

Doenitz's strategy for the rest of the war was (1) to build more U-boats; (2) to continue the U-boat war, mainly in the "softer" sectors, such as the Caribbean or the area southwest of the Azores; and (3) to press for and await scientific developments that would again shift the balance in favor of Germany. He continued to send U-boats to the North Atlantic periodically but never with appreciable success. In the meantime, the U-boats continued to go out and sink Allied ships; however, almost as many U-boats failed to return. From June through August 1943, only 60 Allied freighters were lost—against 79 U-boats.

German science did produce a submarine (Type XXI) that might have been able to defeat the Allied convoy and escort system, but it was developed too late to make any difference. During the D–Day invasion, Doenitz ordered the last, massive commitment of submarines against the Allied navies. In all, 36 U-boats were committed. Fewer than half survived. Between June 6 and August 31, Doenitz continued to feed forces into the battle, in a desperate and fanatical attempt to influence the course of events no matter what his casualties were. His stubborn and unreasonable efforts were futile and were responsible for the needless deaths of hundreds of German sailors. Between June 6 and August 31, German submarines sank five escort vessels, 12 ships totaling 56,845 tons, and four landing craft totaling 8,400 tons. Eighty-two U-boats were lost during the same period.[40] Out of the 820 U-boats the German submarine branch committed to the Battle of the Atlantic from 1939 through 1945, 781 were destroyed in action. Out of 39,000 U-boat men who fought there, 32,000 lost their lives—most of them in the last two years of the war.

During his tenure as grand admiral, Doenitz was a loyal and sometimes enthusiastic supporter of Adolf Hitler, backing his Fuehrer on every possible occasion, including such militarily senseless decisions as holding Tunisia in the spring of 1943; hanging onto the bridgehead in northeastern Sicily in August 1943; defending the Crimean peninsula between October 1943 and April 1944; and keeping Army Group North isolated in Courland in 1944 and 1945, when Germany needed every soldier it could muster to defend the Fatherland. Doenitz also issued propaganda statements echoing Goebbels, Goering, and so on; praised Hitler at every opportunity; called for fanatical offensives in highly inappropriate situations; and made sure that the navy was ideologically "pure" (i.e., pro-Nazi). Whether or not he knew of the mass murders of the Nazi regime is still the subject of debate, but he did use slave labor in his construction program and was at least outwardly friendly with Heinrich Himmler. On April 19, 1945, he evacuated his headquarters (on the outskirts of Berlin) only 24 hours before the

Soviet tanks arrived. He then visited Hitler at the Fuehrer Bunker on April 20—the Fuehrer's 56th and last birthday. Ten days later Hitler shot himself. To the surprise of many, his last will and testament named Grand Admiral Doenitz his successor and head of state.

Doenitz had initially transferred his headquarters to Ploen, but on May 2 he relocated it (and the capital of the Reich) to the Naval Cadet School at Muerwik, near Flensburg, at the far north of the Schleswig-Holstein peninsula. Here he pursued the twin policies of trying to end the war against the Western Allies as soon as possible while simultaneously saving as many Germans as possible from the Soviets. He sent every available naval and merchant vessel to the Baltic ports still in German hands, with orders to bring out every refugee they could. The troop units still fighting were ordered to cover the evacuation of the refugees and then escape to the west themselves. It has been estimated that 2 million civilians escaped Soviet captivity in the eight days that Doenitz prolonged hostilities. However, at 2:30 a.m. on the morning of May 7, Colonel General Jodl was forced to sign the instrument of unconditional surrender. It was to take effect at midnight on May 8–9. Doenitz continued the fiction of governing Germany until 9:45 a.m. on May 23, when he was summoned to the liner *Patria* and arrested by U.S. Major General Lowell W. Rooks of the Allied Control Commission. He was put on trial at Nuremberg as a major war criminal. Interestingly, he was forced to undergo an I.Q. test first. He scored 138 (borderline genius). Had he not been "the last Fuehrer," Karl Doenitz probably would not have been indicted as a major war criminal. On the witness stand (May 8–10, 1946) he put up a strong defense in his own behalf, stating that as an officer it was not his place to decide if a war was "aggressive" or not but that he had to obey orders. After Doenitz finished testifying on May 9, Hermann Goering declared to those around him, "Ah, now I feel great for the first time in three weeks! Now we finally hear a decent German soldier speak for once!"[41]

Unlike most trials, at Nuremberg the defense had to present its case first. Also, defense objections had to be submitted in writing and the court answered them at its leisure—making them practically useless. Doenitz nevertheless held his own. When asked if he was interested in the fact that naval arms had been produced by slave labor, he denied any knowledge of it but added that he was only interested in the production itself, not where the weapons came from. (The debate over whether or not Doenitz lied about not knowing that slave labor produced naval armaments continues to this day, but it seems extremely likely that he did.) He denied having anything to do with the concentration camps but admitted ordering the sinking of neutral ships in war zones, declaring this perfectly proper. They had been warned to stay out, he said, and if they risked entering a war zone for the sake of profit, they should be prepared to suffer the consequences. Even Franklin D. Roosevelt had recognized this fact, the admiral said, when he stated that merchant ships had no right to risk the lives of their crews by entering a war zone just to make a profit. The prosecution countered by bringing out that Doenitz had advocated occupying Spain (to get her ports and Gibraltar) and asserted that he had supported Hitler in various efforts to prosecute the war aggressively. Doenitz could not deny that he advocated seizing Spain, but he justified his "fanatical" Nazi speeches as necessary to keep up morale, since the collapse of the Eastern Front would have meant death for countless German women and children. He attacked the conduct of the Soviets and denied that he had any idea millions of Jews were being murdered. Unlike some of the other defendants, however, he refrained from denouncing Adolf Hitler.[42]

Much of the prosecution's case hinged on the issue of the legality of unrestricted submarine warfare and was deflated by U.S. Admiral Chester A. Nimitz, who supported Doenitz's views on the subject. He submitted written testimony, stating that this type of warfare had been the policy of the U.S. Pacific Fleet from December 8, 1941. Several British prisoners also submitted depositions stating that they had been treated in strict accordance with the Geneva Convention while prisoners of the German Navy. Now, almost 50 years later, it appears that much of the case against Doenitz was rather thin. At the time, however, passions were running high, and the Soviets in particular wanted Doenitz's scalp for rescuing the refugees from the East, for the remarks he made about them from the witness stand, and for his anti-Communist activities, which dated back to the 1920s. The British judge also wanted his head, apparently because his submarines had been too successful. U.S. Judge Francis Biddle thought Doenitz should be acquitted on all counts. The result was a compromise. Doenitz was sentenced to 10 years' imprisonment—the lightest sentence of any of those convicted at Nuremberg. Even this relatively light sentence did not satisfy Major General J. F. C. Fuller, the distinguished British armored theorist and military historian, who a decade later was still describing Doenitz's sentence as a "flagrant travesty of justice resulting from hypocrisy!"[43]

Doenitz was imprisoned at Spandau. He had an easier time of it than the others because of his Spartan self-discipline and work ethic. He was soon devoting himself to growing things and sometimes produced up to 50 tomatoes on a single plant—he was always the classic overachiever! While in prison, he and Admiral Raeder remained distinctly cool toward each other, and his previous friendship with Albert Speer deteriorated into thinly veiled animosity because of the munitions minister's testimony at Nuremberg. Contrary to his hopes, Doenitz served every day of his sentence and was released on October 1, 1956.

Frau Ingeborg Doenitz had been working as a nurse in a Hamburg hospital while her husband was in Spandau. He rejoined her in the nearby residential town of Aumuehle, a quiet, pleasant community where she rented the ground floor of a villa. She had had to struggle to make ends meet, but Karl soon managed to get his pension restored (as an admiral, not as a grand admiral), so they were able to live comfortably. Doenitz spent most of the time immediately after his release hard at work, writing his memoirs, which were published in 1958 under the title *10 Jahre und 20 Tage* (*Ten Years and Twenty Days*), which was later printed in English. Later he wrote *Mein wechselvoltes Leben* (*My Eventful Life*, published in 1968) and *Deutsche Strategie zur See in zweiten Weltkrieg* (*German Naval Strategy in World War II*, published in 1969), which was retitled *40 Fragen an Karl Doenitz* (*Forty Questions to Admiral Doenitz*) in later editions.

His wife died on May 2, 1962, and the rest of his life was lonely. Now a Christian, he had a huge cross erected over her grave. He went to church every Sunday and still attended dinners and enjoyed visiting and receiving old comrades, but he became more introverted and more easily angered. Perhaps this can be partially explained by his Spandau years, his advanced age, and his growing frailness and deafness. He was particularly disappointed with the German people, who, he felt, had unjustly turned against him. He was also annoyed by the Bonn government's continued refusal to clear his name, despite the efforts of various U-boat associations on his behalf. He was also bitterly disappointed when the government refused to grant him a state funeral or to allow uniforms to be worn at a private one.

A man who had outlived his time, Karl Doenitz died of a heart attack at 7:10 p.m. on Christmas Eve, 1980, the last of six German grand admirals. His funeral took place at the Bismarck Memorial Chapel in Aumuehle on January 6, 1981. The German government decreed that no serviceman was allowed to attend his funeral in uniform, but this order was generally ignored. Dozens of his old comrades attended his funeral, including more than 100 Knight's Cross holders. He was buried in the Waldfriedhof Cemetery without military honors.

GUENTHER PRIEN, the son of a judge, was born in Luebeck, an ancient city on the Baltic, in 1908 and spent his formative years there, developing a fervent love for the sea, which remained with him for the rest of his life.

Later his parents separated, and his mother moved to Leipzig with her three children. Apparently Judge Prien made no further financial contribution to his estranged family, because Frau Prien was barely able to make a living selling peasant-lace and pictures she painted. Frequently, she was afraid to open bills because she had no money to pay them. At the age of 15, the stocky, friendly Guenther, who had chubby cheeks and a ready smile, left home so that his mother would have one less burden. It was the era of high inflation, when the value of the German mark fell from 12 per U.S. dollar to more than 4.2 trillion marks per dollar. Using foreign exchange he earned working as a guide during the Leipzig Industrial Fair, young Guenther paid for his admission to the Hamburg-Finkenwaerder Seaman's School (called the Seaman's Factory), where he learned the rudiments of seamanship. He then obtained a job on the SS *Hamburg* as a cabin boy.[44]

The *Hamburg* was lost in a winter gale, but Prien was fortunate enough to reach the coast of Ireland, where he was rescued. Not unduly upset by this shipwreck, young Prien spent the next several years on other ships, learning his trade. By hard labor and concentration he earned his master's ticket but could not find a ship, as the German merchant marine had been overwhelmed by the Great Depression. At age 24, the unemployed sea captain was forced to enlist in the Voluntary Labor Service in order to feed himself. He was very unhappy at this occupation (for which he received room and board, but no money), and when he learned that the German Navy was recruiting merchant officers for a naval reserve, he was quick to sign up. Guenther Prien enlisted at Stralsund as an ordinary seaman in January 1933, beginning his career in the Kriegsmarine.

Prien again worked his way up from the bottom and eventually managed to wangle an appointment to the U-boat school, where he was befriended by Werner Hartmann, the commander of *U-26*. At Hartmann's request Prien was assigned to his submarine, which served in the Spanish Civil War. In 1938, Prien attended the U-boat commanders' course and was given his first command in 1938. His boat was *U-47*. By now Prien was married and had a young daughter. Even so, his love for the sea had not diminished. He once astonished his messmates by announcing, "I would rather have a decent month's maneuvers in the Atlantic than any leave."[45] He distinguished himself in the Bay of Biscay maneuvers and impressed Captain Karl Doenitz, the head of the U-boat arm.

Prien was out on patrol in the North Sea on September 3, 1939, when France and England declared war on Nazi Germany. Two days later Prien sank his first ship, a French steamer, which was followed to the bottom by the British cargo ships *Rio Claro* and *Gartavon*. When he returned to base in mid-September, Admiral Raeder decorated him with the Iron Cross, Second Class, and gave the entire crew of *U-47* a two-week leave. On Sunday, October 1, shortly after he returned to duty, Prien was summoned to the depot ship *Weichsel*, at anchor at Kiel, where he met with Captain Doenitz. The future grand admiral quickly came to the point: "Do you think that a determined commander could get his U-boat inside Scapa Flow and attack the enemy naval forces lying there?" After a short pause, he added, "I don't want you to give me an answer now. Think it over. Report back on Tuesday and let me have your considered opinion then. Whichever way you decide, it will not be a black mark against you. It will not affect the high opinion we have of you."

Prien was temporarily stunned. Scapa Flow was the principal base of the British Home Fleet and a port hitherto considered impenetrable to submarines. This Orkney Islands base also had a special place in German naval history. It was here that the officers of the Kaiser's navy had scuttled the Imperial High Seas Fleet after World War I. A victory here would have a tremendous psychological effect on the German Kriegsmarine. On the other hand, two U-boats had tried to sneak through its defenses during World War I, and neither had come back. But Doenitz had received a communication from a merchant captain who had been to the port of Kirkwall, just north of Scapa Flow, a few weeks before, and he reported having heard that the eastern entrances to the Flow had been neglected. A Luftwaffe photo reconnaissance flight confirmed this fact: there was a 17-meter gap between sunken blockships in Kirk Sound, the northernmost of the eastern passages, by which a bold commander might enter the great basin of Scapa Flow.

Lieutenant Prien reported back to Doenitz the next day: he would do it. They set the time of the attack for the night of October 13–14. *U-47* left Kiel on October 8. On the morning of October 13, Prien submerged outside the British home port and told his crew of their mission. They were enthusiastically in favor of it despite the obvious dangers. Prien surfaced at 7:15 p.m. that evening to find the entire sky illuminated by a brilliant display of the northern lights, which made it almost as bright as day. After suppressing an oath, Prien decided to try it anyway. Slowly the U-boat moved into Scapa Flow, working its way against the current, only just avoiding collision with the blockships. British security, however, was lax, and the German submarine was not sighted. At 12:58 a.m. Prien lined up on what he thought were the battleships *Royal Oak* and *Repulse*. (Actually, what he thought was the *Repulse* was the old seaplane-carrier *Pegasus*.) At a range of

4,000 yards he fired four torpedoes; however, one tube misfired and only one of the other three detonated—on the anchor cable of the *Royal Oak.*

Prien now expected the base to become a beehive of activity, but there were no alarms, searchlights, destroyer attacks, or coastal artillery fire. Were the British asleep? With incredible daring, Prien decided to launch a second attack. He calmly turned south and made a wide circle around the anchorage on the surface, while his torpedomen loaded four fresh "fish."

Prien had no way of knowing that his first attack had caused so little damage that the battleship's captain and the other officers who went to investigate thought the explosion must have been internal. No general alarm was signaled. At 1:16 a.m. Prien launched his second attack, firing all four torpedoes at the *Royal Oak.* Two of them hit the huge battleship and exploded, igniting a magazine. A thunderous explosion ripped the 31,200-ton ship apart, filling the air with flying wreckage. The *Royal Oak* capsized and sank in 13 minutes, taking with her Rear Admiral H. F. C. Blagrove and 832 crewmen. Meanwhile, *U-47*—which was still surfaced—withdrew at high speed. Prien had a bad moment when a destroyer came straight at him with searchlights blazing but miraculously turned away before sighting the vulnerable U-boat. By 2:15 a.m. Prien had again skirted the blockships and was back in the open sea.

When *U-47* returned to friendly waters, it was escorted to dock at Wilhelmshaven by two destroyers. It was met by cheering crowds, a band, and a delegation of VIPs, headed by Doenitz and Grand Admiral Raeder, who came on board and shook hands with every member of the crew: a most unusual gesture for him. He then conferred the Iron Cross, Second Class, on every one of them and announced that Doenitz was promoted to rear admiral. Prien himself was to make a personal report to the Fuehrer. That afternoon Hitler's personal Wulf-Vogel and a Ju-52 landed at Wilhelmshaven: Hitler wanted to see the entire crew. When they landed at Tempelhof the next day, the entire route from the airfield to the Kaiserhof Hotel was black with people screaming, "We want Prien!" Hitler received them in the Reichschancellery the following day and decorated their captain with the Knight's Cross. They were Hitler's guests for lunch and Goebbels's guests at the Wintergarten Theater that evening. Afterward they went night-clubbing and, in their honor, the ban on dancing was lifted for the evening.

Guenther Prien was now an idol of the Third Reich—a far cry from his days of poverty and unemployment just a few years before. He was, however, the same officer he had always been. Fame embarrassed him. Fan letters, which he received by the mailbag, he handled by simply throwing them away unread, stating that he was not a movie star. He still loved to drink beer and tell stories with his comrades and friends and by all accounts had a wonderful gift for humor. On duty, however, he was a different man. Here there was no room for sentiment. Here Guenther Prien was all business, a man who believed in practice, practice, practice, and both he and his officers were scathing in their rebukes for the slightest mistakes. Discipline aboard *U-47* was very strict indeed, but then both morale and pride were quite high. In late 1939 the men painted a bull on the conning tower of *U-47*, and from then on Prien had a permanent nickname: the Bull of Scapa Flow.

U-47 went out on its third wartime patrol in mid-November 1939, heading for the North Atlantic. Its commander was relieved to escape the limelight that his victory at Scapa Flow had inflicted on him. East of the Shetland Islands he fired a torpedo at the British cruiser *Norfolk* and thought he had sunk her, but the torpedo had missed and exploded in the ship's wake. *U-47* had no chance for a thorough investigation, as it was instantly forced to dive and was subjected to depth charges dropped by three destroyers for several hours. After escaping this harrowing experience, Prien resumed his patrol and, five days later, torpedoed a large passenger steamer amidships. She was, however, able to limp away, while *U-47* was again subjected to depth-charging.

Lieutenant Prien's next target was a heavily laden tanker, which did not escape: it exploded in a "terrifying tower of flame" and sank in two minutes.[46] The next day he torpedoed a second tanker with the same result. Finally, on the way home, he fired two torpedoes at a 4,000-ton freighter but missed. To Prien's amusement, the freighter never knew that it had been under U-boat attack.

Due to damage caused by drift ice and depth charges, *U-47* was not ready for action again until mid-March 1940. After an unsuccessful patrol, cut short by fuel pump failure and abysmal weather, Prien returned to Wilhelmshaven on March 29. In the first days of April, he went back to sea with a new mission: steal through the heavily mined waters of the Skagerrak and help screen the German naval forces taking part in the invasion of Norway. On April 7—three days before the invasion began—Prien received a signal announcing the birth of his second daughter. This news did not affect his daring one bit. He closed to within 900 yards of the British battleship *Warspite* and fired two torpedoes, one of which exploded prematurely. The other failed to detonate. He also launched a surprise attack on an Anglo-French convoy of three large transports, two cruisers, and three freighters at anchor in the Bydden fjord—a U-boat commander's dream. Prien fired eight torpedoes into the transports, but all eight either failed to explode or took wildly erratic courses and missed everything except the rocky beaches of Norway. Then Prien ran aground while taking evasive action, damaging his starboard diesel. He only just managed to free his boat and make for the open sea, from which he headed for home. An angry and depressed Prien reported to Doenitz that "it was useless to send him to fight with a dummy rifle."[47]

U-47 was not the only submarine with torpedo difficulties, as we have seen. It did not return to sea until June, when the problem was solved.

With Norway conquered and the torpedoes running true and exploding when they were supposed to again, Doenitz sent his U-boats back to the North Atlantic. He divided them into two battle groups: Prien and Roesing. Prien was given the task of attacking a Halifax convoy, which was returning home. June 1940 was one of Germany's best months in the naval war. The navy and Luftwaffe combined to sink 140 merchant ships—a total of 585,496 tons. Prien alone accounted for more than 10 percent of the total. He fired all his torpedoes and sank 66,587 tons of shipping, including the 15,501-ton *Amndom Stat*. The second-leading U-boat ace that month was Lieutenant Engelbert Endrass, who sank 54,000 tons of enemy shipping. Endrass had been Prien's second-in-command at Scapa Flow.

June to October 1940 was the period of the U-boat aces—Prien, Kretschmer, Endrass, and others. Prien was the first to be credited with sinking more than 200,000 tons of Allied shipping and was the fifth German officer to be decorated with the Oak Leaves to the Knight's Cross. (After the war, when it was possible to calculate actual instead of estimated totals, Prien's figures were reduced to 160,939 tons.[48]) He was soon surpassed by Otto Kretschmer of *U-99*, who would go on to become the leading U-boat ace of the war, sinking 44 ships (266,629 tons). It was the era of "wolf pack" tactics—of concentrated attacks by entire groups of U-boats. On the night of October 17–18, Prien led three other boats in a wolf pack strike against a British convoy. The joint effort, conducted at close range, resulted in the sinking of eight more Allied ships. There were no U-boat losses. Prien's patrols in the winter of 1940–1941 were less successful due to the normal North Atlantic gales, storms, and poor visibility. Even when a target was sighted it was difficult to get off a shot. Meanwhile, the British gradually forged ahead in the field of technological warfare at sea. They developed ASV radar and began systematically training escort commanders and equipping Coastal Command's bombers with depth charges, instead of the heretofore ineffective bombs. Also, the strain of this intensive type of warfare was beginning to tell on the U-boat crews and commanders. No one, however, ever reported detecting any evidence of strain or pressure on the face of Guenther Prien. Now operating out of Lorient, he looked forward to each new mission, although he still enjoyed partying and beer-drinking with comrades. In late January 1941, he took Lieutenant Wolfgang Frank, his officers, and two midshipmen with him on one of his excursions into the interior of France, where they dined in a small village at an inn run by an old Breton woman famous for her cuisine. The submariners consumed bottle after bottle, while Prien regaled them with humorous tales about adventures on yachts, merchant ships, and submarines. Frank recalled that he was "filled with a passionate eagerness to be in action again." The next day, just before he departed, he shook hands with Frank. "This time it is going to be a good trip," he said. "I can feel it in my bones."[49]

After being given flowers by a French female admirer, Guenther Prien began his tenth wartime patrol. It was not like old times, however. On March 8, six weeks after putting to sea, Prien led an attack on Convoy OB-293, outward bound from Liverpool to Halifax. The battle took place south of Iceland. The U-boats sank two merchant ships, but their own losses were devastating. Hans Eckermann's U-boat was so badly damaged that he was forced to drop out of the battle and limp back to Lorient, which he was able to do in the general confusion. Then *U-70* was brought to the surface by depth charges from two corvettes, where it was scuttled by its captain, Lieutenant Commander Joachim Matz. Even *U-99* under Otto Kretschmer was driven off by OB-293's strong escort, which was led by Commander James Rowland in the World War I destroyer *Wolverine*. But the redoubtable Guenther Prien persisted in the attack, sinking his 28th merchantman in the process. In heavy seas and thick weather he struck again at dusk on March 8, penetrating the escort screen in a rain squall. Then, all of a sudden, Prien's luck deserted him. Before he could fire, the squall dissipated, the overcast broke, and *U-47* found itself in the fading sunlight, in full view of the *Wolverine*. Prien crash-dived immediately, but the *Wolverine* reacted with equal swiftness by hurling a pattern of depth charges. At that range, with *U-47* already picked up by Rowland's asdic (sonar), they could hardly miss. *U-47* was badly damaged, and the *Wolverine* picked up the rattle of propeller shafts out of alignment. Prien stayed under water until nightfall, when he surfaced again, about a mile from the point of Rowland's original attack. The *Wolverine* was on him immediately. Prien crash-dived again— for the last time. This time the depth charges blew *U-47* apart. A few minutes later bits and pieces of debris came to the surface—the sure sign of a "kill." There were no survivors.

For some time OKM withheld the news from the nation and the next of kin on the faint hope that Prien's prolonged silence was due to the failure of his wireless transmitter. By early April, however, Doenitz and his staff gave up all hope. Doenitz and Raeder then pressed for a public announcement of Prien's death, but Fuehrer Headquarters would not release the news until May 23. Prien was then posthumously promoted to full commander for gallantry in action.

Prien was such a hero to the German people that a number of incredible rumors began to circulate about his death. Prien and his crew had mutinied and been sent to a penal labor battalion on the Russian Front; Prien and his men were sent to a penal battalion for making false and exaggerated claims of tonnage sunk; Prien had refused to put to sea in an unseaworthy boat, so Doenitz court-martialed him and he was sent to a concentration camp at Esterwegen. Here, according to one story, he starved to death. According to another version, he was executed by a firing squad shortly before the Allies arrived. Most incredibly, Prien had had an accident and drowned—in his bathtub! When it comes to such bizarre and weird stories, Prien's case is not unique. Similar stories were heard about other U-boat commanders, generals, and Luftwaffe aces who were missing in action. Similarly imaginative tales gain currency even today, especially those about deceased rock and roll singers and other pop culture idols. The Bull of Scapa Flow was killed in action against his enemy in the North Atlantic on March 8, 1941. He died exactly as he had lived.

Prien was not the only U-boat ace lost in March 1941. On March 17, *U-100* under Lieutenant JOACHIM SCHEPKE was damaged during an attack on Convoy HX-112. As it limped away, the surfaced U-boat was sighted by a newly developed British radar set and rammed by the destroyer *Vanoc*. Schepke, who had sunk 39 Allied ships (159,130 tons), was on the conning tower when the *Vanoc* struck and was crushed to death by the destroyer's bow. There were few survivors. Schepke, who had been born in Flensburg on March 8, 1912, was a holder of the Knight's Cross with Oak Leaves.

Later on March 17, 1941, the same night on which Joachim Schepke was killed, the British destroyer *Walker* sighted *U-99* with his asdic device. The escort brought the submarine to the surface with depth charges and, with the help of the *Vanoc*, sank the German vessel with gunfire. Among the prisoners fished out of the ocean was Lieutenant Commander OTTO KRETSCHMER, the leading U-boat ace of World War II. He is credited with sinking 47 ships, which displaced 274,333 tons, including a British destroyer. Otto Kretschmer had been born in Heidau, Silesia, near Liegnitz (now Legnica, Poland) on May 1, 1902. As a 17-year-old, he spent almost a year in the United Kingdom, where he became fluent in English. He entered the service as a sea cadet in April 1930, and served aboard the light cruisers *Emden* and *Koeln*, before transferring to the U-boat branch in January 1936. He assumed command of *U-35* in 1937 and operated off the Spanish coast, although he sank no vessels in the Spanish Civil War. Later he commanded *U-23* (a coastal U-boat) and *U-99*.

Kretschmer was known as Silent Otto because of his use of "silent running" tactics (including slow approaches, which minimized propeller noise) and because he did not like to transmit radio dispatches while on patrol. He was also known for his motto "One torpedo, one ship."

Silent Otto was a chivalrous opponent and, in the days before the convoys and the wolf packs, forced lone merchant ships to surrender. He put the crews in lifeboats, provided them with blankets and alcoholic beverages, and gave them a compass and the heading to the nearest land.

A U-boat commander from the beginning of the war, he sank eight ships, totaling 50,000 tons, on a single patrol in the summer of 1940 and was awarded his Knight's Cross by Grand Admiral Raeder in the harbor of Lorient. Ironically, his Knight's Cross with Oak Leaves and Swords was presented to him by the commandant of the prison camp at Bowmanville, Canada. On March 17, 1941, he was forced to surface after repeated depth charges damaged his boat. He found himself in the middle of a British convoy and was forced to scuttle *U-99*. He spent the rest of the war in POW camps.

After the war, he married Dr. Luise-Charlotte Mohnsen-Hinrich (nee Bruns), a war widow. He joined the West German Navy in 1955 and retired in 1970 as a rear admiral, junior grade (*Flotillenadmiral*). He and his wife celebrated their 50th wedding anniversary in 1998 by taking a cruise on the Danube. Here Kretschmer attempted to climb a ladder, as he had done thousands of times before. This time, however, he slipped, fell, and struck his head. Silent Otto never regained consciousness. He died in a hospital in Straubing, Bavaria, on August 5, 1998.

The most highly decorated member of the U-boat arm was Captain **WOLFGANG LUETH**, holder of the Knight's Cross with Oak Leaves, Swords, and Diamonds. Born near Rita in Estonia on October 15, 1913, he joined the German Navy in the mid-1930s, received command of his first submarine (*U-138*) in January 1940, and, as an Oberleutnant zur See, was awarded his Knight's Cross on October 24, 1940, for sinking 49,000 tons of enemy shipping in 27 days.[50] Later, he commanded *U-43* and *U-181*. By the time he left his last undersea command in November 1943, he had sunk 43 ships, totaling 225,712 tons, making him the number two U-boat ace of World War II. He had also sunk an Allied submarine. In August 1944, Lueth was promoted to Kapitaen zur See and named commander of the Naval School at Muerwik/Flensburg, which became Nazi Germany's last seat of government, under Doenitz. He was shot and killed by a German sentry on May 14, 1945, after the war was over but before the rump Doenitz government was disbanded. Captain Lueth was buried at Flensburg on May 16, with full military honors—the last such funeral in the history of the Third Reich. The subsequent court-martial acquitted the sentry: after being challenged, Lueth had given him the wrong password.

The third leading U-boat ace was Commander ERICH TOPP, captain of *U-57*, *U-552*, and *U-2513*. A native of Hanover, he was born on July 2, 1914, and joined the navy in 1934. He was commander of *U-57* from June 5 to September 3, 1940, when it was sunk in a collision with a Norwegian ship. In the meantime, he had sunk six enemy ships. In December 1940, Topp was given a second command: *U-552*. Between July 1940, and August 1942, he sank another 29 Allied merchant ships and brought his total to 197,460 tons. He was awarded the Swords to his Knight's Cross with Oak Leaves on August 17, 1942.

Topp sparked an international incident on October 31, 1941, when he sank the U.S. destroyer *Reuben James*, the first American naval vessel sunk in World War II. He was promptly verbally attacked by U.S. President Franklin D. Roosevelt in his famous "rattlesnakes of the sea" speech. Some observers thought Roosevelt was about to use the incident to ask Congress for a declaration of war against Germany, but he did not. The reasons were simple: Roosevelt "forgot" to mention that the *Reuben James* was escorting a British convoy at the time, was not flying the American flag, and was on a depth-charge run against another U-boat when it sailed in front of Topp's periscope. One of the torpedoes blew off the entire bow and detonated the magazine. It sank instantly. Many of the 115 American sailors who died were killed when their own depth charges detonated. Only 44 survived. It is significant that Topp was never even indicted as a war criminal for the incident, much less convicted.

Years later, at a banquet, Admiral Topp met a survivor, who described the awfulness of the incident to him, and what is was like to be left floating in the burning oil, struggling for his life. Erich Topp was so appalled and horrified by this conversation that he refused to ever discuss the affair again.

Topp commanded *U-552* until October 1942, when he assumed command of the 27th U-boat Flotilla at Gotenhafen, East Prussia (now Gdynia, Poland). Here he helped develop the XXI Elektro submarine, which came too late to help the Third Reich. Topp took personal command of *U-2513* in the last days of the war and sailed it to Horten, Norway, where he surrendered it to the Western Allies.

After the war, Topp became a fisherman and had a second career as an architect in Remegen. He joined the West German Navy when it was formed in 1955 and retired as a Konteradmiral (two-star admiral) in 1969. For many years thereafter, he visited Texas every Christmas, to visit his daughter and grandchildren. He died in Suessen on December 26, 2005. He was 91 years old.

ENGELBERT ENDRASS, who was born in Bamberg on March 2, 1911, was Prien's watch officer and second-in-command at Scapa Flow. Shortly thereafter, he was given command of his own submarine (*U-46*) and became a leading U-boat ace himself, rising to the rank of lieutenant commander and sinking 22 ships (128,879 tons). As commander of *U-567* he was killed in action on December 26, 1941, while he was attempting to sink the British aircraft carrier *Audacity*. Depth-charged by escort vessels, *U-567* vanished northeast of the Azores. There were no survivors.[51]

The leading U-boat ace of all time was LOTHAR VON ARNAULD DE LA PERIERE. His family was French until 1757, when his great-grandfather, a 26-year-old artillery lieutenant, cut down a prince of the House of Bourbon in a duel and fled the country one step ahead of the police. Jean-Gabriel Arnauld de la Periere then joined Frederick the Great's army and rose to the rank of full general. The Arnaulds served Prussia and Germany from then on.

Lothar was born in Posen, Prussia (now Poznan, Poland), on March 18, 1886. He attended the cadet schools at Wahlstatt and Gross-Lichterfelde, and joined the Imperial Navy in 1903. After eight years service on three different battleships, Arnault became a torpedo officer aboard the light cruiser *Emden* in 1911. After that, he was adjutant to Admiral Hugo von Pohl, the chief of the Admiralty Staff and an early advocate of U-boat development and unrestricted submarine warfare.[52] Arnauld transferred to the U-boat branch in 1915, and assumed command of *U-35* in November. He sank a record 194 ships (453,716 Gross Registered Tons) during World War I, and received the Pour le Merite in 1916.

Most of Arnauld's "kills" were undramatic. He would stop a merchant vessel, inspect its papers, allow the crew to board lifeboats, and then sink it with his 88mm deck gun. Sometimes this procedure was not practical. Arnauld fired a total of 74 torpedoes during the war and scored 39 hits.

Arnauld remained in the navy during the Weimar era, where he served as a navigation officer on old pre-dreadnoughts and as commander of the *Emden* (1928–1930). Promoted to captain, he retired in 1931, and then taught at the Turkish Naval Academy from 1932 to 1938. He also briefly joined an anti-Nazi political party in the early 1930s.

Captain von Arnauld was recalled to active duty when World War II began. Promoted to rear admiral on June 1, 1940, he was naval plenipotentiary for Danzig and the Polish Corridor (September 1939–March 1940). He became Naval Commander, Belgium-Netherlands (May–June 1940); Naval Commander, Brittany (June–December 1940); and Naval Commander, Western France (December 1940–February 1941). He was promoted to vice admiral on February 1, 1941.

Admiral von Arnauld was named naval commander south on February 19, 1941. He was en route to his new command when he was killed in an airplane accident at the Paris-Le Bourget Airport on February 24. He is buried at the *Invalidenfriedhof* (the German national cemetery) in Berlin.

8

THE WAFFEN-SS

**Theodor Eicke. Paul Hausser. Josef "Sepp" Dietrich.
Helmut Becker. Michael Wittmann. Gustav Knittel.**

THEODOR EICKE was a major figure in the history of the SS. Charles Syndor described him as "the architect, builder and director of the pre-war German concentration camp system."[1] He also created the *Totenkopf* ("Death's Head") Division of the Waffen-SS (armed SS), which he drew largely from his own concentration camp guards. Eicke was born in Huedingen, in the then-German province of Alsace, on October 17, 1892, the eleventh child of Heinrich Eicke, a railroad stationmaster. Little is known of his early life except that he grew up in relative poverty and was a poor student. In 1909, he dropped out of *Realschule* (roughly the equivalent of high school) to enlist in the Imperial Army. He joined the Rhineland-Palatinate 23rd Infantry Regiment, then stationed at Landau, but was transferred to the Bavarian 3rd Infantry Regiment in 1913 and to the 22nd Bavarian Infantry Regiment in 1914.[2] He took part in the Lorraine campaign of 1914, the Ypres battles (1914–1915), and in the trench warfare in Flanders (1914–1916), serving at various times as a clerk, assistant paymaster, and frontline infantryman. In 1916, he was again transferred, this time to the 2nd Bavarian Foot Artillery Regiment of the 2nd Bavarian Infantry Division, which suffered 50 percent casualties in the battle of Verdun.[3] From 1917 until the end of the war he served in the reserve machine-gun company (*Ersatz-Maschinengewehr-Kompanie*) of the II Army Corps on the Western Front. He emerged from the war with the Iron Cross, First and Second classes,[4] very high decorations indeed for an enlisted man in the Imperial Army of this era. In late 1914, Eicke's commanding officer gave him leave and approved his request to marry Bertha Schwebel of Ilmenau.

She gave him two children: a daughter, Irma, born in 1916, and a son, Hermann, born in 1920. Eicke's family life seems to have had little impact on his subsequent career, however. When he returned to Germany after four years on the Western Front, Eicke was a very violent and embittered man. The Second Reich that he had served had ceased to exist, and Germany was in the throes of revolution, which filled Eicke with hatred and disgust. He had no desire to serve in the "new" army of the Weimar Republic; like many disillusioned men of his day, such as Adolf Hitler, Eicke blamed the democrats, leftists, Communists, Jews, and other "November criminals" who, in their view, "stabbed Germany in the back" and caused her defeat. When he was discharged from the army on March 1, 1919, Theodor Eicke had almost nothing to show for 10 years' service and had no career prospects whatsoever. He initially attended the technical school in Ilmenau, Thuringia, but had to drop out due to a lack of funds. Apparently he had hoped to receive financial assistance from his father-in-law but was disappointed. Unemployment was rampant in revolutionary Germany, and Eicke finally grew desperate enough to take a job as a paid police informer. He was fired in July 1920, for political agitation against the Weimar Republic and the "November criminals." He had, however, developed a love for police work. For the next three years, Eicke wandered to at least four cities (Cottbus, Weimar, Sorau-Niederausitz, and Ludwigshafen). At least twice he secured employment as a policeman, only to be fired for anti-government activities. Finally, in January 1923, Eicke became a security officer for the I. G. Farben corporation in the small Rhineland city of Ludwigshafen. Here his fierce nationalism and hatred for the republic did not hinder him, and he remained with Farben until he became a full-time SS man in 1932.[5] Meanwhile, he joined the Nazi Party and the Stormtroopers (SA) in 1928 and transferred to the more highly disciplined SS (*Schutzstaffel*), then part of the SA, in 1930. In November of that year, Heinrich Himmler appointed him *Untersturmfuehrer* (second lieutenant of SS) and gave him command of the 147th SS Platoon (Sturm) in Ludwigshafen.[6]

Eicke threw himself into his new work with fanatical energy. Within three months of joining the SS, his recruiting efforts had been so successful that Himmler promoted him to *SS-Sturmbannfuehrer* (major) and ordered him to recruit a second battalion for the 10th *SS-Standarte* (regiment), then being formed in the Rhineland-Palatine. Again he was extremely successful—so much so that Himmler promoted him to *SS-Standartenfuehrer* (colonel) and named him commander of the 10th Standarte on November 15, 1931. Although he had joined the Nazis rather late, Eicke was climbing rapidly indeed.

About this time, Eicke left I. G. Farben. One source suggests that he was fired, perhaps because his political activities caused him to neglect his job, but this cannot be confirmed. In any event, he embarked upon a career of political violence that led to his arrest and conviction for illegal possession of high explosives and conspiracy to commit political assassination. Fortunately for him, the Bavarian minister of justice—a Nazi-sympathizer— granted him a temporary parole for reasons of health in July 1932. Eicke promptly resumed his violent activities, but the police were soon after him, and he was forced to flee to Italy in September, using a false passport. To console him, Himmler promoted him to *SS-Oberfuehrer*[7] and named him commandant of the SA- and SS-Refugee Camp at Bozen-Gries, Italy,[8] but Eicke was not able to return to Germany until Adolf Hitler became chancellor in 1933. While Eicke was in exile, one of his many enemies, Josef Buerckel, the Gauleiter of the Palatinate, tried to have him replaced as commander of the 10th Standarte. When he returned, Eicke, as usual, acted without restraint. On March 21, 1933, he and a group of armed followers stormed the Ludwigshafen party headquarters and locked Buerckel—who held a position roughly equivalent to a U.S. governor—in a broom closet for two or three hours, until he was rescued by the local police.

Once again Eicke had gone too far, and the humiliated Buerckel extracted full revenge. He had Eicke arrested, declared mentally ill, and thrown into a psychiatric facility at Wuerzburg as a "dangerous lunatic."[9] Heinrich Himmler was also furious at Eicke (it must be remembered that the Nazis had not yet consolidated their power, and this incident was a major embarrassment to the party). On April 3, 1933, the Reichsfuehrer-SS struck Eicke's name off the roles of the SS and approved his indefinite confinement to the mental institution.

Finally cowed, Eicke managed to keep his fierce temper under control for several weeks and even succeeded in acting as if he were normal—a tremendous feat of acting! He also wrote to Himmler several times and, with the assistance of a Wuerzburg psychiatrist, finally persuaded the former chicken farmer to have him released and restored to his former rank. Himmler, of course, knew better than to send Eicke back to the Palatinate, so, on June 26, 1934, SS-Oberfuehrer Theodor Eicke left the mental institution and went directly to his new assignment: commandant of Dachau, the first German concentration camp for political prisoners.

When Eicke arrived at the camp, located about 12 miles northwest of Munich, Dachau was a mess from the Nazis' point of view. The original commandant was being prosecuted for the murder of several inmates, and the guards were corrupt, undisciplined, brutal, and prone to brag about their activities in public places. Eicke soon discovered that Josef "Sepp" Dietrich, SS regional district commander, had "dumped" his worst men (thieves, antisocial types, etc.) on Dachau. Eicke quickly replaced or dismissed half the staff (about 60 out of 120 men) and established the code of conduct that became the model for all concentration camps in Nazi Germany. Undisciplined brutality was replaced by disciplined, well-organized brutality, based upon the principle of unquestioned and absolute obedience to all orders from superior SS officers. Eicke subjected prisoners to close confinement, solitary confinement, beatings, and other corporal punishment. Usually this amounted to 25 lashes with a whip in front of the assembled prisoners and SS staff. The whippings were administered on a rotating basis by all officers, NCOs, and privates in order to toughen them so that they could torture their prisoners impersonally, without remorse or conscience. "Under Eicke's experienced direction," Heinz Hoehne wrote later, "anyone who still retained a shred of decency and humanity was very soon brutalized."[10] Eicke was particularly hard on Jewish prisoners, whom he hated most of all. Roger Manvell and Heinrich Faenkel called him "one of Himmler's most trusted adherents on racial matters."[11] He frequently delivered anti-Semitic lectures to the staff and had *Der Stuermel*, a violently racist Nazi newspaper, displayed on bulletin boards in both the camp and the barracks. He even tried to incite hatred and anti-Semitism among the prisoners.[12]

Heinrich Himmler was so impressed by Eicke's "success" at Dachau that he promoted him to *SS-Brigadefuehrer* on January 30, 1934, and once again came to look upon him as a loyal and valuable servant.

Loyal to Himmler and the Fuehrer he certainly was. When Hitler purged the SA in the so-called Night of the Long Knives, Eicke played a major role in the planning and helped draw up the death lists. His men formed some of the death squads, and Eicke was selected by Himmler to personally execute Ernst Roehm, the chief of the Brownshirts. He obeyed this order without question on the evening of July 1.[13] Apparently this order was much to Eicke's liking, for he shot the SA chief and then taunted him as he lay dying. For his services during the purge, Eicke was appointed the first inspector of concentration camps and commander of SS guard units (*Inspekteur der Konzentrationslager und Fuehrer der SS Wachverbaende*) on July 5. Six days later he was promoted to *SS-Gruppenfuehrer* (equivalent to lieutenant general in the German Army).[14]

Eicke established his headquarters on the Friedrichstrasse in Berlin, assembled a staff, and began work on the task of converting the Nazis' dispersed and locally directed concentration camps into one centralized system. Soon he moved his offices to the Sachsenhausen concentration camp at Oranienburg, north of Berlin, where the inspectorate remained until the fall of the Reich in 1945. By 1937, Eicke had closed several smaller camps and had set up four large camps: Dachau, Sachsenhausen, Buchenwald (near Weimar), and Lichtenburg. After the Anschluss (the annexation of Austria) in 1938, he established a fifth camp at Mauthausen, near Linz, to handle Austrian political prisoners, Jews, and other people arrested by the Gestapo. Perhaps more important, he imposed the Dachau model of conduct on all the camps. "By 1937," Snydor wrote, "Eicke had a formidable reputation among his SS colleagues as a tough and vicious figure. Ever suspicious, quarrelsome, cruel, humorless, and afflicted with a cancerous ambition, Eicke was a genuinely fanatic Nazi who had embraced the movement's political and racial liturgy with the zeal of a late convert."[15]

Once he had the new camp system fully operational, Eicke turned his attention to converting his SS Death's Head guard units (the *SS Totenkopfverbaende*, or SSTV) into Nazi Party paramilitary formations. Skillfully worming his way through the political jungle of the Third Reich, Eicke had formed and equipped six motorized SSTV battalions by early 1935. By the end of 1938, he had expanded these into four regiments, each named after a region and headquartered at a major concentration camp.[16] By the time the war broke out, several other Standarte were on the drawing boards or in the process of forming.[17]

Eicke's SSTV guards spent one week each month guarding prisoners and three weeks in training, which involved rigorous physical exercise, military maneuvers, weapons familiarization, and political indoctrination aimed at making them insensitive and unquestioning political soldiers for Adolf Hitler. Eicke imposed a ruthless discipline on his men, most of whom were fanatical young Nazis, aged 17 to 22. Those who did not measure up or were not sufficiently obedient were dismissed or transferred to the *Allgemeine-SS* (General SS). Eicke also brought about an indefinable camaraderie among officers, NCOs, and men, who were much closer than their counterparts in the German Army. Simultaneously, Eicke waged a war against Christianity, because he hated any form of religion, not just Judaism. Adolf Hitler was his god, and he wanted men who felt the same way. By 1937, the overwhelming majority of his troops had officially renounced their religion. When this led to a permanent breach between a young SS man and his family (which it frequently did), Eicke would open his own home to a lonely young SS man who was on leave and wanted to spend time with a family. He also encouraged his officers, NCOs, and men to make special efforts to befriend comrades who were, in his view, badly treated by their parents.

When World War II broke out, Eicke mobilized three of his regiments (Oberbayern, Brandenburg, and Thuringen—about 7,000 men in all) and followed the army into Poland. His men behaved like robots and killing machines, just as Eicke had trained them to do. They did no fighting against the Polish Army (except to run down an occasional straggler) but rather along with Reinhard Heydrich's SD formed the infamous Einsatzgruppen ("action groups" or murder squads), which confiscated livestock and engaged in acts of terrorism, extortion, and murder against Polish civilians, especially aristocrats, political figures, clergymen, intellectuals, and especially Jews. One Standarte commander burned all the synagogues in a Polish community and then had the local Jewish leaders beaten until they signed a confession stating that they had set the fires. He then fined them thousands of marks for arson. As brutal as this incident was, these victims were luckier than many. Most of those who fell into the hands of the Einsatzgruppen were simply "shot while attempting to escape." Entire lunatic asylums were emptied and their helpless inmates gunned down, and there were dozens of other atrocities.

Many German generals were sickened and outraged by the excesses of the SSTV and SD, and at least three lodged formal protests. These were quickly hidden by Colonel General Walter von Brauchitsch, the commander-in-chief of the army, who lacked the intestinal fortitude to stand up to Adolf Hitler. Instead of punishing Eicke and company, Hitler acted on the advice of Heinrich Himmler and decided to create a Totenkopf motorized infantry division! Naturally, Theodor Eicke was selected to command it. By mid-October he was back at Dachau, organizing his new command, which soon had a strength of more than 15,000 men.

The *SS Totenkopfdivision* (SSTK) consisted of three motorized infantry regiments, an artillery regiment, signals, engineer, anti-tank and reconnaissance battalions, and all the administrative and support units found in an army motorized division. The motorized infantry regiments came from the old concentration camp guard units Oberbayern, Brandenburg, and Thuringen, while the artillerymen came mainly from SS Heimwehr Danzig (the Danzig Home Guard). The other units were manned by new recruits and men from the *Verfuegungstruppen* (Special Purpose SS), the General SS, the Order Police (i.e., civilian policemen), and the new SSTV that were still forming in 1939. These new units, which included more than half the men in the division, were all poorly trained, badly equipped, and, by Eicke's standards, inadequately disciplined.

Eicke showed true talent in equipping his division and became known as the greatest "scrounger" in the SS. Discipline he handled in the usual manner. Men who committed the slightest violation were transferred back to the concentration camps as guards. One former guard, dissatisfied with the rigorous training, requested a transfer back to his former camp. Eicke quickly approved the request—but sent the man back to the concentration camp as an inmate instead of as a guard! Equally significant, the man was given an indefinite sentence. There were no further requests for transfer.[18] The new men had little choice but to try to adapt to their situation and apply themselves to their training. By the time Hitler invaded Holland, Belgium, and France on May 10, 1940, the men of the SSTK were ready.

Their officers, however, were not. Few had military training or experience appropriate to their assignments, and there was not one properly trained General Staff officer in the entire division. In fact, the only really competent officer on the divisional staff at this time was the Ia (operations officer and senior divisional staff officer), SS-Standartenfuehrer Baron Cassius von Montigny—until he collapsed due to exhaustion and overwork.[19] Due to poor logistical management, traffic jams in the divisional rear were so monumental that the combat units were out of supply for at least three days and had to rely on food taken from the French or borrowed from Erwin Rommel's 7th Panzer Division, which was then advancing in the neighboring sector. Nowhere, however, was the lack of adequate officer training more evident than in the case of the divisional commander. Eicke, more often than not, acted on fragmentary and insufficient information rather than letting the situation develop properly. He tended to fly into rages in crisis situations, issuing now one order, countermanding it 15 minutes later and giving another, diametrically opposing order, and then giving a third, contradictory order, without retracting the second. The confusion that radiated from divisional headquarters definitely had a negative effect on the division's performance in the Western campaign of 1940. Fortunately for Eicke, the fanatical bravery of his troops, coupled with their superb physical conditioning and fierce hatred for anyone who opposed the Fuehrer's will, won the division victories that his own tactical ineptitude put in jeopardy. Casualties were nevertheless higher than they should have been. In justice to Eicke, however, it must be noted that he had trained these fanatically brave (though pitiless) men and that his own performance as a divisional commander improved remarkably after the French campaign, indicating that he learned a great deal from his mistakes. Even so, the battlefield is not the proper place for a divisional commander to receive on-the-job training.

As the German panzer spearhead drove on the English Channel, SSTK was used to prevent the escape of units from the Dunkirk Pocket to the main French armies south of the Somme. On May 21, SSTK and

Rommel's 7th Panzer Division met and, in the vicinity of Arras, turned back the main Allied counterattack of the entire campaign. During this battle the SS anti-tank battalion alone knocked out 22 British tanks—most of them at point-blank range. The division's assault on the La Bassee Canal line the following day was less successful, largely because of Eicke's ham-fisted conduct of the battle. He attacked across the canal with one unsupported infantry battalion, without reconnaissance or artillery preparation, and ran into an unexpectedly strong British force, which drove the SS back across the canal with heavy losses. Eicke launched a second unsuccessful attack on May 24, which was again mishandled. After this check his corps commander, General of Panzer Troops Erich Hoepner, bitterly reprimanded Eicke, calling him a "butcher" to his face in front of his divisional staff and accusing him of caring nothing about the lives of his men.[20] Even Himmler was angry at Eicke because of the high casualties.

After the reduction of the Dunkirk Pocket, both Eicke and the SSTK had an easier time, pursuing the disintegrating French armies all the way to Orleans. After the French surrendered at Compiègne on June 22, the Totenkopf was sent to Hosten, a village 25 miles southwest of Bordeaux, for occupation duties. Later it was transferred to Avallon, then to Biarritz, and finally to Bordeaux, from which it boarded trains in early June 1941 for transport to East Prussia. It crossed into the Soviet Union on June 24, 1941, two days after Operation Barbarossa, Hitler's invasion of the Soviet Union, had begun. As part of Field Marshal Ritter Wilhelm von Leeb's Army Group North, the Death's Head Division crossed the Dvina at Dvinsk, overran bitter resistance in central Lithuania, penetrated the Stalin Line, and earned the enthusiastic praise of General Erich von Manstein, the commander of the LVI Panzer Corps and one of Germany's greatest military brains.[21] Eicke was not with the division throughout all these actions, however. On July 6, while the battles of the Stalin Line were still in progress, he was returning to his command post after a day at the front with his men. Near the CP his vehicle hit a Soviet mine. His right foot was shattered and his leg was badly mutilated. After emergency surgery he was evacuated back to Berlin, where it took him three months to recover—and even then not completely. As late as mid-1942, he still limped and had to walk with the aid of a cane.

Had Eicke now rested on his laurels and taken a staff appointment, no one in the government, army, or the SS would have said a single negative word about it. Indeed, a less fanatical man would not have wanted to go back to the Russian Front. Eicke rushed back to it even though he had not fully recuperated from his wounds. He resumed command of the SSTK on

September 21, 1941.[22] As part of Manstein's corps, he turned back repeated human-wave attacks near Lushno, south of Lake Ilmen, from September 24 through 27. The battle continued until the 29th, with less intensity. Through the fanatical resistance of its men, Totenkopf alone smashed three Soviet divisions. For his own personal bravery in preventing a Soviet breakthrough, Eicke was recommended for the Knight's Cross.[23] By now, however, the Death's Head had lost 6,600 men since the campaign began but had received only 2,500 replacements. Even though it was in serious need of more soldiers, rest, new equipment, and time for maintenance, Totenkopf remained in the forefront of the advance. Its situation was not much worse than that of most German divisions in Russia. By the end of November, it had suffered its 9,000th casualty since June 22 and was at about 60 percent of its original strength.

On December 6, 1941, Stalin launched a massive winter offensive on all sectors of the Eastern Front. Although the SS men held their lines, the Soviets achieved penetrations elsewhere on the front and gradually worked their way around the city of Demyansk. Field Marshal von Leeb urgently requested permission to fall back, but Hitler refused to allow a retreat. On February 8, 1942, the Russians finally succeeded in encircling Demyansk. Inside the pocket were six divisions—103,000 Germans, including the SS Totenkopf Division—all under the overall direction of Army General of Infantry Count Walter von Brockdorff-Ahlefeldt, the commander of the II Corps.

Brockdorff-Ahlefeldt positioned Eicke's motorized division on the critical western edge of the perimeter, where the Soviet 34th Army threatened to break through and collapse the pocket. The winter fighting was bitter and desperate as the two ruthless ideologies struggled to the death in the snow and swamps west of Demyansk. At one point Eicke had to lead the walking wounded back into combat, but despite odds heavily stacked against him, he turned back every Soviet attack and virtually annihilated the elite Soviet 7th Guards Division. Losses in Totenkopf had not been light, however: the division lost more than 6,000 men by April 1942, and now had fewer than 10,000 soldiers. This figure would dwindle to 6,700 in the weeks ahead, and a third of these would be exhausted and unfit for duty after months of combat. SSTK had started Barbarossa with more than 17,000 men. Nevertheless, it was the Totenkopf Division that broke the Soviet encirclement and linked up with the army's relief force in May 1942, establishing a tenuous link between Demyansk and the rest of the German Wehrmacht. Still, II Corps was boxed in on three sides, and the veteran SS division was desperately needed to keep the supply corridor open.

Totenkopf beat back several fresh attacks, but by the end of July, fewer than 3,000 SS men remained.

To Theodor Eicke, there was only one real crime: physical cowardice. Not even Eicke's fiercest detractors ever questioned his physical courage. During the Demyansk battles, Eicke suffered every privation his men suffered. He camped in the snow, wore soggy clothes for days on end, repeatedly exposed himself to enemy fire, and subsisted on poor and meager rations. (For six months, all supplies had to be airlifted into the pocket.) As a reward for his outstanding services at Demyansk, Eicke was decorated with the Knight's Cross on December 26, 1941. He was promoted to *SS-Gruppenfuehrer und General der Waffen-SS* (equivalent to lieutenant general, U.S. Army) and was awarded the Oak Leaves to the Knight's Cross on April 20, 1942—Hitler's birthday. These gestures of confidence did not placate the former concentration camp commander, however. He was very unhappy over the loss of so many men he had trained, was furious about what he regarded as the army's indifference to the fate of his division, and raged about its willingness to fight to the last SS man. Eicke had earlier charged that Brockdorff was deliberately sacrificing his division by committing it to all the critical situations, while sparing army units from heavy combat whenever possible. As the weeks wore on and the situation did not change, Eicke's criticisms became more and more outspoken.

It seems quite likely that Eicke was right. Count von Brockdorff-Ahlefeldt had been a part of the anti-Hitler conspiracy since before the war and certainly wasted no love on the SS.[24] Eicke also railed at Himmler, demanding that the remnants of his elite division be withdrawn from the Russian Front. He even secured a private audience with Adolf Hitler at the Wolf's Lair (his headquarters near Rastenburg, East Prussia) on June 26, 1942, and bluntly described the situation to him. The Fuehrer promised Eicke that he would withdraw the division in August if the situation south of Lake Ilmen remained stable. He also promised to send it to France, where it would be rebuilt to its pre-Barbarossa strength. Not until August 26, however, did Hitler even authorize the withdrawal of the SSTK from the Russian Front—and by then it had suffered even more casualties. Then the tactical situation at Demyansk made immediate withdrawal impossible. Theodor Eicke became more and more critical of SS headquarters in Berlin for not sending him enough replacements. This Himmler was unwilling to do, since he had already started assembling men for the new (i.e., rebuilt) Totenkopf Division, and his manpower reserves were not unlimited at this stage of the war. Eicke's demands became so outspoken and persistent that

Himmler sent him on indefinite convalescent leave. It seems likely that Eicke was suffering from combat fatigue. In any event, in the last battles in the Demyansk salient, the SSTK was commanded by its senior regimental commander, Oberfuehrer Max Simon. When he finally brought the remnants out of the salient in October, it had repulsed several more major Soviet attacks. All its noncombat units had been dissolved and their men incorporated into the infantry. Fewer than 2,000 men remained.[25]

In the winter of 1942–1943, the SSTK was completely rebuilt as a panzer grenadier division. It took part in the occupation of Vichy France in November 1942, and then remained in the Angouleme area in the south of France, where it went through its paces. A refreshed Eicke, as usual, relentlessly and ruthlessly trained his new men in accordance with his own ideas. During this period Hitler decided to enlarge Eicke's panzer battalion into a regiment, and the Totenkopf became, in effect, a panzer division, although it retained the official designation *SS-Panzergrenadier-Division "Totenkopf."*[26]

The rebuilt Death's Head Division was hurried back to the Russian Front after the fall of Stalingrad and in February 1943, joined Obergruppenfuehrer Paul Hausser's SS Panzer Corps, which was retreating from the Second Battle of Kharkov. The SSTK then took part in Field Marshal von Manstein's brilliant counteroffensive, which led to the recapture of that Ukrainian city, and the division distinguished itself in this fast-moving armored operation. Theodor Eicke did not live to see the end of it, however. On the afternoon of February 26, 1943, he became alarmed when he could not make radio contact with his panzer regiment, so he boarded a Fieseler Storch (a single-engine light reconnaissance airplane) to see if he could find out what was happening from the air. Eicke and his pilot spotted an SS tank company near the village of Michailovka but could not tell from the air that the adjoining village of Artelnoye—less than half a mile away—was still in Soviet hands. As the Storch dropped to an altitude of 300 feet, it began a slow turn directly over the well-camouflaged Red Army positions. As it did so, the Soviets opened up with a hail of machinegun, rifle, and anti-aircraft fire, instantly destroying the small airplane. It crashed and burned between the two villages.

The next day the SS recovered Eicke's charred body and buried it at the nearby village of Otdochnina with full military honors—covering the SS general with the soil of the country that he hated so much. In his eulogy to the fallen commander, Adolf Hitler renamed one of the Totenkopf's units the 6th SS Panzer Grenadier Regiment "Theodor Eicke." Very few outside the SS mourned his death, however.

When the war in the East again turned against Germany, Himmler had Eicke's remains moved to the Hegewald Cemetery at Zhitomir, to keep them out of Soviet hands. When the Red Army overran Ukraine in the spring of 1944, however, Eicke's remains were left behind.[27] It was customary for the Soviets to bulldoze or otherwise desecrate the graves of German soldiers, and this is almost certainly what happened to Eicke. In any event, his remains have disappeared. A brutal and violent man had met the violent end that he richly deserved.

PAUL HAUSSER, the man who had perhaps the single greatest influence in the military development of the Waffen-SS, was born in Brandenburg on October 7, 1880, the son of a Prussian officer. He was educated in military prep schools and in 1892 enrolled in Berlin-Lichterfelde, Imperial Germany's equivalent of West Point. Among his classmates were future field marshals Fedor von Bock and Guenther von Kluge.

Hausser graduated in 1899 and, as a second lieutenant, was assigned to the 155th Infantry Regiment in Ostrow, Posen. After eight years of regimental service he entered the War Academy in 1907 but did not graduate until 1912. In the interval he returned to his regiment and also underwent coastal defense and aerial observer training. He was assigned to the Greater General Staff in 1912 and was promoted to captain in 1914. Later that year, when the German Army mobilized for World War I, Hausser was assigned to the staff of the 6th Army, commanded by Crown Prince Rupprecht of Bavaria. Later he served on the staff of the VI Corps, as Ia of the 109th Infantry Division; with the I Reserve Corps (also as Ia); and as a company commander in the 38th Fusilier Regiment. He fought in France, Hungary, and Rumania and was awarded both classes of the Iron Cross. At the close of hostilities, he was Ia of the 59th Reserve Command at Glogua, Germany. After the war he served with a Freikorps unit on the eastern frontier before joining the Reichsheer in 1920.

During the Reichswehr era, Hausser was on the staff of the 5th Infantry Brigade (1920–1922); Wehrkreis II at Stettin, Pomerania (1922–1923); 2nd Infantry Division, also at Stettin (1925–1926); and the Saxon 10th Infantry Regiment at Dresden (1927). He also served as commander of the III Battalion, 4th (Prussian) Infantry Regiment at Deutsch-Krone (1923–1925), and 10th Infantry Regiment (1927–1930), and ended his army career as Infantry Commander IV (*Infanteriefuehrer IV*) at Dresden, a post he held from 1930 to 1932. In this last post he was simultaneously one of the two deputy commanders of the 4th Infantry Division. He retired as a major general on January 31, 1932, at the age of 51, with the honorary rank of lieutenant general. At this point in his career, Paul Hausser—who had always been a fervent German nationalist—became involved with the

Nazi Party. By 1934 he was an SA Standartenfuehrer and brigade commander in the Berlin-Brandenburg area, when Heinrich Himmler offered him the job of training his SS-*Verfuegunstruppe* (SS-VT, or Special Purpose Troops)—the embryo of the Waffen-SS. Hausser entered the SS as a Standartenfuehrer of November 15, 1934. His first assignment was that of commandant of the SS-Officer Training School (*SS-Junkerschule*) at Braunschweig (Brunswick).

In the SS-VT, Hausser found enthusiastic but untrained young Nazis who were fanatically dedicated to their Fuehrer and were most willing to be shaped into a cohesive military organization. As a former General Staff officer, Hausser possessed command and organizational experience, both of which were needed and appreciated. He quickly organized the curriculum of the school into a model copied by all SS officers, NCOs, and weapons schools throughout Germany—and later throughout Europe. Hausser's program emphasized physical fitness, athletic competition, teamwork, and a close relationship between the ranks—a degree of comradeship that did not exist in the German Army at that time. Hausser himself was a noted sportsman and equestrian who could successfully compete with men 30 years his junior. Under his leadership, the SS elite soon exceeded anything the army could field—at least in appearance. Himmler was so impressed that he named Hausser inspector of SS Officer Schools, in charge of the officer training establishments at Brunswick and Bad Toelz, as well as the SS Medical Academy in Graz. He was promoted to Oberfuehrer on April 20, 1936 (Hitler's birthday) and to Brigadefuehrer in May 1936. Later that year, due to the rapid expansion of the SS, he was appointed chief of the Inspectorate of SS-VT and was responsible for the military training of all SS units except those belonging to Theodor Eicke.

Hausser proved to be an intelligent and professionally broad-minded director of training. It was he, for example, who saw to it that the SS-VT were the first troops to wear camouflaged uniforms in the fields, and he stuck to his decision, even though the army's soldiers laughed and called the SS men "tree frogs." (These uniforms were very much like the present-day U.S. Army battledress uniforms [BDUs, or "fatigues"].) During the next three years he oversaw the organization, development, and training of the SS regiments "Deutschland," "Germania," and "Der Fuehrer," as well as smaller combat support, service, and supply units. Paul Hausser was quick to see the potential of the blitzkrieg and, as a consequence, most of the SS units were motorized. In the autumn of 1939, he was in the processes of forming the SS-VT Division, but the outbreak of the war caught him by surprise, and not all his units had completed their training; consequently, no SS division as such fought in Poland. Most of the combat-ready SS-VT units (and Hausser personally) were attached to the ad hoc Panzer Division "Kempf," led by army Major General Werner Kempf. After this campaign the first full Waffen-SS division was established at the Army Maneuver Area Brdy-Wald, near Pilsen, on October 10, 1939.[28] Its commander was the recently promoted SS-Gruppenfuehrer Paul Hausser.

Hausser trained his SS-VT Motorized Infantry Division throughout the winter of 1939–1940 and led it with some distinction in the conquests of Holland, Belgium, and France in 1940, during which it pushed all the way to the Spanish frontier. As a result of the successes of the Waffen-SS units in these battles, Hitler authorized the formation of the new SS combat divisions in the winter of 1940–1941. The SS-VT Division (now on garrison duty in Holland) provided the nucleus for these divisions, giving up a motorized infantry regiment and several smaller units in the process. Meanwhile, in December 1940, the SS-VT was transferred to Vesoul in southern France and redesignated SS Division Deutschland; however, this name was too easily confused with the regiment of the same name, so in early 1941 it became SS Panzer Division "Das Reich."

Paul Hausser did not complain about losing almost half his veteran soldiers, but rather devoted himself to training their inexperienced replacements for the planned invasion of England. In March 1941, however, the Reich Division was transferred to Rumania and took part in the conquest of Yugoslavia in April. Hurried back to Germany, it was quickly refitted for Operation Barbarossa and was then sent to assembly areas in Poland, where it was still in the process of reforming on June 15.

The invasion of the Soviet Union began on June 22, 1941. Hausser crossed the border near Brest-Litovsk and took part in the battles of encirclement in the zone of Army Group Center. The Reich Division distinguished itself in extremely heavy combat. In July alone it destroyed 103 tanks and smashed the elite Soviet 100th Infantry Division. By mid-November the Reich had suffered 40 percent casualties, among them the divisional commander. Paul Hausser was severely wounded in the face and lost his right eye in a battle near Gjatsch on October 14. He was evacuated back to Germany, where it took him several months to recover.

Hausser (now an Obergruppenfuehrer) returned to active duty in May 1942, as commander of the newly created SS Motorized Corps, which became the SS Panzer Corps on June 1, 1942. Hausser was thus the first SS man to become a corps commander. He spent the rest of 1942 in northern France, controlling the 1st, 2nd, and 3rd SS divisions (the Leibstandarte, Das Reich, and Totenkopf divisions, respectively). Among other things, these superbly equipped units were given a panzer battalion and a company of the first PzKw V ("Tiger") tanks.

While Hausser prepared his new command for its next campaign, disaster struck on the Russian Front. Stalingrad was surrounded, the Don sector collapsed, and the Red Army poured through Axis lines, heading west. In January 1943, Hitler rushed the SS Panzer Corps to Kharkov, the fourth-largest city in the Soviet Union, which, for reasons of prestige, he ordered to be held to the last man. "Now at last Hitler was reassured," Paul Carell wrote later. "He relied on the absolute obedience of the Waffen-SS Corps and overlooked the fact that the corps commander, General Paul Hausser, was a man of common sense, strategic skill, and with the courage to stand up to his superiors."[29]

By noon on February 15, Hausser was almost surrounded by the Soviet 3rd Tank and 69th armies. Rather than sacrifice his two elite SS divisions (Totenkopf had not yet arrived from France), Hausser ordered his corps to break out to the southwest at 1 p.m., regardless of Hitler's commands or those of the army generals.

Hausser's immediate superior, Army General Hubert Lanz, was horrified by this development. A Fuehrer Order was being deliberately disobeyed! At 3:30 p.m. he signaled Hausser: "Kharhov will be defended under all circumstances!"[30]

Paul Hausser ignored this order as well. The last German rearguard left Kharkov on the morning of February 16. Hausser had made good his escape and had saved the army's 320th Infantry Division and its elite Grossdeutschland Panzer Grenadier Division in the process. The question now was how Hitler would react to this piece of deliberate insubordination.

Adolf Hitler's mentality demanded that a scapegoat be found for this latest disaster, but Hausser was not a candidate for public disgrace. After all, he was an SS officer, a loyal Nazi, and a holder of the Golden Party Badge, which Hitler had conferred on him just three weeks before. Instead, Hitler sacked none other than Hubert Lanz, the very officer who had insisted to the last that the Fuehrer's order be obeyed. Contrary to usual practice, however, Lanz was given command of a mountain corps shortly thereafter, instead of being permanently retired.[31]

Hitler did not forgive Hausser quickly, however, even after reports and events of the next few days made the correctness of his actions clear for all to see—even at Fuehrer Headquarters. As punishment, a recommendation that Hausser be decorated with the Oak Leaves to his Knight's Cross was not acted upon.

Meanwhile, Field Marshal Erich von Manstein, the commander of Army Group South, devised a brilliant plan to restabilize the southern sector of the Eastern Front. Realizing that the overconfident Soviets were in danger of outrunning their supply lines, he allowed them to surge forward, while he hoarded his armor for a massive counterattack. This stroke would entail a pincer movement to cut off the massive Soviet penetration south of Kharkov, followed by an attempt to recapture the city. Hausser, now reinforced with the SS Totenkopf Division, would command the left wing of the pincer.

The Third Battle of Kharkov began on February 21, 1943. The fighting was fierce, but by March 9 the Soviet 6th Army and Popov Armored Group had been destroyed—a loss of more than 600 tanks, 400 guns, 600 anti-tank guns, and tens of thousands of men. That day Paul Hausser's spearheads reentered the burning city of Kharkov, beginning the most controversial battle of the general's career. Military historians generally agree that Kharkov was now doomed and that Hausser should have encircled the city; instead, he attacked it frontally from the west and began six days of costly street fighting against fanatical resistance. The conquest of Kharkov was not complete until March 14. During the battle, the SS Panzer Corps suffered 11,000 casualties, against 20,000 for the Red Army.

Hausser redeemed his military reputation that July, during the Battle of Kursk—the greatest tank battle in history. His command, now designated II SS Panzer Corps, penetrated farther than any other German unit and destroyed an estimated 1,149 Soviet tanks and armored vehicles in the process. Colonel General Hermann Hoth, the commander of the 4th Panzer Army, recommended him for the Oak Leaves, stating that despite being handicapped by his previous wounds, he "untiringly led all day from the front. By his presence, his bravery and his humor, even in the most difficult situations, he imbued his troops with buoyancy and enthusiasm, yet he kept command of the corps tightly and in his hand. . . . [Hausser] again distinguished himself as an unusually qualified commanding general."[32]

While the Germans were being defeated at Kursk, Italian dictator Benito Mussolini was overthrown on July 25. Hitler ordered the II SS Panzer Corps to transfer to northern Italy on the same day, although in the end only the corps headquarters and the 1st SS Panzer Grenadier Division ever left the Eastern Front. Hausser remained in Italy until December 1943, without engaging in any fighting; then he was transferred to France, where his corps took charge of the recently organized 9th SS Panzer Division "Hohenstaufen" and the 10th SS Panzer Division "Frundsberg."

Hausser's corps was supposed to be held in reserve to oppose the D-Day invasion, but when the 1st Panzer Army was surrounded in Galicia in April 1944, Hausser was sent back to the Eastern Front to rescue it.

This was accomplished without too much difficulty, thanks to Manstein, Hausser, and the army's commander, Hans Valentin Hube. Instead of sending the SS corps back to France, however, Hitler sent it to Poland, where it formed a reserve against the Soviets. It was not until June 11—five days after the Allies' D-Day landings—that Hitler ordered the corps back to France. It was assigned a sector west of Caen, with the mission of holding the critical Hill 112.

The Battle of Normandy was the most difficult and exacting of General Hausser's career. Badly outnumbered, he faced an enemy with devastating air and naval supremacy, which made it difficult for him to either move or resupply his troops. Hausser nevertheless held his positions despite heavy casualties on both sides.

Meanwhile, the left half of the German front in Normandy, which was the responsibility of Colonel General Friedrich Dollmann's 7th Army, was in serious trouble. At the end of June, shortly after the fall of Cherbourg, the hard-pressed general dropped dead of a heart attack (see chapter 4). He was replaced by Paul Hausser, who shortly thereafter was promoted to SS-*Oberstgruppenfuehrer und Generaloberst der Waffen-SS*—the equivalent of an American four-star general. He was the first SS man to be assigned to the command of an army on a permanent basis.[33]

Hausser's army, which included the LXXXIV Corps and II Parachute Corps, was much weaker than its sister army, the 5th Panzer, on its right. It had only 50 medium and 26 Panther tanks, for example, against 5th Panzer's 250 medium and 150 heavy tanks, and it had only about one-third of the artillery and anti-aircraft guns as the 5th Panzer. It did, however, have the advantage of excellent defensive terrain, and Hausser's men took full advantage of that situation. They were gradually pushed back, however, and Hausser's divisions were slowly ground to bits. By July 11, for example, his elite 2nd Parachute Division was down to 35 percent of its authorized manpower, and most of his other divisions were also down to *Kampfgruppe* (regimental) strength. By mid-July Hausser was restoring to tactical patchwork to establish any kind of reserve at all.

The decisive breakthrough of the Normandy campaign occurred in Hausser's sector of July 25, 1944. That day, in Operation Cobra, 2,500 Allied airplanes—1,800 of which were heavy bombers—dropped approximately 5,000 tons of high explosives, jellied gasoline (napalm), and white phosphorus on a six-square-mile block, mostly in the zone of the Panzer Lehr Division. Panzer Lehr's forward units were virtually annihilated. By the end of the day, it had only about a dozen tanks and assault guns left, and a parachute regiment attached to it had vanished under the bombs.

There is little doubt that Hausser mishandled the entire Operation Cobra. Several days before the bombs fell, Field Marshal Guenther von Kluge (who had replaced a critically wounded Rommel a week before) had suggested that Hausser replace the Panzer Lehr with the 275th Infantry Division, which Hausser then held in army reserve. Meanwhile, on the far left flank, LXXXIV Corps had managed to pull the 353rd Infantry Division out of the line. Kluge suggested than Hausser use it to replace the 2nd SS Panzer Division "Das Reich" at the front, thus establishing an army reserve of two armored divisions. The SS general, however, ignored both of his former classmates' suggestions. "Hausser did little more than clamor for battlefields replacements, additional artillery, and supplies, and the sight of air cover," according to the American official history records.[34]

When the American ground forces began to advance at 11 a.m. on July 25, Hausser reacted slowly because he did not initially appreciate the magnitude of the disaster that had overtaken his army. By late afternoon, however, he realized that his front had been penetrated in seven places in the Lessay–St. Lô sector, and without an armored reserve, he could do little to seal the gaps. He therefore requested permission to conduct a general withdrawal to Coutances. Kluge, however, also misread the situation and would approve only a limited withdrawal. As a result, LXXXIV Corps was soon cut off on the west coast of the Cotentin peninsula and only broke out (on Hausser's orders) with heavy losses. Meanwhile, the Americans were in the rear of the 7th Army; SS Oberfuehrer Christian Tychesen, the commander of Hausser's old Das Reich Division, was killed near his command post by an American patrol; and Hausser himself only narrowly escaped death from an American armored car that fired on him near Gavray. There was little he could do but withdraw the remnants of his disintegrating command to the east, while the rapidly advancing Americans captured Avranches (at the base of the Cotentin peninsula) and broke out into the interior of France. In doing so they unknowingly came within a few hundred yards of the 7th Army's forward command post, which was located 3.5 miles north of Avranches. Cut off, Hausser and many of his key staff officers had to escape on foot by infiltrating through the regularly spaced intervals between American troop convoys. There was, of course, nothing Hausser could do to influence the course of the battle, which was totally out of hand.

When he finally learned of the extent of the 7th Army's disaster, Kluge's dissatisfaction with the 7th Army's leadership reached a head. On July 30, he inspected Hausser's headquarters and found it "farcical, a complete mess," and concluded that "the whole army [is] putting up a poor show."[35] Lacking the authority to relieve the SS general (or perhaps not daring to do so, given his own previous association with the conspirators who had tried to assassinate Adolf Hitler a few days before), Kluge sacked Hausser's chief of staff and the commander of the LXXXIV Corps—who was less responsible for the disaster than Kluge himself—and replaced them with his own men. Kluge also took active charge of the left flank himself.[36] It was too late by then, however; the battle was already lost.

Paul Hausser had little influence on the campaign in Normandy after July 28. As General George S. Patton's U.S. 3rd Army advanced south and east of Mortain and threatened to encircle the 5th Panzer and 7th armies south of Caen, Hausser joined Kluge in objecting to Hitler's unrealistic plan to concentrate nine depleted panzer divisions in the western edge of the salient, with the objective of thrusting west to the coast, to cut off Patton. Instead, Kluge and Hausser wanted to fall back behind the Seine while there still might be time to do so. Kluge was overruled, however, and it is significant that, on the orders of Adolf Hitler, the final effort to reach the west coast was directed by an ad hoc panzer group under Army General Heinrich Eberbach, the former commander of the 5th Panzer Army, and not by Hausser. In any event it was defeated, and the bulk of Army Group B was surrounded in the Falaise Pocket on August 17.[37] Hausser, still with his men inside the pocket, ordered all units capable of action to break out in individual combat groups on the night of August 19–20.

Hausser's actions saved about one-third of his army, which was on the far side of the encirclement. (A considerably larger portion of the 5th Panzer Army was saved because it did not have as far to go to reach friendly lines.) The general himself joined the 1st SS Panzer Division Liebstandarte Adolf Hitler and, on August 20, was marching on foot with a machine pistol draped around his neck when an Allied artillery shell landed in front of him, and a piece of shrapnel hit him right in the face. Some soldiers from the Leibstandarte placed him on the stern of a tank and eventually succeeded in getting the seriously wounded commander back to German lines, after a number of narrow escapes.[38] He was taken to the Luftwaffe hospital at Greifswald, where he slowly began to recover.

Six days after he was wounded, Hausser was awarded the Swords to his Knight's Cross; however, he was unable to return to active duty until January 23, 1945, when he became acting commander of Army Group Oberrhein (Upper Rhine), replacing Heinrich Himmler. Six days later this headquarters was dissolved, and Hausser was given command of Army Group G, controlling the 1st and 19th armies and later 7th Army as well. He was given the task of defending southern Germany. The war, however, was already lost, and Hausser could do little but fight a delaying action through the Saar and Palatinate. By now thoroughly disillusioned with the Nazi leadership, Hausser became increasingly frustrated by Hitler's constant interference in the details of operations of his forces and especially with his hold-at-all-costs orders—one of which cost Hausser much of his command, which had not been allowed to retreat across the Rhine in time. The personal relationship between the two men, which had begun to deteriorate during the Second Battle of Kharkov, had reached a new low in early 1945, due to a heated argument they had over tactical matters. On March 30, 1945, Hitler remarked to Dr. Joseph Goebbels, the minister of propaganda, that neither Sepp Dietrich nor Hausser had any real operational talent and that "no high-class commander has emerged from the SS."[39] Three days later a dispatch from Hausser arrived, suggesting that a gap between the 1st and 7th armies be closed by another retreat into southern Germany. Furious, Hitler immediately relieved Hausser of his command and replaced him with General of Infantry Friedrich Schulz. Unemployed for the rest of the war, Hausser surrendered to the Americans in May. At Nuremberg he was the most important defense witness for the Waffen-SS, stating that his men were soldiers like any other. Nevertheless the entire SS, including the Waffen-SS, was condemned as a criminal organization. Hausser himself was not subjected to a long imprisonment, however.

As a general, Paul Hausser proved to be an above-average divisional commander and a gifted—and sometimes brilliant—corps commander, although his conduct of the Third Battle of Kharkov is hardly above criticism. As a trainer, he had few equals anywhere. He was largely responsible for establishing the Waffen-SS as a potent combat force, and it bore his influence throughout its existence. As the commander of the 7th Army in Normandy, however, his performance left a great deal to be desired. It is not possible to objectively evaluate his direction of Army Group G, except to say that it would have been more effective had he been left to his own devices, rather than receiving "help" from Adolf Hitler. It would probably have been better for Nazi Germany if he had been left in command of an SS panzer corps—or as director of training for the Waffen-SS—from 1943 on.

In the postwar years, Paul Hausser was an active member of the Mutual Aid Society of the Waffen-SS (*Hilfsorganization auf Gegenseitigkeit der Waffen-SS*, or HIAG), the Waffen-SS veterans organization, and wrote numerous articles for its magazine, *Wiking Ruf* (*Viking Call*), now *Dei Freiwillige—The Volunteer*. In 1953 he wrote his first book, *Waffen-SS im Einsatz* (*The Waffen-SS in Operation*), which he expanded in 1966 and subtitled *Soldaten wie Andere Auch* (*Soldiers like Any Other*). He died on December

28, 1972, at the age of 92. His funeral was attended by thousands of his former soldiers.

Besides Paul Hausser, the only SS man to reach the rank of SS-colonel general (SS-Oberstgruppenfuehrer und Generaloberst der Waffen-SS) was JOSEF "SEPP" DIETRICH, a close personal friend of Adolf Hitler in the early years of the Nazi Party and an advocate of removing him as Supreme Commander in 1944.

Sepp Dietrich was born in the village of Hawangen (near Memmingen) in Swabia on May 28, 1892, one of three boys born to Palagius Dietrich, a master meat packer, and his wife. Described as good Catholics, the Dietrichs also had three daughters. Both of Sepp's younger brothers were killed in action in World War I. Young Sepp attended school for eight years and then dropped out to become an agricultural driver. As a teenager he succumbed to wanderlust and at the age of 15 traveled to Austria, Italy, and Switzerland, where he found employment as an apprentice in the hotel trade. He was drafted into the Royal Bavarian Army in 1911 but stayed only a few weeks due to a training injury he suffered when he fell from a horse. Invalided out, he returned to Kempten (where his parents now lived) and became a baker's errand boy. Like so many Germans, however, he quickly rushed to the colors when World War I broke out. As a member of the 7th Bavarian Field Artillery Regiment, he fought at Ypres in 1914 and was wounded by shrapnel in the lower leg and by a lance thrust above his left eye. He was wounded again in the Battle of the Somme, when a shell splinter struck the right side of his head. Nevertheless, Sepp Dietrich volunteered for an elite assault (*Sturm*) battalion and ended the war in one of Germany's few tank units.

Like so many restless young veterans, Sepp Dietrich joined Freikorps after the war. When the Poles (supported by French advisers) invaded Silesia in 1920, Dietrich paid his own way to the scene of the fighting and took part in the partially successful German attempt to prevent the Polish annexation of that province. Then he returned to Bavaria, where he married for the first time, joined the Landespolizei (provincial, or Green, police), and actually settled down for the first time. Like his marriage, however, it did not last.

Sepp joined the right-wing Bund Oberland and took part in Hitler's unsuccessful Beer Hall Putsch, which ended in the November 9, 1923, gun battle between the Nazis and their supporters (including the Bund) on one side and the green police on the other. This incident probably explains Dietrich's sudden discharge from the provincial police the following year.

From 1924 until 1929 he remained in Munich and worked in a variety of jobs, including tobacco clerk, waiter, and gas station attendant. Meanwhile, he joined the Nazi Party and the SS and soon became a favorite of Adolf Hitler, who nicknamed him "Chauffeureska" and carried him along on his automobile tours throughout Germany. As the Nazi Party gained in popularity, Sepp Dietrich advanced as well. He became a member of the Reichstag in 1930 and in late 1931 was promoted to Gruppenfuehrer in the SS.[40] Burly, tough, powerful, solid, and stocky, Dietrich was noticed for his down-to-earth manner and his "robust" sense of humor.[41]

Hitler considered him an excellent bodyguard and, in March 1933, only a few weeks after assuming power, the new chief of state charged Sepp with the task of forming an SS unit for the protection of the Reich Chancellery. On March 12 Dietrich formed up 117 men on the Friesenstrasse, in front of the Kaiserin Augusta-Victoria Barracks in Berlin. From this modest beginning evolved the mighty 1st SS Panzer Division Leibstandarte Adolf Hitler, which eventually exceeded a strength of 20,000 men and distinguished itself on dozens of bloody battlefields all across Europe. From the ranks of the young men who formed up that morning, the Waffen-SS eventually drew three divisional commanders and at least eight regimental commanders.[42]

As a commanding officer, Sepp Dietrich was considered likable, enthusiastic, and courageous but not overly bright. Field Marshal Gerd von Rundstedt called him "decent but stupid," and SS General Willi Bittrich, who was his chief of staff in 1939, recalled, "I once spent an hour and a half trying to explain a situation to Sepp Dietrich with the aid of a map. It was quite useless. He understood nothing at all."[43] Undoubtedly an officer with inadequate training, he nevertheless ended up in charge of an entire SS panzer army at the end of the war. Fortunately for him, he had the natural shrewdness of a Bavarian peasant and a deep-seated common sense, which partially made up for his lack of education and training. He also had a habit of selecting excellent chiefs of staff, a talent that helped him immeasurably.

On June 30, 1934, during the Night of the Long Knives, Dietrich personally commanded the firing squad that executed many senior members of the SA. "You have been condemned to death by the Fuehrer for high treason! Heil Hitler!" he shouted at each new victim. One of them was a long-time personal friend. "Sepp, my friend, what is happening? We are completely innocent!" cried SA Obergruppenfuehrer August Schneidhuber, as the SS put him up against the wall. Dietrich treated him like all the others; however, he became nauseated and left just before the SS riflemen opened up on Schneidhuber.[44]

For his services during the Blood Purge, Dietrich was promoted to SS-Obergruppenfuehrer (equivalent to a full general in the German Army). He led Hitler's elite bodyguard unit in the reoccupation of the Saarland (1935), in the Anschluss (1938), in the march into the Sudetenland (1938), and in the occupation of Bohemia and Moravia (1939). He continued to direct it in the invasions of Poland (1939); Holland, Belgium, and France (1940); and Yugoslavia, Greece, and Russia (1941). During this period, the Leibstandarte was progressively upgraded into a motorized infantry division.

Sepp Dietrich played a most credible role in the Battle of Rostov on the Eastern Front in November and December 1941. After this battle (which Germany lost), Hitler arrived in southern Russia with the intention of sacking Colonel General Ewald von Kleist, the aristocratic commander of the 1st Panzer Army. Dietrich, however, stood up for Kleist and bluntly told the Fuehrer that he, Adolf Hitler, and not Kleist, had been wrong in the conduct of the battle. He also added that Hitler had been wrong to relieve Field Marshal von Rundstedt of his command for wanting to evacuate Rostov a few days earlier. Dietrich's courageous intervention saved Kleist's career and that of his chief of staff, Colonel (later Colonel General) Kurt Zeitzler, and eventually led to Rundstedt's being recalled to active duty in March 1942. This would not be the last time Hitler's former bodyguard saved an army comrade. In 1944, Dietrich's personal intervention secured mercy for Lieutenant General Hans Speidel, Rommel's former chief of staff, who had been arrested by Himmler's security service in connection with the July 20 attempt to assassinate Adolf Hitler. Since Speidel was, in fact, guilty, Dietrich's actions almost certainly saved his life.

At Rostov, Dietrich suffered first- and second-degree frostbite on the toes of his right foot. In January 1942, he returned to Germany to recover and, while home, married his second wife, Ursula Moninger, the daughter of a famous Karlsruhe brewery owner. Ursula had given birth to Dietrich's first son, Wolf-Dieter, in 1939.[45] Meanwhile, the Leibstandarte was withdrawn to France to rebuild and reequip. Dietrich joined it there in 1942 and led it back to the Russian Front in December. By that time it was an SS panzer grenadier division and had a strength of 21,000 men. Sepp Dietrich spent most of the rest of the war in combat. He assumed command of the I SS Panzer Corps on July 22, 1943, and of the 6th Panzer Army (later 6th SS Panzer Army) in late September 1944. In August 1944, he was promoted to Oberstgruppenfuehrer and became the 16th soldier (and one of only 27 in the war) to receive the Diamonds to his Knight's Cross with Oak Leaves and Swords.

Despite the many honors provided to him by the Nazi government, Dietrich became increasingly disillusioned with Hitler's leadership as the war progressed and was especially critical of his tendency to meddle in the detailed affairs of his generals. In July 1944, he told Field Marshal Erwin Rommel that he would obey his orders even if they conflicted with those of the Fuehrer. Whether he would have sided with the Desert Fox and the conspirators of July 20 in a showdown is anybody's guess, because Rommel was critically wounded on July 17 and was still in a coma when the plot misfired.

Whatever else can be said of Dietrich, he genuinely liked his men and took care of them. In 1936, for example, he had occasion to order the arrest of a young SS lieutenant who lost his temper in a discussion in the officers' mess and poured a stein of beer on a colleague's head, thus provoking a fist-fight. The normal disciplinary action for such conduct was a court-martial and dismissal from the Leibstandarte. However, when Dietrich learned that the young man's wife was pregnant, he quietly had the charges dropped. This young officer was Kurt Meyer, who later became a Brigadefuehrer and, as one of Nazi Germany's most decorated warriors, brilliantly led the 12th SS Panzer Division "Hitler Youth" in the Normandy campaign.[46] Army General Friedrich Wilhelm von Mellenthin related another typical incident, which occurred in the campaign in Hungary near the end of the war. An 18-year-old boy who had been very much pampered by his mother was posted to a Waffen-SS tank crew; the men naturally had little sympathy for him and made life difficult for the spoiled youth. The boy soon deserted and headed for his home and his mother but was arrested en route. Duly tried, he was convicted and sentenced to death. It was up to his army commander, SS-Oberstgruppenfuehrer Dietrich, to confirm the sentence.

Instead of merely signing the death warrant, as many of Hitler's commanders would have done at that stage of the war, Dietrich studied the records and ordered the condemned boy to appear before him. After listening to the lad's tale of woe and mental anguish, the SS general rose and soundly boxed his ears. (This was the traditional, pre–World War I method Prussian officers used to handle minor infractions—and break eardrums!) He then sent the young private on a one-week leave to his mother's, with orders to return to the 6th SS Panzer at the end of that time as a good soldier. The lad did as he was told and apparently grew up considerably in the process, as one might imagine. In any event he was a good soldier after that. And the record of the court-martial and death sentence disappeared.[47]

Dietrich put up a tenacious defense in Normandy and, like several of his army colleagues, called for a timely retreat from the Falaise sector before the Anglo-Americans could close the pocket. Ignored by Hitler, he did what he could to minimize the damage and was almost captured by a British patrol as a result. Dietrich was then sent back to Germany to organize the newly authorized 6th Panzer Army for the Hitler's Ardennes counteroffensive. The SS general argued against this overly ambitious scheme, but when Hitler would not relent, Dietrich tried to make it work, without achieving any notable successes. He and his army were easily outperformed by General Baron Hasso von Manteuffel's 5th Panzer Army to the south. Following this failure, Dietrich was sent to the East with his headquarters and was charged with conducting the Lake Balaton counteroffensive of 1945. Even though he attacked before all his units were ready, Dietrich did not achieve surprise and was soon defeated by the Red Army, which had a vast numerical superiority in every material category.

Furious over the lack of success of his elite SS troops in another fruitless counterattack in April 1945, Hitler issued an order stripping the 1st, 2nd, 3rd, and 9th SS Panzer divisions of their cuff bands. All four divisions were part of the 6th SS Panzer Army at the time. Dietrich retaliated by going one step further: he and his officers filled a chamber pot with their medals and prepared to send it to the Fuehrer Bunker in Berlin. Dietrich then instructed them to tie a Goetz von Berlichingen Division ribbon on it. (In Goethe's drama *Goetz von Berlichingen*, the Knight tells the Bishop of Bamberg, "You can kiss my ass!" Dietrich knew that Hitler would fully understand the implications of his gesture.) As Louis Snyder wrote, "The incident expressed perfectly the personality of Sepp Dietrich."[48] As for the order to remove the cuff bands, the panzer army commander saw to it that it was not relayed to the rank and file (i.e., he ignored the order). Unfortunately, Hitler's reaction to the chamber pot apparently was not recorded.

In spite of the chamber pot (or perhaps because of it), Sepp Dietrich was directed to hold Vienna at all costs from the onrushing Soviets in early April 1945. Dietrich knew that this was a hopeless mission. "We call ourselves *Panzerarmee 6* because we have only six panzers left," he sneered grimly to his headquarters staff.[49]

Of course the hard-bitten and disillusioned but sensible commander had no intention of obeying such a ridiculous order. Despite Hitler's directive that "he who gives the order to retreat is to be shot on the spot,"[50] Dietrich pulled the remnants of his panzer army out of the Austrian capital on April 13. Fearing a possible reaction by Hitler, he surrounded himself and his headquarters with a heavily armed SS detachment, which was loyal to him personally. It turned out to be a needless precaution, because the Third Reich ended without Hitler trying to take any retaliatory action against his former favorite. Even so, Dietrich's precautions were unquestionably sensible steps to take.

SS Colonel General Dietrich surrendered his army to the Americans in Austria on May 8, 1945, and was soon charged with murder in connection with the Malmedy massacre, where 86 American prisoners were executed by a group of SS men during the Battle of the Bulge. Since then, Charles Whiting has proven almost beyond question that Dietrich was nowhere near Malmedy at the time and knew nothing about the atrocity. Nevertheless, he was convicted and sentenced to 25 years' imprisonment on July 16, 1946. Ironically, he was confined in the fortress of Landsberg, where Adolf Hitler had written *Mein Kampf* 22 years before. After the passions generated by the war died down somewhat, the former SS man was paroled on October 22, 1955.

Josef Dietrich's legal problems were not over, however, because the West Germans were soon after him for another crime—and this time it was one he undoubtedly did commit. Duly convicted by a Munich court, he began serving an 18-month sentence on August 2, 1958, for his part in the Blood Purge of 1934. Again confined to Landsberg, he was released after only five months due to circulatory problems and a serious heart condition. He then returned to his family at Ludwigsburg—but not to his wife. She had apparently broken off her relationship with Dietrich during his first imprisonment, and they remained estranged. (She died in 1983.)

Now left alone in retirement, the former general of SS devoted himself to hunting and the activities of the HIAG. Unfortunately, because he could have told us much, he left no memoirs. Sepp Dietrich died suddenly in his bed (and perhaps in his sleep) of a massive heart attack on April 21, 1966. He was 73 years old.

HELMUT BECKER, a protégé of Theodor Eicke, is typical of the controversy surrounding some of the leading members of the Waffen-SS today—especially those associated with the 3rd SS Panzer Division "Totenkopf." He was born at Alt-Ruppin, Brandenburg province, on August 12, 1902, the son of Hermann Becker, a local housepainter. He graduated from the local high school (*Volksschule*) and started vocational training in Alt-Ruppin before he was accepted into the Reichsheer on August 1, 1920, as a private in the Prussian 5th Infantry Regiment, stationed at Neu-Ruppin in Brandenburg. The minimum service period in the Reichswehr at this time was 12 years, so Becker's enlistment constituted a career choice. He served with the 16th Company of the 5th Infantry at Greifswald and with the 5th Company at Angermuende (70 miles northeast of Berlin), gradually rising to the rank of sergeant. By 1928 he was on the staff of the 2nd Artillery Regiment (2nd Infantry Division) at Stettin. When his enlistment expired in 1932, however, he was not selected for retention in the 100,000-man army. Naturally he was disappointed, but the Reichsheer was in a position to accept or retain only those it considered to be the very best, and they obviously did not consider Helmut Becker to be in this category. There is, however, no stigma attached to this; in fact, it was in the Reichsheer's interests not to retain many of their experienced NCOs so that there would be vacancies for younger men, and the Reichsheer would not become an army of older people. Future SS generals Hermann Priess and Wilhelm Bittrich (who later smashed the British 1st Airborne Division at Arnhem) were among those not selected for retention.[52]

In any event, Becker soon put on a new uniform: that of an *SS-Mann* (private of SS), which he joined on February 27, 1933. As we have seen, the SS at this time was full of enthusiastic young men but woefully short on people who could provide them with good (or even adequate) military training. Because of his experience in the Reichsheer and his own forceful personality Becker rose rapidly and within a year was an *Oberscharfuehrer* (equivalent to an Army *Feldwebel*, or sergeant first class in the present-day U.S. Army) and adjutant of the 74th SS-Standarte. He performed his tasks in this position so well that he was promoted to *Hauptscharfuehrer* (master sergeant) in March and, on June 17, 1934, became an SS–Untersturmfuehrer (second lieutenant of SS). Nine months later he was promoted to first lieutenant of SS (*SS-Obersturmfuehrer*). In the meantime, Helmut Becker served as a military trainer at Greifswald and as adjutant of the II Battalion of the SS-Standarte Germania.[53] He seems to have found his home, however, when he was transferred to the 1st SS-Totenkopf-Standarte Oberbayern—one of Eicke's paramilitary Death's Head regiments of concentration camp guards—in 1935.

In his new unit, Becker served as commander of the 9th (Replacement and Training) Company of the Oberbayern and was responsible for the physical training and sports program of the entire regiment. He was also in charge of the regimental NCO training course. Becker excelled in his new jobs and in 1936 was promoted to *Hauptsturmfuehrer* (SS captain) and given command of the battalion. Later that year he was promoted to Sturmbannfuehrer (SS major) and in early 1938 was advanced to SS lieutenant colonel (*SS-Obersturmbannfuehrer*). He took part in all the peacetime operations of the 1st Totenkopf, including the occupations of Austria, the Sudetenland, and Czechoslovakia. When the Sudetenland crisis reached its high point (before Britain and France gave in to Hitler's demands at

Munich), Becker was busy forming the I SS Battalion (Bann) of the Sudeten Freikorps, which he was preparing for use against the Czechs. Returning to his own command (I/1st Totenkopf), Becker and his battalion followed the army into Poland in 1939, where it was employed as one of the dreaded Einstazgruppen.

What part it played in the subsequent atrocities is difficult to determine, but he no doubt did just as he was told—no matter what that entailed. In any event, Becker's battalion was motorized in the winter of 1939–1940, as part of the Death's Head (later 3rd SS Panzer) Division.

SS Lieutenant Colonel Becker first saw combat in the Western campaign of 1940 and fought bravely, winning both grades of the Iron Cross. Sent to Russia in 1941, he was for a time commander of the division's motorcycle battalion and played a significant role in the German victory at Lushno. It was during the battles of the Demyansk Pocket, however, that Becker really distinguished himself. Demyansk was hell on earth for the Totenkopf Division, which held the vital western edge of the pocket. Helmut Becker—now commanding a *Kampfgruppe* (battle group)—beat back attack after attack, despite odds of about five to one against him. The temperature was 30 degrees below zero Fahrenheit as the inadequately clothed SS men huddled in their trenches and foxholes, holding out through blizzards and human-wave attacks on pure willpower, starvation rations, and lack of supplies of every kind. During the siege, Helmut Becker appeared to be everywhere, extolling and cajoling, keeping his men on their toes and their spirits high, despite the fact that their situation appeared to be hopeless on more than one occasion.

His efforts were successful in every respect. When the spring thaw came, Becker and his ragtag survivors still held their position with their morale unbroken. Becker's personal contribution to this amazing feat did not go unnoticed by his superiors, including Theodor Eicke and Adolf Hitler. For his leadership in the Demyansk crises, Becker was awarded the German Cross in Gold, was promoted to Standartenfuehrer (SS colonel), and was earmarked for higher command. In the fall of 1942, when the Totenkopf was withdrawn to France to rebuild, Becker was named commander of the 6th Panzer Grenadier Regiment. Meanwhile, Helmut Becker had already run afoul of Heinrich Himmler, who, like most in the Nazi hierarchy, was engaging in empire building. Specifically, Himmler and his deputy, Gruppenfuehrer Gottlob Berger, the chief of the Waffen-SS recruiting office, were enrolling hundreds of *Volksdeutsche* ("racial" or ethnic Germans from the occupied territories) into the SS—many against their will. This was an obvious compromise of the SS ideal of an elite, volunteer body of Aryan supermen. Some of these new-breed SS men were sent to Becker as replacements, and he was not at all satisfied with them—especially with their poor training and inadequate state of physical fitness—and he said so, in writing.

In a report that was highly critical of Himmler's methods, Becker categorically stated that the SS recruiters should exercise greater selectivity in order to preserve the racially elite status of the Waffen-SS. He also described the situation in the Demyansk Pocket, criticized the lack of support the Totenkopf had received from higher SS headquarters, and recommended that the division be withdrawn at once. When the report reached Himmler's desk, the Reichsfuehrer-SS angrily forbade reports of this nature to be written in the future. In retaliation, Himmler later ordered an investigation of Becker on charges of sexual and military misconduct. It was alleged (among other things) that he had repeatedly been drunk on duty, had raped Russian women, had kept prostitutes in his forward command post, and had ridden a horse to death inside an officers' club in France in 1942, while members of his staff fornicated with French whores on the tables.[54] Nothing was ever proven, however, and Himmler was unable to bring Becker up on charges or to even prevent his advancement—indicating that Becker stood high in the opinion of the Fuehrer and suggesting that the allegations were questionable. In any event, the Becker case does demonstrate that some members of the Waffen-SS had achieved at least a degree of distinctiveness from the rest of Himmler's crowd and that many members of the Waffen-SS—Helmut Becker among them—held the Reichsfuehrer-SS in ill-concealed contempt.

Meanwhile, the 6th SS Panzer Grenadier Regiment returned to Russia in early 1943 and fought in the Third Battle of Kharkov, at Kursk, and in the subsequent retreats on the southern sector of the Eastern Front. Following the death of the original divisional commander, it received the honorary designation "Theodor Eicke." Meanwhile, in August, Helmut Becker received his Knight's Cross for the skill and personal courage he exhibited in smashing a Soviet breakthrough attempt in the Mius sector. Three of his company commanders received the same decoration for their courage in this action. Shortly thereafter, Becker was transferred to Italy where he directed the formation of a regiment of the 16th SS Panzer Grenadier Division "Reichsfuehrer-SS." Becker's stay in Italy was relatively brief, however. When Gruppenfuehrer Hermann Priess was appointed commander of the newly formed XIII SS Corps in mid-1944, Helmut Becker succeeded him as commander of the 3rd SS Panzer Division Totenkopf. He was promoted to SS-Oberfuehrer on June 21 and to SS-Brigadefuehrer und Generalmajor der Wuffen-SS on October 1, 1944.

SS General Becker exhibited considerable tactical skill as he led the Death's Head Division in its last campaigns. Hurriedly rushed from Rumania to help the rapidly disintegrating Army Group Center, the 3rd SS Panzer launched a series of counterattacks and conducted a well-planned delaying action as it helped stabilize the front in Poland in July and August 1944. On August 26 alone Totenkopf was attacked by eight Soviet rifle divisions and several squadrons of Red Air Force fighters. Despite its lack of air support and its growing casualty lists, Totenkopf did not break but fell back slowly on Warsaw. On September 11 it turned on its tormentors and delivered a vicious counterattack, which took the Soviets by surprise and threw them out of Praga, Warsaw's northeastern suburb. The depleted SS division continued to hold its positions there until the Soviet summer offensive had at last been checked by the end of the month. For his part in this campaign, Becker received the Oak Leaves to his Knight's Cross on September 21.

The 3rd SS Panzer Division continued to fight in the successful defensive battles in Poland until late December 1944, when it was hurried to Hungary and assigned to Army Group South, then trying to break the Siege of Budapest. This it was unable to do. The division then fell back across Hungary, took part in Hitler's abortive Lake Balaton offensive in March 1945, and fought its last battles in and around Vienna in April. After Hitler's death, Becker led what was left of his battered division west across Austria and on May 9, 1945, surrendered to elements of the U.S. 3rd Army. The next day, on the grounds that it had fought only on the Eastern Front, the local American commander acceded to Soviet demands and handed the survivors of the SS Totenkopf Division over to the Red Army. This move condemned most of them to death through overwork, malnutrition, or summary execution. Among those to die was the last Death's Head commander, Brigadefuehrer Helmut Becker. Shortly after he arrived in the Soviet Union, Becker and many of his men were subjected to "show trials" and were sentenced to 25 years' imprisonment. Becker had always been an implacable foe of Communism and now he took the attitude that, no matter what his captors did to him, they would not break his spirit. Although not the senior POW at his camp (which was located in Siberia, near the Arctic Circle), he assumed the role of leader and intervened on behalf of the prisoners at every opportunity. "Helmut retained a courageous attitude in captivity," SS Brigadefuehrer Gustav Lombard wrote later. "He helped make the days in the barracks of our prison camps a little less tough for all the men. His fellow generals-in-captivity thought the Soviets paid special attention to the last commander of the unbeaten 'Totenkopf' Division: he was a thorn in the Russians' eyes."[55] They removed this thorn on February 28, 1953, when they summarily executed General Becker, having accused him of sabotaging a building project. His widow, Lieselotte, and their five children were not informed of his death until 20 years later.

Today historians of the Nazi era are generally divided into two camps. The traditional (or "establishment") historians hold that the Waffen-SS was part of a criminal organization, and its members were, therefore, guilty of being criminals by association, if not by specific deeds. The other group, the revisionist (or "apologist") historians, holds that the vast majority of the members of the Waffen-SS (and some say all of them) were soldiers like any other. The second group has achieved a considerable following in Germany today and is growing in number in the United States and other countries. Since history is truly argument without end, the debate will no doubt go on for years to come. In any event, there is little middle ground in the case of Helmut Becker: he was either an unsung military hero who was murdered by the Soviets, or he was a filthy Nazi monster who finally got what he deserved. Readers, of course, must draw their own conclusions.

MICHAEL WITTMANN, one of the greatest warriors in history, was born on April 22, 1914, at Vogelthal in the Oberpflaz district. After completing his high school education, he worked for his father (a local farmer) and joined the Volunteer Labor Services[56] for a short time in 1934, before being accepted into the Reichsheer in October that same year. After serving two years with the 19th Infantry Regiment in the Munich area, he was discharged as a corporal (*Gefreiter*). He volunteered for the Waffen-SS in 1937 and was assigned to Hitler's bodyguard unit, the Leibstandarte Adolf Hitler (the LAH, later the 1st SS Panzer Division), based at Berlin Lichterfelde.

Quiet, unassuming, cool-headed, and conscientious, Wittmann gravitated into the SS because of its stress on comradeship, the friendliness that existed between the ranks, and (one surmises) its handsome black uniforms, which attracted many young Germans into its ranks during this era. (Even Manfred Rommel, the only son of the Desert Fox, considered joining the SS as a teenager—due to the effectiveness of its recruiting campaigns and the attractiveness of its uniforms.) The opportunity for more rapid promotion did not hurt, either. By the time World War II broke out, Wittmann was an *SS-Unterschurfuehrer* (sergeant) in the divisional assault gun battalion. After seeing action in Poland, France, and Belgium, he was given his own assault gun, which he directed in the Greek campaign. He did not come into his own, however, until the Leibstandarte crossed into the Soviet Union in June 1941.

Unlike the panzers, the German assault guns were used primarily as infantry support vehicles, as anti-tank weapons in close defensive situations, and as a divisional commander's organic mobile reserves. Sergeant Wittmann soon acquired a reputation for cool determination and incredible bravery because he liked to let enemy tanks get very close before opening fire on them. In fact, most of Wittmann's kills were with the first shell, at very close range. There was certainly nothing wrong with his nerve! He destroyed several Soviet tanks in this manner in the summer and fall of 1941, although not without taking hits himself. (He was wounded, though not seriously, in August.) At one point he was attacked by eight Soviet tanks. He coolly engaged them at close range, blowing away one after another, until six were burning and the other two were fleeing.

In 1941, he was decorated with both grades of the Iron Cross, as well as the Panzer Assault Badge. In mid-1942, after the LAH was transferred back to France to rest and rebuild, Wittmann was sent to Germany to attend the SS-Junkerschule at Bad Toelz. After successfully completing his training he was commissioned SS-Untersturmfuehrer (second lieutenant) on New Year's Eve, 1942. He then returned to the Eastern Front. When Wittmann rejoined the LAH in southern Russia, he was given a platoon of Tigers in the 13th (Heavy) Tank Company of the 1st SS Panzer Regiment. Although these monsters were slow, poor in maneuverability and prone to breakdown, they were heavily armored and packed tremendous punch in the long-barreled 88mm guns. Michael Wittmann soon became the acknowledged master of this deadly weapon. On the first day of the Kursk offensive (July 5, 1943), he personally destroyed eight Soviet tanks and seven artillery pieces. Always coolly methodical, he let the situation—not his own personality—dictate his tactics and the extent of his daring at any given time. This attitude, plus his great bravery and the courage and teamwork of his well-trained crew soon propelled Wittmann to near legendary status as the greatest tank warrior in military history. During the Battle of Kursk alone he destroyed 30 Soviet tanks and 28 guns.

Following the failure of Operation Citadel, all roads led backward for Hitler's legions in the East. Michael Wittmann was one of those who remained at or near the front, covering the retreat and counterattacking when the opportunity arose. In one engagement during the winter campaign of 1943–1944, for example, he personally destroyed 10 Soviet tanks in a single day. Remarkably, he was not awarded his Knight's Cross until January 14,

1944; however, he was presented his Oak Leaves only 16 days later. A few weeks later he was promoted to SS-Obersturmfuehrer (first lieutenant) and, in April 1944, was named commander of the 1st (Heavy) Company of the 501st SS Panzer Battalion, a Tiger unit attached directly to Headquarters, I SS Panzer Corps. By the time he left the Russian Front in the spring of 1944, Michael Wittmann had 119 Soviet tanks to his credit. He now, however, faced his most challenging battles on the Western Front.

The 501st was stationed at Beauvais, France, on June 6, 1944, when the Allied D-Day invasion came ashore. The following day the SS heavy tank battalion began its march to join the I SS Panzer Corps in Normandy. This was no easy task. Allied airplanes had destroyed most of the bridges south of Paris and made daytime travel an extremely hazardous business. After the 2nd Company had been caught in the open near Versailles and smashed by fighter-bombers on June 8, the 501st traveled only at night. The battalion's spearhead—Wittmann's company—arrived in the combat zone during the night of June 12–13 and took up camouflaged positions northeast of Villers-Bocage, in the extreme left-rear of Dietrich's corps. Wittmann intended to spend the next day repairing some of the bomb damage his tanks had suffered in the approach march. However, the British quickly changed his plans.

On the morning of June 13, a strong combat group from the British 7th Armoured Division found a gap in the too-thin German line, advanced past the left flank of the Panzer Lehr Division, penetrated into the German rear, and passed Villers-Bocage. They had turned the flank of the I SS Panzer Corps and were clearly heading for Caen, the key German position in Normandy and the major obstacle between Montgomery and Paris. They were about three miles east of Villers-Bocage when they were spotted by Lieutenant Wittmann, whose position was far from enviable. He had only five Tiger tanks—all that were still operational after his harrowing approach march. The rest of his battalion was still some distance away, and both Panzer Lehr and I SS Panzer had committed all their reserves to contain fierce British attacks in Tilly and Caen sectors. In other words, Wittmann's handful of tanks was all that stood between Montgomery and the envelopment of most of the SS panzer corps and the capture of Caen. The SS lieutenant decided to attack immediately. This decision began one of the most spectacular feats of arms in the entire Normandy campaign.

The British column—which included the 22nd Armoured Brigade and elements of the 1st Infantry Brigade—did not expect to meet opposition here and was lax in its security measures. Wittmann opened up on the first British Sherman from a range of 80 meters, instantly reducing it to a mass of flaming metal. Within moments he had knocked out three more Shermans and was closing in on the British column at full throttle.

Consternation broke out in the British ranks as Wittmann's Tiger blasted its first armored personal carrier (APC). Many British soldiers abandoned their vehicles and fled as Wittmann closed to within 10 to 30 meters of an APC, stopped, fired, watched his target explode into a million pieces, and then moved on to his next victim. A British Cromwell tank fired on Wittmann's Tiger with its 75mm main battle gun, but the shell bounced harmlessly off the thick armored plating of the German giant. Wittmann turned his 88 on the Cromwell and blew it away. Meanwhile his crew machine-gunned other British soldiers and vehicles that had failed to maintain a proper march interval and were now packed together much too closely. Simultaneously to the south, the light tanks of the British 8th Hussars Regiment (which had come up to help the main column) were attacked by the other four Tigers of Wittmann's company, and several more Allied tanks were soon abandoned and on fire. Wittmann continued to tear up the enemy spearhead as he proceeded slowly toward Villers-Bocage, destroying at least seven more tanks and several APCs in the process. Meanwhile, SS Captain Rudolf Moebius of the 501st SS Panzer arrived with eight more Tigers, was joined by Wittmann's other four, and headed straight for Villers-Bocage. He broke into the town and fought a running battle in the narrow streets with British tanks, an anti-tank gun unit, and the now dismounted infantry in the ruins of the French town.

Firing bazookas from windows and doorways, the British destroyed two Tigers and damaged others but were totally smashed in the process. Meanwhile, however, they managed to knock out Wittmann's Tiger as he entered Villers-Bocage from the other direction. Unable to join Moebius due to the British infantry, Wittmann abandoned his wrecked tank and headed north, where the Panzer Lehr Division was still holding on at last report. The lieutenant and his crew, however, traveled about 10 miles before they reached German lines.

Wittmann's counterattack had broken the back of the British breakthrough, and Villers-Bocage was back in German hands by nightfall. "Through his determined act," Sepp Dietrich wrote of Michael Wittmann that night, "against an enemy deep behind his own lines, acting alone and on his own initiative with great personal gallantry, with his tank he destroyed the greater part of the British 22nd Armoured Brigade and saved the entire front of the I SS Panzer Corps from the imminent danger which threatened." He recommended Wittmann for the Swords to his Knight's Cross.[57]

Lieutenant General Fritz Bayerlein, the commander of the Panzer Lehr Division, wrote a similar recommendation. Wittmann received this decoration on June 22 and a few days later was promoted to SS-Hauptsturmfuehrer (captain). As of June 14, he had destroyed 138 enemy tanks and 132 guns.

Despite the urgings of von Rundstedt, Rommel, von Kluge, Dietrich, and others, Adolf Hitler refused to allow Army Group B to retreat from the hedgerow country of Normandy to positions behind the Seine. As a result, the German forces were slowly ground to pieces. On August 8, the II Canadian Corps, supported by 500 British heavy bombers and 700 American airplanes, decimated the German 89th Infantry Division and broke through the German front. They were, however, slow in committing their armored reserve—the 4th Canadian and 1st Polish Armored divisions. Grasping this fact immediately, SS Major General Kurt "Panzer" Meyer realized that the proper course of action would be to launch a sharp counterattack with his 12th SS Panzer Division "Hitler Youth" to pin down the Allies before they could begin to roll south, into the German rear. After two months of constant combat, however, the 12th SS had only 50 operational tanks left, including Michael Wittmann's company, which had recently been loaned to Meyer by corps headquarters. The young SS general divided his assault forces into two battle groups (under Wittmann and SS Major Hans Waldmueller)[58] and attacked at once.

On the last day of his life, Captain Wittmann led the Hitler Youth battle group that recaptured Cintheaux and took the steam out of the Allied drive. The Allies tried to regain their momentum by counterattacking the ruined village with 600 tanks and, after a battle of several hours, actually succeeded in retaking the position. They were too late to take advantage of their earlier success, however, because the Germans had brought up reinforcements. When Panzer Meyer fell back behind the 85th Infantry Division, the German front was no longer in imminent danger of collapse. Michael Wittmann was not with him, however. He had last been seen directing the rearguard, where his lone Tiger was engaged in a fierce combat with five Shermans. He was reported as missing in action that evening and remained missing for the next 43 years.

In 1987, a French highway crew was widening a road near Cintheaux when it unearthed an unmarked grave. In it, they found the remains of Michael Wittmann, the greatest tank ace of all time. He is now buried in the Soldiers Cemetery at La Cambe.

★   ★   ★

GUSTAV KNITTEL is a good example of the kind of young man who joined the Waffen-SS.

Gustav and his twin brother, Bernhard, were born on November 27, 1914, in Neu–Ulm, Bavaria, the sons of a baker.[59] Gustav's life's ambition was to be a soldier, so he joined the *Allgemeine-SS* (General-SS) and the Nazi Party in the spring of 1934, because he thought membership in these organizations would help him when he applied to join the Reichswehr. It did not. Gustav received his *Abitur* (school leaving certificate, roughly equivalent to today's high school diploma) in 1934 and promptly tried to enlist in the army but was rejected. (He was one year too early. Hitler's military expansion did not begin in earnest until 1935.) Disappointed, he enlisted in the Waffen-SS instead and was assigned to the SS-Standarte "Deutschland" of the SS-VT in Ellwangen. He was promoted to SS corporal in 1936 and SS sergeant in 1937.

In a sense, advancement in the Waffen-SS was easier than in the more class-conscious army, and Knittel took advantage of this fact. He applied for officer training and was sent to the SS-Junkerschule at Bad Toelz, where he graduated 7th in his class in 1938. Commissioned SS second lieutenant on November 9, 1938, he returned to the SS Deutschland Regiment. The following summer, he was named adjutant of the SS Reserve Motorcycle Battalion "Ellwangen." He was promoted to SS first lieutenant on November 9, 1939.

Knittel first saw action in France, as a platoon leader in the 15th (Motorcycle) Company of the LAH, where he did well until he was severely wounded in the left thigh during the attack on St. Pourcain on June 19, 1940. After he recovered, he was given command of the 3rd Company of the Leibstandarte's Reconnaissance Battalion (later redesignated 1st SS Panzer Reconnaissance Battalion "Liebstandarte Adolf Hitler"). He led this company in the conquests of Yugoslavia and Greece, and in Operation Barbarossa, until July 10, 1941, when he was wounded by shrapnel and shot through the right shoulder as the Leibstandarte stormed the heights at Marchlewsk. After stops at various hospitals, he was sent to the SS replacement and training battalion at Dachau to recover.

Promoted to SS captain on November 9, 1941, Knittel was back in action on the Eastern Front later that month, where he distinguished himself in the capture of Rostov. He continued to lead his company in the retreat to the Mius, after which he was given command of the 3rd (light half-track) company of the 1st SS Recon. This unit was sent to the Sennelager Maneuver Area in Germany, where it was rebuilt and reequipped following its heavy losses on the Russian Front. Knittel and his men were then sent to Normandy, where they recovered from the winter fighting and trained new replacements until after the 6th Army was encircled at Stalingrad. The Leibstandarte was then hurried to the southern sector of the Eastern Front, where it took part in the battles around Kharkov. Knittel was wounded in the leg near Bereka on February 15 and in the left arm near Teterewino on July 11, but he remained with his troops.

In the spring of 1943, Kurt "Panzer" Meyer, the commander of the 1st SS Reconnaissance, was earmarked to command the 25th SS Panzer Grenadier Regiment of the 12th SS Panzer Division "Hitler Youth." Knittel succeeded him as commander of the 1st SS Recon and led it in the Battle of the Kursk and the subsequent retreats through Russia and Ukraine. He was promoted to SS major on April 23, 1943.

In March 1944, Knittel's battalion held Hill 300 against five major Soviet attacks and enabled the army's 68th Infantry Division to escape encirclement. For this and other actions, Gustav Knittel was awarded the Knight's Cross. Shortly thereafter, he returned to Germany for a short leave and married 21-year-old Raymonde Gauthier on May 6. They would have one child, a son named Bruno, who was born on May 28, 1946. Knittel, meanwhile, returned to the war.

After three years on the Eastern Front, Knittel and his men were thrown into the Battle of Normandy a few days after D-Day. Here they were in action almost daily, and the Leibstandarte was again smashed. It was here, as he witnessed the devastating power of the Allied air forces, that SS Major Knittel realized that the war was lost. He nevertheless continued fighting—in Normandy, in the Falaise Pocket, and in the retreat across France to the Siegfried Line. After the retreat ended, Knittel finally managed to secure a noncombat position. Following a brief furlough at Neu-Ulm, Knittel took charge of the 1st SS Field Replacement Battalion at Luebbecke in Westphalia.

Because he knew that the war was lost, Gustav Knittel did not want to return to the front. Meanwhile, however, the brutal Wilhelm Mohnke replaced the badly wounded Theodor Wisch (who lost both of his legs) as commander of the 1st SS Panzer Division.[60] It was Mohnke—who had obviously been impressed by Knittel's performance in Russia—who insisted that he be reassigned as commander of the 1st SS Reconnaissance Battalion. Knittel arrived back at the Western Front on December 13, 1944, where he was named commander of *Schnell Gruppe Knittel* (Fast Group Knittel), a battle group built around the 1st SS Recon. Knittel asked Mohnke to give the command to another, but his appeal was rejected.

The Battle of the Bulge began on December 16. By this point of the war, the 1st SS was almost completely brutalized, especially under Mohnke's command, and at least a dozen atrocities were committed. On December 17, at Wereth, members of Knittel's battalion murdered 11 African American soldiers from the U.S. 333rd Artillery Battalion after they had surrendered. It is not clear whether or not Knittel knew about this, but it seems fairly certain that he was aware of atrocities against civilians at Stavelot, Parfondruy, and Renardmont on December 19. It is not certain that he sanctioned these murders, but it is certain that he did little to restrain his men. His battalion was not involved in the Malmedy Massacre, as its route of advance that day was south of Kampfgruppe Peiper, which did the killing. Later in the battle, Knittel covered the retreat of the remnants of Joachim Peiper's regiment.

For Gustav Knittel, the war ended on December 31, 1944, when American airplanes bombed his command post near Vielsahn. The SS major suffered a serious concussion (his fifth wound of the war). He had not returned to active duty when Adolf Hitler committed suicide on April 30, 1945.

Following the surrender, Knittel hid out at a farm near Stuttgart. On January 5, 1946, he attempted to visit his wife at Neu-Ulm, but found that agents of the American CIC (Counter Intelligence Service) were waiting for him. He was taken to Schwaebisch Hall, where he was a defendant in the Malmedy trials. He confessed to the murder of American prisoners, but later averred that the CIC obtained the confession as a result of physical abuse and psychological torture. The CIC agents naturally denied this, and Knittel was found guilty and was sentenced to life imprisonment on July 16. Six weeks later, his wife filed for divorce.

Gustav Knittel filed at least three appeals and his sentence was progressively reduced. He was released as part of an amnesty on December 7, 1953. Shortly thereafter, he went to work for Opel as a car salesman.

Knittel suffered his first heart attack in 1968 and the rest of his life was characterized by ill health, which forced his retirement in 1970. He died of heart failure during surgery in an Ulm hospital on June 30, 1976.

Appendix I

EQUIVALENT OFFICER RANKS

U.S. Army	German Army and Luftwaffe
(none)	Reichsmarschall (Luftwaffe only)[a]
General of the Army	Field Marshal (Generalfeldmarschall)
General	Colonel General (Generaloberst)
Lieutenant General	General (General)[b]
Major General	Lieutenant General (Generalleutnant)
Brigadier General	Major General (Generalmajor)
Colonel	Colonel (Oberst)
Lieutenant Colonel	Lieutenant Colonel (Oberstleutnant)
Major	Major (Major)
Captain	Captain (Hauptmann)
First Lieutenant	First Lieutenant (Oberleutnant)
Second Lieutenant	Leutnant
Officer Cadet, Officer Candidate	Faehnrich (Senior Officer Candidate), Fahnenjunker (Officer-cadet)

SS Rank	German Army Equivalent
Reichsfuehrer-SS[c]	Commander-in-Chief of the Army
(none)	Field Marshal
Oberstgruppenfuehrer	Colonel General
Obergruppenfuehrer	General
Gruppenfuehrer	Lieutenant General
Brigadefuehrer	Major General
Oberfuehrer	(none)
Standartenfuehrer	Colonel
Obersturmbannfuehrer	Lieutenant Colonel
Strumbannfuehrer	Major
Haupsturmfuehrer	Captain

299

Obersturmfuehrer
Untersturmfuehrer

First Lieutenant
Second Lieutenant

U.S. Navy Rank	German Navy
Admiral of the Fleet	Grossadmiral (Grand Admiral)
(none)	Generaladmiral
Admiral	Admiral
Vice Admiral	Vizeadmiral
Rear Admiral	Konteradmiral
Captain	Kapitaen zur See
Commander	Fregattenkapitaen
Lieutenant Commander	Korvettenkapitaen
Lieutenant	Kapitaenleutnant
Lieutenant (junior grade)	Leutnant
Ensign	Leutnant zur See

---

[a] Held only by Hermann Goering (July 19, 1940–April 23, 1945).

[b] In the German military, the rank of General was followed by the branch of the officer; for example, General of Infantry, General of Panzer Troops, General Artillery, General of Mountain Troops, General of Flyers, General of Engineers, and so on.

[c] Held only by Heinrich Himmler.

Appendix II

GENERAL STAFF POSITIONS
AND ABBREVIATIONS

Ia	Staff Officer, Operations
Ib	Chief Supply Officer
Ic	Staff Officer, Intelligence (subordinate to Ia)
IIa	Chief Personnel Officer (adjutant)
IIb	Second Personnel Officer (subordinate to IIa)
III	Chief Judge Advocate
IVa	Chief Administrative Officer (subordinate Ib)
IVb	Chief Medical Officer (subordinate to Ib)
IVc	Chief Veterinary Officer (subordinate to Ib)
IVd	Chaplain (subordinate to IIa)
V	Motor Transport Officer (subordinate to Ib)

Special Staff Officers included the Chief of Artillery; Chief of Projector (Rocket Launcher) Units; Senior Military Police Officer; Gas Protection Officer; National Socialist Guidance Officer (added in 1944); and others.

Appendix III

CHARACTERISTICS OF
SELECTED OPPOSING TANKS

Model	Weight (tons)	Speed (mph)	Range (miles)	Armament	Crew
BRITISH					
Mark IV *Churchill*	43.1	15	120	1 6-pounder	5
Mark VI *Crusader*	22.1	27	200	1 2-pounder	5
Mark VIII *Cromwell*	30.8	38	174	1 75 mm	5
AMERICAN					
M3A1 *Stuart*	14.3	36	60	1 37mm	4
M4A3 *Sherman*	37.1	30	120	1 76mm	5
				3 MGs	
GERMAN					
PzKw II	9.3	25	118	1 20mm	3
				1 MG	
PzKw III	24.5	25	160	1 50mm	5
				2 MGs	
PzKw IV	19.7	26	125	1 75mm	5
				2 MGs	
PzKw V *Panther*	49.3	25	125	1 75mm	5
				2 MGs	
PzKw VI *Tiger*	62.0	23	73	1 88mm	5
				2 MGs	
SOVIET					
T-34/85	34.4	32	250	1 85mm	4
				2 MGs	
JS II *Stalin*	45.3	23	150	1 122mm	4
				4 MGs	
ITALIAN					
L 3	3.4	26	75	2 MGs	2
L 11	10.8	21	124	1 37mm	2
				2 MGs	

Appendix IV

LUFTWAFFE AVIATION UNIT STRENGTHS AND CHAIN OF COMMAND

Unit	Composition	Rank of Commander
OKL[a]	All Luftwaffe units	Reichsmarschall
Air Fleet	Air corps and air and flak divisions	General to Field Marshal
Air Corps	Air and flak divisions plus miscellaneous units	Major General to General
Air Division	2 or more wings	Colonel to Major General
Wing	2 or more groups 100 to 120 aircraft	Major to Major General
Group	2 or more squadrons 30 to 36 aircraft	Major to Lieutenant Colonel
Squadron	2 or more sections 9 to 12 aircraft	Lieutenant to Captain
Section[b]	3 or 4 aircraft	Lieutenant

[a]Oberkommando der Luftwaffe: The High Command of the German Air Force and the command organ of the Luftwaffe. Headed by Goering; day-to-day operations were directed by the chief of the General Staff of the Luftwaffe.

[b]The section (*Kette*) was called a *Schwarm* in fighter units only.

Appendix V

LUFTWAFFE
TACTICAL ABBREVIATIONS

Jagdgeschwader: a single-engine fighter wing, abbreviated JG. The 1st Fighter Wing would be abbreviated JG 26, and so on.

Kampfgeschwader: a bomber wing, abbreviated KG. The 1st Bomber Wing would be abbreviated KG 1.

Nachtjagdgeschwader: a night fighter wing, abbreviated NJG. 2nd Night Fighter Wing would be abbreviated NJG 2.

Stukageschwader: a Ju-87 "Stuka" wing. Abbreviated StG 1, StG 2, and so on.

Zerstoerergeschwader: literally, "destroyer wing"; a twin-engine fighter wing, abbreviated ZG 2.

Gruppe: a group; the basic combat and administrative aviation unit of the Luftwaffe. Largely self-contained, the entire Gruppe was usually based at a single airfield. It could be (and frequently was) detached from its parent wing. Gruppen were abbreviated by Roman numerals; for example, the II Group, 77th Bomber Wing would be II/KG 77; III Group 3rd (Single-Engine) Fighter Wing would be III/JG 3, etc.

Staffel: a squadron—the smallest operational air unit. Normally commanded by a captain or a lieutenant, it had a full-time adjutant, but its other branches (signal, technical, navigation, etc.) were supervised by flying officers in their spare time. They were represented by Arabic numbers. For example, the 7th Squadron of the II Group, 77th Fighter Wing would be 7, II/JG #77. Also, 3, I/KG 100 would represent the 3rd Squadron, I Group, 100th Bomber Wing.

Appendix VI

ACRONYMS

APC	armored personal carrier
FdU	*Fuehrer der U-boote* (U-boat Fuehrer)
HIAG	*Hilfsorganization auf Gegenseitigkeit der Waffen-SS* (Mutual Aid Society of the Waffen-SS)
HPA	*Heerespersonelamt* (Army Personnel Office)
HWA	*Heereswaffenamt* (Army Weapons Office)
JG	*Jagdgeschwader* (single-engine fighter wing)
LAH	*Leibstandarte* Adolf Hitler
NCO	noncommissioned officer
NJG	*Nachtjagdgeschwader* (night fighter wing)
NSFOs	National Socialist Leadership Officers
OB West	*Oberbefehlshaber* West
OKH	*Oberkommando des Heeres* (High Command of the Army)
OKL	*Oberkommando der Luftwaffe* (High Command of the Air Force)
OKM	*Oberkommando der Kriegsmarine* (High Command of the Navy)
OKW	*Oberkommando der Wehrmacht* (High Command of the Armed Forces)
POW	prisoner of war
RAF	Royal Air Force
SA	*Sturmabteilung* (Stormtroopers)
SD	*Sicherheitsdienst* (Security Service)
SKL	*Seekriegsleitung* (German Supreme Naval Staff)
SS	*Schutzstaffel* (Protection Squadron)
SSTK	*SS Totenkopfdivision* (Death's Head Division)
SSTV	*SS Totenkopfverbaende* (SS Death's Head guard units)
SS-VT	*SS-Verfuegunstruppe* (Special Purpose Troops)
TVA	*Torpedo-Versuchs-Anstalt* (Torpedo Testing Institute)

NOTES

CHAPTER 1: THE GENERALS OF THE HIGH COMMAND

1. Although the terms are frequently used interchangeably, the *Reichsheer* (army) differs from the *Reichswehr*, as the armed forces of the Weimar Republic were called. The Reichswehr consisted of both the Reichsheer (army) and *Reichsmarine* (navy), which only had 15,000 men. Because of its much greater size and importance, the army dominated the Reichswehr establishment.

2. Walter Goerlitz, *Keitel, Verbrecher Oder Offizier, Erinnerungen, Briefe und Dokumente des Chef OKW* (Goettingen: Muster-Schmidt Verlag, 1961), p. 71.

3. *Trial of the Major War Criminals before the International Military Tribunal* (Washington, D.C.: United States Government Printing Office, 1946–1948), volume 10, p. 502 (hereafter cited as *IMT*).

4. Count von Helldorf was born in Merseburg, East Prussia, in 1896. He served as a lieutenant in the artillery during World War I and joined the Nazi Party in the 1920s. By 1931, he was the chief of the Berlin SA (Brownshirts) and, in 1933, became a member of the Reichstag and Police President of Potsdam. He became Police President of Berlin in 1935. He was famous for arresting wealthy Jews and then accepting bribes from them to release them and get them out of Germany. He often used the proceeds to help support his mistresses and to pay his gambling debts. He nevertheless played a prominent role in the anti-Hitler conspiracy and was executed at Ploetzensee Prison on August 15, 1944.

5. Walter Warlimont, *Inside Hitler's Headquarters, 1939–45*, R. H. Barry, trans. (New York: Frederick A. Praeger, 1966), p. 13 (hereafter cited as Warlimont, *Inside Hitler's Headquarters*).

6. Bodewin Keitel (1888–1953) was chief of the Army Personnel Office from February 4, 1938, to September 1942, when his older brother fell into temporary disfavor with Hitler, and Bodewin was replaced by Hitler's adjutant, Major General Rudolf Schmundt. He later commanded Wehrkreis XX (March 1, 1943, to

November 30, 1944). He was promoted to major general effective March 1, 1938, to lieutenant general two years later, and to general of infantry in 1941.

7. Kurt von Schuschnigg (1897–1977) was chancellor of Austria from 1934 until 1938, when his country was absorbed by the Third Reich. He spent the next seven years in concentration camps. Freed by the U.S. Army in 1945, he emigrated to the United States, where he became a professor of political science at St. Louis University.

8. See Gene Mueller, *The Forgotten Field Marshal: Wilhelm Keitel* (Durham, N.C.: Moore Publishing Co., 1979) (hereafter cited as Mueller, *Keitel*).

9. Louis L. Snyder, *Encyclopedia of the Third Reich* (New York: McGraw-Hill, 1976), p. 242 (hereafter cited as Snyder, *Encyclopedia*).

10. Interview with General Warlimont, June 1972.

11. Albert Speer, *Inside the Third Reich*, Richard and Clara Winston, trans. (New York: Macmillan, 1970), p. 389 (hereafter cited as Speer, *Inside the Third Reich*).

12. Field Marshal von Witzleben was hanged on August 8, 1944, and Erich Fritz Fellgiebel was hanged on September 4, 1944. Rommel was forced to commit suicide on October 14, 1944, and Colonel General Friedrich Fromm was shot for cowardice in March 1945.

13. Mueller, *Keitel*, pp. 256–58.

14. Ferdinand Jodl (1896–1956) was chief of staff of the XXXIX Mountain Corps (1940–1941) in Yugoslavia and Russia, chief of staff of the 20th Mountain Corps (1942–1944) on the far north sector of the Eastern Front, and commander of the XIX Mountain Corps in Lapland (1944). He was commander of Army Detachment Narvik at the end of the war.

15. Eugene Davidson, *The Trial of the Germans* (New York: Macmillan, 1966), p. 346 (hereafter cited as Davidson, *Trial*).

16. Jodl was promoted to lieutenant colonel on October 1, 1933, and to colonel on August 1, 1935.

17. Viebahn (1888–1980) barracked himself in his office, threw ink bottles at the door, and threatened to shoot anyone who tried to enter. He eventually recovered and commanded the 257th Infantry Division in the French campaign and the LX Corps in occupied France. He retired as a general of infantry in 1942.

18. *IMT*, volume 25, p. 300.

19. Walter Goerlitz, "Keitel, Jodl and Warlimont," in Correlli Barrett, ed., *Hitler's Generals* (London: Weidenfeld and Nicolson, 1989), p. 157 (hereafter cited as Goerlitz, "Keitel, Jodl and Warlimont").

20. Group XXI was the reinforced XXI Armee Korps (XXI Corps) (see chapter 4). Hereafter, all corps are understood to be infantry (*Armee*), unless otherwise specified.

21. Interview with Alfred Speer, June 1972.

22. Warlimont, *Inside Hitler's Headquarters*, p. 232.

23. *IMT*, volume 19, p. 300.

24. List (1880–1971) was relieved of his command on September 10, 1942 and was never reemployed. He was a talented leader.

25. Goerlitz, "Keitel, Jodl and Warlimont," p. 161.

26. Davidson, *Trial*, p. 363. Louise Jodl succeeded in officially rehabilitating General Jodl's reputation and annulling the German penalties against his property at the proceedings carried on by the West German government regarding the properties of those tried by the International Military Tribunal at Nuremberg.

27. Hugh Trevor-Roper, *The Last Days of Hitler* (New York: Macmillan, 1947), pp. 120–27.

28. Speer, *Inside the Third Reich*, p. 515.

29. Percy Schramm, *Hitler: The Man and the Myth*, Donald Detwiler, trans. (Chicago: Quadrangle, 1971), p. 204.

30. David Irving, *Hitler's War* (New York: Viking Press, 1977), volume 1, p. 112 (hereafter cited as Irving, *Hitler's War*).

31. Fritz von Lossberg (April 30, 1868–May 4, 1942) was chief of staff of the 2nd, 3rd, 6th, and 4th armies on the Western Front during World War I. A troubleshooter, he was normally sent wherever there was a crisis. He was the first officer to put the concept of the "elastic defense" or "defense in depth" into practice during the Battle of Arras in April 1917. Awarded the Pour le Merite with Oak Leaves, he was the commander of Group Command I (one of the Reichsheer's two army-level commands) when he retired in 1926.

32. The German *Wehrkreis*, or military district, had no exact American equivalent. Prior to the outbreak of the war, it had two components: a tactical component and a secondary or deputy component. When the army was mobilized, the tactical component became a corps headquarters and directed combat units in the field. The deputy component (which consisted mainly of older officers and soldiers) became the Wehrkreis. Its missions were extremely important and included recruiting, drafting, inducting and training soldiers, training officers and administering Army schools, as well as mobilizing divisions and providing them with replacements. The number of Wehrkreise increased from seven in 1932 to 18 in 1943.

33. Irving, *Hitler's War*, volume 1, p. 110.

34. Lossberg married Ella Schmidt in Berlin in 1934. They had two children (both sons), of which Fritz was the oldest.

35. Irving, *Hitler's War*, volume 1, p. 177.

36. Wilhelm Deist, *The Wehrmacht and the German Rearmament* (Buffalo, N.Y.: University of Toronto Press, 1981), p. 94 (hereafter cited as Deist, *Wehrmacht*).

37. Deist, *Wehrmacht*, pp. 94–95.

38. John W. Wheeler-Bennett, *The Nemesis of Power: The German Army in Politics, 1918–1945* (New York: St. Martin's Press, 1967), p. 432 (hereafter cited as Wheeler-Bennett, *Nemesis*).

39. Peter Hoffmann, *The History of the German Resistance, 1933–1945*, Richard Barry, trans. (Cambridge, Mass.: MIT Press, 1977), p. 111 (hereafter cited as Hoffmann, *German Resistance*).

40. Ulrich von Hassell, *The Von Hassell Diaries, 1938–1944*, Hugh Gibson, ed. (London: Hamish Hamilton, 1948), p. 195.

41. Richard Brett-Smith, *Hitler's Generals* (Novato, Calif.: Presidio Press, 1977), p. 211; Wheeler-Bennett, *Nemesis*, p. 560n.

42. Warlimont, *Inside Hitler's Headquarters*, p. 232.

43. Warlimont, *Inside Hitler's Headquarters*, p. 404.

44. Joachim Kramarz, *Stauffenberg: The Life and Death of an Officer, 15th November 1907–20th July 1944* (London: Deutsch, 1967), p. 76.

45. Speer, *Inside the Third Reich*, p. 420.

46. Joseph Goebbels, *Final Entries, 1945: The Diaries of Joseph Goebbels*, Hugh Trevor-Roper, ed., Richard Barry, trans. (New York: G. P. Putnam's Sons, 1978), p. 128 (hereafter cited as Goebbels, *Final Entries*).

47. Wheeler-Bennett, *Nemesis*, p. 680.

48. Gerhard Boldt, *Hitler's Last Days*, Sandra Bance, trans. (London: Arthur Barker, 1973; reprint ed., London: Sphere Books, Ltd., 1973), p. 161.

49. Gerald Reitlinger, *The SS: Alibi of a Nation, 1922–1945* (New York: Viking Press, 1968), p. 178 (hereafter cited as Reitlinger, *SS*).

50. Reitlinger, *SS*, p. 179.

51. Robert Lee Quinnett, "Hitler's Political Officers: The National Socialist Leadership Officers" (unpublished Ph.D. dissertation, Norman: University of Oklahoma, 1973), p. 180. Ernst Maisel (1896–1978) had commanded a battalion in 1939 and the 42nd Infantry Regiment on the Eastern Front (1941–1942), where he fought at Brest-Litovsk, Bialystok, Gomel, Moscow, and Juchnov, among other battles. Later, as deputy chief of the Army Personnel Office, he played an unsavory role in forcing Erwin Rommel, the Desert Fox, to commit suicide.

52. Hoffmann, *German Resistance*, pp. 487, 528. Hase was hanged in the Ploetzensee prison on the afternoon of August 8, 1944, along with Field Marshal von Witzleben and several others.

53. Quinnett, "Hitler's Political Officers," p. 235.

54. For Reinecke's sentence, as well as his opening and final statements and extracts from the prosecution's case and his defense, see *Trials of the War Criminals before the Nuremberg Military Tribunals* (Washington, D.C.: United States Government Printing Office, 1950), volumes 10 and 11.

55. Gene Mueller, "Generaloberst Friedrich Fromm," in Gerd R. Ueberschaer, ed., *Hitlers militaerische Elite*, vol. 1 (Darmstadt: Primus Verlag, 1998), p. 76.

CHAPTER 2: THE WARLORDS OF THE EASTERN FRONT

1. W. E. Hart, *Hitler's Generals* (Garden City, N.Y.: Doubleday, 1944), p. 154 (hereafter cited as W. E. Hart, *Hitler's Generals*).

2. Axis Biographical Research, "Fedor von Bock," www.geocities .com/~orion47 (accessed 2011).

3. W. E. Hart, *Hitler's Generals*, p. 160.

4. W. E. Hart, *Hitler's Generals*, p. 160.

5. Fabian von Schlabrendorff, *Revolt against Hitler*, Gero von S. Gaevernitz, ed. (London: Eyre and Spottiswoode, 1948), p. 58.

6. United States Army, Intelligence Section of the General Staff, American Expeditionary Force, *Histories of Two Hundred and Fifty-One Divisions of the German Army Which Participated in the Great War (1914–1918)* (Washington, D.C.: United States Government Printing Office, 1920), p. 647 (hereafter cited as AEF, *Divisions of the German Army*).

7. W. E. Hart, *Hitler's Generals*, p. 177.

8. James Lucas, *War on the Eastern Front, 1941–1945* (Briarcliff Manor, N.Y.: Stein and Day, 1979), p. 176 (hereafter cited as Lucas, *Eastern Front*).

9. See Lucas, *Eastern Front*, p. 176. Paul Carell, *Hitler Moves East, 1941–43*, Ewald Osers, trans. (Boston: Little, Brown, 1965; reprint ed., New York: Bantam Books, 1966), pp. 84–85 (hereafter cited as Carell, *Hitler Moves East*); Albert Seaton, *The Russo-German War, 1941–1945* (New York: Praeger, 1970), p. 130 (hereafter cited as Seaton, *Russo-German War*); and Albert Seaton, *The Battle for Moscow* (Briarcliff Manor, N.Y.: Stein and Day, 1980; reprint ed., New York: Playboy Press Paperbacks, 1981), pp. 43–45.

10. Carell, *Hitler Moves East*, p. 134. From north to south, Bock's forces included the 3rd Panzer Army (Hoth), 9th Army (Strauss), 4th Army (von Kluge), 4th Panzer Army (Hoepner), 2nd Army (von Weichs) and 2nd Panzer Army (Guderian).

11. Carell, *Hitler Moves East*, pp. 134–42.

12. John Shaw and the editors of Time-Life Books, *Red Army Resurgent* (Alexandria, Va.: Time-Life Books, 1979), p. 35 (hereafter cited as Shaw et al., *Red Army*); Seaton, *Russo-German War*, pp. 260–61; and Earl F. Ziemke, *Stalingrad to Berlin: The German Defeat in the East*, Office of the Chief of Military History (Washington, D.C.: United States Government Printing Office, 1966), p. 33 (hereafter cited as Ziemke, *Stalingrad to Berlin*).

13. Lieutenant General Hermann Plocher (MS 1944) says that Bock's death occurred on May 5, while Brett-Smith (*Hitler's Generals*, pp. 84–85) gives it as May 2 and Keilig (Wolf Keilig, *Die Generale des Heeres* [Friedberg: Podzun-Pallas Verlag, 1983], p. 38 [hereafter cited as Keilig, *Die Generale*]) states that he was killed on May 3. Most other sources give the date as May 4. In the confusion of the German collapse, it is unlikely that anyone is certain. See the bibliography for details on the Plocher manuscripts.

14. Christopher Chant, Richard Humble, William Fowler, and Jenny Shaw, *Hitler's Generals and Their Battles* (New York: Chartwell Books, 1976), p. 98.

15. Brett-Smith, *Hitler's Generals*, p. 53.

16. Harold C. Deutsch, *The Conspiracy against Hitler in the Twilight War* (Minneapolis: University of Minnesota Press, 1978), p. 210.

17. www.lexikon-der-wehrmacht.de/Personenregister/K/KuechlerGu.htm.

18. Two divisions went to Army Group Center. The third division, the Spanish 250th (Blue) Infantry Division, was sent home at the demand of the Spanish dictator, Franco.

19. The 36th Infantry Division was later destroyed at Bobruisk in June 1944, during Operation Bagration, which the Germans called the Battle of White Russia.

20. James D. Carnes, "A Study in Courage: German General Walter von Seydlitz' Opposition to Hitler" (unpublished Ph.D. dissertation, Tallahassee: Florida State University, 1976), p. 317 (hereafter cited as Carnes, "Seydlitz' Opposition").

21. Irving, *Hitler's War*, volume 1, p. 77.

22. *Kriegstagebuch des Oberkommando des Wehrmacht (Wehrmachtfuehrungstab)* (Frankfurt-am-Main: Bernard and Graefe Verlag fuer Wehrwesen, 1961), January 1, 1943 (hereafter cited as KTB OKW).

23. Georg Tessin, *Verbaende und Truppen der deutschen Wehrmacht und Waffen-SS in Zweiten Weltkrieg, 1939–1945* (Frankfurt/Main: Verlag E. S. Mittler und Sohn, 1976), volume 3, pp. 5–6 (hereafter cited as Tessin, *Verbaende*); Keilig, *Die Generale*, p. 227.

24. Iron Rations were a concoction of chocolate laced with caffeine.

25. Lieutenant General Friedrich-August Weinknecht was born in Breslau in 1895 and entered the service as a war volunteer in 1914. Originally an engineer officer (he was commissioned in late 1915), he later joined the General Staff and commanded the 596th Infantry Regiment (1942–1943) and the 82nd Infantry Division (1943) on the Eastern Front. He assumed command of the 79th Infantry on October 25, 1943, and surrendered to the Russians on August 29, 1944. Released in October 1955, he retired to Goettinger, where he died on October 26, 1964.

26. For the story of the last days of the IV Corps and more detailed descriptions of the encirclement of the 6th Army, see Seaton, *Russo-German War*, pp. 467–86, and Walter Rehm, *Jassy* (Neckargem: K. Vowinckel, 1959).

27. AEF, *Divisions of the German Army*, p. 655.

28. Heinrici had served as acting commander of the VII Corps from January 31 to February 12, 1940, while General of Infantry Ritter Eugen von Schobert was on leave.

29. Ludwig Kuebler (born 1889) previously commanded the XXXX Mountain Corps. He returned to duty as commander of Security Troops and Rear Area Center in the summer of 1943. He commanded LXXXVII Mountain Corps in the Balkans from the fall of 1944 until the end of the war. The Yugoslavians hanged him after a show trial in 1947.

30. Kurt von Tippelskirch (1891–1957) previously commanded the 30th Infantry Division (1941–1942) and the XII Corps (1943–1944). After serving as deputy commander of the 1st Army in France (1944) and the 14th Army in Italy (1944–45), he was named commander of the 25th Army in April 1945.

31. Island Farm Prisoner of War Camp website, www.islandfarm.fsnet.co.uk (accessed 2011).

CHAPTER 3: THE GENERALS OF STALINGRAD

1. "Friedrich Paulus" in German Army Personnel Records, World War II Records Division, National Archives, Washington, D.C. (hereafter cited as Paulus personnel file).

2. Paulus personnel file.

3. Walter Goerlitz, *Paulus and Stalingrad* (Westport, Conn.: Greenwood Press, 1974), pp. 10–12 (hereafter cited as Goerlitz, *Stalingrad*).

4. Shaw et al., *Red Army*, p. 136.

5. William Craig, *Enemy at the Gates: The Battle of Stalingrad* (New York: E. P. Dutton, 1973), p. 11 (hereafter cited as Craig, *Enemy*).

6. When the war broke out, there were 18 Wehrkreise, numbered I through XVIII. All had territorial responsibilities except Wehrkreise XIV, XV, and XVI, which controlled Germany's motorized infantry, light, and panzer divisions, respectively. These had no deputy components and ceased to be Wehrkreise when the war began.

7. Victor von Schwedler personnel file. Married in 1910, Schwedler had a daughter (Ruth), born in 1914, and a son, Detlof, born in 1922.

8. Irving, *Hitler's War*, volume 1, p. 16.

9. Uli Haller, *Lieutenant General Karl Strecker* (Westport, Conn.: Praeger, 1994), pp. 2–3. This book is the source of much of the information on Strecker (hereafter cited as Haller, *Strecker*).

10. The Prussian police totaled men in 1920. There were 150,000 policemen in all of Germany (including Prussia).

11. Haller, *Strecker*, p. 25.

12. Haller, *Strecker*, pp. 41–42.

13. The permanent corps commander, General of Infantry Karl Hollidt, was on leave.

14. Carnes, "Seydlitz' Opposition," p. 3.

15. Carnes, "Seydlitz' Opposition," pp. 1–8.

16. Seydlitz joined the service as a Fahnenjunker on September 18, 1908. Service record of Walter von Seydlitz-Kurzbach, Air University Archives.

17. Keilig, *Die Generale*, p. 323.

18. Seydlitz personnel file, Air University Archives.

19. The fact that his death sentence was commuted did Count Sponeck little good. He was executed by the SS in 1944 (see chapter 2).

20. Carnes, "Seydlitz' Opposition," pp. 92–93.

21. Carell, *Hitler Moves East*, pp. 490–97.

22. Wolfgang Pickert was born on February 3, 1897, and entered the military service on August 2, 1914, as a member of the 73rd Field Artillery Regiment during the first "rush to the colors" on the eve of World War I. He served on both the Eastern and Western fronts. He apparently received his commission during the war; in any event, he was retained in the 100,000-man army. From 1921 to 1935 he was primarily associated with the 1st Artillery Regiment in East Prussia. During this period he underwent General Staff training, was detailed to the Soviet Army during their maneuvers and became interested in anti-aircraft artillery. After that he was a tactics instructor at the AA school (1934–1935), on the staff of the AA inspectorate at the Air Ministry (1935–1937), and commander of the I Battalion, 49th Anti-Aircraft Regiment at Mannheim (1937–1938). He was chief of staff of the XIII Luftwaffe Administrative Command (1938–1939), during which he underwent pilot training.

He was a General Staff officer on the staff of the Rhine-Ruhr Air Defense District when the war broke out. In May, 1940, Pickert became chief of staff of the I Flak Corps and a few months later rose to chief of staff of Air Fleet Reich. He held this post until May 1942, when he assumed command of the 9th Flak Division. General Pickert was married and had three children (Pickert personnel file).

23. Carell, *Hitler Moves East*, p. 634.

24. Carnes, "Seydlitz' Opposition," pp. 151–52.

25. Carnes, "Seydlitz' Opposition," pp. 158, 166–67.

26. Plocher, MS 1942.

27. Plocher, MS 1942, citing Schroeter, *Stalingrad*, pp. 92–94.

28. F. W. von Mellenthin, *German Generals of World War II* (Norman: University of Oklahoma Press, 1977), p. 115 (hereafter cited as Mellenthin, *German Generals*).

29. Plocher, MS 1942.

30. Paulus personnel file; Keilig, *Die Generale*, p. 303.

31. V. I. Chuikov, *The Battle for Stalingrad* (New York: Holt, Rinehart and Winston, 1964; reprint ed., New York: Ballantine Books, 1969), p. 254.

32. Erich von Manstein, *Lost Victories*, Anthony G. Powell, trans. and ed. (Novato, Calif.: Presidio Press, 1982), pp. 332–34 (hereafter cited as Manstein, *Lost Victories*). Eismann later served on the staff of the rebuilt 6th Army. Promoted to full colonel, he was Ia of Army Group Vistula.

33. Craig, *Enemy*, p. 363.

34. Haller, *Strecker*, p. 50.

35. Haller, *Strecker*, p. 52.

36. Haller, *Strecker*, p. 54.

37. Stemmermann, the commander of XI Corps, was killed on February 18, 1944, during the breakout attempt.

38. Speer, *Inside the Third Reich*, p. 394n.

39. Axis Biographical Research, "Wolfgang Pickert," www.geocities .com/~orion47 (accessed 2011). Rudolf Absolon, comp., *Rangliste der Generale der deutschen Luftwaffe Nach dem Stand vom 20. April 1945* (Friedberg: Podzun-Pallas Verlag, 1984), p. 30 (hereafter cited as Absolon, *Rangliste*).

40. Craig, *Enemy*, p. 335.

41. Friedrich von Stauffenberg, personal communication, 1985.

42. According to General Plocher (MS 1943). Keilig (*Die Generale*, p. 156) says it was LXXXII Corps.

43. Ziemke, *Stalingrad to Berlin*, pp. 293–94.

44. Josef Folttmann and Hanns Moeller-Witten, *Opfergang der Generale* (Berlin: Verlag Bernard & Graefe, 1952), p. 133.

45. Haller, *Strecker*.

46. Haller, *Strecker*.

47. Haller, *Strecker*.

48. For a detailed account of this incident from one of the officers who accompanied Hube, see Samuel W. Mitcham, Jr., and Friedrich von Stauffenberg, *The Battle of Sicily* (New York: Crown Publishers, 1991).

CHAPTER 4: THE COMMANDERS IN THE WEST

1. E. H. Stevens, ed., *The Trial of Nikolaus von Falkenhorst* (London: William Hodge and Company, 1949), p. xxxv.

2. Erich Dethleffsen was born in Kiel in 1904 and entered the Reichsheer as a Fahnenjunker in 1923. Commissioned in the 8th Infantry Regiment in 1927, he transferred to the East Prussian 1st Infantry Regiment, where he became a battalion adjutant. Later he was adjutant to the fortress commander in Koenigsberg. He attended General Staff training at the War Academy (1935–1937) and occupied a variety of General Staff positions, including group leader in the Army Training Department (1939–1941), Ia of the LVI Corps (1941), and Ia of the 330th Infantry Division on the Eastern Front, where he was seriously wounded in February 1942. He returned to duty in August as an instructor at the War Academy, where he was promoted to colonel in the spring of 1943. He was then named chief of staff of the XXXIX Panzer Corps (June 1943), chief of staff of 4th Army (May 1944), and chief of operations of OKW's operations staff (March 1945). He briefly commanded an ad hoc division and became chief of staff of Army Group Vistula the day Hitler committed suicide. Promoted to major general on November 9, 1944, he surrendered to the British in May 1945, and was released from the POW camps in the spring of 1948. He died in Munich in 1980.

3. Harry R. Fletcher, "Legion Condor: Hitler's Military Aid to Franco, 1936–1939 (unpublished M.A. thesis, Madison: University of Wisconsin, 1961), pp. 143–47 (hereafter cited as Fletcher, "Legion Condor"); Karl Drum, *The German Air Force in the Spanish Civil War*, United States Air Force Historical Studies Number 150, United States Air Force Historical Division, Aerospace Studies Institute, Maxwell Air Force Base (Montgomery, Ala.: The Air University, 1965).

4. Fletcher, "Legion Condor," pp. 147–48.

5. After a career as an army engineer, Helmuth von Volkmann transferred to the Luftwaffe in 1934 and, after commanding the Condor Legion, directed the Air War Academy and rose to the rank of general of fliers. He fell out with Hermann Goering and transferred back to the army as a general of infantry in early 1940. Despite his rank, Volkmann commanded the 94th Infantry Division in France. He died in a hospital in Berlin on August 21, 1940, as a result of injuries sustained in an automobile accident. He was born in 1889.

6. Brett-Smith, *Hitler's Generals*, p. 124.

7. Cajus Bekker, *The Luftwaffe War Diaries*, Frank Ziegler, trans. and ed. (New York: Macdonald and Company, 1966; reprint ed., New York: Ballantine Books, 1969), pp. 156–59.

8. *Jagdfliegerfuehrer* 1—literally "Fighter Leader 1"—is translated here as 1st Fighter Command, to conform to the English language.

9. Winston S. Churchill, *Their Finest Hour* (Boston: Houghton Mifflin, 1949), p. 331.

10. Robert Wistrich, *Who's Who in Nazi Germany* (New York: Macmillan, 1982), pp. 294–95 (hereafter cited as Wistrich, *Who's Who*).

11. Interrogation of Lieutenant General Karl Veith, Air University Archives. Veith (1894–1979) commanded Air Defense Command Black Forest (1940), 5th Flak Brigade (1940–1942), and 17th Flak Division (1942–1944). He ended the war as commander, Flak Schools Division, Brunswick (1944–1945). He briefly commanded all flak artillery schools in 1944.

12. Wistrich, *Who's Who*, pp. 294–95.

13. Paul Joseph Goebbels, *The Goebbels Diaries*, Louis P. Lochner, ed. (Garden City, N.Y.: Doubleday, 1948; reprint ed., New York: Universal-Award House, 1971), March 9, 1943.

14. Hans Speidel, *Invasion 1944* (New York: Henry Regnery, 1950; reprint ed., New York: Paperback Library, 1968), p. 46 (hereafter cited as Speidel, *Invasion*).

15. Charles B. MacDonald and Martin Blumenson, "Recovery of France," in Vincent J. Esposito, ed., *A Concise History of World War II* (New York: Frederick A. Praeger, 1964), p. 80.

16. Lionel F. Ellis, *Victory in the West*, Volume I, *The Battle of Normandy* (London: HMSO, 1962), p. 111 (hereafter cited as Ellis, *Victory*).

17. Ellis, *Victory*, p. 111.

18. Speidel, *Invasion*, p. 46; Interrogation of Field Marshal Erhard Milch, Air University Archives. Also see Brett-Smith, *Hitler's Generals*, p. 127.

19. David Irving, *The Rise and Fall of the Luftwaffe: The Life of Field Marshal Erhard Milch* (Boston: Little, Brown, 1973), p. 336.

20. Richard Suchenwirth, *Command and Leadership in the German Air Force*, United States Air Force Historical Studies Number 189, Maxwell Air Force Base (Montgomery, Ala.: The Air University, 1969) (hereafter cited as Suchenwirth, *Command*).

21. Ellis, *Victory*, p. 490.

22. Interrogation of field marshals Milch and Sperrle. Milch did almost all of the talking in this interview. Sperrle said virtually nothing.

23. Otto E. Moll, *Die deutschen Generalfeldmarschaelle, 1939–1945* (Rastatt/Baden: Erich Pabel Verlag, 1961), p. 245.

24. Wistrich, *Who's Who*, p. 294.

25. Friedrich Dollmann Personnel File.

26. Matthew Cooper, *The German Army, 1933–1945* (Briarcliff Manor, N.Y.: Stein and Day, 1978; reprint ed., Chelsea, Mich.: Scarborough House, 1990), pp. 47–48; Richard J. O'Neill, *The German Army and the Nazi Party, 1933–1939* (New York: James H. Heinemann, 1966), p. 101.

27. Brett-Smith, *Hitler's Generals*, pp. 102–3.

28. Brett-Smith, *Hitler's Generals*, p. 102.

29. Oberbefehlshaber West does not have an exact English translation. It roughly translates as "Supreme Commander, West," but the term *OB West* was used to refer to either the commander-in-chief or his headquarters.

30. Friedrich Ruge, *Rommel in Normandy* (San Rafael, Calif.: Presidio Press, 1979), p. 82.

31. Paul Carell, *Invasion: They're Coming!* Ewald Osers, trans. (New York: E. P. Dutton, 1963; reprint ed., New York: Bantam Books, 1964), p. 112 (hereafter cited as Carell, *Invasion*).

32. Tony Foster, *Meeting of the Generals* (Agincourt, Canada: Methuen Publications, 1986), p. 331 (hereafter cited as Foster, *Meeting*).

33. A few sources have reported that Dollmann took poison, but this is unproven and seems unlikely.

34. Gordon A. Harrison, *Cross-Channel Attack*, United States Army in World War II, European Theater of Operations (Washington, D.C.: United States Government Printing Office, 1951), p. 395.

35. Rudolf Bacherer (1895–1964) served in the 22nd (3rd Baden) Dragoons Regiment in World War I. He was discharged in 1919, but returned to active duty as a first lieutenant in the 18th Cavalry Regiment at Cannstadt in 1935. He was a captain in the 156th Reconnaissance Battalion during the Polish campaign. Later he fought in Belgium, in France, and in the drive on Moscow. As a battalion commander in the 234th Infantry Regiment, he was severely wounded on the Eastern Front on January 4, 1943. Returning to Germany in October, he briefly commanded the 1026th Grenadier Regiment (late 1943) before assuming command of the 1049th Grenadier on February 6, 1944. He was captured on August 15, 1944. He was never promoted to major general, probably because of his reserve status.

36. Otto Theodor von Manteuffel (1805–1882) was minister of the interior (1848–1850) and foreign minister and prime minister (December 19, 1850 to November 6, 1858) under King Friedrich Wilhelm IV of Prussia. General Baron Edwin von Manteuffel (1809–1885) commanded the I Corps and the Army of the South in the Franco-Prussian War (1870–1871). He was promoted to field marshal at the conclusion of that conflict. He was governor of Alsace-Lorraine at the time of his death.

37. Donald Grey Brownlow, *Panzer Baron: The Military Exploits of General Hasso von Manteuffel* (North Quincy, Mass.: The Christopher Publishing House, 1975), p. 30 (hereafter cited as Brownlow, *Panzer Baron*).

38. Mellenthin, *German Generals*, p. 240.

39. B. H. Liddell Hart, *The German Generals Talk* (New York: William Morrow, 1948), p. 70 (hereafter cited as Liddell Hart, *German Generals*).

40. Brownlow, *Panzer Baron*, p. 97.

41. Mueller's interviews with Albert Speer and Hasso von Manteuffel, June 1972, and subsequent correspondence.

42. Interview with Hasso von Manteuffel.

43. Liddell Hart, *German Generals*, p. 274.

44. Mellenthin, *German Generals*, p. 245.

45. Liddell Hart, *German Generals*, p. 214.

46. Interview with General Burkhart Mueller-Hillebrand, June 1972. Mueller-Hillebrand (1904–1987) became a lieutenant general in the West German Army in 1965 (a three-star general under the new rank structure).

47. Mueller, *Keitel*, p. 287.

48. Brownlow, *Panzer Baron*, p. 158.

49. Much of the information on Baron Heinrich von Luettwitz has been extracted from the papers of the late Friedrich-Theodor von Stauffenberg, part of which are in the possession of Dr. Mitcham.

50. Keilig, *Die Generale*, p. 212. Smilo von Luettwitz was born in 1895 (one year before Heinrich). He was commander of the III Corps in the Bundeswehr in 1958.

51. John S. D. Eisenhower, *The Bitter Woods* (New York: G. P. Putnam's Sons, 1969), p. 16ff.

52. Walter Duevert (1893–1972) was nevertheless promoted to lieutenant general effective January 1, 1943, and was given command of the 265th Infantry Division in occupied France on June 1, 1943. He held this post for more than a year but had to be relieved again in July 1944. Never reemployed, he was retired in November.

53. Vollrath Luebbe (1894–1969) was considered a better infantry and training officer than a panzer commander. After leading the 2nd Panzer, he briefly commanded the 81st Infantry Division (April–July 1944) on the northern sector of the Eastern Front and then the 462nd Replacement Division at Metz, where he did a fine job against Patton's 3rd Army. He suffered a stroke in October, but returned to duty in late December, as commander of an infantry division on the Eastern Front. He surrendered to the Russians at the end of the war and was a Soviet prisoner until 1955.

54. Henning Schoenfeld (1894–1958) was a cavalry officer. After commanding a reconnaissance battalion in the Polish campaign, he held staff positions at OKH for most of the war. He owed his appointment as commander of the 2nd Panzer to his friends in the High Command, and there were dozens of officers more qualified to lead the division than he. After being relieved, Schoenfeld was unemployed for the rest of the war.

55. Robert E. Merriam, *The Battle of the Bulge* (New York: Ballantine Books, 1957), p. 138.

56. Stauffenberg Papers.

57. Stauffenberg Papers.

58. Stauffenberg Papers.

59. S. L. A. Marshall, *Bastogne: The First Eight Days* (Washington, D.C.: Infantry Journal Press, 1946; reprint ed., Washington, D.C.: Zenger Publishing Co., 1979), pp. 175–76.

CHAPTER 5: THE PANZER COMMANDERS

1. Oswald Lutz was the first ever general of panzer troops. Born in Oehringen, Baden-Wuerttemberg, in 1876, he joined the army as a Fahnenjunker in the Bavarian Railroad Battalion in 1894 and was commissioned in the 1st Bavarian Engineer

Battalion in 1896. During World War I, he commanded the motorized troops of the 6th Army (1915–1917) and was in General Staff positions. During World War II, he was briefly recalled to active duty but only held one position: commander of a special transportation staff at Frankfurt/Oder (1941–1942). He died in Munich on February 26, 1944.

2. See Samuel W. Mitcham, Jr., *The Rise of the Wehrmacht* (Westport, Conn.: Praeger Publishing, 2008), volume 2, pp. 459–96.

3. Kluge later commanded OB West and Army Group B on the Western Front (1944). He was marginally involved in the anti-Hitler conspiracy and committed suicide near Metz on August 19, 1944, three days after Hitler relieved him of his command.

4. Guderian's new assignment did not include assault guns, which remained with the artillery.

5. It seems likely that Zeitzler (1895–1963) did know that Stauffenberg was planning to blow up the Fuehrer on July 20. He was nowhere to be seen when the bomb detonated, and Zeitzler's deputy, Lieutenant General Adolf Heusinger, never forgave Zeitzler for leaving him in the conference room when the bomb exploded. Zeitzler, who had already suffered a nervous breakdown from working with Hitler, never held another assignment and was expelled from the army in January 1945.

6. Georgi K. Zhukov (1896–1974), spent his life in the army. Born into the peasant class, Zhukov rose through the ranks to become a marshal. He commanded the defense of both Leningrad and Stalingrad and participated in the Russian offensive against Germany (1944–1945). He accepted German surrender on May 8, 1945. He was one of Russia's greatest military heroes of World War II, and served as defense minister after World War II under Nikolai Bulganin and Nikita Khrushchev (1955–1957).

7. Friedrich von Mellinthin (1904–1997) served as a staff officer during the German invasion of France. He remained on occupation duty after the German victory. His next combat assignment took him to the Balkans as a staff officer. He also served as a staff officer under Erwin Rommel in North Africa. Mellinthin then transferred to Russia, where he served as chief staff officer of the XXXXVIII Panzerkorps (1942–1944); then in August 1944, he served as chief of staff to General Balck. Mellinthin's last assignment was as chief of staff of the 5th Panzer Army in 1945. He was captured by the British on May 3, 1945.

8. Axis Biographical Research, www.geocities.com/~orion47 (accessed 2011).

9. Johannes Blaskowitz (1883–1948) served as commander of the 8th Army from August 1939 thru October 1939. He also served as commander of the 1st Army, October 1940 to May 1944. Blaskowitz was then assigned command of Army Group G in France, May 1944 to September 1944. Following Balck's dismissal as commander-in-chief of Army Group G in December 1944, Blaskowitz replaced him until January 28, 1945, when he took command of Army Group H. He held that post until March 21, 1945, when he took command of the German 25th Army. His last command was of Fortress Holland until his capture on May 5,

1945. Blaskowitz was accused of war crimes by the Allies. He committed suicide on February 5, 1948.

10. Walton Walker (1889–1950) was a major general in 1942 and commanded the 3rd Armored Division. Later, he commanded the XX Corps in Patton's 3rd Army and remained its commander until the end of the war. The XX Corps liberated Buchenwald concentration camp and pushed into Austria in May 1945, the same month Walker was promoted to lieutenant general. After World War II, Walker commanded the 8th Army in Japan and then in Korea to turn back the invading North Koreans. Walker died in an automobile crash on December 23, 1950, just north of Seoul, Korea.

11. John Nelson Rickard, *Patton at Bay: The Lorraine Campaign, 1944* (Washington D.C.: Brassey, 2004), pp. 259–64.

12. KTB OKW, volume 4, p. 1455.

13. Heinz Guderian, *Panzer Leader*, Constantine Fitzgibbon, trans. (New York: Ballantine Books, 1957), p. 109.

14. Mellenthin, *German Generals*, pp. 259–61.

15. Craig, *Enemy*, p. 218.

16. Mellenthin, *German Generals*, p. 263; Craig, *Enemy*, p. 218.

17. Alan Clark, *Barbarossa: The Russian-German Conflict, 1941–1945* (New York: William Morrow, 1965), p. 436.

18. KTB OKW, volume 4, p. 1454.

19. Mueller, *Keitel*, p. 282.

20. Mueller, *Keitel*, p. 285.

21. Walter Duevert (1893–1972) briefly commanded the 20th Panzer Division (July 1–October 9, 1942), but again cracked under the strain. He was then furloughed for eight months and then was given command of the 265th Infantry Division in France (June 1, 1943 to July 27, 1944), but was retired before his unit became involved in combat against the Anglo-Americans. He was promoted to lieutenant general in 1943.

22. Ferdinand Schaal (1889–1962) was a cavalry officer but he had commanded the 10th Panzer Division since before the war began. He later directed the XXXIV Corps Command in France, the LVI Panzer Corps on the Eastern Front, and Wehrkreis Bohemia and Moravia. He was arrested for his cooperation in the July 20, 1944, plot to assassinate Adolf Hitler and spent the rest of the war in prison, but was liberated by the Allies on April 28, 1945. A general of panzer troops since October 1, 1941, he was released from prison in August 1945.

CHAPTER 6: THE LORDS OF THE AIR

1. Bruno Loerzer remained a close friend of Hermann Goering until the latter's death. Despite his lack of qualifications, Loerzer commanded the II Air Corps in the first half of World War II. Later he became chief of personnel (subsequently chief of

personnel armaments) of the Luftwaffe. Promoted to colonel general on February 2, 1943, he retired on December 20, 1944. At his own request, he testified for Hermann Goering at Nuremberg in 1946. Goering allowed him to do so only reluctantly and almost certainly regretted it, because the Allied lawyers had no trouble tying him in knots. Loerzer died in Hamburg on August 22, 1960 (Absolon, *Rangliste*, p. 18).

2. According to Colonel Killinger of the Luftwaffe General Staff, to his British interrogators (CSDIC [U.K.] SRGG 1243 [C], dated 22 May 1945), on file at the Historical Research Center, Air University Archives, Maxwell Air Force Base, Alabama.

3. Ritter von Greim commanded the 6th Air Fleet on the Eastern Front in World War II. On April 25, 1945, he was promoted to field marshal and named commander-in-chief of the Luftwaffe. He committed suicide on May 24, 1945.

In the early 1920s, Greim took Hitler (then a minor political agitator and community organizer) on his first flight. Hitler became airsick and swore he would never fly again. He later changed his mind.

4. Suchenwirth, *Command.*

5. August-Albert Ploch (1894–1967) was forced into retirement by Milch in late 1942.

6. Gablenz was born in Erfurt, Thuringia, in 1893. He served as an aerial observer, bomber pilot, and instructor pilot in World War I. After the war, he joined the Freikorps and worked for Junkers and Lufthansa as an aviation executive and technical consultant. He was commander of the 172nd Bomber Wing when the war began, and directed the Luftwaffe's Instrument Flying School from late 1939 until the spring of 1941. Chief of the Air Force Equipment Office at the time of Udet's suicide, he later became chief of the Generalluftzeugmeister's planning office. He was killed in an airplaine crash near Muehlberg/Elbe on August 21, 1942 (Absolon, *Rangliste*, p. 79).

7. Suchenwirth, *Command*; Werner Baumbach, *The Life and Death of the Luftwaffe*, Frederick Holt, trans. (New York: Coward-McCann, 1960; reprint ed., New York: Ballantine Books, 1967), p. 17.

8. Overburdened by his responsibilities, political infighting, and the bullying of Hermann Goering, Jeschonnek committed suicide on August 19, 1943.

9. Trevor J. Constable and Raymond Toliver, *Horrido! Fighter Aces of the Luftwaffe* (London: Arthur Barker, 1968), p. 262 (hereafter cited as Constable and Toliver, *Horrido*).

10. Major Wick, who had 55 kills, was the leading German ace when he crashed into the English Channel on November 28, 1940. (Werner Moelders had 54 and Adolf Galland had 52 on that date.) Wick's body was never found. Captain Karl-Heinz Greisert was acting wing commander until Balthasar assumed command on February 16, 1941.

11. Constable and Toliver, *Horrido*, p. 221.

12. Constable and Toliver, *Horrido*, p. 222. Trautloff (1912–1995) shot down 58 aircraft during the war. He later became a lieutenant general (under the new rank structure) in the West German Air Force.

13. Nowotny was killed in action on November 8, 1944, while trying to get his damaged jet away from several American fighters. He was buried in a grave of honor in the Zentralfriedhof (Central Cemetery) in Vienna. His honor status was revoked by an initiative led by the Austrian Green Party in 2003, on the incredibly thin grounds that Nowotny had fought for Germany, not for Austria. He was 23 years old at the time of his death.

14. Constable and Toliver, *Horrido*, p. 222.

15. Colonel Helmut Lent (commander of the 3rd Night Fighter Wing) shot down 110 enemy airplanes (102 of them at night) before being fatally injured in an air accident on October 5, 1944. Colonel Werner Streib (1911–1986) had 65 night kills and one day victory. The last commander of NJG 1, he survived the war and retired from the West German Air Force as a *Brigadegeneral* in 1966.

16. Constable and Toliver, *Horrido*, p. 104.

17. Constable and Toliver, *Horrido*, p. 93. Macki Steinhoff (1913–1994) shot down 176 enemy aircraft in World War II and was shot down 12 times himself. He was severely burned in the last days of the war. Steinhoff became a full general and chief of staff of the Luftwaffe after the war. He was President Ronald Reagan's escort officer during the Bitburg cemetery controversy of 1985. The German 73rd Fighter Wing "Steinhoff" is named in his honor.

18. Heinz Joachim Nowarra, *Marseille: Star of Africa* (Sun Valley, Calif.: John W. Caler Publications, 1968), n.p.

19. www.powcamp.fsnet.co.uk/Generalmajor%20Kurt%20Abderseb%20(Luftwaffe).htm (accessed 2011). This is the Island Farm (Special Camp 11) website, which is one of the best World War II websites on the Internet.

CHAPTER 7: THE NAVAL OFFICERS

1. Dr. Raeder and his wife, Gertraudt Hartmann Raeder, both died in 1932.

2. Erich Raeder, *My Life*, Henry W. Drexel, trans. (New York: Arno Press, 1980), pp. 3–5 (hereafter cited as Raeder, *My Life*). Until that time, young Raeder had planned to study medicine. His father nevertheless fully supported his son's decision and wrote to the Oberkommando der Marine on his behalf.

3. Hart, *Hitler's Generals*, p. 198.

4. Charles S. Thomas, *The German Navy in the Nazi Era* (London: Unwin Hyman, 1990), pp. 21–22 (hereafter cited as Thomas, *German Navy*). Also see Keith W. Bird, *Weimar the German Naval Officer Corps and the Rise of National Socialism* (Amsterdam: B. R. Gruener, 1977).

5. Snyder, *Encyclopedia*, p. 280.

6. W. E. Hart, *Hitler's Generals*, p. 200. Kapp (1858–1922) was an East Prussian right-wing civil servant and political activist and an associate of Admiral Alfred von Tripitz. Along with General Walter von Luettwitz (commander of Group Command 1) and the Freikorps' Ehrhardt Brigade, he attempted to overthrow

the government but was foiled by a general strike. He died of cancer shortly after returning to Germany in 1922.

7. "Erich Raeder" in Maxine Block, ed., *Current Biography 1941* (New York: H. W. Wilson Company, 1941), p. 695.

8. Thomas, *German Navy*, p. 54.

9. See Thomas, *German Navy*, pp. 68–69.

10. Raeder, *My Life*, p. 241.

11. For the best description of Navy-Nazi relations in both the Raeder and Doenitz eras, see Thomas, *German Navy*.

12. Heinz Hoehne, *Canaris*, I. Maxwell Brownjohn, trans. (Garden City, N.Y.: Doubleday, 1979), p. 162. The father of this young woman was reportedly a close friend of Raeder's (Thomas, *German Navy*, p.92).

13. Deposition by Rear Admiral Karl Kuehlenthal, a.D., reprinted in Raeder, *My Life*, pp. 416–17.

14. Raeder, *My Life*, pp. 262–63.

15. Cajus Bekker, *Hitler's Naval War* (Garden City, N.Y.: Doubleday, 1974; reprint ed., New York: Zebra Books, 1977), p. 34 (hereafter cited as Bekker, *Hitler's Naval War*). Both Vice Admiral Guenther Guse and Captain Hellmuth Heye of the Naval High Command (OKM) warned Raeder of the dangers inherent in Hitler's policy but could not convince the Grand Admiral. See Manfred Messerschmidt, "German Military Effectiveness between 1919 and 1939," in Allan R. Millett and Williamson Murray, eds., *Military Effectiveness*, volume 2, *The Interwar Period* (Boston: Allen and Unwin, 1988), p. 234.

16. The previous four were Hans von Koester (appointed in 1905), Prince Heinrich of Prussia (1909), Alfred von Tirpitz (1911), and Henning von Holtzendorff (1918). See Hans H. Hildebrand and Ernest Henriot, *Deutschland's Admirale, 1849–1945* (Osnabrueck: Biblio Verlag, 1988–1990), volume 2, p. xxiv (hereafter cited as Hildebrand and Henriot, *Deutschland's Admirale*).

17. David Irving, *The War Path: Hitler's Germany, 1933–1939* (New York: Viking Press, 1979), pp. 213–14.

18. Hildebrand and Henriot, *Deutschland's Admirale*, volume 1, pp. 126–27.

19. Hildebrand and Henriot, *Deutschland's Admirale*, volume 2, pp. 434–36.

20. Bekker, *Hitler's Naval War*, p. 53.

21. A small, Type II U-boat, *U-56* was considered a coastal submarine of the type not normally used in the Atlantic. It fired only three torpedoes on October 30 because it had only three tubes.

22. Bekker, *Hitler's Naval War*, p. 138. Vice Admiral Goetting (who was born in Berlin in 1886) was forced into retirement by Admiral Doenitz in 1943 and died in Soviet captivity in 1946. Admiral Wehr (1886–1968) was held in fortress detention at Germersheim for a time. He was serving as an adviser to the Luftwaffe at the end of the war.

23. Earl F. Ziemke, "The German Northern Theater of Operations, 1940–1945," United States Department of the Army Pamphlet # 20–271 (Washington, D.C.: United States Department of the Army, 1959), pp. 104–5.

24. Hildebrand and Henriot, *Deutschland's Admirale*, volume 2, p. 435.

25. Bekker, *Hitler's Naval War*, pp. 235–36.

26. G. M. Gilbert, *Nuremberg Diary* (New York: Farrar, Strauss and Cudahy, 1947; reprint ed., New York: Signet Books, 1961), pp. 308–9 (hereafter cited as Gilbert, *Nuremberg Diary*).

27. Bekker, *Hitler's Naval War*, p. 219.

28. Bekker, *Hitler's Naval War*, p. 219.

29. Bekker, *Hitler's Naval War*, p. 227.

30. Bekker, *Hitler's Naval War*, pp. 224–25.

31. Bekker, *Hitler's Naval War*, p. 164.

32. Hildebrand and Henriot, *Deutschland's Admirale*, volume 2, pp. 434–36.

33. Peter Padfield, *Doenitz: The Last Fuehrer* (New York: Harper and Row, 1984), p. 23 (hereafter cited as Padfield, *Doenitz*). Padfield cites Doenitz, *Mein Wechselvolles*, p. 24.

34. Lieutenant Klaus Doenitz was born on May 14, 1920, and was killed on his 24th birthday when the reconnaissance boat *S-141* was sunk off the coast of Cherbourg. Ensign Peter Doenitz, who was born on March 20, 1923, was lost with *U-954* in the North Atlantic on May 19, 1943. Doenitz also had a daughter, Ursula, who was born on April 3, 1917. Apparently she was his favorite child. In November 1937, she married Guenther Hessler, a U-boat captain who distinguished himself by sinking 14 vessels (86,699 tons) during a cruise to South America in the summer of 1941. This record for a single cruise was never equaled. Doenitz then made Hessler his first staff officer, and he remained on Doenitz's staff until the end of the war. Hessler (1909–1968), who fathered Doenitz's two grandchildren, later helped the grand admiral assemble materials for his memoirs. After the war, he worked as a historian for the Royal Navy.

35. Walter Forstmann (1883–1973) conducted 47 patrols and sank 146 ships, for a total of 384,304 tons, making him the second leading submarine ace in history. He became a captain during World War II.

36. Wolfgang Frank, *The Sea Wolves*, R. O. B. Long, trans. (New York: Rinehart and Company, 1955; reprint ed., New York: Ballantine Books, 1958), p. 13.

37. Lieutenant Commander Herbert Schultze (1909–1987) later won the Knight's Cross with Oak Leaves. At the end of the war, he ranked sixth highest on the "ace" list with 171,122 tons (26 ships) sunk. He was deeply respected by the British because of his practice of broadcasting his sinkings to them, so that they could rescue their stranded crews.

38. At the turn of the year (1941–1942), the U-boat arm had 91 operational boats. After deducting those employed in the Mediterranean, off Gibraltar, and in Norwegian waters, 55 remained for the tonnage war in the North Atlantic. Of these, 60 percent were undergoing lengthy repairs. Half of the remaining 22 were on their way to or from the battle area. See Peter Cremer, *U-Boat Commander* (Annapolis, Md.: Naval Institute Press, 1984), p. 52 (hereafter cited as Cremer, *U-Boat Commander*).

39. Generaladmiral Rolf Carls was born in Rostock on May 29, 1885, and joined the navy as a sea cadet in 1903. He spent his early career on battleships and heavy cruisers, but commanded a U-boat in 1918. He held a number of important assignments from the 1920s until 1943, including chief of the training department (1928–1930), chief of staff of the Naval Command (1930–1932), commander of the battleship *Hessen* (1932–1933), chief of staff of the High Seas Fleet (1933–1934), commander of battleships (1934–1936), fleet commander (1936–1938), commander-in-chief of Naval Group Baltic (1938–1940), and commander-in-chief of Naval Group North (1940–1943). Officially retired on May 31, 1943, he was never reemployed. He was killed in an Allied air raid on Bad Oldesloe, Schleswig-Holstein, on April 24, 1945. He was promoted to Generaladmiral on July 19, 1940.

40. Cremer, *U-Boat Commander*, p. 185.

41. Gilbert, *Nuremberg Diary*, p. 300.

42. See *IMT*, volume 13, for Doenitz's testimony.

43. Padfield, *Doenitz*, p. 484, citing the London *Sunday Times*, January 25, 1959.

44. Wolfgang Frank, *Enemy Submarine* (London: William Kimber, 1954), pp. 21–22 (hereafter cited as Frank, *Enemy Submarine*). Frank, a lieutenant in a naval propaganda company and a classmate of Prien's brother, wrote this book mainly from Prien's diaries and is the main source for this part of *Hitler's Commanders*.

45. Frank, *Enemy Submarine*, p. 25.

46. Frank, *Enemy Submarine*, p. 78.

47. Eddy Bauer, *Illustrated World War II Encyclopedia*, Peter Young, ed. (Westport, Conn.: H. S. Stuttmann, Publishers, 1978), volume 3, p. 298.

48. Barrie Pitt and the editors of Time-Life Books, *The Battle of the Atlantic* (Alexandria, Va.: Time-Life Books, 1980), p. 67.

49. Frank, *Enemy Submarine*, pp. 189, 198.

50. John R. Angolia, *On the Field of Honor: A History of the Knights Cross Bearers* (San Jose, Calif.: R. James Bender Publishing, 1979), volume 1, p. 69 (hereafter cited as Angolia, *Field of Honor*).

51. Bekker, *Hitler's Naval War*, p. 380; Angolia, *Field of Honor*, volume 2, pp. 30–31.

52. Admiral von Pohl (born 1855) became commander of the High Seas Fleet after the Battle of Dogger Bank. He almost immediately authorized unrestricted submarine warfare (February 1915). He died of illness in early 1916.

CHAPTER 8: THE WAFFEN-SS

1. Charles W. Syndor, Jr. *Soldiers of Destruction* (Princeton, N.J.: Princeton University Press, 1977), p. 3 (hereafter cited as Syndor, *Destruction*).

2. Ernst-Guenther Kraetschmer, *Die Ritterkreuztraeger der Waffen-SS* (Preussisch Oldendorf: Verlag K. W. Schuetz KG, 1983), p. 231 (hereafter cited as Kraetschmer, *Ritterkrueztraeger*).

3. AEF, *Divisions of the German Army*, p. 65.

4. Kraetschmer, *Ritterkreuztraeger*, p. 231.

5. Syndor, *Destruction*, p. 6; Kraetschmer, *Ritterkreuztraeger*, pp. 231–32.

6. Nikolaus von Preradovich, *Die Generale der Waffen-SS* (Berg am See: Kurt Vowinckel Verlag, 1985), pp. 26–27 (hereafter cited as Preradovich, *Waffen-SS*).

7. No U.S. equivalent. Oberfuehrer would be a grade between colonel and brigadier general, U.S. Army.

8. Preradovich, *Waffen-SS*, p. 27.

9. Heinz Hoehne, *The Order of the Death's Head*, Richard Barry trans. (New York: Ballantine Books, 1971), p. 228 (hereafter cited as Hoehne, *Death's Head*).

10. Hoehne, *Death's Head*, p. 229. Among Eicke's guards during this period was Adolf Eichmann, the Gestapo's future "Jewish specialist" in the Reich Main Security Office and the man charged with implementing the "Final Solution" to the "Jewish Problem." Another guard trained by Eicke during this period was a Rudolf Hoess, the future commandant of the Auschwitz extermination camp.

11. Roger Manvell and Heinrich Faenkel, *Himmler* (New York: G. P. Putnam's Sons, 1965; reprint ed., New York: Paperback Library, 1968), p. 45.

12. At this time, approximately 80 percent of the inmates at Dachau were political prisoners. Probably less than one-quarter of all of Dachau inmates were Jewish at this time.

13. Roehm was shot simultaneously by Eicke and Eicke's adjutant, SS-Strumbannfuehrer Michael Lippert, at the Stadelheim prison in Munich. In accordance with Hitler's orders, Eicke had first given Roehm the opportunity to commit suicide, but he refused. As the badly wounded chief of the Stormtroopers lay on the floor of his cell, he gasped, "My Fuehrer! My Fuehrer!" Eicke replied, "You should have thought of that earlier; it's too late now." A bullet in the chest then put Roehm out of his misery. See Hoehne, *Death's Head*, pp. 140–44. In 1957, Lippert and Sepp Dietrich (who had commanded a firing squad) were tried by a Munich court and were given prison sentences for their parts in the affair.

14. Preradovich, *Waffen-SS*, p. 27.

15. Syndor, *Destruction*, pp. 22–23.

16. The 1st SS Totenkopfstandarte, Oberbayern, was based at Dachau; the 2nd (Brandenburg) was at Sachsenhausen; the 3rd (Thuringen) at Buchenwald; and the 4th (Ostmark) at Mauthausen.

17. Most of these never joined the Totenkopf Division. The 6th and 7th SS Totenkopf Infantry regiments, for example, were assigned to the 6th SS Mountain Division "Nord" and fought in Russia and Finland. The 8th and 10th Totenkopf regiments formed the 1st SS Motorized Infantry Brigade and, after two years on the Russian Front, formed the nucleus of the 18th SS Panzer Grenadier Division "Horst Wessel." The 1st and 2nd Totenkopf Cavalry regiments formed the SS Cavalry Brigade, which was later expanded to a division and finally became the famous 8th SS Cavalry Division "Florian Geyer," which fought so well in the Siege of Budapest and, when the city finally fell, was killed almost to the last man. For

more detailed histories of these and other Totenkopf units, see Roger J. Bender and Hugh P. Taylor, *Uniforms, Organization, and History of the Waffen-SS* (Mountain View, Calif.: R. James Bender Publishing, 1969–1982), volumes 1–5 (hereafter cited as Bender and Taylor, *Waffen-SS*); and Richard Landwehr, "Budapest: The Stalingrad of the Waffen-SS," *Siegrunen*, volume 7, number 1 (1985): pp. 3–35.

18. Syndor, *Destruction*, p. 62.

19. During his most unusual career, Baron von Montigny served as a U-boat officer in World War I, in the Freikorps fighting Poles and Communists (1919–1920), as a police officer in several cities (1920–1935), and in the army (1935–1937), where he reached the rank of colonel and commanded a regiment. He joined the SS in 1938 as an instructor in military tactics and was assigned to the Totenkopf in October 1939. Montigny had apparently recovered on July 15, 1940, when Himmler appointed him commandant of the SS Officer Training School at Bad Toelz. On November 8, 1940, he suddenly dropped dead of a massive heart attack. See Syndor, *Destruction*, pp. 48–49, 105n.

20. Reitlinger, *SS*, p. 148. Hoepner later commanded the 4th Panzer Army on the Eastern Front (1941–1942) and was hanged in August 1944, for his part in the July 20, 1944, attempt to assassinate Adolf Hitler.

21. Manstein, while commenting that Totenkopf's officers and NCOs "lacked solid training and proper experience" nevertheless praised the division's bravery and discipline and wrote that it "always showed great dash in the assault and was steadfast in the defense. . . probably the best Waffen-SS division I ever came across" (Manstein, *Lost Victories*, pp. 187–88).

22. During Eicke's absence, the division was commanded by SS-Brigadefuehrer Matthias Kleinheisterkamp, the senior regimental commander. When Kleinheisterkamp was given command of his own division (the "Das Reich" SS Motorized Infantry Division), SS-Brigadefuehrer Georg Keppler became acting commander until Eicke returned. Kleinheisterkamp later commanded the XI SS Panzer Corps and was reported as missing in action on the Eastern Front on May 2, 1945, and presumably was killed. Keppler also later commanded Das Reich (1942–1943) and ended the war commanding the XVIII SS Corps. He died in Hamburg in 1966 (Kraetschmer, *Ritterkreuztruegen*, pp. 52–59, 270–72).

23. He received this decoration on December 26, 1941 (Kraetschmer, *Ritterkreuztruegen*, p. 227).

24. An aristocrat of the old school, Count von Brockdorff-Ahlefeldt planned to use his command (the 23rd Infantry Division, based at Potsdam, near Berlin) against the Nazi Party and the SS during the Sudetenland crisis of 1938. This coup, which was under the overall command of Colonel General Erwin von Witzleben, was aborted only after the British and French signed the Munich Agreement, in effect abandoning Czechoslovakia to the Nazis. Brockdorff escaped the hangman's noose only by dying of natural causes in 1943 (Keilig, *Die Generale*, p. 52).

25. Max Simon (1899–1961) later became an SS-Gruppenfuehrer and commanded the 16th SS Panzer Grenadier Division "Horst Wessel" on the Italian Front

(1943–1944) and the XIII SS Corps on the Western Front (late 1944–1945). He was later sent to prison for anti-partisan activities in Italy but was released in 1954.

26. On the orders of the Fuehrer, the Death's Head Division was officially redesignated 3rd SS Panzer Division Totenkopf on October 22, 1943 (Tessin, *Verbaende*, volume 2, pp. 212–13).

27. The Soviets desecrated German war graves with bulldozers as a matter of standard procedure, so it must be assumed that Eicke's remains have been lost.

28. Bender and Taylor, *Waffen-SS*, volume 2, p. 80.

29. Paul Carell, *Scorched Earth*, Ewald Osers, trans. (Boston: Little, Brown, 1966; reprint ed., New York: Ballantine Books, 1971), p. 196 (hereafter cited as Carell, *Scorched Earth*).

30. Carell, *Scorched Earth*, p. 198.

31. Until the fall of Kharkov, Lanz was commander of the ad hoc Army Detachment Lanz (*Armee Abteilung Lanz*), which included the remnants of Army Group B and Hausser's corps. Lanz was replaced by Werner Kempf. The army detachment headquarters was upgraded to 8th Army shortly thereafter. Lanz took command of the XXII Mountain Corps, then stationed in Greece (Keilig, *Die Generale*, pp. 166 and 197; Tessin, *Verbaende*, volume 4, p. 175).

32. Mark C. Yeager, *SS-Oberstgruppenfuehrer and Generaloberst der Waffen-SS Paul Hausser* (Winnipeg, Canada: John Fedorowicz, 1986), p. 11.

33. The first SS man to be in acting command of an army-level headquarters was "Sepp" Dietrich, who directed the remnants of Headquarters, Panzer Group West (later rebuilt as Headquarters, 5th Panzer Army) on June 9 and 10, 1944. The group commander, General of Panzer Troops Baron Leo Geyr von Schweppenburg, had been seriously wounded when the headquarters was struck by an Allied saturation bombing raid on June 9, shortly after its location had been pinpointed by radio intercepts. It was so badly smashed that it had to be withdrawn from the battle the following day and rebuilt.

34. Martin Blumenson, *Breakout and Pursuit*, United States Army in World War II, European Theater of Operations, United States Army, Office of the Chief of Military History (Washington, D.C.: United States Government Printing Office, 1961), p. 226 (hereafter cited as Blumenson, *Breakout and Pursuit*).

35. Albert Seaton, *The Fall of Fortress Europe, 1943–1945* (New York: Holmes & Meier, 1981), p. 121.

36. Blumenson, *Breakout and Pursuit*, p. 328. Major General Max Pemsel, Hausser's chief of staff, was replaced by Colonel Baron Rudolf-Christoph von Gersdorff. Lieutenant General Otto Elfeldt assumed acting command of the LXXXIV Corps and was captured in the Falaise Pocket on August 20. The man he replaced, Dietrich von Choltitz, was officially promoted to general of infantry three days after he was sacked by Kluge, giving us a clue about what Berlin thought of Kluge's measures. Named Wehrmacht commander of the Greater Paris area, Choltitz surrendered the city on August 24.

37. Hitler relieved Kluge of his command and, at 7:30 p.m. on August 15, ordered Hausser to take charge of the army group until Kluge's replacement, Field Marshal Walter Model, arrived. Model did so on August 17.

38. Carell, *Invasion*, p. 297.

39. Goebbels, *Final Entries*, March 30, 1945.

40. Snyder, *Encyclopedia*, p. 66; Charles Messenger, *Hitler's Gladiator* (London and Washington: Brassey's Defense Publishers, 1988), pp. 38–49 (hereafter cited as Messenger, *Gladiator*).

41. Mellenthin, *German Generals*, p. 226.

42. Rudolph Lehmann, *The Leibstandarte*, Nick Olcott, trans. (Winnipeg, Canada: J. J. Fedorowicz Publishing, 1987), volume 1, p. 1.

43. Messenger, *Gladiator*, p. 71.

44. Max Gallo, *The Night of the Long Knives*, Lily Emmet, trans. (New York: Harper and Row, 1972; reprint ed., New York: Warner Books, 1973), p. 268.

45. A second son, Lutz, was born in 1943 and a third, Goetz-Hubertus, was born in 1944.

46. Foster, *Meeting*, pp. 129–30. Dietrich himself selected Meyer for this post—another example of his ability to select talented subordinates.

47. Mellenthin, *German Generals*, p. 236.

48. Snyder, *Encyclopedia*, p. 66.

49. Messenger, *Gladiator*, p. 170.

50. Robert Goralski, *World War II Almanac: 1931–1945* (New York: G. P. Putnam's Sons, 1981), p. 397.

51. See Charles Whiting, *Massacre at Malmedy* (Briarcliff Manor, N.Y.: Stein and Day, 1971).

52. Richard Landwehr, "SS- Brigadefuehrer Helmuth Becker," *Siegrunen*, volume 4, number 6 (24) (1981): p. 3 (hereafter cited as Landwehr, "Becker").

53. Preradovich, *Waffen-SS*, p. 112.

54. Syndor, *Destruction*, pp. 317–18 and 318n.

55. Landwehr, "Becker," p. 4.

56. The *Freiwilligearbeitsdienst* (FAD) was the forerunner of the less voluntary *Reichs-arbeitsdienst* (Reich Labor Service, or RAD).

57. Gordon Williamson, *Aces of the Third Reich* (London: Arms and Armour Press, 1989), p. 88.

58. Obersturmbannfuehrer Hans Waldmueller (born in Bamberg on September 13, 1912) was the commander of the I Battalion, 25th SS Panzer, Grenadier Regiment. He was awarded the Knight's Cross on August 27 and was killed in action on September 8, 1944 (Kraetschmer, *Ritterkreuztraeger*, p. 731).

59. Bernhard Knittel did not share his brother's ambitions. He was killed in action on the Eastern Front in early 1945 as a sergeant in an army combat engineer battalion.

60. SS Major General (SS-Brigadefuehrer) Wilhelm Mohnke (1911–2001) was one of the original 133 members of Hitler's elite bodyguard, the LAH, which

was formed in 1933. He fought with the Waffen-SS in Poland (where he was wounded), the Netherlands, Belgium, France, and the Balkans, where he lost a foot. He nevertheless led a battalion in Russia (where he apparently committed several atrocities) and was with the 1st SS Panzer Division until 1943, when he assumed command of the 26th SS Panzer Grenadier Regiment of the 12th SS Panzer Division. He led this unit in Normandy, in the Falaise Pocket, and in the retreat across France. He led the 1st SS Panzer Division from August 31, 1944, to February 1945, when he was wounded in an air attack in Hungary. After he recovered, he was named commandant of Fuehrer Headquarters in Berlin. He was captured when the city fell in May 1945. A Soviet prisoner until October 1955, he went into private business and, despite repeated calls for his prosecution as a war criminal, he was never tried. He died a wealthy man in the village of Damp, Schleswig-Holstein, at the age of 90. The ill-tempered Mohnke was disliked even by his SS peers because of his harshness.

BIBLIOGRAPHY

Absolon, Rudolf, comp. *Rangliste der Generale der deutschen Luftwaffe Nach dem Stand vom 20. April 1945.* Friedberg: Podzun-Pallas Verlag, 1984.

Angolia, John R. *On the Field of Honor: A History of the Knights Cross Bearers.* San Jose, Calif.: R. James Bender Publishing, 1980. 2 volumes.

Axis Biographical Research, www.geocities.com/~orion47 (accessed 2011).

Barrett, Correlli, ed. *Hitler's Generals.* London: Weidenfeld and Nicolson, 1989.

Bauer, Eddy. *Illustrated World War II Encyclopedia.* Peter Young, ed. Westport, Conn.: H. S. Stuttmann Publishers, 1978. 24 volumes.

Baumbach, Werner. *The Life and Death of the Luftwaffe.* Frederick Holt, trans. New York: Coward-McCann, 1960. Reprint ed., New York: Ballantine Books, 1967.

Bekker, Cajus. *Hitler's Naval War.* Garden City, N.Y.: Doubleday, 1974. Reprint ed., New York: Zebra Books, 1977.

Bekker, Cajus. *The Luftwaffe War Diaries.* Frank Ziegler, trans. and ed. New York: Macdonald and Company, 1966. Reprint ed., New York: Ballantine Books, 1969.

Bender, Roger James, and Hugh P. Taylor. *Uniforms, Organization, and History of the Waffen-SS.* San Jose, Calif.: R. James Bender Publishing, 1969–1982. 5 volumes.

Bird, Keith W. *Weimar: The German Naval Officer Corps and the Rise of National Socialism.* Amsterdam: B. R. Gruener, 1977.

Block, Maxine, ed. *Current Biography 1941.* New York: H. W. Wilson Company, 1941.

Blumenson, Martin. *Breakout and Pursuit.* United States Army in World War II, European Theater of Operations. United States Army Office of the Chief of Military History. Washington, D.C.: United States Government Printing Office, 1961.

Boehmer, Rudolf, and Werner Haupt. *Fallschirmjaeger.* Dorheim: Verlag Hans-Henning Podzun, 1971.

Boldt, Gerhard. *Hitler's Last Days.* Sandra Bance, trans. London: Arthur Barker, 1973. Reprint ed., London: Sphere Books, 1973.

Brett-Smith, Richard. *Hitler's Generals.* Novato, Calif.: Presidio Press, 1977.

Brownlow, Donald G. *Panzer Baron: The Military Exploits of General Hasso von Manteuffel.* North Quincy, Mass.: The Christopher Publishing House, 1975.

Carell, Paul. *Hitler Moves East, 1941–43.* Ewald Osers, trans. Boston: Little, Brown, 1965. Reprint ed., New York: Bantam Books, 1966.

Carell, Paul. *Invasion: They're Coming!* Ewald Osers, trans. New York: E. P. Dutton, 1963. Reprint ed., New York: Bantam Books, 1964.

Carell, Paul. *Scorched Earth.* Ewald Osers, trans. Boston: Little, Brown, 1966. Reprint ed., New York: Ballantine Books, 1971.

Carnes, James D. "A Study in Courage: General Walther von Seydlitz' Opposition to Hitler." Unpublished Ph.D. dissertation. Tallahassee: Florida State University, 1976.

Chant, Christopher, Richard Humble, William Fowler, and Jenny Shaw. *Hitler's Generals and Their Battles.* New York: Chartwell Books, 1976.

Chuikov, V. I. *The Battle for Stalingrad.* New York: Holt, Rinehart and Winston, 1964. Reprint ed., New York: Ballantine Books, 1969.

Churchill, Winston S. *Their Finest Hour.* Boston: Houghton Mifflin, 1949.

Clark, Alan. *Barbarossa: The Russian-German Conflict, 1941–1945.* New York: William Morrow, 1965.

Constable, Trevor J., and Raymond Toliver. *Horrido! Fighter Aces of the Luftwaffe.* London: Arthur Barker, 1968.

Cooper, Matthew. *The German Army, 1933–1945.* Briarcliff Manor, N.Y.: Stein and Day, 1978. Reprint ed., Chelsea, Mich.: Scarborough House, 1990.

Craig, William. *Enemy at the Gates: The Battle of Stalingrad.* New York: E. R. Dutton, 1973. Reprint ed., New York: Ballantine Books, 1974.

Cremer, Peter. *U-Boat Commander.* Annapolis, Md.: Naval Institute Press, 1984.

Davidson, Eugene. *The Trial of the Germans.* New York: Macmillan, 1966. Reprint ed., New York: Collier Books, 1972.

Davis, Brian L. *German Parachute Forces 1935–45.* New York: Arco Publishing Company, 1974.

Deist, Wilhelm. *The Wehrmacht and German Rearmament.* Buffalo, N.Y.: University of Toronto Press, 1981.

Deutsch, Harold C. *The Conspiracy against Hitler in the Twilight War.* Minneapolis: University of Minnesota Press, 1978.

Drum, Karl. *The German Air Force in the Spanish Civil War.* United States Air Force Historical Studies Number 150. U.S. Air Force Historical Division, Aerospace Studies Institute, Maxwell Air Force Base. Montgomery, Ala.: The Air University, 1965.

Eisenhower, John S. D. *The Bitter Woods.* New York: G. P. Putnam's Sons, 1969.

Ellis, Lionel F. *Victory in the West.* Volume 1, *The Battle of Normandy.* London: HMSO, 1962.

Esposito, Vincent J., ed. *A Concise History of World War II.* New York: Frederick A. Praeger, 1964.

Fletcher, Harry R. "Legion Condor: Hitler's Military Aid to Franco, 1936–1939." Unpublished M.A. thesis. Madison: University of Wisconsin, 1961.

Folttmann, Josef, and Hanns Moeller-Witten. *Opfergang der Generale*. Berlin: Verlag Bernard & Graefe, 1952.

Foster, Tony. *Meeting of Generals*. Agincourt, Canada: Methuen Publications, 1986.

Frank, Wolfgang. *Enemy Submarine*. London: William Kimber, 1954.

Frank, Wolfgang. *The Sea Wolves*. R. O. B. Long, trans. New York: Rinehart and Company, 1955. Reprint ed., New York: Ballantine Books, 1958.

Der Freiwillige. Osnabrueck: Minin-Verlag. Various numbers.

Gallo, Max. *The Night of the Long Knives*. Lily Emmet, trans. New York: Harper and Row, 1972. Reprint ed., New York: Warner Books, 1973.

Gilbert, G. M. *Nuremberg Diary*. New York: Farrar, Strauss and Cudahy, 1947. Reprint ed., New York: Signet Books, 1961.

Goebbels, Paul Joseph. *Final Entries, 1945: The Diaries of Joseph Goebbels*. Hugh Trevor-Roper, ed., Richard Barry, trans. London: Martin Secker & Warburg, 1978. Reprint ed., New York: G. P. Putnam's Sons, 1978.

Goebbels, Paul Joseph. *The Goebbels Diaries*. Louis P. Lochner, ed. Garden City, N.Y.: Doubleday, 1948. Reprint ed., New York: Universal-Award House, 1971.

Goerlitz, Walter. "Keitel, Jodl and Warlimont." In Correlli Barrett, ed., *Hitler's Generals*. London: Weidenfeld and Nicolson, 1989.

Goerlitz, Walter. *Keitel, Verbrecher Oder Offizier, Erinnerungen, Briefe und Dokamente des Chef OKW*. Gottingen: Musterschmidt-Verlag, 1961.

Goerlitz, Walter. *Paulus and Stalingrad*. Westport, Conn.: Greenwood Press, 1974.

Goralski, Robert. *World War II Almanac: 1931–1945*. New York: G. P. Putnam's Sons, 1981.

Guderian, Heinz. *Panzer Leader*. Constantine Fitzgibbon, trans. New York: Ballantine Books, 1957.

Halder, Franz. *The Halder War Diary 1939–1942*. Charles Burdick and Hans-Adolf Jacobsen, eds. Novato, Calif.: Presidio Press, 1988.

Haller, Uli. *Lieutenant General Karl Strecker*. Westport, Conn.: Praeger, 1994.

Harrison, Gordon A. *Cross-Channel Attack*. United States Army in World War II, European Theater of Operations. Washington, D.C.: United States Government Printing Office, 1951.

Hart, W. E. (pseudo.). *Hitler's Generals*. Garden City, N.Y.: Doubleday, 1944.

Hassell, Ulrich von. *The Von Hassell Diaries, 1938–1944*. Hugh Gibson, ed. London: Hamish Hamilton, 1948.

Hildebrand, Hans H., and Ernest Henriot. *Deutschland's Admirale, 1849–1945*. Osnabrueck: Biblio Verlag, 1988–1990. 3 volumes.

Hoehne, Heinz. *Canaris*. J. Maxwell Brownjohn, trans. Garden City, N.Y.: Doubleday, 1979.

Hoehne, Heinz. *The Order of the Death's Head*. Richard Barry, trans. New York: Ballantine Books, 1971.

Hoffmann, Peter. *The History of the German Resistance, 1933–1945*. Richard Barry, trans. Cambridge, Mass.: MIT Press, 1977.

Hoyt, Edwin R. *The U-Boat Wars*. New York: Arbor House, 1984.

Interrogation Reports, Air University Archives:
  Killinger, Colonel
  Milch, Field Marshal Erhard
  Sperrle, Field Marshal Hugo
  Veith, Lieutenant General Karl

Interviews:
  Manteuffel, General of Panzer Troops Baron Hasso von
  Speer, Albert
  Stauffenberg, Theodor-Friedrich von
  Warlimont, General of Artillery Walter

Irving, David. *Hitler's War*. New York: Viking Press, 1977. 2 volumes.

Irving, David. *The Rise and Fall of the Luftwaffe: The Life of Field Marshal Erhard Milch*. Boston: Little, Brown, 1973.

Irving, David. *The War Path: Hitler's Germany, 1933–1939*. New York: Viking Press, 1979.

Island Farm Prisoner of War Camp: www.islandfarm.fsnet.co.uk (accessed 2011).

Keegan, John. *Waffen-SS: The Asphalt Soldiers*. New York: Ballantine Books, 1970.

Keilig, Wolf. *Die Generale des Heeres*. Friedberg: Podzun-Pallas Verlag, 1983.

Kennedy, Robert M. *The German Campaign in Poland (1939)*. United States Department of the Army Pamphlet No. 20–255. Washington, D.C.: United States Department of the Army, 1956.

Kraetschmer, Ernst-Guenther. *Die Ritterkreuztraeger der Waffen-SS*. 3rd ed. Preussisch Oldendorf: Verlag K. W. Schuetz KG, 1983.

Kramarz, Joachim. *Stauffenberg: The Life and Death of an Officer 15th November 1907–20th July 1944*. London: Deutsch, 1967.

Kriegstagebuch des Oberkommando des Wehrmaeht (Wehrmachtfuehrungstab). Frankfurt-am-Main: Bernard und Graefe Verlag fuer Wehrwesen, 1961. 4 volumes.

Landwehr, Richard. "Budapest: The Stalingrad of the Waffen-SS." *Siegrunen*. Volume 7, number 1 (1985): pp. 3–35.

Landwehr, Richard. *Narva 1944: The Waffen-SS and the Battle for Europe*. Silver Spring, Md.: Bibliophile Legion Books, 1981.

Landwehr, Richard, ed. *Siegrunen*. Brookings, Ore. Various numbers.

Landwehr, Richard. "SS-Brigadefuehrer Helmuth Becker." *Siegrunen*. Volume 4, number 6 (24) (1981): pp. 3–4.

Lehmann, Rudolf. *The Leibstandarte*. Nick Olcott, trans. Winnipeg, Canada: J. J. Fedorowicz Publishing, 1987.

Liddell Hart, B. H. *The German Generals Talk*. New York: William Morrow, 1948.

Lucas, James. *War on the Eastern Front, 1941–1945*. Briarcliff Manor, N.Y.: Stein and Day, 1979. Reprint ed., New York: Bonanza Books, n.d.

MacDonald, Charles B. *The Last Offensive*. United States Army in World War II, European Theater of Operations. United States Army Office of the Chief Military History. Washington, D.C.: United States Government Printing Office, 1973.

MacDonald, Charles B., and Martin Blumenson. "Recovery of France," In Vincent Esposito, ed., *A Concise History of World War II*. New York: Frederick A. Praeger, 1964. Pp. 70–96.

Manstein, Erich von. *Lost Victories*. Anthony G. Powell, trans. and ed. Novato, Calif.: Presidio Press, 1982.

Manvell, Roger, and Heinrich Fraenkel. *Himmler*. New York: G. P. Putnam's Sons, 1965. Reprint ed., New York: Paperback Library, 1968.

Marshall, S. L. A. *Bastogne: The First Eight Days*. Washington, D.C.: Infantry Journal Press, 1946. Reprint ed., Washington, D.C.: Zenger Publishing Co., 1979.

Mellenthin, F. W. von. *German Generals of World War II*. Norman: University of Oklahoma Press, 1977.

Mellenthin, F. W. von. *Panzer Battles*. Norman: University of Oklahoma Press, 1956. Reprint ed., New York: Ballantine Books, 1971.

Merriam, Robert E. *The Battle of the Bulge*. New York: Ballantine Books, 1957.

Messenger, Charles. *Hitler's Gladiator*. London and Washington: Brassey's Defense Publishers, 1988.

Messerschmidt, Manfred. "German Military Effectiveness between 1919 and 1939." In Allan R. Millett and Williamson Murray, eds., *Military Effectiveness*. Volume 2, *The Interwar Period*. Boston: Allen and Unwin, 1988. Pp. 218–55.

Millett, Allan R., and Williamson Murray, eds. *Military Effectiveness*. Volume 2, *The Interwar Period*. Winchester, Mass.: Allen and Unwin, 1988.

Mitcham, Samuel W., Jr. *The Rise of the Wehrmacht*. Westport: Conn.: Praeger, 2008. 2 volumes.

Mitcham, Samuel W., Jr., and Theodor-Friedrich von Stauffenberg. *The Battle of Sicily, 1943*. New York: Crown Publishers, 1991.

Moll, Otto E. *Die deutschen Generalfeldmarschaelle, 1939–1945*. Rastatt/Baden: Erich Pabel Verlag, 1961.

Mollo, Andrew. *The Armed Forces of World War II*. New York: Crown Publishers, 1981.

Mueller, Gene. *The Forgotten Field Marshal: Wilhelm Keitel*. Durham, N.C.: Moore Publishing Company, 1979.

Mueller, Gene. "Generaloberst Friedrich Fromm." In Gerd R. Ueberschaer, ed., *Hitlers militaerische Elite*. Volume 1. Darmstadt: Primus Verlag, 1998.

Nowarra, Heinz Joachim. *Marseille: Star of Africa*. Sun Valley, Calif.: John W. Caler Publications, 1968.

O'Neill, Richard J. *The German Army and the Nazi Party, 1933–1939*. New York: James H. Heinemann, 1966.

Padfield, Peter. *Doenitz: The Last Fuehrer*. New York: Harper and Row, 1984.

Personal Extracts, Air University Archives, United States National Archives, and the records of the late Friedrich von Stauffenberg for the following officers:
Erwin Jaenecke
Ritter Wilhelm von Leleb
Friedrich Paulus
Victor von Schwedler

Pfannes, Charles E., and Victor A. Salamone. *The Great Admirals of World War II.* Volume 2, *The Germans.* New York: Zebra Books, 1984.

Pitt, Barrie, and the editors of Time-Life Books. *The Battle of the Atlantic.* Alexandria, Va.: Time-Life Books, 1980.

Plocher, Hermann. "The German Air Force versus Russia, 1941." United States Air Force Historical Studies Number 154. United States Air Force Historical Division, Aerospace Studies Institute, Maxwell Air Force Base. Montgomery, Ala.: The Air University, 1965.

Plocher, Hermann. "The German Air Force versus Russia, 1942." United States Air Force Historical Studies Number 155. United States Air Force Historical Division, Aerospace Studies Institute, Maxwell Air Force Base. Montgomery, Ala.: The Air University, 1965.

Plocher, Hermann. "The German Air Force versus Russia, 1943." United States Air Force Historical Studies Number 156. United States Air Force Historical Division, Aerospace Studies Institute, Maxwell Air Force Base. Montgomery, Ala.: The Air University, 1965.

Porten, Edward P. von der. *The German Navy in World War II.* New York: Crowell, 1969.

Preradovich, Nikolaus von. *Die Generale der Waffen-SS.* Berg am See: Kurt Vowinckel Verlag, 1985.

Quinnett, Robert Lee. "Hitler's Political Officers: The National Socialist Leadership Officers." Unpublished Ph.D. dissertation. Norman: University of Oklahoma, 1973.

Raeder, Erich. *My Life.* Henry W. Drexel, trans. New York: Arno Press, 1980.

Rehm, Walter. *Jassy.* Neckargem: K. Vowinckel, 1959.

Reitlinger, Gerald. *The SS: Alibi of a Nation, 1922–1945.* New York: Viking Press, 1957. Reprint ed., Viking Press, 1968.

Rickard, John Nelson. *Patton at Bay: The Lorraine Campaign, 1944.* Washington, D.C.: Brassey, 2004.

Rohwer, J., and G. Hummelchen. *Chronology of the War at Sea 1939–1945.* Derek Masters, trans. New York: Arco Publishing Co., 1973–1974. 2 volumes.

Ruge, Friedrich. *Rommel in Normandy.* San Rafael, Calif.: Presidio Press, 1979.

Salewski, Michael. *Die deutsche Seekriegsleitung 1935–1945.* Munich: Bernard & Graefe, 1970–1975. 3 volumes.

Scheibert, Horst. *Die Traeger des Deatschen Kreuzes in Gold.* Friedberg: Podzun-Pallas Verlag, 1983.

Schlabendorff, Fabian von. *Revolt against Hitler*. Gero von S. Gaevernitz, ed. London: Eyre and Spottiswoode, 1948. Reprint ed., New York: AMS Press, 1948.

Schliephake, Hanfried. *The Birth of the Luftwaffe*. Chicago: Henry Regnery, 1971.

Schramm, Percy E. *Hitler: The Man and the Myth*. Donald Detwiler, trans. Chicago: Quadrangle, 1971.

Seaton, Albert. *The Battle for Moscow*. Briarcliff Manor, N.Y.: Stein and Day, 1980. Reprint ed., New York: Playboy Press Paperbacks, 1981.

Seaton, Albert. *The Fall of Fortress Europe, 1943–1945*. New York: Holmes & Meier, 1981.

Seaton, Albert. *The Russo-German War, 1941–1945*. New York: Praeger, 1970.

Shaw, John, and the editors of Time-Life Books. *Red Army Resurgent*. Alexandria, Va.: Time-Life Books, 1979.

Snyder, Louis L. *Encyclopedia of the Third Reich*. New York: McGraw-Hill, 1976.

Speer, Albert. *Inside the Third Reich*. Richard and Clara Winston, trans. New York: Macmillan, 1970.

Speidel, Hans. *Invasion 1944*. New York: Henry Regnery, 1950. Reprint ed., New York: Paperback Library, 1968.

Stauffenberg, Theodor-Friedrich von. Papers and personal communications, 1986–1988.

Stein, George H. *The Waffen-SS: Hitler's Elite Guard at War*. Ithaca, N.Y.: Cornell University Press, 1966.

Stevens, E. H., ed. *The Trial of Nikolaus von Falkenhorst*. London: William Hodge and Company, 1949.

Suchenwirth, Richard. *Command and Leadership in the German Air Force*. United States Air Force Historical Studies Number 189. Maxwell Air Force Base. Montgomery, Ala.: The Air University, 1969.

Syndor, Charles W., Jr. *Soldiers of Destruction*. Princeton, N.J.: Princeton University Press, 1977.

Taylor, Telford. *The Breaking Wave*. New York: Simon & Schuster, 1967.

Taylor, Telford. *March of Conquest*. New York: Simon & Schuster, 1958.

Tessin, Georg. *Verbaende und Truppen der deutschen Wehrmacht und Waffen-SS in Zweiten Weltkrieg, 1939–1945*. Osnabrueck: Biblio Verlag, 1974. 16 volumes.

Thomas, Charles S. *The German Navy in the Nazi Era*. London: Unwin Hyman, 1990.

Trevor-Roper, Hugh. *The Last Days of Hitler*. New York: Macmillan, 1947.

Trial of the Major War Criminals before the International Military Tribunal. Washington, D.C.: United States Government Printing Office, 1946–1948. 42 volumes.

Trial of the War Criminals before the Nuremberg Military Tribunals. Washington, D.C.: United States Government Printing Office, 1950. 14 volumes.

United States Army, Intelligence Section of the General Staff, American Expeditionary Force. *Histories of Two Hundred and Fifty-One Divisions of the German Army Which Participated in the War (1914–1918)*. Washington, D.C.: United States Government Printing Office, 1920.

Warlimont, Walter. *Inside Hitler's Headquarters, 1939–45*. R. H. Barry, trans. New York: Frederick A. Praeger, 1966.

Wheeler-Bennett, John W. *The Nemesis of Power: The German Army in Politics, 1918–1945*. New York: St. Martin's Press, 1967.

Whiting, Charles. *Massacre at Malmedy*. Briarcliff Manor, N.Y.: Stein and Day, 1971.

Wikipedia. "Hans Graf von Sponeck." en.wikipedia.org/wiki/Hans_Graf_von_Sponeck (accessed 2011).

Williamson, Gordon. *Aces of the Reich*. London: Arms and Armour Press, 1989.

Wistrich, Robert. *Who's Who in Nazi Germany*. New York: Macmillan, 1982.

Yeager, Mark C. *SS-Oberstgruppenfuehrer und Generaloberst der Waffen-SS Paul Hausser*. Winnipeg, Canada: John Fedorowicz, 1986.

Young, Peter, ed. *Illustrated World War II Encyclopedia*. Based on the original text by Eddy Bauer. Westport, Conn.: H. S. Stuttman, 1978.

Young, Peter, ed. *The World Almanac of World War II*. New York: Bison Books, 1981. Reprint ed., New York: World Almanac, 1986.

Ziemke, Earl F. "The German Northern Theater of Operations, 1940–1945." United States Department of the Army Pamphlet No. 20–271. Washington, D.C.: United States Department of the Army, 1959.

Ziemke, Earl F. *Stalingrad to Berlin: The German Defeat in the East*. Office of the Chief of Military History. Washington, D.C.: United States Government Printing Office, 1966.

INDEX